Ultimate Docker for Cloud Native Applications

Unleash Docker Ecosystem by Optimizing Image Creation, Storage and Networking Management, Deployment Strategies to Revolutionize Workflow, Scalability, and Security"

Meysam Azad

www.orangeava.com

First published: February 2024

Published by: Orange Education Pvt Ltd, AVA™

Address: 9, Daryaganj, Delhi, 110002

ISBN: 978-81-96815-12-7

www.orangeava.com

Dedicated To

My beloved Parents:

Mohamad Reza Azad
Masoumeh Khorami

and

My wife Yenni

About the Author

In "*Ultimate Docker for Cloud Native Applications*," Meysam Azad presents his journey as a seasoned Senior Site Reliability Engineer, drawing from over 6 years of professional experience. Throughout his career, he has navigated diverse industries, from social media with latency-intensive services to machine learning and AI deployments, demonstrating versatile expertise both within and beyond public cloud environments.

With a steadfast commitment to excellence, the author shares his profound insights into provisioning and maintaining production workloads, spanning the evolution from the pre-Kubernetes era to the present day. Containerization has revolutionized modern computing, and Meysam Azad has been at the forefront, leveraging firsthand experience from customer-facing services to inter-organizational tooling.

Proficient in continuous delivery methodologies, the author employs a spectrum of tools and technologies, including GitHub Actions, GitLab CI, and Travis CI. Automation is not merely a convenience but a cornerstone of his daily operations, from orchestrating complex deployments to ensuring seamless integration with GitOps principles using FluxCD.

With adept system administration skills, Meysam Azad adeptly manages virtual and bare-metal infrastructure using Ansible and Terraform, fortifying reliability and robustness at every turn. Rooted in practical experience, *Ultimate Docker for Cloud Native Applications* offers a treasure trove of knowledge for professionals seeking to navigate Docker and containerization in real-world scenarios with confidence and competence.

Technical Review Partner

Thinknyx® Technologies is a team of professionals with years of experience in IT technology, ranging from Software Development to the Management of IT Infrastructure, Cloud, Automation, Container Management, Web and APP Development, Security, and Professional Services. Recognized as a reputable brand, Thinknyx® Technologies provides IT consulting services, offering comprehensive Information Technology and Soft Skills' Training. Additionally, they offer Talent Acquisition and Recruitment solutions to diverse organizations worldwide.

Mr. Yogesh Raheja, the Founder and CEO of Thinknyx® Technologies, is a certified expert in DevOps, SRE, Cloud, and Containerisation, with two decades of IT experience. He has expertise in technologies such as Public/Private Cloud, Containers, Automation tools, Continuous Integration/Deployment/Delivery tools, Monitoring and Logging tools, and more. Mr. Raheja is passionate about sharing his technical expertise with a global audience through various forums, conferences, webinars, blogs, and LinkedIn. Moreover, he has authored multiple books, including *Effective DevOps with AWS*, *Automation with Puppet 5*, and *Automation with Ansible*, and has published his online courses on various platforms. Furthermore, he has reviewed multiple books for Packt, including *Implementing Splunk 7, Third Edition* and *Splunk Operational Intelligence Cookbook, Third Edition*, among others.

Acknowledgements

I extend my deepest gratitude to my parents, whose unwavering support has been my anchor throughout the creation of *Ultimate Docker for Cloud Native Applications*. Their encouragement and belief in my abilities have fueled my passion for technology. Without their guidance, this endeavor would not have been possible. I am truly fortunate to have such pillars of strength in my life.

To my beloved wife, your understanding, patience, and unwavering support have been the driving force behind every late-night coding session and countless hours spent immersed in the world of containers. Your love and companionship are the bedrock upon which I have built this achievement. I am profoundly grateful for your presence in my life.

A special acknowledgment goes to the editors of Orange AVA publication, whose dedication turned a challenging process into a collaborative and enriching experience. Their patience and keen insights have left an indelible mark on every page of *Ultimate Docker for Cloud Native Applications*.

I would also like to express my heartfelt thanks to the technical editor, Nicolas De Loof. His sharp eyes and dedication to the betterment of this book have been invaluable. Nicolas, your meticulous attention to detail and commitment to excellence have significantly enhanced the quality of the content. I am grateful for your contributions to ensuring the technical accuracy and clarity of *Ultimate Docker for Cloud Native Applications*.

Finally, a note of appreciation to myself. This journey of writing a book has been one of self-discovery, growth, and resilience. Through the challenges and triumphs of crafting *Ultimate Docker for Cloud Native Applications*, I have not only honed my technical skills but also cultivated a deeper understanding of the subject matter. This accomplishment is a testament to the power of perseverance and continuous learning.

Preface

Welcome to *Ultimate Docker for Cloud Native Applications*, a comprehensive guide that navigates the ever-evolving landscape of containerization, providing a roadmap from the fundamentals to advanced concepts. In the ever-evolving universe of software engineering and system administration, Docker has emerged as a transformative force, simplifying the deployment, scaling, and management of applications. This book is your companion on a journey from zero to hero, covering the latest changes and updates in Docker up to the year of writing, 2023.

Whether you are a recent graduate eager to delve into the world of containers or a seasoned engineer aiming to keep your skills sharp, this book caters to all levels of expertise. Docker has become a cornerstone in modern software development, and understanding its intricacies is essential for anyone involved in building, deploying, or maintaining software systems.

Our exploration begins with the basics, ensuring a solid foundation for those new to Docker. We gradually progress through intermediate topics, exploring advanced container orchestration with Kubernetes, understanding Docker networking, and optimizing container performance. Every concept is accompanied by practical examples and real-world scenarios to enhance your hands-on experience.

In this edition, we take a thorough look at the latest changes and updates in the Docker ecosystem. From the newest features in Docker Engine to advancements in orchestration tools and ecosystem tooling, you will gain insights that reflect the state of Docker in 2023.

Ultimate Docker for Cloud Native Applications is not just a book; it's a learning journey designed to empower you with the skills needed to excel in today's fast-paced software industry. Whether you're embarking on your first containerization project or looking to refine your expertise, the knowledge within these pages will guide you toward mastering Docker and staying at the forefront of technological innovation. Enjoy the adventure!

Chapter 1. Introduction to Docker: This chapter introduces the fundamental concepts of Docker. Covering the historical context of containerization, the chapter explores Docker's installation process, providing a solid foundation for beginners and setting the stage for the subsequent chapters.

Chapter 2. Docker Architecture and Components: This chapter takes a deep dive into the inner workings of Docker. Readers gain insights into the architecture, understanding the roles and interactions of key components. This chapter equips readers with a comprehensive understanding of how Docker functions.

Chapter 3. Building and Managing Docker Images: This chapter is a practical guide to image creation and management. From crafting images from scratch to implementing best practices for efficient image management, this chapter empowers readers to master the art of handling Docker images effectively.

Chapter 4. Docker Networking: This chapter explores the intricacies of Docker's networking capabilities. The chapter provides an overview of Docker networking, covering container communication and customization of network configurations. Readers gain practical insights into optimizing Docker networking.

Chapter 5. Persistent Data Management with Docker: This chapter focuses on the critical aspect of data within Docker containers. Strategies for managing persistent data, including handling volumes and implementing backup and recovery, are explored. This chapter ensures readers are well-versed in maintaining data integrity.

Chapter 6. Docker Compose for Simplified Application Deployment: This chapter introduces readers to Docker Compose. This tool simplifies multi-container application deployment, orchestrating services seamlessly. Readers learn practical strategies for creating cohesive application deployment scenarios.

Chapter 7. Scaling Applications with Docker Swarm: This chapter delves into Docker Swarm, a container orchestration tool. The chapter provides an overview and practical guidance on creating and managing Swarm clusters, enabling readers to scale applications effectively.

Chapter 8. Securing Docker Deployments: This chapter emphasizes the importance of security in Docker environments. Best practices for securing Docker deployments, including securing container images, runtime security, and role-based access control, are thoroughly covered.

Chapter 9. Docker in Continuous Integration and Deployment: This chapter explores the integration of Docker into CI/CD pipelines. Readers gain insights into automating deployment processes, testing strategies, and monitoring in Dockerized environments, ensuring a seamless CI/CD workflow.

Chapter 10. Docker on Cloud Platforms: This chapter extends Docker knowledge to cloud environments. Readers explore deployment considerations on major cloud providers, understanding cloud-native features, integration possibilities, and optimization strategies for Docker in the cloud.

Chapter 11. Introduction to Kubernetes: This chapter provides a comprehensive introduction to Kubernetes. Readers gain insights into Kubernetes' architecture, deployment management, and interactions with Docker, enhancing their knowledge of container orchestration.

Chapter 12. Exploring Advanced Docker Concepts: This chapter builds upon foundational knowledge. It covers topics such as advanced container orchestration, a deep dive into Docker networking, and strategies for optimizing container performance. This chapter equips readers with advanced Docker skills.

Chapter 13. Future Trends in Containerization: This chapter explores emerging technologies and trends. Readers gain insights into the evolving landscape of container orchestration, predicting the future of Docker and container technology. This chapter prepares readers for staying ahead in the dynamic field of containerization.

Each chapter is meticulously crafted to provide a comprehensive and hands-on learning experience, ensuring that readers at every level find value in *Ultimate Docker for Cloud Native Applications.*

Downloading the code bundles and colored images

Please follow the links or scan the QR codes to download the **Code Bundles and Images** of the book:

https://github.com/ava-orange-education/Ultimate-Docker-For-Cloud-Native-Applications

The code bundles and images of the book are also hosted on ***https://rebrand.ly/ktruao9***

In case there's an update to the code, it will be updated on the existing GitHub repository.

Errata

We take immense pride in our work at **Orange Education Pvt Ltd,** and follow best practices to ensure the accuracy of our content to provide an indulging reading experience to our subscribers. Our readers are our mirrors, and we use their inputs to reflect and improve upon human errors, if any, that may have occurred during the publishing processes involved. To let us maintain the quality and help us reach out to any readers who might be having difficulties due to any unforeseen errors, please write to us at :

errata@orangeava.com

Your support, suggestions, and feedback are highly appreciated.

DID YOU KNOW

Did you know that Orange Education Pvt Ltd offers eBook versions of every book published, with PDF and ePub files available? You can upgrade to the eBook version at **www.orangeava.com** and as a print book customer, you are entitled to a discount on the eBook copy. Get in touch with us at: **info@orangeava.com** for more details.

At **www.orangeava.com**, you can also read a collection of free technical articles, sign up for a range of free newsletters, and receive exclusive discounts and offers on AVA™ Books and eBooks.

PIRACY

If you come across any illegal copies of our works in any form on the internet, we would be grateful if you would provide us with the location address or website name. Please contact us at **info@orangeava.com** with a link to the material.

ARE YOU INTERESTED IN AUTHORING WITH US?

If there is a topic that you have expertise in, and you are interested in either writing or contributing to a book, please write to us at **business@orangeava.com**. We are on a journey to help developers and tech professionals to gain insights on the present technological advancements and innovations happening across the globe and build a community that believes Knowledge is best acquired by sharing and learning with others. Please reach out to us to learn what our audience demands and how you can be part of this educational reform. We also welcome ideas from tech experts and help them build learning and development content for their domains.

REVIEWS

Please leave a review. Once you have read and used this book, why not leave a review on the site that you purchased it from? Potential readers can then see and use your unbiased opinion to make purchase decisions. We at Orange Education would love to know what you think about our products, and our authors can learn from your feedback. Thank you!

For more information about Orange Education, please visit **www.orangeava.com**.

Table of Contents

CHAPTER 1

Introduction to Docker

Figure 1.1: *A ship of containers.*
source: https://unsplash.com/photos/HjBOmBPbi9k

Introduction

In an era where technological advancements are transforming every aspect of our lives, Docker has emerged as a game-changer in application development. With its unique approach to containerization, Docker has revolutionized how developers build, deploy, and manage applications. In this book, we embark on a journey to explore the world of Docker, understanding its concepts, features, and practical use cases. Whether you are a seasoned developer or a newcomer to the world of containerization, this book aims to provide you with a comprehensive understanding of Docker and empower you to leverage its capabilities effectively.

Docker has gained widespread popularity due to its ability to solve many challenges developers face in the software development lifecycle. Docker addresses these problems by encapsulating applications and their dependencies into lightweight, self-contained containers. These containers can be deployed across different operating systems, cloud platforms, and local development environments, ensuring consistency and eliminating the need for complex setup procedures.

Structure

In this chapter, we will cover the following topics:

- History of Docker
- Understanding Containerization and Its Advantages
- Overview of Docker and Its Key Features
- Docker Terminology and Concepts
- Use Cases and Benefits of Docker in Real-World Scenarios

History of Docker

In this section, we will delve into the intriguing history of Docker, tracing its origins and the driving factors that led to its creation. We'll explore the pivotal events and technological advancements that laid the foundation for Docker's birth and its subsequent rise as a transformative force in the world of containerization and application development.

Pre-Docker Era

The history of Docker can be traced back to the concept of containerization, which has its roots in the early 1970s. In those years, chroot, a Unix utility, allowed users to create isolated environments by changing the root directory for a process. However, it's important to note that while chroot provided a form of isolation, it primarily customized the visible filesystem, which was indeed a significant aspect of the "environment necessary for running applications." Nonetheless, this approach fell short of encapsulating the environment required to run applications effectively.

Fast forward to the early 2000s, and containerization technologies began to emerge with the introduction of FreeBSD Jails and Solaris Containers, primarily known as Solaris Zones. FreeBSD Jails, introduced in 2000, created lightweight virtualized environments within a single operating system instance. Similarly, Solaris Containers, introduced by Sun Microsystems in 2004, provided operating system-level virtualization, enabling the creation of isolated environments called zones.

Birth of Docker

These early containerization technologies laid the foundation for the concepts that Docker would later build upon. They were the predecessors of Docker, with Linux Containers (LXC) being one notable example. However, these technologies, including LXC, were limited in cross-platform compatibility and often required more user-friendly tooling to simplify container creation and management. It's important to note that Docker, like LXC before it, leveraged Linux kernel features inspired by these earlier containerization technologies. Docker aimed to provide a unified and user-friendly platform for containerization. While it introduced innovations such as the Docker container runtime, it also faced the challenge of balancing complexity with usability in its user experience (UX). This delicate balance became a defining aspect of Docker's journey and its impact on the software development industry.

The birth of Docker in 2013 marked a significant milestone in the evolution of containerization. Docker was initially released as an open-source project by Solomon Hykes and his team under the name **dotCloud**. The project aimed to address developers' challenges in building and deploying applications consistently across different environments.

As dotCloud gained traction, it became evident that the containerization technology they developed had far-reaching potential beyond their original platform-as-a-service (PaaS) offering. In 2013, dotCloud rebranded its containerization technology as Docker, emphasizing its focus on creating portable, self-contained containers that could run virtually anywhere. The name "Docker" was inspired by the shipping industry, where standardized containers revolutionized the transportation of goods worldwide.

Docker v1.0

The release of Docker 1.0 in June 2014 marked a turning point in adopting containerization. Docker provided an intuitive command-line interface, a declarative configuration file called Dockerfile, and a centralized repository called Docker Hub, where developers could share and distribute container images. These features, combined with Docker's emphasis on portability, consistency, and efficiency, garnered significant attention and rapidly gained popularity among developers, DevOps teams, and organizations.

Docker's rise in popularity also led to the development of additional tools and platforms that extended its capabilities. Docker Compose simplified the management of multi-container applications, allowing developers to define and deploy complex, interconnected services with ease. The introduction of Docker Swarm provided native container orchestration capabilities, enabling the management of container clusters and facilitating high availability and scalability. Moreover, the rise of Kubernetes, an open-source container orchestration platform, further solidified Docker's position as a foundational technology in the containerization ecosystem.

Today, Docker has become the de facto standard for containerization, transforming how applications are built, deployed, and managed. Its impact is visible across various industries, from small startups to large enterprises. Docker's versatility, coupled with its vast ecosystem and robust community support, has made it a fundamental tool for developers, enabling them to embrace a container-first approach and achieve faster, more scalable, and more reliable application development and deployment processes.

Figure 1.2: *Two birds sitting next to each other and enjoying the view. source: https://unsplash.com/photos/yhicgIlXP20*

Understanding Containerization

Containerization is a revolutionary technology that has transformed the way software is developed and deployed. At its core, containerization allows applications and their dependencies to be packaged together into isolated, lightweight units called containers. These containers encapsulate everything needed to run the application, including libraries, runtime environments, and configurations.

The advantages of containerization are significant. First and foremost, it enables portability and consistency across different environments. Containers provide a consistent runtime environment, ensuring that applications behave the same way regardless of the underlying infrastructure. This eliminates the "it works on my machine" problem and streamlines the development and deployment process.

Moreover, containerization promotes scalability and resource efficiency. Containers are highly scalable, allowing applications to be easily replicated and deployed across various servers or cloud environments. They also consume fewer resources compared to traditional virtual machines, leading to improved utilization and cost savings.

Additionally, containerization facilitates faster deployment and enhanced development workflows. Containers can be created, started, and stopped quickly, allowing for rapid iteration and continuous integration. They enable developers to work independently without worrying about conflicting dependencies or system configurations.

Overall, containerization offers numerous advantages, including portability, consistency, scalability, resource efficiency, and streamlined development processes. Organizations can realize these benefits by adopting containerization technologies such as Docker, transforming how they build, deploy, and manage their applications.

Introduction to Docker

Docker, a powerful containerization platform, has transformed the software development and deployment world. Its fundamental purpose lies in simplifying the packaging and distribution of containerized applications. By encapsulating applications and their dependencies into lightweight and portable containers, Docker enables self-contained, infrastructure-independent application deployment. This focus on streamlined packaging & distribution, one of Docker's major advantages, revolutionizes how software is managed and deployed.

With Docker, developers can create consistent and reproducible environments for their applications, regardless of the target operating system or hosting environment. It eliminates the complexities and challenges of managing dependencies, compatibility issues, and conflicting configurations that often arise in traditional software development.

Docker simplifies the process of deploying and managing applications, enabling rapid and scalable deployments across various environments, such as local machines, cloud servers, and clusters. It offers a streamlined workflow, allowing developers to focus on writing code and iterating on their applications, while Docker takes care of the environment setup and management.

By leveraging Docker, organizations can achieve increased productivity, improved collaboration between development and operations teams, efficient resource utilization, and faster time-to-market for their applications. With its ease of use, flexibility, and wide adoption in the industry, Docker has become an essential tool for modern software development and deployment.

Benefits of Docker

Docker offers numerous benefits that have contributed to its widespread adoption and revolutionized the software development landscape. Here are some of the key advantages:

- **Portability and Consistency**: Docker provides a lightweight, portable platform for packaging and distributing applications. By encapsulating an application and its dependencies within a container image, Docker ensures consistency across different environments. Developers can create a containerized application on their local machine and be confident that it will run seamlessly on any system that supports Docker, whether a developer's laptop, a testing environment, or a production server. This portability eliminates compatibility issues, streamlining the deployment process and improving collaboration between development and operations teams.
- **Efficiency and Resource Utilization**: Docker's containerization approach enables efficient resource utilization by isolating applications within containers. Unlike traditional virtualization, Docker containers share the host operating system's kernel. This lightweight approach allows for higher density and faster startup times, enabling organizations to run more containers on a single host machine. Docker also manages container resources, enabling fine-grained control over CPU, memory, and I/O limits.
- **Scalability and Agility**: Docker's scalability features make it ideal for managing applications in dynamic and evolving environments. With Docker, developers can quickly scale applications horizontally by replicating containers across multiple hosts or vertically by adjusting resource allocation to meet changing demands. Docker's orchestration tools, such as Docker Swarm or Kubernetes, facilitate the management of containerized applications at scale, automatically distributing containers, handling load balancing, and ensuring high availability. This scalability and agility enable organizations to respond quickly to spikes in traffic, accommodate growth, and adapt to changing business needs.
- **Rapid Application Deployment**: Docker streamlines the application deployment process, significantly reducing the time and effort required to package, distribute, and deploy applications. With Docker, developers can create reproducible container images that contain all the necessary dependencies, configurations, and libraries. These images can be

easily shared and deployed across different environments, making the deployment process consistent and reliable. Docker's fast startup times and efficient resource utilization allow applications to be deployed quickly, enabling rapid iteration and deployment cycles and facilitating continuous integration and continuous deployment (CI/CD) workflows.

- **Isolation and Security**: Docker containers provide strong isolation between applications and the underlying host system. Each container operates in its own isolated environment, with its own filesystems, network interfaces, and resource limits. This isolation ensures that applications running in separate containers do not interfere with each other, enhancing security and stability. Docker achieves this security isolation using built-in Linux kernel features, such as namespace isolation and control groups (cgroups), to prevent unauthorized access and mitigate potential vulnerabilities. Additionally, Docker images can be scanned for vulnerabilities, allowing developers to proactively address security concerns before deploying applications.
- **Ecosystem and Community**: Docker has fostered a thriving ecosystem and community, contributing to its continuous improvement and adoption. The Docker Hub, a centralized repository for Docker images, provides access to a vast library of pre-built images for various applications and technologies, enabling developers to leverage existing solutions and accelerate development processes. The Docker community actively shares knowledge, best practices, and troubleshooting techniques, making it easier for developers to learn and solve problems. The broad adoption of Docker has also led to integrating Docker support into various development tools, platforms, and cloud providers, further enhancing its capabilities and ease of use.

These additional benefits reinforce Docker's position as a transformative technology in the software development industry. By facilitating rapid deployment, ensuring strong isolation and security, and fostering a vibrant ecosystem, Docker empowers developers to deliver applications faster, improve security, and collaborate more effectively, ultimately driving innovation and efficiency in developing and deploying modern software systems.

Docker vs Competitors

Now, we focus on the competitive landscape and compare Docker with other solutions that emerged alongside it. We'll examine how Docker's unique features and innovations set it apart from its competitors, paving the way for its widespread adoption and establishing it as the industry's de facto standard for containcrization.

Distinguishing Features of Docker

Docker's rise to prominence is not without competition. Before Docker's widespread adoption, various approaches to application deployment existed, each with its own advantages and limitations. Traditional virtualization technologies, such as hypervisors, allowed for the creation of isolated virtual machines (VMs), but they incurred significant resource overhead and lacked the efficiency and agility needed for modern application development.

Docker emerged as a clear winner in containerization due to its numerous advantages over competitors. Unlike heavyweight VMs, Docker containers are lightweight and share the host operating system's kernel, leading to faster startup times, efficient resource utilization, and higher container density. This efficient utilization of resources translates into cost savings, increased scalability, and improved organizational performance.

Docker's Best Selling Point: Portability

Another critical factor that sets Docker apart is its emphasis on portability and consistency. Docker containers encapsulate an application and its dependencies into a single, self-contained unit, ensuring the application runs consistently across different environments. This portability eliminates compatibility issues and facilitates seamless deployment on diverse systems, including local development machines, cloud providers, and production servers. Docker's standardized format for packaging applications, coupled with its expansive ecosystem and repository of pre-built container images, known as Docker Hub, has propelled its adoption and made it the go-to choice for developers worldwide.

Furthermore, Docker's user-friendly tooling and intuitive command-line interface have contributed to its popularity. Docker provides developers with a straightforward and accessible way to create, manage, and deploy containers through commands that are easy to learn and use. Additionally, Docker's declarative configuration file, Dockerfile, allows developers to define the desired state of a containerized application, automating the image build process and enabling reproducibility across different environments.

Besides, Docker offers an efficient and scalable solution for managing applications at scale. With Docker, developers can easily replicate and distribute application environments, enabling seamless collaboration and reducing the time it takes to onboard new team members. Additionally, Docker provides robust tools for automating the deployment and orchestration of containers, allowing applications to scale horizontally, adapt to fluctuating demands, and handle high-traffic loads efficiently. By harnessing the power of Docker, developers can streamline their workflows, enhance productivity, and deliver applications faster, all while maintaining the desired level of reliability and consistency.

In addition to its practical benefits, Docker has had a profound impact on the software development community and the industry as a whole. It has democratized the application deployment process and made it more accessible to developers of all levels of expertise. Docker's open-source nature and vibrant community have fostered a culture of collaboration, knowledge sharing, and innovation. Developers worldwide have embraced Docker, creating a rich ecosystem of pre-built containers, tools, and frameworks that extend its capabilities and provide solutions for various use cases.

The World Needs Microservices: Docker's Contributions

Moreover, Docker has played a pivotal role in advancing the concept of microservices architecture. By breaking down monolithic applications into smaller, loosely coupled services, Docker enables organizations to build scalable and resilient systems. With Docker's lightweight containers, each microservice can be independently developed, deployed, and scaled, improving agility, scalability, and fault tolerance. The flexibility and modularity offered by Docker have paved the way for modern application architectures, empowering teams to build complex, distributed systems that can adapt and evolve with the ever-changing demands of the digital landscape.

In the following chapters of this book, we will explore Docker in-depth, covering its fundamental concepts, installation and setup, container management, networking, orchestration, and best practices for leveraging Docker effectively. Whether you are an individual developer, part of a small team, or working in a large enterprise, understanding Docker and harnessing its potential will undoubtedly enhance your ability to develop, deploy, and maintain robust and scalable applications.

Figure 1.3: *A cat gazing at the cameraman.*
source: https://unsplash.com/photos/tEMU4lzAL0w

Limitations of Docker

There is no free lunch! Whether in life or especially in technology, everything has a downside, and Docker is no exception.

While Docker has revolutionized the world of containerization and application development, like any technology, it has its share of limitations. Understanding these limitations is crucial for developers and organizations to make informed decisions and identify appropriate mitigating solutions. Here are some of them:

- **Performance Overhead**: One challenge associated with Docker primarily pertains to network performance due to the use of virtual network interfaces, while CPU and memory performance remain largely unaffected and operate at native levels. Running applications within Docker containers incurs a slight performance penalty compared to running them natively on the host operating system. This overhead is mainly attributed to isolation and resource management mechanisms provided by the Linux kernel that Docker relies on. However, several solutions have emerged to address this issue. Notably, `containerd`, introduced to refactor the Docker daemon into a reusable and flexible component, played a pivotal role in optimizing container execution and reducing overhead. CRI-O, another container runtime, relies on `containerd` to enhance the efficiency of containerized environments, aiming to provide faster and more efficient container execution.
- **Limited Compatibility with Windows**: Although Windows containers are supported within Docker, it's important to note that Docker's primary focus has historically been on Linux containers, with Windows containers being a supported but less emphasized feature. Docker was originally designed for

Linux-based environments, and while support for Windows has improved over the years, it still lags behind its Linux counterpart. This limitation poses challenges for organizations with Windows-centric infrastructures or requiring seamless integration with Windows-based applications. To address this, Microsoft developed Windows Subsystem for Linux (WSL), allowing running Linux distributions natively on Windows, enabling Docker to run on Windows systems more smoothly.

- **Complexity in Networking and Storage Configuration**: Networking and storage configuration in Docker can be complex, especially when dealing with more advanced networking scenarios or persistent storage requirements. Docker's default networking options, such as bridge networks and overlay networks, may only sometimes meet the specific needs of complex distributed systems. Similarly, managing the persisting data within Docker containers can be challenging, as containers are typically ephemeral by design. To address these challenges, complementary tools and frameworks have emerged. Kubernetes, for example, offers advanced networking capabilities through its Container Networking Interface (CNI) plugins and provides robust storage management with features like persistent volumes and storage classes through its Container Storage Interface (CSI) plugins. Additionally, Docker itself provides solutions like Docker volumes and related plugins for simplified data management and persistence within containers. Container orchestration platforms like Docker Swarm and Nomad also offer simplified networking and storage management for Docker deployments.
- **Security Concerns**: While Docker provides isolation between containers, it is not impervious to security vulnerabilities. Running multiple containers on a single host poses potential risks, as a compromised container may have access to the underlying host system. Moreover, container images obtained from external sources may contain security vulnerabilities, which can be inadvertently introduced into the environment. To mitigate these risks, it is crucial to implement best practices such as regularly updating and patching container images, performing vulnerability scanning, and implementing proper network segmentation. Additional security-focused tools like container security scanners, such as Anchore and Clair, can be used to identify and address vulnerabilities in container images.

Learning Curve

One of the first questions in every technology is, "How easy is it to learn?". The learning curve of Docker can be considered both an advantage and a disadvantage, depending on the perspective and experience of the users.

Advantages of Docker's Learning Curve

- **Rapid Onboarding**: Docker's learning curve can be relatively quick and straightforward, especially for developers familiar with containerization concepts or those experienced with Linux-based systems. Docker provides intuitive command-line tools and a user-friendly interface that simplifies creating, managing, and deploying containers. This enables developers to quickly adopt Docker and leverage its benefits, such as improved application portability, scalability, and faster deployment cycles.
- **Skills Reusability**: Once developers gain proficiency in Docker, their knowledge and skills become highly transferable. The concepts and practices learned while working with Docker can be applied across different projects, teams, and organizations. This reusability of Docker skills can improve collaboration, consistent deployment practices, and streamlined workflows.

Disadvantages of Docker's Learning Curve

- **Complexity for Novice Users**: For users new to containerization or with limited experience with command-line interfaces, Docker's learning curve can be perceived as steep. Understanding the fundamental concepts of containerization, learning Docker's terminology, and mastering the various commands and configuration options can require significant time and effort. This complexity can challenge beginners, potentially leading to frustration and slower adoption.
- **Understanding Advanced Features**: While the basics of Docker can be grasped relatively quickly, mastering advanced features and more complex aspects of Docker can be more challenging. Docker offers a wide range of features, such as networking, volume management, and container orchestration, which require a deeper understanding and experience to utilize effectively. Learning these advanced features may require additional research, experimentation, and exploration of complementary tools and technologies like Docker Swarm or Kubernetes.

Docker and Software Development Lifecycle

In the realm of software development, Docker has emerged as a game-changing technology that significantly impacts the Software Development Lifecycle (SDLC). By providing a powerful containerization platform, Docker revolutionizes the way applications are developed, tested, and deployed. In this section, we explore the profound influence of Docker on the SDLC, examining its role in enabling faster iterations, improved collaboration, enhanced scalability, and streamlined deployment processes.

Advantage: Streamlined Development and Deployment Process

One significant advantage that Docker has brought to the software development lifecycle is streamlining the development and deployment process. Docker's containerization technology allows developers to package their applications and dependencies into self-contained containers. These containers encapsulate the entire runtime environment, including the application code, libraries, and system tools, ensuring consistency across different environments.

This advantage brings several benefits to the software development lifecycle. Firstly, Docker simplifies setting up development environments by eliminating the need for complex configuration steps. Developers can define the desired state of their application in a Dockerfile, which serves as a blueprint for building containers. This lets team members quickly spin up identical development environments, reducing compatibility issues and minimizing time spent on environment setup.

Secondly, Docker enables seamless collaboration and deployment across the development and operations teams. With Docker, developers can package their applications and share them as container images, ensuring that the same application on a developer's machine will run consistently in different deployment pipeline stages. This promotes smoother handoffs between development, testing, and production environments.

Disadvantage: Increased Complexity in Container Orchestration

One disadvantage that Docker has introduced to the software development lifecycle is the increased complexity of container orchestration. While Docker simplifies the packaging and deployment of individual containers, managing and orchestrating multiple containers in complex distributed systems can become challenging.

As organizations adopt microservices architectures and deploy applications composed of numerous interconnected services, the need for container orchestration arises. Container orchestration platforms like Kubernetes, Docker Swarm, and Apache Mesos have emerged to manage the lifecycle, scaling, and coordination of containers across clusters of hosts. However, configuring, monitoring, and managing these container orchestration platforms adds a layer of complexity to the development and deployment process.

Container orchestration requires understanding concepts like service discovery, load balancing, scaling, and fault tolerance. It also involves additional tooling and infrastructure considerations to ensure high availability, efficient resource allocation, and reliable service orchestration. The learning curve associated with container orchestration platforms and the complexities of managing distributed systems can pose challenges for teams transitioning to containerized architectures.

Organizations can mitigate this disadvantage by investing in training and education to upskill their teams in container orchestration. Additionally, leveraging managed container orchestration services provided by cloud providers can offload some operational complexity and allow developers to focus more on application development and less on infrastructure management.

Figure 1.4: *Different stages of the life of a flower.*
source: https://unsplash.com/photos/VlTJdP8ZY1c

Docker Affects Different Roles

The adoption of Docker has brought about transformative changes across various roles in the software development and operations landscape. This section delves into how Docker affects different roles, shedding light on the specific advantages and challenges individuals face in their respective positions. By understanding Docker's impact on different roles, we can appreciate its role in driving collaboration, efficiency, and innovation within cross-functional teams.

Software Engineer

For software engineers, Docker has become an indispensable tool in their toolkits. It empowers them to build applications in a consistent and isolated environment, eliminating the "works on my machine" problem and ensuring smoother collaboration across the development team. By leveraging Docker, software engineers can focus on writing code without worrying about the underlying infrastructure, enabling faster development cycles, improved code quality, and easier application maintenance.

Advantage: Application Portability and Consistency

Docker brings the advantage of application portability and consistency to software engineers. With Docker, software engineers can package their applications and dependencies into containers, ensuring the application runs consistently across different environments. This portability eliminates compatibility issues and "it works on my machine" problems. It allows software engineers to focus more on writing code and less on environment setup and configuration.

Challenge: Learning Curve and Containerization Complexity

One challenge software engineers may face when adopting Docker is introducing new concepts, such as containerization, Dockerfiles, and container orchestration platforms. Software engineers must invest time and effort in learning these concepts and adapt their workflows accordingly.

DevOps Engineer

DevOps engineers are critical in bridging the gap between development and operations. Docker has become a valuable asset for DevOps engineers, enabling them to streamline the deployment and management of applications. By leveraging Docker's containerization technology, DevOps engineers can create standardized deployment pipelines, automate infrastructure provisioning, and ensure consistent environments across development, testing, and production stages. Docker's container-based approach aligns with the principles of DevOps, facilitating collaboration, accelerating time-to-market, and enhancing the overall efficiency of software delivery processes.

Advantage: Streamlined Deployment and Scalability

Docker provides DevOps engineers with a streamlined deployment process and improved scalability. With Docker containers, DevOps engineers can package applications and their dependencies into portable units that can be easily deployed across different environments. Docker's container orchestration platforms, like Kubernetes, enable efficient scaling and management of containers, ensuring high availability and performance. This allows DevOps engineers to automate deployment pipelines, scale applications seamlessly, and manage resources effectively.

Challenge: Infrastructure Management and Complexity

Adopting Docker introduces challenges for DevOps engineers regarding infrastructure management and complexity. DevOps engineers need to manage container orchestration platforms, handle networking and storage configurations specific to containers, and ensure proper resource allocation. Orchestrating containers at scale requires understanding concepts like service discovery, load balancing, and automated scaling. DevOps engineers must also monitor and troubleshoot containerized environments to ensure smooth operations and efficient resource utilization.

It's important to note that the challenges mentioned can vary based on the specific context, organization, and project requirements. Nonetheless, Docker provides significant advantages to software, DevOps, and hardware engineers alike, revolutionizing how applications are developed, deployed, and managed across different roles in the software development lifecycle.

Docker's Security Considerations

Docker container security is more challenging, largely because a typical Docker environment contains a lot more moving pieces that need to be secured. These components are as follows:

- **Container Isolation**: While Docker containers provide isolation, it is not foolproof. Containers share the same underlying operating system kernel, meaning a compromise within one container could potentially impact other containers or the host system. It is essential to configure appropriate isolation mechanisms, such as namespaces and control groups, and regularly update the host operating system to mitigate security risks.
- **Container Image Vulnerabilities**: Docker relies on container images often obtained from public registries or third-party sources. These images may contain vulnerabilities, outdated software versions, or malicious code. It is crucial to regularly update and patch container images, perform vulnerability scanning and image signing, and enforce strict image verification processes to minimize the risk of running compromised or insecure container images.
- **Inadequate Container Configurations**: Improper configurations within Docker containers can lead to security vulnerabilities. For instance, misconfigured network settings, weak access controls, or excessive container privileges can expose sensitive information or grant unauthorized access to attackers. Following security best practices, such as employing minimal and least-privileged access, utilizing secure

network configurations, and conducting regular security audits to identify and address misconfigurations, is essential.

- **Docker Daemon Security**: The Docker daemon, responsible for managing and running containers, is a critical component with potential security implications. Securing the Docker daemon involves restricting access to privileged Docker APIs, enabling transport encryption for API communications, and implementing strong authentication and access control mechanisms. Monitoring Docker daemon logs regularly and applying security patches promptly to protect against known vulnerabilities is essential.
- **Multi-tenancy Risks**: In multi-tenant environments, where multiple applications or users share the same Docker infrastructure, one tenant risks affecting the security and performance of others. Adequate isolation mechanisms, such as using separate Docker networks and storage volumes for each tenant, can help mitigate these risks. Additionally, implementing fine-grained access controls and monitoring solutions can provide visibility into tenant activities and enable timely responses to any suspicious or malicious behavior.

We will talk more in detail about the security aspect of Docker in Chapter 8, "*Securing Docker Deployments*".

Examples of Docker in the Real World

Some real-world examples of Docker are explicated as follows:

- A popular streaming platform, Netflix, leverages Docker to enhance its development and deployment processes. They use Docker to containerize their microservices, allowing for rapid scalability and efficient resource utilization. By adopting Docker, Netflix has achieved faster application deployment, improved system resilience, and increased flexibility in managing its infrastructure.
- Spotify, a leading music streaming service, relies on Docker to streamline its continuous integration and delivery pipeline. They use Docker containers to package their applications and dependencies, ensuring consistency across development, testing, and production environments. Docker enables Spotify's development teams to work independently, easily deploy services, and quickly respond to customer needs.
- eBay, an e-commerce platform, adopted Docker to modernize its infrastructure and optimize resource utilization. They migrated a significant portion of their applications to Docker containers, resulting in improved scalability, faster deployment, and better utilization of server resources. Docker's containerization has allowed eBay to achieve higher

availability, isolate applications for enhanced security, and efficiently manage its diverse application ecosystem.

- GE Appliances, a major appliance manufacturer, utilizes Docker for its development and testing processes. They employ Docker containers to create isolated environments for testing software on various operating systems and configurations. This approach ensures consistent and reproducible testing conditions, accelerates the development lifecycle, and delivers high-quality products faster.
- Visa, a global payments technology company, embraces Docker for its cloud infrastructure management. By containerizing its applications and services, Visa achieves better resource utilization, scalability, and portability across different cloud providers. Docker allows Visa to deploy and manage its microservices architecture efficiently, enabling rapid innovation and seamless integration with its payment systems.

Figure 1.5: *A pinpoint in a geography map.*
source: https://unsplash.com/photos/Z8UgB80_46w

Conclusion

In this chapter, we explored Docker's introduction, benefits, history, and impact on application development. Docker introduced containerization technology, revolutionizing the development, deployment, and management of applications.

We began by discussing the introduction of Docker, highlighting its ability to package applications and their dependencies into portable units called containers. This portability allows consistent deployment across different environments, simplifying the development and deployment process.

Next, we delved into the benefits of Docker. These include improved application portability, streamlined development and deployment processes, and enhanced collaboration between development and operations teams. Docker's containerization technology enables rapid onboarding, reusability of skills, and consistent development and testing environments.

The history of Docker provided insights into the evolution of containerization technologies and the factors that led to Docker's emergence. We traced the roots of containerization back to operating system-level virtualization and discussed how Docker addressed the limitations of previous technologies, leading to its widespread adoption.

We then explored the security concerns and considerations associated with Docker. These include container isolation, container image vulnerabilities, container configuration risks, Docker daemon security, and multi-tenancy risks. It is crucial to address these concerns by following best practices, implementing secure configurations, regularly updating components, and employing security-focused tools.

Finally, we provided official references for further reading, including the Docker Documentation, Docker Blog, and CNCF resources. These sources offer detailed and up-to-date information on Docker technology, use cases, and industry insights.

This chapter has laid the foundation for understanding Docker's significance in application development. In the subsequent chapters, we will explore Docker's core concepts, container management, orchestration, and advanced features, enabling readers to harness the full potential of Docker for their projects.

References

1. **Docker Documentation**: The official documentation provided by Docker itself is an excellent reference for information about Docker's introduction, benefits, history, and security considerations. Refer to the official Docker documentation website for detailed and up-to-date information: https://docs.docker.com.

2. **Docker Blog**: The Docker Blog is an official source where Docker publishes articles, tutorials, and updates related to Docker technology. It covers various aspects of Docker, including its introduction, benefits, use cases, and industry impact. Refer to the Docker Blog for insightful articles that provide valuable insights and information: https://www.docker.com/blog/

3. **CNCF (Cloud Native Computing Foundation) Resources**: Docker is an essential component of the cloud-native ecosystem, and the CNCF hosts valuable resources related to containerization, including Docker. The CNCF website offers whitepapers, case studies, and presentations on containerization technologies and their impact on application development. You can explore the CNCF resources section for authoritative information: https://www.cncf.io/resources/

Chapter 2
Docker Architecture and Components

***Figure 2.1**: The Zentrum Paul Klee Museum, located in Bern.*
source: https://unsplash.com/photos/opFPVxMRpP8

Introduction

This chapter will delve into Docker's architecture and key components, the leading containerization platform. Understanding Docker's architecture is crucial for effectively utilizing its capabilities and harnessing the full power of containerization. By comprehending how Docker works under the hood and each component's role, you will gain the knowledge needed to orchestrate and manage containers confidently. This chapter will explore the core concepts that form the foundation of Docker's architecture, empowering you to become a master of containerization.

Structure

In this chapter, we will cover the following topics:

- Introduction to Docker architecture and its significance
- Installation of Docker
- Overview of Docker's client-server model and the role of Docker client and daemon
- Exploration of crucial Docker components: images, containers, and registries

Architecture Significance

Docker's architecture embodies a client-server model that enables seamless communication between users and the Docker daemon, facilitating the efficient deployment and scaling of applications.

The significance of Docker's architecture lies in its ability to isolate and package applications, along with their dependencies, into self-contained units called containers. Docker's architecture provides a lightweight and consistent runtime environment that ensures applications run reliably across different operating systems and platforms. By encapsulating applications and their dependencies, Docker eliminates compatibility issues and simplifies deploying and scaling applications, making it an ideal solution for both development and production environments.

Moreover, Docker's architecture enables efficient resource utilization through containerization. Containers leverage the host system's resources while maintaining isolation from other containers, maximizing resource efficiency and minimizing overhead. Docker's architecture also allows for rapid application deployment and scalability, enabling organizations to respond quickly to changing demands and streamline their development and deployment processes.

Docker's architecture provides seamless communication between containers and the outside world. Docker implements network namespaces, allowing containers to have their isolated network stack. This enables easy connectivity between containers, facilitating the creation of complex distributed applications. Docker's networking capabilities and architecture empower developers to build scalable, microservices-based architectures and orchestrate containers. In *Chapter 4, "Docker Networking," we will dive deeper into networking.*

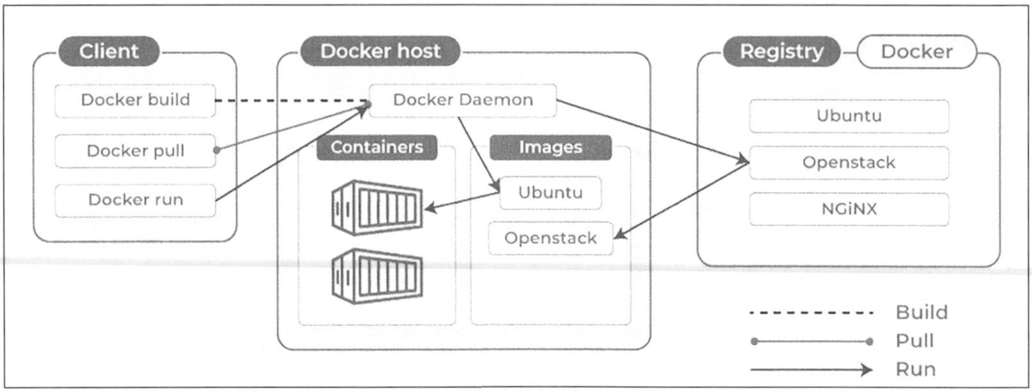

***Figure 2.2**: Docker architecture.*
source: https://docs.docker.com/get-started/overview/

Architecture Components

Docker's architecture comprises several vital components that provide a powerful containerization platform. Each part is crucial in Docker's overall functionality and efficiency, contributing to the bigger picture of seamless application deployment and management.

- **Docker Daemon**: The Docker daemon, also known as the Docker engine, is the heart of Docker's architecture. It runs as a background service on the host system and listens for requests from the Docker client. The daemon is responsible for building, running, and managing containers. It interacts directly with the host's operating system and controls CPU, memory, and storage resources for efficient container execution.
- **Docker Client**: The Docker client is the primary interface for users to interact with Docker daemon. It allows users to issue commands and manage Docker resources using the Docker CLI or a graphical user interface (GUI). The Docker client sends requests to the Docker daemon, instructing it to perform various tasks such as building images, creating containers, and managing networks and volumes. The client can be either on the same machine as the one running the Docker Daemon or a remote machine, sending requests to the Daemon from another host.
- **Docker Images**: Docker images are the building blocks of containers. They contain everything needed to run a specific piece of software, including the operating system, runtime environment, libraries, dependencies, and application code. Images are created from scratch or by pulling existing images from image registries. Images are immutable, meaning they cannot be modified once created. Instead, new images are made based on existing ones, allowing for versioning and reproducibility.

- **Docker Containers**: Containers are lightweight, isolated runtime environments created from Docker images. Each container represents a running instance of an image. Containers encapsulate the application and its dependencies, providing a consistent and isolated environment for execution. They are portable and can run on any host system with Docker installed, making application deployment and scaling effortless.
- **Image Registries**: Docker registries act as repositories for storing and sharing Docker images. They provide a centralized location where users can push their custom images or pull public images shared by the community. Docker Hub is the default public registry, offering a vast collection of pre-built images. Users can also set up private registries to store proprietary images within their organization, ensuring control and security over their container images.

The collaboration of these components forms the foundation of Docker's architecture. Users interact with the Docker client, which communicates with the Docker daemon to build, run, and manage containers based on Docker images. With their layered and immutable structure, Docker images provide the necessary environment for applications, while containers offer lightweight isolation and portability. Docker registries serve as centralized repositories for sharing and distributing images.

Installation of Docker

As you will see in the rest of this chapter, Docker has multiple components that must be installed in the host machine. These components can be cumbersome to install if you wish to do them one by one and manually, which is why the recommended and modern practice is installing Docker Desktop. Another common practice is using the system package manager (for example, `apt`, `yum`, and more) to install, which is handy if you're installing Docker on a server machine.

For the sake of this book, we will use Docker from a desktop machine, which is why Docker Desktop installation is the best option here. It also comes with some helpful other components that we shall use later in this book.

To install Docker Desktop, visit the official documentation from the following URL:

https://docs.docker.com/desktop/

For every platform, there is a bundled package available for download. For example, we will need to download the `.deb` format for Ubuntu-based Linux machines.

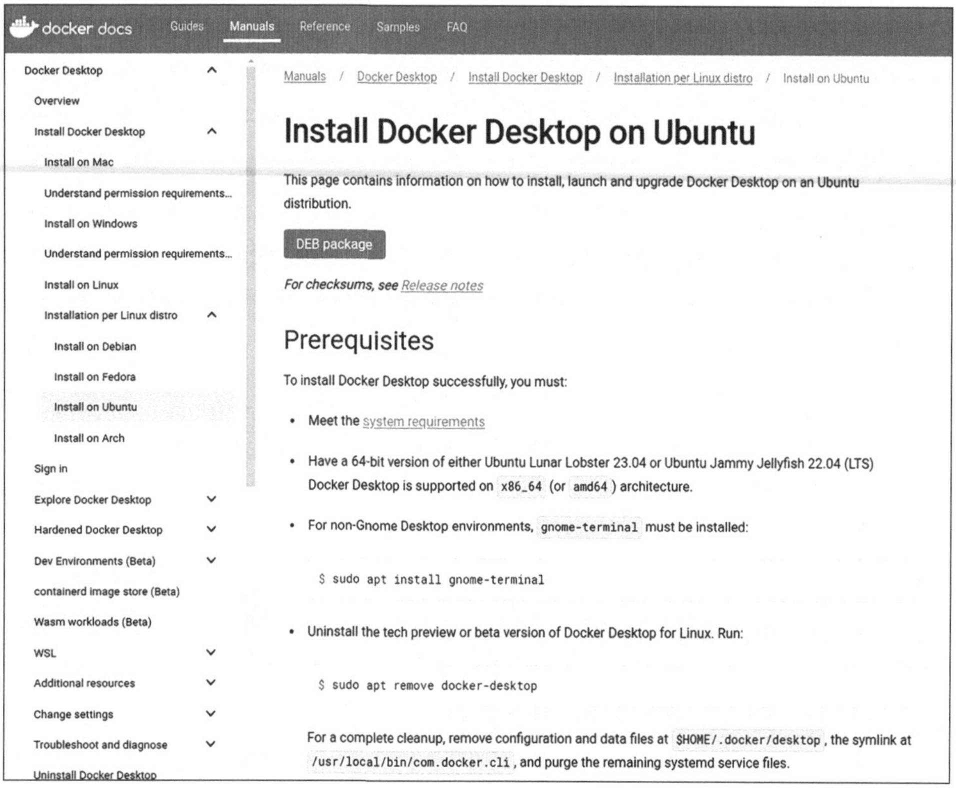

***Figure 2.3**: Docker Desktop installation*

Pressing on the **`DEB package`** in the preceding screen will download a Debian package that can be used to install Docker Desktop. This constitutes the final set of steps, which looks like the following:

1. **`Add the Docker repository to the system package manager`** (https://docs.docker.com/engine/install/ubuntu/#install-using-the-repository).
2. Perform some clean-ups before the installation (shown below).
3. Install the package using the downloaded Debian bundle.

```
$ # First, clean up old installations (if any)
$ sudo apt install gnome-terminal
$ sudo apt remove docker-desktop
$ rm -r $HOME/.docker/desktop
$ sudo rm /usr/local/bin/com.docker.cli
```

```
$ sudo apt purge docker-desktop
$
$ # Second, the installation itself
$ sudo apt-get update
$ sudo apt-get install ./docker-desktop-*.deb
```

Using these steps, we now have a Docker Desktop application, Docker engine, Docker CLI, and many other components installed into our system that we shall use for the remainder of this book.

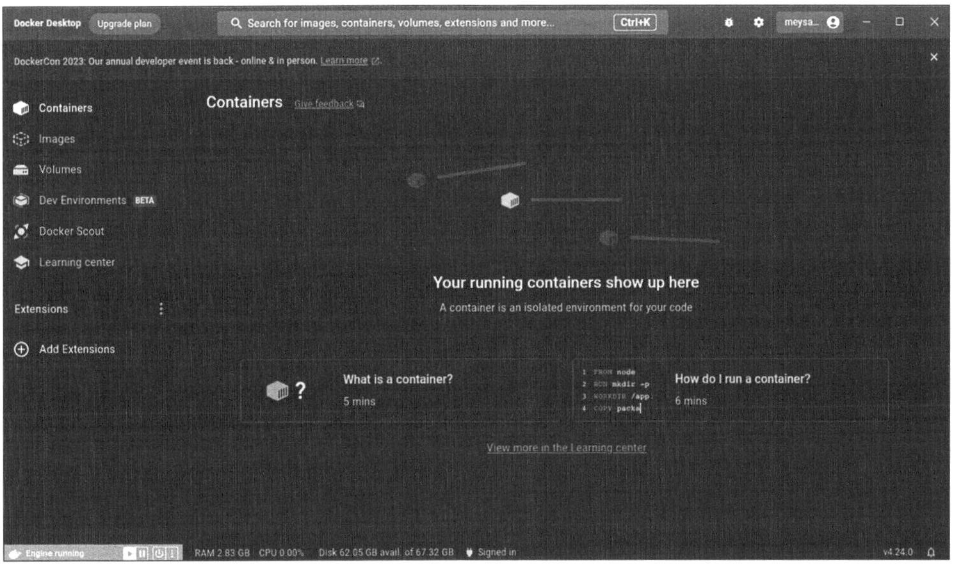

***Figure 2.4**: Docker Desktop*

With the introduction of each component, it's time to explain each in more detail to give you an understanding of how they play a role in the bigger picture.

Docker Daemon

The Docker Daemon, also known as the Docker Engine, is a critical component of Docker's architecture. It is a background service that runs on the host system and plays a central role in managing containers and coordinating containerization processes. Let's delve into the details of the Docker Daemon and its significance.

Primary Role of Docker Daemon

The Docker Daemon is the intermediary between the user and the underlying operating system. Its primary role is to receive user commands, orchestrate container operations, and translate them into appropriate `syscalls` to achieve the desired state of containers. The Docker Daemon ensures that the user's instructions, such as creating, starting, or stopping containers, are correctly translated into `syscalls` that interact with the host operating system to perform the necessary actions.

The Docker Daemon is necessary as it is responsible for the core functionalities of Docker, such as container creation, management, and execution. It interacts with the host operating system to create and manage lightweight, isolated containers. Without the Docker Daemon, Docker's containerization capabilities would not be available.

Without Docker Daemon, alternative containerization technologies like LXC (Linux Containers) would require more manual management. The Docker Daemon automates the process of container creation, deployment, and resource management. Other containerization technologies may need users to manually configure and manage container environments, which can be more complex and time-consuming.

Docker Daemon Delegation of Responsibility

While the Docker Daemon is crucial in managing containers, it delegates specific responsibilities to the operating system. For example, the Docker Daemon uses the operating system's process isolation mechanisms, such as Linux namespaces, to create isolated container environments. It also leverages control groups (`cgroups`) to allocate and manage resources for individual containers, such as CPU and memory. Docker benefits from the underlying kernel's robust and efficient implementations of these features by delegating these responsibilities to the host operating system.

To understand the technical aspects of the primary role and delegation of responsibility within Docker's architecture, it is essential to delve into how Docker leverages system calls (`syscalls`) to create the desired state requested by the user. `Syscalls` provide an interface between user-level processes and the operating system kernel, allowing programs to request services from the kernel. Docker leverages `syscalls` to interact with the underlying operating system and delegate specific responsibilities. Let's explore this further.

Overview and Background

Docker's core is a powerful engine called Docker Daemon, often referred to as `dockerd`. This engine is responsible for the heavy lifting that makes Docker's containerization work. While Docker provides user-friendly interfaces like the Docker CLI and SDKs, Docker Daemon is the workhorse behind the scenes.

Docker simplifies the complexities of interacting with the underlying operating system, making it user-friendly.

You need to know Linux Kernel's namespaces and chroot to understand how Docker creates isolation between the processes inside the container and the host operating machine.

Namespaces and Chroot

Two fundamental concepts drive Docker's containerization: `namespace` and `chroot`. These ideas are the foundation that allows Docker to create isolated operating environments.

Think of namespaces as creating virtual compartments within an operating system. Each compartment, or namespace, is isolated from the others. For example, Docker uses namespaces to create separate spaces for processes, network interfaces, mount points, and more. This isolation ensures that each container operates independently, with its process space, network setup, and filesystem view.

`Chroot`, short for "change root," is another essential concept. It enables Docker to change the root directory of a process, effectively isolating it from the rest of the filesystem. In Docker's world, when you run a container, it operates in its isolated filesystem, separate from the host system.

Now, let's put these concepts into perspective with a simple example.

When you run a Docker container, you trigger Docker Daemon to perform a set of steps. Docker Daemon creates a separate, isolated environment for your application. It uses namespaces to isolate your application's processes from the host and other containers. It also employs `chroot` to give your application its private filesystem.

For instance, imagine you run a web server in a Docker container. Thanks to namespaces and chroot, that web server operates as if it's the only thing on the system, even though it shares the same host OS with other containers.

Now that we have introduced how Docker achieves its level of isolation for containers, let's bring an example so that you understand it by heart.

```
# source: https://btholt.github.io/complete-intro-to-containers/namespaces
# First, installing the prerequisites
apt-get update -y
apt-get install debootstrap -y
debootstrap --variant=minbase bionic /better-root

# Head into the new namespace'd, chroot'ed environment
unshare --mount --uts --ipc --net --pid --fork --user --map-root-user
chroot /better-root bash # this also chroot's for us
mount -t proc none /proc # process namespace
mount -t sysfs none /sys # filesystem
mount -t tmpfs none /tmp # filesystem
```

After creating the chroot and running a new bash from it, any new command will be completely isolated from the host machine.

You can try running the command `ps aux` from the newly `chroot`'ed environment to see that only the processes inside that environment are visible.

While namespaces and chroot are vital, Docker builds upon the foundation provided by the Linux kernel. It utilizes control groups (`cgroups`) for resource management, capabilities for fine-grained permissions, and creates a secure runtime environment. These elements are integral to Docker's capabilities and are made possible by the Linux kernel's support for **cgroups** and other low-level features.

The beauty of Docker is that it hides these complexities from you. You don't need to worry about the technical details; you can focus on managing and deploying your applications efficiently. Docker translates your high-level commands into the necessary actions, making it accessible and user-friendly.

Now that you have seen the theories and a practical example implementation let's try to discover how expensive running the Docker Daemon is.

Figure 2.5: *An old man with a long beard working on an anvil.*
source: https://unsplash.com/photos/2MuZ23gkFKo

Performance Impact of the Docker Daemon

The Docker Daemon is a background service that runs on the host system and manages containers and their resources. As with any system component, it is essential to consider the potential performance impact of running the Docker Daemon alongside other workloads. Here are some factors to consider.

Resource Utilization

The Docker Daemon utilizes system resources such as CPU, memory, and disk I/O to manage containers and perform various tasks. Docker is designed to be resource-efficient; however, the primary factors affecting resource utilization are the number of containers actively defined and running on the host system. Each container consumes a fixed amount of resources, directly correlated with the number of containers used. While the size of container images affects disk usage, it doesn't directly impact the Docker Daemon's resource footprint. Additionally, the workload running within containers can influence resource usage, especially CPU and memory, as it determines the demands placed on individual containers. When the host system has limited resources or is under heavy load from other applications, the Docker Daemon may compete for resources, potentially affecting overall system performance.

To provide a tangible example of resource utilization and its impact on performance, let's consider a scenario where the Docker Daemon runs alongside other workloads on a host system. Suppose the host system has a quad-core CPU, 8GB of RAM, and a standard spinning hard drive.

Assuming that the Docker Daemon is actively managing several containers, each running a web application, we can analyze the resource utilization and its potential impact:

- **CPU Utilization**: The Docker Daemon's CPU utilization varies based on workload and container activity. While it typically remains dormant once containers are running, its CPU usage may temporarily increase during intensive container orchestration, such as managing numerous CPU-intensive containers. The specific percentage can vary widely and is not fixed, but it should not be a significant concern under normal conditions. Monitoring resource utilization and adjusting container workloads is critical to maintaining optimal performance.
- **Memory Utilization**: The Docker Daemon also requires memory to maintain container metadata, manage network configurations, and execute container-related operations. Memory consumption varies based

on the number and size of containers and the containerized applications' complexity. On average, the Docker Daemon may utilize around 100–200MB of RAM for managing a moderate number of containers. However, the total memory footprint can increase significantly if numerous containers actively run and consume memory resources.

- **Disk I/O**: The Docker Daemon utilizes disk I/O for various operations, such as pulling and caching container images, managing container storage, and persisting container logs. The impact on disk I/O depends on the size and frequency of image pulls, container updates, and log writes. The actual disk I/O impact can vary widely. Still, as a rough estimate, the Docker Daemon may generate disk I/O operations in the range of a few hundred to a few thousand IOPS (Input/Output Operations Per Second) during image pulls and container-related operations.
- **Impact on Other Workloads**: Running the Docker Daemon alongside other workloads on the same host system may result in resource competition. If the host system is already under heavy load from other applications, Docker Daemon's resource consumption may impact the performance of those workloads. For example, suppose the host system utilizes 80% of its CPU capacity from other applications. In that case, the Docker Daemon's additional CPU utilization may lead to increased contention and potential performance degradation for both the Docker Daemon and the existing workloads.

To mitigate resource contention and optimize performance, it is crucial to carefully monitor resource utilization, adjust container resource limits, and consider scaling strategies. Employing techniques like horizontal scaling, where containers are distributed across multiple host systems, can help spread resource usage and alleviate the impact on any single host.

Container Isolation

Docker provides container process isolation, ensuring each container operates independently without interfering with other containers or the host system. However, this isolation requires some overhead in terms of system resources. Each container has its filesystem, network stack, and resource allocations, which may result in additional resource consumption compared to running the same workload directly on the host operating system.

The Overhead of Containerization

Containerization itself incurs some performance overhead due to Docker's additional layers of abstraction and isolation. While the overhead is generally minimal, it is essential to consider that running an application within a container adds an extra layer of virtualization and introduces some performance trade-offs compared to running the application directly on the host system.

Scaling and Resource Allocation

Docker's ability to scale applications by running multiple containers in parallel can affect resource allocation. When scaling horizontally, numerous containers may compete for system resources, increasing resource usage and potential performance impact. Proper resource management and scaling strategies, such as setting resource limits and utilizing container orchestration platforms like Kubernetes, can mitigate these issues and optimize performance.

System Tuning and Optimization

To minimize the performance impact of the Docker Daemon, it is crucial to consider system tuning and optimization techniques. This may involve adjusting container resource limits, optimizing container configurations, and fine-tuning the host system to ensure efficient resource utilization. Additionally, keeping Docker and its components up to date with the latest versions can help leverage performance improvements and bug fixes.

It's important to note that the performance impact of the Docker Daemon can vary based on the specific workload, system configuration, and resource availability. While some overhead may be associated with running the Docker Daemon, Docker's containerization benefits, such as isolation, portability, and scalability, often outweigh the potential performance trade-offs. By carefully monitoring system resources, optimizing configurations, and employing best practices, it is possible to mitigate any adverse performance impact and achieve efficient containerization with Docker.

Figure 2.6: *Woman's hands drawing a wireframe.*
source: https://unsplash.com/photos/gcHFXsdcmJE

Docker Clients

The Docker Daemon provides various interfaces and APIs that enable users to interact with it and manage Docker resources effectively. These interfaces offer different levels of abstraction and flexibility, catering to a wide range of user requirements. Let's explore the interfaces and APIs available to communicate with the Docker Daemon:

Docker Command-Line Interface (CLI)

The Docker CLI is the most common and user-friendly interface to interact with the Docker Daemon. It provides a command-line interface that allows users to issue commands and manage Docker resources conveniently. With the Docker CLI, users can build, run, and manage containers, manage networks and volumes, access logs, and perform various other tasks. The CLI abstracts the underlying complexity of Docker's operations and provides a straightforward way to interact with the Docker Daemon.

Docker Remote HTTP API

The Docker Daemon exposes a RESTful API that allows programmatic communication with the Docker Daemon. This API provides a powerful interface for developers to integrate Docker into their applications and build custom solutions. The Docker Remote API allows users to perform various operations, including managing containers, images, networks, and volumes. It offers endpoints for creating and deleting containers, inspecting container details, pulling and pushing images, and managing various Docker resources. The reference for writing the API's can be found in this link.

Docker SDKs and Client Libraries

Docker provides Software Development Kits (SDKs) and client libraries for several programming languages, making it easier for developers to interact with the Docker Daemon programmatically. These SDKs and libraries encapsulate the Docker Remote API and provide a higher-level abstraction for application developers. They offer functions, classes, and methods that simplify interacting with the Docker Daemon, allowing developers to focus on building their applications rather than handling low-level API calls.

At the time of writing this book, there are two official SDKs provided by Docker itself in Golang and Python. There are many other community-supported libraries for different programming languages as well. You can check the complete list at this link.

Third-Party Tools and Utilities

In addition to the Docker CLI and official SDKs, numerous third-party tools and utilities exist that leverage the Docker API to provide additional functionality or user interfaces. These tools range from graphical user interfaces (GUIs) for managing containers and images to advanced orchestration and deployment frameworks. They often utilize the Docker Remote API to interact with the Docker Daemon and extend Docker's capabilities.

Docker Desktop

Docker Desktop is a versatile application designed for various operating systems, offering a Graphical User Interface (GUI) that enhances user experience. This tool is precious for those running Docker on non-Linux systems, as it provides a straightforward way to manage and interact with Docker containers and services.

For readers eager to experiment with the examples in this book, it's essential to understand that while Docker is typically associated with Linux environments, Docker Desktop extends its support to other platforms like Windows and macOS. This means that even if you're using a non-Linux system, you can still utilize Docker Desktop to run the examples provided in this book seamlessly.

Furthermore, it's worth noting that Docker Desktop for Linux also exists, although Linux users may be more accustomed to interacting with Docker through command-line interfaces. In this context, Docker Desktop is an option for those who prefer a GUI-based approach to container management.

You can install the desktop application from the official website, whether you're using Mac, Windows, or Linux.

The availability of these interfaces and APIs enables a wide range of possibilities for interacting with the Docker Daemon. Users can choose the interface that best suits their needs, whether it's the user-friendly Docker CLI, the flexibility of the Docker Remote API for programmatic control, or the convenience of SDKs and client libraries for application development.

By providing these interfaces, Docker promotes interoperability and extensibility, allowing users to build custom solutions, integrate Docker into existing systems, and automate Docker-related tasks. These interfaces empower developers and system administrators to leverage the power of Docker's containerization capabilities in a way that aligns with their workflow and technical requirements.

Docker Images: Structure and Composition

Docker images are the building blocks of containers, providing a portable and reproducible way to package applications, along with their dependencies and configurations. Understanding the structure of a Docker image is essential for effectively working with containers. Let's explore the high-level design of Docker images, including the concept of Docker layers and how they contribute to efficient image building. We'll conclude by building a Docker image for a sample application.

Docker Image Structure

A Docker image comprises multiple layers, each representing specific changes or additions to the underlying filesystem. These layers are stacked on each other, each building upon the previous one. The layers are read-only and immutable, ensuring the image's integrity and reproducibility.

Docker's layered architecture is pivotal in optimizing image creation and distribution. When a new layer is added to an existing image, only the changes made in that layer are stored, while the unchanged parts are shared across multiple images. This approach dramatically reduces the storage footprint and speeds up image creation, as subsequent builds only need to focus on the modified layers.

Docker leverages layers to build images efficiently by utilizing a technique called copy-on-write. When a new layer is created during the build process, it references the underlying layers, and any changes made are stored as new data without modifying the original layers. This copy-on-write mechanism ensures that image creation remains fast and resources are utilized optimally.

Docker images result from a couple of instructions written in a file named `Dockerfile`. This file and the instructions inside are parsed and mapped to predefined commands instructing Docker Daemon to create an immutable image. These so-called "images" are the templates you can use later to run isolated container environments, each with its setup and configurations.

It allows you to run the same image with different needs and environments. Once you create and store an image, you can use it countless times to create running containers doing the specific job they were supposed to do.

An example includes the Docker image of the Nginx web server. It is only built once but used many times in different deployments with different configurations and environment variables.

For example, imagine writing an application that uses environment variables and behaves differently with different configurations. Docker images are the closest representation to that written application (acting as a template), and the running application with the configuration and environment variables are "containers" in Docker terminology.

Building a Docker Image

Let's walk through building a Docker image for a sample application. Suppose we have a simple web application with one or more source code files in your favorite programming language. To create a Docker image for this application, we follow these steps:

1. **Create a Dockerfile**: The Dockerfile is a plain text file containing instructions for building the image. It specifies the base image, adds the necessary dependencies, copies the application files, and configures the container.
2. **Define the Base Image**: The Dockerfile starts with specifying a base image that forms the initial layer of the image. The base image includes the operating system and pre-installed packages or libraries that the application relies on.
3. **Add Application Files**: Next, the Dockerfile includes instructions to copy the application files into the image. This creates a new layer that contains the application code, ensuring it is isolated and portable.
4. **Configure the Container**: The Dockerfile allows specifying additional configuration steps, such as exposing network ports, setting environment variables, and defining the command to run when the container starts.
5. **Build the Image**: With the Dockerfile ready, the Docker CLI provides the docker build command to build the image. This command reads the instructions from the Dockerfile and executes them sequentially, creating a layered image based on those instructions.

Hello World in Docker

Now that you have seen the outline let's build a Docker image together to make sense of all the theories.

Imagine having the following Python applications.

```
import os
from fastapi import FastAPI
app = FastAPI()
GREETER = os.getenv("GREETER", "Docker")
@app.get("/")
async def index(name: str = None):
    greetee = name or "Friend"
    return {"message": f"Hello {greetee}! I am {GREETER}."}
if __name__ == "__main__":
    import uvicorn
    uvicorn.run(app, host="0.0.0.0", port=8000)
```

If you want to run this app locally, a simple `python main.py` will run the application.

But as your application grows, so does its dependency graph, and so does every other piece that makes it a fully functional and feature-rich app.

That's why putting this app in a containerized and isolated environment with all the dependencies installed can go a long way in simplifying and streamlining the application deployments.

It reduces operational overhead by building the image once and shipping it to many deployment environments.

To build a Docker image for this application, we only need a **`Dockerfile`**. A sample **`Dockerfile`** could look like this for a Python application.

```
FROM python:3.11-alpine
WORKDIR /app
RUN pip install "fastapi<1" "uvicorn<1"
COPY main.py .
CMD ["uvicorn", "main:app", "--host", "0.0.0.0", "--port", "8000"]
```

In the next chapter, we will discuss how to write an efficient **`Dockerfile`** to optimize your Docker images, but for the sake of simplicity, these instructions will be enough to create an image for us.

As you can see, the instructions are human-readable and quite intuitive. Even people unfamiliar with Docker or containerization technology can understand the declarative instructions specified in this file.

Let's briefly explain the different instructions since this book is entirely dedicated to Docker and deserves great detail for such a title.

The first line is where we specify the base image. If we don't set the Python base image here, we would need to build the Python from the source code ourselves and put it in the **`Dockerfile`**.

This may be desirable if you want to build it with a special feature flag, but optional for a typical use case.

The second line is the same as the `cd` command (that is, "change directory in a Linux machine). We delegate the same task to the Docker Daemon when creating the image.

In the third line, we are installing the dependencies. This is where the magic happens, so your Docker image is portable across different machines. When you install the dependencies in your Docker image, anyone else who uses this image will not have to reinstall them because of missing libraries. Still, they will have the app and all its dependencies in one isolated and self-contained unit called image.

Different applications will likely need their specific dependency installations and commands. But it'll do for our sample demo application.

We copy the source code to the ultimate Docker image in the fourth line. It's important to note that you must run the `docker build` command from the same directory as the Dockerfile. We will provide the alternatives when you want otherwise in a later chapter.

The last line is just an instruction to the Docker Daemon, saying, "If no other command were specified by the user of this image when running the container, this command would be the default to run."

Imagine running a `cd` in a Linux machine from any non-home directory. If you don't provide any arguments to the command, the default argument is the home directory; an empty `cd` will get you to your user's home directory.

The same applies to Docker images. You can specify `CMD` in your `Dockerfile` if nothing else was set to provide a default argument.

Now that we have written the app and its `Dockerfile`, it's time to create the Docker image.

One crucial piece of information we have kept to ourselves so far is that creating an image from a `Dockerfile` is called **build**. It essentially converts those human-readable instructions to an immutable image that can only be used to run the app but not modified unless rebuilt again!

The command to build a Docker image is:

```
$ docker build --tag greeter .
```

Here, **`greeter`** is the name of the image and can be anything arbitrary that you prefer. The dot you see at the end is the **context**. We will talk about the context later, but for now, all you need to know is that the Dockerfile must be present at the specified location; the dot refers to the current working directory.

This will create an immutable image in the host machine with the name specified (greeter). Once built, we're ready to make a running container from this image in the next section.

Docker Containers

It's essential to recognize their roles and relationships within the containerization ecosystem to understand the distinction between Docker images and containers. Docker images serve as the building blocks, providing a snapshot of a specific application, its dependencies, and configurations. On the other hand, Docker containers are the instances created from these images, running and executing the application in an isolated and portable environment.

Think of Docker images as blueprints or templates that define the application's environment, while Docker containers are the actual instances derived from those blueprints.

Consider the analogy of a bakery. Imagine a baker preparing a variety of pastries. The recipes for these pastries are akin to Docker images. Each recipe contains a list of ingredients, instructions, and a defined outcome. The baker can create multiple instances of pastries based on the same recipe. These pastries represent Docker containers, each running independently in an isolated environment.

For example, in the last section, let's consider the Docker image based on the Python web application. This image includes the necessary Python runtime, application code, and required libraries. Using the Docker CLI, we can create a container from this image, essentially an isolated runtime environment running our Python web application. We can start, stop, and manage this container independently of other applications.

The relationship between Docker images and containers can be visualized as follows: an image acts as a blueprint or a snapshot of a specific state, providing all the necessary components and instructions to run the application. Containers, on the other hand, are the live instances created from these images, enabling the execution of the application in an isolated and self-contained manner.

Docker containers are temporary, which means they can be created, started, stopped, and destroyed as needed. This flexibility allows for easy scaling, migration, and reproducibility. Multiple containers can be made from the same Docker image, enabling the deployment of multiple instances of an application across different environments.

Docker images are the immutable building blocks that define the environment and dependencies of an application, while Docker containers are the running instances created from these images. The image-container relationship provides a powerful mechanism for encapsulating applications, ensuring consistency, portability, and scalability throughout the development, deployment, and operational lifecycle.

Running a Docker Container

After building the Python web app in the previous section, we can run it in a Docker container. This will give us a running process over the app we have written, whatever programming language.

This is the simplest way to run the container from the previously created image:

```
$ docker run greeter
```

But you won't be able to access the exposed 8000 port from your host machine just yet!

To be able to send an HTTP request to the running Docker container, you would have to "expose" the port on the host machine, and that is done with this command:

```
$ docker run -p 8000:8000 greeter
```

After running this command, sending an HTTP request to the container from the host machine using `curl` or any other HTTP client of your preference is possible:

```
$ curl localhost:8000
{"message":"Hello Friend! I am Docker."}
```

This is our Hello World application, written in Python and deployed in a Docker container. You can get more advanced usage, and I invite you to get curious and change things slightly to see how it'll affect different parts.

Running a Docker container can be more advanced when specifying different options and flags to the `docker run` command.

Here are examples of creating other containers based on the same immutable image:

```
# Run the container, specifying a unique name for it
docker run --name mygreeter greeter


# Run the container and expose its port on the host machine
docker run --publish 8000:8000 greeter


# Run the container with a different environment variable
docker run --env GREETER="Mastering Docker" greeter


# Run the container, but remove it when it stops
docker run --rm greeter


# Run the container in the background
docker run --detach greeter
```

These examples are not exhaustive, but they'll give you an idea of what is possible. A complete guide of all the possible options will be provided later on.

Inner Working of a Docker Container

It's helpful to draw parallels between Docker containers and regular processes running on a host machine to understand the inner workings of a Docker container. While Docker containers provide isolation and portability, they fundamentally leverage existing operating system mechanisms to achieve these features. Let's explore the similarities between Docker containers and regular processes and the role of namespaces and cgroups in container isolation.

At its core, a Docker container behaves similarly to a traditional process running on a host machine. Like any process, a Docker container has its runtime environment, file descriptors, network interfaces, and process tree. This similarity allows Docker containers to be managed, monitored, and controlled using familiar system tools.

Docker achieves container isolation primarily through the use of namespaces. Namespaces provide a way to virtualize system resources, creating isolated instances independent of one another. Docker leverages various namespaces, such as the PID namespace for process isolation, the network namespace for network isolation, the mount namespace for filesystem isolation, and others. Using namespaces, Docker ensures that each container operates in its isolated environment, separate from other containers and the host system.

For example, to see this isolation in effect, a container will be run, and the running processes will be queried from inside the container using the following CLI terminal commands:

```
$ docker run --rm -d --name nginx nginx:1-alpine
```

```
$ docker exec -it nginx ps -ef
```

Don't worry if you don't know the command or the flags; we'll cover them later in this book.

All you need to know for now is that a container was run, and an attempt was made to see the processes running inside it.

Here's what the output will look like:

```
PID   USER     TIME  COMMAND
    1 root      0:00 nginx: master process nginx -g daemon off;
   30 nginx     0:00 nginx: worker process
   31 nginx     0:00 nginx: worker process
   32 nginx     0:00 nginx: worker process
   33 nginx     0:00 nginx: worker process
   34 nginx     0:00 nginx: worker process
   35 nginx     0:00 nginx: worker process
   36 nginx     0:00 nginx: worker process
   37 nginx     0:00 nginx: worker process
   38 nginx     0:00 nginx: worker process
   39 nginx     0:00 nginx: worker process
   40 nginx     0:00 nginx: worker process
   41 nginx     0:00 nginx: worker process
   42 nginx     0:00 nginx: worker process
   43 nginx     0:00 nginx: worker process
   44 nginx     0:00 nginx: worker process
   45 nginx     0:00 nginx: worker process
   46 root      0:00 ps -ef
```

Figure 2.7: *Query processes inside a container*

You can see in the screenshot that only the running container can see the processes running inside the container and nothing more. That is the level of isolation Docker and the underlying technologies are providing. This is what is going to empower the security isolation (more on that later).

Additionally, Docker utilizes control groups (**`cgroups`**) to manage resource allocation and container utilization. **`cgroups`** allow for fine-grained control over resource limits, such as CPU, memory, and I/O. This enables Docker to allocate resources to containers and prevent any container from monopolizing the system's resources. **`cgroups`** ensure that containers operate within their designated resource boundaries, providing isolation and preventing resource contention among containers.

The combination of namespaces and **`cgroups`** allows Docker to provide a highly isolated and resource-controlled environment for containerized applications. The namespaces ensure that each container has its isolated view of system resources, while **`cgroups`** ensure fair and efficient allocation of resources among containers.

To summarize, Docker containers share similarities with normal processes running on a host machine, leveraging namespaces and **`cgroups`** for isolation and resource management. Namespaces enable the creation of isolated environments for containers, while **`cgroups`** ensure resource allocation and prevent resource abuse. Understanding the inner workings of Docker containers helps grasp the underlying mechanisms that enable their portability, scalability, and efficient utilization of system resources.

Now that you know what Docker image and container is, it's time to explore Docker Registries, a place to store Docker images, whether privately or publicly.

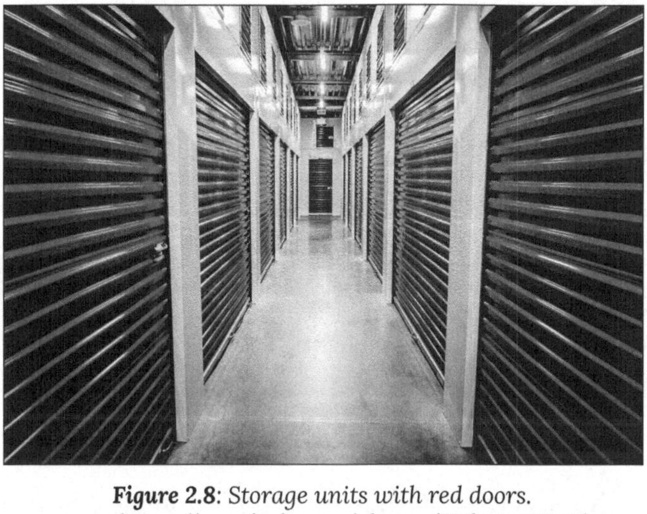

***Figure 2.8**: Storage units with red doors.*
source: https://unsplash.com/photos/ZVkDLrXGMdw

Docker Registry: Facilitating Image Storage and Distribution

Docker Registry plays a crucial role in the ecosystem by providing a centralized repository for storing and distributing Docker images. It is a reliable and scalable solution for managing container images, facilitating the seamless sharing of images across different environments. Let's explore how Docker Registry enables efficient image storage and pulling and how it accommodates both private and public registries. We'll also highlight its significance in CI/CD pipelines.

Image Storage and Distribution

Docker Registry is a dedicated image storage platform allowing users to upload, store, and manage their Docker images. It provides a centralized location where images can be securely stored and versioned. With Docker's push command, users can upload their local images to a Docker Registry, making them accessible for deployment on various systems. Docker Registry ensures that images are readily available and can be pulled on demand, facilitating seamless distribution across hosts.

If you know Google Drive or Dropbox, Docker Registry acts the same way, only for Docker images!

Private and Public Registries

Docker Registry supports private and public registries, offering flexibility in sharing and accessing images. Organizations typically use private registries to store their proprietary or sensitive images securely. They provide controlled access, allowing authorized users or teams to retrieve images for deployment within their infrastructure. On the other hand, public registries like Docker Hub serve as a vast collection of publicly available Docker images, allowing users to share their images with the broader community. Public registries offer a rich ecosystem of community-contributed images, making it easy to discover and utilize pre-built images for various purposes.

CI/CD Pipelines

One of the key selling points of Docker Registry is its seamless integration with CI/CD pipelines. CI/CD pipelines automate the process of building, testing, and deploying applications, and Docker Registry plays a vital role in streamlining the image management aspect of these pipelines. By leveraging the Docker Registry, developers can publish their application images to a central repository, enabling continuous integration and delivery. CI/CD pipelines can retrieve these images from the registry, ensuring consistent and reliable deployments across different environments. Docker Registry's support for versioning and tagging further enhances the traceability and reproducibility of images in CI/CD workflows.

In summary, Docker Registry is a reliable and scalable solution for storing and distributing Docker images. It accommodates private and public registries, providing flexible options for image sharing and access control. Its integration with CI/CD pipelines enables seamless automation and deployment of containerized applications. Docker Registry's central role in the Docker ecosystem highlights its significance in helping efficient image management and fostering collaboration among developers and organizations.

Setting Up a Private Docker Registry: An Example

To illustrate the inner workings of a private Docker registry, let's walk through setting up a registry on a server. This example assumes a Linux-based environment and demonstrates the basic steps in configuring and accessing a private registry.

Server Setup

Begin by setting up a dedicated server hosting the private Docker registry. This server should have sufficient resources to handle image storage and network traffic. Install Docker on the server to enable registry functionality.

For a small organization's private Docker registry, it is recommended to have a host with a dual-core CPU, 4GB of RAM, at least 100GB of storage space, and a network connection with a minimum of 100 Mbps upload and download speed. These specifications should be sufficient to handle the workload of up to 100 employees, ensuring smooth operation, efficient image storage, and responsive image transfers between the registry and the clients.

Generate SSL Certificates

To ensure secure communication between the registry and clients, generate SSL certificates.

If you're not an advanced user and don't know much about certificates, step CLI is a recommended tool with friendly and intuitive API with reasonable defaults.

If you know your way around advanced tools, use tools like OpenSSL to create self-signed certificates or obtain valid certificates from a trusted certificate authority (for example, with certbot). These certificates will encrypt the communication between the clients and the registry.

For your reference, here's how to create a self-signed certificate with the aforementioned tools.

```
# https://github.com/smallstep/cli

step certificate create docker.example.com docker.crt docker.key --profile
root-ca


openssl req -x509 -newkey rsa:4096 -keyout docker.key -out docker.crt
-sha256 -days 3650 -nodes -subj "/CN=docker.example.com"
```

Configure Registry (Optional)

Next, configure the Docker registry by creating a configuration file, typically `config.yml`. This file specifies basic settings such as storage location, authentication mechanisms, and TLS configurations. Customize the configuration to suit your requirements. Ensure that the storage path specified in the configuration has enough disk space to accommodate the Docker images.

The complete reference of available keys can be found in this link.

This step is not required for local development but is highly recommended for production and internet-exposed environments.

Start Registry Container

Create and start a Docker container using the generated SSL certificates and the configuration file based on the registry image. This container will run the private registry and make it accessible to clients. The command to start the container might look like this:

```
docker run -d -p 5000:5000 --restart=always --name my-registry \
  -v /path/to/ssl/certs:/certs \
  -v /path/to/registry/data:/var/lib/registry \
  -v /path/to/config.yml:/etc/docker/registry/config.yml \
```

```
-e REGISTRY_HTTP_ADDR=0.0.0.0:443 \
-e REGISTRY_HTTP_TLS_CERTIFICATE=/certs/domain.crt \
-e REGISTRY_HTTP_TLS_KEY=/certs/domain.key \
registry:2
```

Push and Pull Images

With the private registry up and running, Docker images can now be pushed to and pulled from the registry. To push an image, tag it with the registry's address and port and then use the 'docker push' command. For example:

```
docker tag greeter docker.example.com:5000/greeter
docker push docker.example.com:5000/greeter
```

To pull an image from the private registry, use the `docker pull` command:

```
docker pull docker.example.com:5000/greeter
```

Clients accessing the private registry must have their SSL certificates added to their trusted certificate store to avoid certificate validation errors.

The method will vary depending on the operating system and the software importing the self-signed certificate into the trusted certificate store. Here are some common approaches:

- **Graphical User Interface (GUI)**: On some operating systems, you can import the certificate using a GUI tool. This typically involves opening the certificate file, viewing its details, and selecting an option to import it into the trusted store. Follow the on-screen instructions provided by the GUI tool.
- **Command Line Interface (CLI)**: You can use command-line tools to import the certificate. For example, on Linux systems, you can use the `update-ca-certificates` command or the trust command to add the certificate to the trusted store. You can use the `certutil` command or the `Import-Certificate` PowerShell cmdlet on Windows.

A private Docker registry can be set up by following these steps, providing a secure and controlled environment for storing and sharing Docker images. The registry allows for the seamless pushing and pulling of images, enabling teams to collaborate and deploy applications in a controlled manner.

For your reference, here's how you would add a certificate to a host machine using the command line:

```
# copy the certificate to the client host machine
sudo cp docker.crt /usr/local/share/ca-certificates/

# update the certificate store
sudo update-ca-certificates

# check the certificate is trusted
sudo trust list
```

Figure 2.9: *Man with a leather bag and book.*
source: https://unsplash.com/photos/mO9vKbG5csg

Conclusion

This chapter provides a comprehensive overview of Docker's architecture and its components. We explored the significance of Docker's architecture in enabling efficient containerization and discussed how Docker differentiates itself from other containerization technologies. By understanding the inner workings of Docker's architecture, readers can gain valuable insights into how it operates and leverages various components to deliver its containerization capabilities.

We delved into the Docker daemon, which serves as the core engine of Docker and is responsible for managing and executing container-related tasks. We examined its necessity, discussed the consequences of its absence, and explored the interfaces and APIs available to communicate with the daemon. We also explored the performance impact of running the Docker daemon alongside other workloads, highlighting the importance of resource allocation and optimization.

Furthermore, we discussed Docker images and their structure, shedding light on the layered approach that enables efficient building and sharing of images. We examined the distinction between Docker images and containers, showcasing their relationship and how containers are instantiated from images. Additionally, we explored the Docker registry, both public and private, as a vital component for storing and distributing Docker images. We highlighted the benefits of private registries, including facilitating CI/CD pipelines for seamless integration and deployment. In the upcoming chapters, we will dive deeper into specific aspects of Docker, including image optimization techniques, container orchestration, and advanced Docker features. Stay tuned to enhance your mastery of Docker further and unlock its full potential in your development and deployment workflows.

References

- The source codes presented in this chapter and the entire book can be found at this link: https://github.com/ava-orange-education/Ultimate Docker for Cloud Native Applications
- This book heavily relies on the official documentation at https://docs.docker.com/
- The interactive version of this book is available freely on this URL: https://killercoda.com/meysam/course/mastering-docker

CHAPTER 3

Building and Managing Docker Images

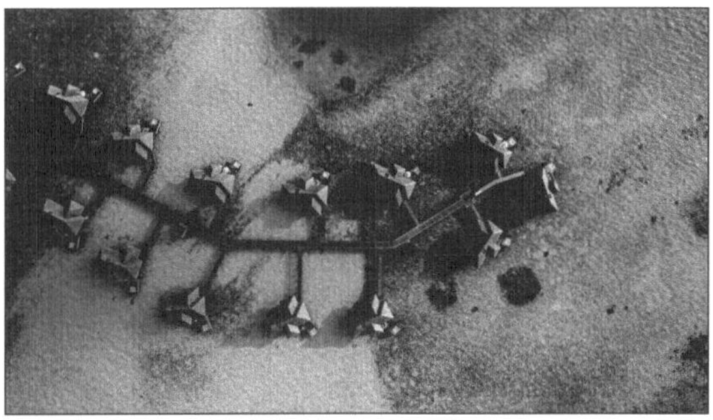

***Figure 3.1**: Aerial photography of resort villa on water.*
source: https://unsplash.com/photos/GSZQ_eupukE

Introduction

Welcome to Chapter 3 of "*Mastering Docker*"! In this chapter, we dive deep into the world of Docker images. Docker images are the foundation of containerization, allowing you to package your applications and dependencies into a portable and reproducible format. This chapter will equip you with the knowledge and techniques to create, manage, and optimize Docker images.

Docker images are the building blocks of Docker containers. They contain everything required to run your application, **including the code, runtime, libraries, and system** tools. In this chapter, we will explore various aspects of working with Docker images, providing you with a solid understanding of how to create and customize them to meet your specific requirements. By the end of this chapter, you will be equipped with the necessary skills to build efficient and robust Docker images for your applications.

Structure

In this chapter, we will discuss the following topics:

- Docker Image Basics
- Creating Docker Images
- Image Management and Distribution
- Advanced Techniques

By the end of this chapter, you will have a comprehensive understanding of Docker image creation, management, and optimization, enabling you to build and deploy containerized applications with Docker confidently. So, let's dive in and embark on this exciting journey of mastering Docker images!

Docker Image Basics

In this section, we will lay the foundation of Docker image understanding by exploring the anatomy of a Docker image, delving into the significance of different layers, harnessing the power of the Docker image cache, and learning techniques to optimize image size and complexity. Building upon this knowledge, we will move on to creating Docker images, diving into the core concepts and best practices that will empower you to craft efficient and tailored images for your applications.

Understanding the Anatomy of a Docker Image

A Docker image is a self-contained unit that encapsulates everything needed to run an application. To comprehend the inner workings of a Docker image, it's crucial to grasp its anatomy. At its core, a Docker image comprises a series of read-only layers stacked on top of each other. Each layer represents a specific modification or addition to the underlying filesystem. These lightweight layers share common components, fostering efficient disk usage and facilitating rapid image creation and distribution.

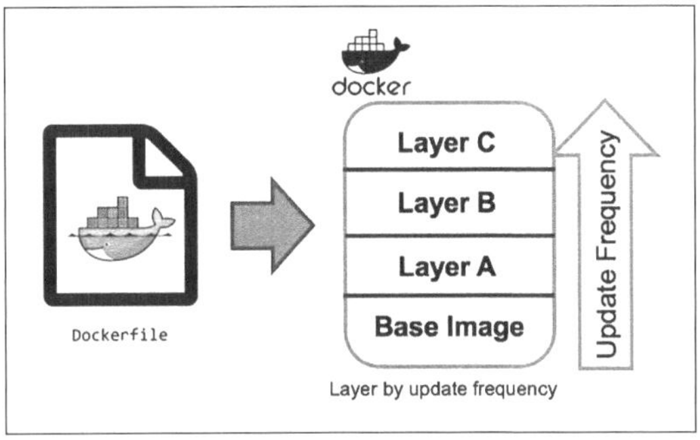

Figure 3.2: *Representation of Docker layers.*
source: https://medium.com/@pratyush.mathur/understanding-dockerfile-b17807981833

The Docker image layers adopt a hierarchical structure, with the base layer forming the foundation and subsequent layers building upon it. Each layer captures changes made to the filesystem, such as adding files, modifying configurations, or installing software packages. This layer-based approach enables Docker to optimize storage usage by reusing unchanged layers across different images, reducing duplication and conserving disk space.

By inspecting a Docker image's layers, you can gain insights into its construction and understand the dependencies and components it contains. Docker employs a union file system, such as OverlayFS, to create a unified view of the layers, presenting them as a cohesive filesystem to the container. This union filesystem efficiently merges the different layers and offers them as a unified directory structure, providing a seamless environment for running applications [source: https://docs.docker.com/storage/storagedriver/].

Understanding the anatomy of a Docker image empowers you to make informed decisions about image management, optimization, and troubleshooting. By comprehending how the layers contribute to the overall image, you can employ techniques like layer caching, image layer pruning, and minimizing layer size to enhance build performance, reduce image footprint, and improve overall application deployment speed.

To get a hands-on experience as a warm-up, head over to the lab of this section, accessible at the following URL:

https://killercoda.com/meysam/course/mastering-docker/chapter3.1

A Practical Example

To put the theories into practice, we'll create a Docker image for a Python web application and explain how layers make the build process efficient.

The app's contents are not our main concern, and the code is not included here for brevity. Still, if you're curious to take a look at the code, it's all available at the GitHub repository of the book, accessible from the following link:

https://github.com/ava-orange-education/Ultimate Docker for Cloud Native Applications

To summarize, here are the details of what the app does:

1. During the boot-up stage, fetch the top currencies' conversion rates and save them in a Redis server.
2. When a request comes in, fetch the conversion rate saved in the Redis server and respond to the client.
3. Frequently update the Redis server in a background worker process to keep the conversion rates current.

For this app, we can write a simple Dockerfile, as follows:

```
FROM python:3.11-alpine AS base
WORKDIR /app
COPY requirements.txt /
RUN pip install -r /requirements.txt -U pip
COPY *.py ./
CMD ["python", "main.py"]
```

There are a couple of reasons for choosing the structure of the Dockerfile such as this.

Firstly, in the first line, you see the `FROM` instruction. The base image is selected from an Alpine version of the Python docker image. This will help us get a smaller ultimate image for the app because only the required dependencies are installed. Not all these dependencies are needed by the app, and that's why it's an excellent idea to have the minimum amount of required libraries installed and packaged into the Docker image. This approach provides the following advantages:

- Avoid security risks of outdated packages.
- Achieve the most minimal ultimate Docker image.
- Reduce the size of the final Docker image and make deployments faster and easier.

For these reasons, here's the official recommendation from the Docker website [source: https://docs.docker.com/develop/dev-best-practices/]:

```
Small images are faster to pull over the network and faster to load into
memory when starting containers or services. [...] Start with an appro-
priate base image. For instance, if you need a JDK, consider basing your
image on a Docker Official Image, which includes OpenJDK, such as eclipse-
temurin, rather than building your own image from scratch.
```

The following line, `WORKDIR`, ensures that the app contents have their dedicated directory and are not placed at the root. We want to keep our files in their specific place and avoid mixing them with other directories in the Docker image. If you don't specify any WORKDIR, it will be considered root or `/` in the UNIX filesystem by default.

The third line is particular, where `COPY` of the requirements is performed. It is recommended to keep the layers of the Docker image as few as possible (as you will see later on in this chapter). However, you might notice that it could have been a good idea if we merged the two `COPY` statements from the third and fifth lines.

However, we're refraining from doing that for one important reason: we want to take advantage of Docker layers.

Here's the rationale: once we start our project, we rarely change the dependencies; at least, the dependencies (add or delete of a library) are not as frequent as modifications to our code.

That's why a file such as `requirements.txt` can safely be considered to be infrequently updated and, therefore, can be moved to the top of the Dockerfiles so that, once executed, it won't re-run if the dependencies (contents of the requirements file) haven't changed.

This means it will install the dependencies for the first run and take the usual time for installation (based on network bandwidth, storage IO, and more). Any subsequent execution (building of the Docker image) will only re-run the line if the contents of `requirements.txt` have changed, using the caches from previous builds. Otherwise, it will use the **layers** of a previously built image.

If you're still hesitant about whether or not this is the case, it is highly recommended to go through the lab exercise accessible at the following URL:

https://killercoda.com/meysam/course/mastering-docker/chapter3.2

Exploring the Different Layers and Their Significance

In Docker, each layer within an image plays a crucial role in containerized applications' overall functionality and efficiency. By exploring the different layers and understanding their significance, you can gain insights into how Docker images are structured and optimized.

The initial layer, also known as the base layer, forms the foundation of the Docker image. It typically contains the operating system, runtime environment, and essential system libraries required for the application to run. The base layer sets the stage for subsequent layers and provides a starting point for building the image.

As additional layers are added on top of the base layer, each layer represents a specific change or modification to the filesystem. These changes include adding application code, installing dependencies, or configuring the environment. Docker allows for efficient image sharing and storage by breaking the image into multiple layers, as **unchanged layers can be reused across multiple images.**

The significance of individual layers lies in their ability to be independently cached and retrieved. Docker employs a layer caching mechanism that stores intermediate layers locally. When a new image is built, Docker reuses the existing layers that haven't changed, significantly speeding up subsequent builds. This caching mechanism enhances build efficiency and optimizes disk usage, making the overall process faster and more resource-friendly.

Understanding the significance of different layers is crucial for optimizing Docker image builds and managing their lifecycles. By designing images with a transparent layer separation and minimizing unnecessary changes, you can effectively leverage the Docker image cache, reducing build times and network transfers. Furthermore, this layer-based approach allows for granular control over image updates and enables quicker deployments by only propagating the modified layers rather than rebuilding the entire image.

Leveraging the Docker Image Cache for Faster Builds

The Docker image cache is a powerful tool that can significantly speed up image builds by reusing intermediate layers. Each instruction in the Dockerfile contributes to a new layer when building a Docker image. Docker intelligently caches these intermediate layers, allowing subsequent builds to **skip unchanged steps** and **retrieve the cached layers directly**. This caching mechanism accelerates the build process and reduces the time and resources required for image creation.

You can optimize your build workflow and improve development productivity by leveraging the Docker image cache. When a Dockerfile is modified, Docker compares each instruction against the cached layers. If an instruction matches a cached layer, Docker uses the cached layer instead of executing the instruction again. This bypasses the need to repeat time-consuming processes, such as installing dependencies or compiling code, resulting in faster builds.

To take advantage of the Docker image cache, it's essential to structure your Dockerfile to maximize cache utilization. **Start with instructions that change less frequently**, such as installing system dependencies, before moving on to instructions that change more often, like copying application code. By ordering the instructions this way, you can ensure that cached layers are reused as much as possible, reducing the build time.

However, it's important to note that certain instructions invalidate the cache for subsequent layers. For example, if an instruction modifies a file or directory referenced in a later instruction, Docker considers the cache for subsequent layers invalid. To mitigate this, consider grouping related instructions to minimize cache invalidation. Additionally, using Docker's layer caching wisely requires careful consideration of the dependencies between instructions, ensuring that changes in one instruction do not inadvertently impact the caching of subsequent layers.

To provide a strong foundation and understanding of how caching works, we will take a Dockerfile, optimize its structure to the point where the builds are optimized, and take advantage of the caching mechanism in the Docker build process.

Optimizing Image Size and Reducing Complexity

When working with Docker, optimizing the size of your Docker images is crucial for efficient storage usage and faster deployment. Additionally, reducing the complexity of your images simplifies management and enhances overall performance. In this section, we will explore techniques to optimize image size and streamline the content of your Docker images.

One key strategy for reducing image size is minimizing the number of layers. Each layer adds overhead to the image regarding storage space and processing time. Combining multiple related instructions into a single layer can consolidate the image's content and reduce size. This can be achieved by chaining multiple commands using the `&&` operator in the Dockerfile or using tools like the `RUN` command with multi-line scripts.

Another approach to optimize image size is to select the base image carefully. Choosing a lightweight base image, such as Alpine Linux, can significantly reduce the size of your final image. These minimalistic base images contain only the essential components needed to run your application, eliminating unnecessary overhead. However, ensure that the chosen base image matches your application's requirements and dependencies.

Furthermore, removing unnecessary files, directories, and dependencies from your image can further reduce its size. Remember to include only the essential components required to run your application, avoiding superfluous files or unnecessary system libraries. Tools like `.dockerignore` can exclude specific files and directories during the image build process, ensuring that only the necessary files are included (similar to the functionality of `.gitignore`).

Additionally, consider leveraging multi-stage builds to separate the build environment from the runtime environment. This technique allows you to build application artifacts in one stage and copy only the necessary files into the final runtime image. By excluding build-time dependencies and intermediate files from the final image, you can significantly reduce its size while maintaining the runtime functionality.

Optimizing image size improves storage efficiency and enhances network transfer speeds, especially when distributing images across different environments or deploying to remote servers. Smaller image sizes lead to faster image pull and deployment times, enabling rapid scaling and efficient utilization of resources.

You have already seen some of the Dockerfile examples so far, having the base image of Alpine to make the final image lighter. This reduces the final image size and the number of bytes you need to ship to your production environment when deploying the image. That said, not all applications can use Alpine as their base image due to their system dependencies and the effort required to install the same dependencies on a minimalistic base image.

Regardless, by reducing the complexity and optimizing the size of your Docker images, you can create lean and efficient containers that facilitate faster deployments, improved resource utilization, and seamless scalability. Applying these techniques empowers you to streamline containerized applications, ultimately enhancing their performance and maintainability.

Figure 3.3: *A young athlete climbing a rock.*
source: https://unsplash.com/photos/4BhHIfljLdE

Creating Docker Images

This section delves into the exciting process of creating Docker images. Building upon the foundation of Docker image basics, we explore the core concepts and techniques required to craft custom Docker images tailored to your application's specific requirements. From understanding Dockerfile syntax to incorporating best practices for image creation, this section equips you with the knowledge and tools necessary to create efficient and reproducible Docker images that serve as the backbone of your containerized applications. Let's embark on this journey of image creation and discover the art of seamlessly crafting containers that encapsulate your applications and their dependencies.

Building Docker Images Using Dockerfiles

Dockerfile provide a declarative and reproducible approach to building Docker images. They serve as blueprints that define the steps and configurations required to create a Docker image. In this section, we will explore the ins and outs of Dockerfile syntax and uncover best practices for creating efficient and well-structured Docker images.

A Dockerfile begins with a base image, typically chosen to match the operating system and runtime environment required by your application. From there, each instruction in the Dockerfile represents a step in the image-building process. Instructions like `RUN, COPY, ADD, and EXPOSE` allow you to install dependencies, copy files into the image, and expose network ports for communication.

One of the key advantages of using Dockerfiles is the ability to version and track changes in your image configurations. By documenting the necessary steps in a Dockerfile, you can maintain a transparent and auditable history of image creation, making it easier to reproduce and troubleshoot issues.

Docker employs a caching mechanism to optimize the build process based on the instructions in the Dockerfile, much like the same way compilers build their binaries incrementally to reduce build time. **Docker checks each instruction against the cached layers when an image is built**. If an instruction matches a cached layer, Docker reuses that layer, skipping the execution of the instruction. This caching mechanism significantly speeds up subsequent builds when the Dockerfile remains unchanged.

When creating Dockerfiles, it is advised to follow best practices. This includes using minimal and specific `RUN` commands to minimize layer size, leveraging multi-stage builds to separate build-time dependencies from the final image, and carefully managing image layers to improve caching efficiency. Additionally, documenting the purpose of each instruction and using comments can enhance the readability and maintainability of the Dockerfile.

You gain fine-grained control over the image creation process by mastering the art of building Docker images using Dockerfiles. With the ability to define dependencies, configurations, and build steps, Dockerfiles allow you to create consistent, repeatable, and efficient images that encapsulate your application and its requirements effectively. So, let's roll up our sleeves and dive into Dockerfile creation to build powerful and robust images.

The following list highlights some of the most common instructions in a Dockerfile:

- `FROM`: Specifies the base image for the Docker image being built. It sets the starting point for your image and defines the operating system and environment.
- `RUN`: Executes commands within the Docker image. This instruction installs packages, sets up dependencies, and runs any other necessary scripts or commands during the image build process.
- `COPY`: Copies files and directories from the build context (local machine) into the Docker image. This instruction allows you to include application code, configuration files, and other necessary assets within the image.
- `ADD`: Similar to the `COPY` instruction, `ADD` also copies files and directories into the Docker image. However, it has additional features like extracting tar archives and downloading files from URLs. It is generally recommended to use `COPY` instead of `ADD` for straightforward file copying.
- `ENV`: Sets environment variables within the Docker image. The running container can access these variables and help configure application-specific settings or provide runtime parameters.

- `EXPOSE`: Informs Docker that the container listens on specific network ports at runtime. This instruction will enable you to expose your Docker image ports to the host machine and random ports using the -P flag (capital p). If you prefer, you can still expose other ports of the container by specifying -p and the exact port you want exposed.
- `CMD`: Specifies the default command to run when a container is created from the image. This instruction can be overridden when starting a container, allowing flexibility in running different commands or processes.
- `ENTRYPOINT`: Similar to `CMD`, `ENTRYPOINT` specifies the command to run when a container starts. However, unlike `CMD`, it is not easily overridden and serves as the primary executable for the container. It is commonly used for the first binary the container will run on. One example is provided in the next section.
- `WORKDIR`: Sets the working directory within the Docker image where subsequent instructions will be executed. It allows you to define a specific directory for running commands, copying files, or performing other file-related operations.
- `VOLUME`: Declares a mount point in the container for external volumes or directories. It enables data persistence by linking specific directories or files from the host machine to the container, allowing them to be accessed or modified by the container. Similar to `EXPOSE`, this will not bind any volume to the running container by default but will instead serve as documentation for users of the container to know where to mount a volume to persist their data.

The full list of available commands can be found from the following URL:

https://docs.docker.com/engine/reference/builder/

Difference Between ENTRYPOINT and CMD

The main difference between `ENTRYPOINT` and `CMD` in a Dockerfile is how they handle the command or executable to run when a container is created.

`ENTRYPOINT` is used to specify the primary executable or command that should be run when a container starts. It sets the default behavior of the container and is typically used for running an application or service within the container. Command-line arguments do not easily override the command specified in `ENTRYPOINT` passed when starting the container.

For example, let's consider a `Dockerfile` for a Python web application. We can set the `ENTRYPOINT` as follows:

```
ENTRYPOINT [“python”, “app.py”]
```

Whenever a container is created from the image, it will automatically start the Python web application by executing the `app.py` file. The `ENTRYPOINT` instruction sets the primary executable for the container, and any additional arguments passed when starting the container will be appended to the `ENTRYPOINT` command.

On the other hand, `CMD` provides default arguments for the `ENTRYPOINT` or specifies a command to run when starting the container if no `ENTRYPOINT` is defined. It can be overridden with command-line arguments when starting the container.

Building upon the previous example, we can add a `CMD` instruction after the `ENTRYPOINT`:

```
CMD ["--port", "8080"]
```

In this case, the `CMD` instruction sets default command-line arguments for the `ENTRYPOINT` command. When the container starts, it will execute the specified `ENTRYPOINT` command (in this case, running the Python web application). It will use the default arguments specified in CMD if no additional command-line arguments are provided.

For instance, running the container without any additional command-line arguments:

```
docker run my-app-image
```

The container will start the Python web application (`app.py`) as specified in `ENTRYPOINT` and use the default port argument (`--port 8080`) from `CMD`.

However, when starting the container, `CMD` can be overridden by explicitly specifying command-line arguments. For example:

```
docker run my-app-image --port 9090
```

In this case, the CMD default arguments will be replaced with the provided `--port 9090` argument.

In summary, `ENTRYPOINT` sets **the primary executable** or command for the container. At the same time, `CMD` provides default arguments for the `ENTRYPOINT` or specifies a command to run if no `ENTRYPOINT` is defined. `ENTRYPOINT` provides the primary behavior, while `CMD` offers the flexibility to modify or override that behavior with command-line arguments when starting the container.

Modifying the default `ENTRYPOINT` is also possible, although not as straightforward as overriding the `CMD`. To do so, you would have to use a dedicated flag when running the container, as follows:

```
docker run --entrypoint /bin/sh my-app-image id
```

This will override the `ENTRYPOINT` with `/bin/sh` and the `CMD` with the shell command id.

Defining the Application Environment and Dependencies

In building Docker images, it's essential to accurately define the application environment and dependencies. This involves specifying the necessary runtime environment, configuring system libraries, and installing dependencies required for the application to run successfully.

To define the application environment, you can leverage the `FROM` instruction in your Dockerfile to choose a base image that provides the required operating system and runtime environment. For example, if you're building a Node.js application, you can set the base image as:

```
FROM node:20-alpine
```

This instruction selects the Node.js base image with the desired version and a lightweight Alpine Linux distribution. Choosing an appropriate base image ensures compatibility and sets the foundation for the application's runtime environment.

Next, you can use package managers such as npm or pip within the `Dockerfile` to install the necessary dependencies for your application. For instance, to install Node.js dependencies using npm, you can include the following instruction:

```
COPY package.json package-lock.json ./
RUN npm ci
```

In this example, the package.json and `package-lock.json` files are copied into the image, and the npm ci command is run to install the dependencies specified in the `package-lock.json` file. This ensures consistent and reproducible installations within the Docker image.

Additionally, environmental variables can be set within the `Dockerfile` using the `ENV` instruction. These variables allow you to define configuration values or provide runtime parameters that the application might require. For instance:

```
ENV PORT=8080
```

This instruction sets the environment variable `PORT` to 8080 within the Docker image, allowing the application to reference this value during runtime the same way you would access an environment variable in your terminal using a dollar sign: `$PORT`

By defining the application environment and managing dependencies within Docker images, you ensure that the necessary runtime components and dependencies are encapsulated within the image. This enables the image to run consistently across different environments and provides a self-contained package for deploying the application. Defining the environment and dependencies accurately within the Dockerfile ensures reproducibility, simplifies deployment, and reduces potential compatibility issues.

Incorporating Best Practices for Image Creation

When building Docker images, following best practices to ensure efficiency, security, and maintainability is crucial. By incorporating these practices, you can create high-quality Docker images optimized for performance, adhere to security guidelines, and facilitate seamless deployment and management. This section will explore some essential best practices for image creation and provide strong examples to illustrate their implementation:

1. **Use a Minimal Base Image**: Choosing a lightweight and minimal base image, such as Alpine Linux, can significantly reduce the image size and minimize potential security vulnerabilities. For example, if you are not familiar with Linux distributions, you can use the mainstream Ubuntu as the base for your Docker images, which is only ~25MB in size. Alternatively, instead of using a general-purpose Linux distribution as the base image, you can opt for a specific and minimal image, as follows:

```
FROM busybox
```

Busybox provides a small footprint and focuses on security and simplicity.

2. **Leverage Layer Caching**: Take advantage of Docker's layer caching mechanism to improve build times. Structure your Dockerfile to allow the maximum reuse of cached layers. For instance, if your application has dependencies specified in a separate `requirements.txt` file, you can copy and install them before copying the rest of the code. This way, the dependencies layer can be cached and reused if the requirements file hasn't changed.

```
COPY requirements.txt .
RUN pip install -r requirements.txt
COPY . .
```

3. **Clean Up Unnecessary Files**: Remove any unnecessary or temporary files within the Docker image to reduce its size. This practice minimizes storage requirements and helps maintain a cleaner and more focused image. For example, after installing dependencies, you can remove the `requirements.txt` file and any build artifacts:

```
RUN rm requirements.txt
```

4. **Implement Multi-Stage Builds**: Utilize multi-stage builds to separate the build environment from the runtime environment. This approach allows you to keep the final image small by discarding any build-time dependencies and intermediate files that are unnecessary for runtime. For example, in a Java application, you can build the application in one stage and then copy the build artifact into a smaller runtime image:

```
# Build Stage
FROM maven:3-openjdk-18 AS builder
COPY . .
RUN mvn clean install
# Runtime Stage
FROM openjdk:11-jre-slim
COPY --from=builder /path/to/artifact.jar /app.jar
CMD [“java”, “-jar”, “/app.jar”]
```

Further explanation on multi-stage builds will be provided later, and this only serves as a quick example for the moment.

5. **Apply Security Practices**: Incorporate security practices into your Docker image creation process. This includes regularly updating the base image, installing security patches, and scanning for vulnerabilities in your dependencies using tools like Clair or Trivy. For example, you can edit the base image and perform package upgrades in your Dockerfile:

```
FROM python:3.11-slim
RUN apt-get update && \
  apt-get upgrade -y && \
  rm -rf /var/lib/apt/lists/*
```

6. **Use** `.dockerignore`: Create a `.dockerignore` file to exclude unnecessary files and directories from being copied into the Docker image during the build process. This reduces the image size and improves build performance. For example, you can ignore files and directories like tests, documentation, or build artifacts:

```
# .dockerignore
# This will be in the same directory as Dockerfile
tests/
docs/
*.log
```

Anything that is not necessary for your application's runtime should be excluded for several good reasons, with the top ones being security vulnerabilities of deprecated packages and reducing the size of your final image.

Incorporating these best practices allows you to create optimized, secure, and maintainable Docker images. These practices help reduce image size, improve build times, enhance security, and ensure consistency across different environments. Remember to continually evaluate and refine your Docker image creation process as new best practices and tools emerge in the ever-evolving container ecosystem.

If you would like to know more about these optimizations, it is highly recommended to read this article from 2020 that is still relevant today:

https://meysam.io/10-tips-on-writing-a-proper-dockerfile-13956ceb435f

Understanding Docker Context

Docker context refers to the files and directories accessible to Docker during build operations. The context is sent to the Docker daemon, allowing it to include relevant files in the container image. Properly managing the Docker context can optimize build performance and minimize the size of the resulting image. Here's an explanation of the Docker context and best practices for effective usage:

- **Context Scope**: The Docker context typically consists of the current directory and subdirectories. The entire context is sent to the Docker daemon when executing Docker commands like docker build. Hence, including only the necessary files is crucial to avoid performance degradation and unnecessary image bloating.
- **Best Practices for Docker Context**: To make the most out of Docker context, follow these best practices:

  - **Exclude irrelevant files**: Utilize a `.dockerignore` file in the root directory of your project to specify files and directories that should be excluded from the Docker context. This prevents them from being sent to the Docker daemon unnecessarily.
  - **Optimize file paths**: Instead of copying entire directories, selectively copy only required files and directories using specific paths in the Dockerfile. This reduces the context size and improves build efficiency.
  - **Leverage build context caching**: Docker caches the context between builds, avoiding redundant file transfers. Utilize this caching mechanism by keeping the context stable unless necessary files have changed, accelerating subsequent builds.

Practical Example

Let's consider an example where you have a Python Flask application with the following directory structure:

```
myapp/
├── app.py
├── requirements.txt
├── templates/
│   └── index.html
└── tests/
└── test_app.py
```

To optimize the Docker context, create a `.dockerignore` file in the `myapp/` directory with the following content:

```
tests/
*.pyc
```

This `.dockerignore` file excludes the `tests/` directory and any compiled Python files (`*.pyc`) from the Docker context. Consequently, the image build process will include only the necessary files (app.py, requirements.txt, and templates).

To get a hands-on experience, head over to the lab exercise accessible from the following link:

https://killercoda.com/meysam/course/mastering-docker/chapter3.3

Automating the Build Process with Build Hooks and ARGs

Automating the build process of Docker images can save time and effort by streamlining repetitive tasks and allowing for flexibility in image customization.

Docker provides features like build hooks, ARGs (build-time variables), and the ONBUILD instructions to automate and parameterize the image-building process. This section will explore effectively leveraging these features to automate and customize the Docker image build process.

Build Hooks

Build hooks are scripts or commands executed during specific stages of the image build process. They allow you to automate tasks such as downloading additional resources, running tests, or generating configuration files. Build hooks are defined in the Dockerfile using the RUN instruction with a command that executes the desired script. For example:

```
RUN /scripts/setup.sh
```

Here, the setup.sh script will be executed during the image build process, automating custom setup tasks.

You can imagine the contents of such a script as being as simple as the following, or as a large file with many complex tasks to set up an application's runtime environment.

```
# !#/bin/bash
# /scripts/setup.sh
# Install dependencies
apt-get update
apt-get install -y curl wget

# Install Node.js
curl -sL https://deb.nodesource.com/setup_8.x | bash -
apt-get install -y nodejs

# Install Yarn
curl -sS https://dl.yarnpkg.com/debian/pubkey.gpg | apt-key add -
echo "deb https://dl.yarnpkg.com/debian/ stable main" | tee /etc/apt/
sources.list.d/yarn.list
apt-get update && apt-get install -y yarn
```

ARGs (Build-Time Variables)

ARGs are build-time variables that can be passed to the Docker build command using the `--build-arg` flag. They allow you to parameterize the build process and make it more flexible. `ARGs` are defined in the Dockerfile using the `ARG` instruction.

```
ARG APP_VERSION
ENV VERSION=$APP_VERSION
```

With this configuration, the value of `APP_VERSION` can be passed as a build argument during the image build process. This allows for dynamic image customization, such as specifying different versions or configurations for other builds.

ONBUILD Instruction

The `ONBUILD` instruction adds a trigger that specifies additional actions to be performed when the image is used as the base for another image. These additional actions are defined in the subsequent Dockerfile that uses the image as its base. This feature enables customization of the build process for derived images. Here's an example:

```
ONBUILD COPY . /app
ONBUILD RUN pip install -r /app/requirements.txt
```

With these instructions in a "parent" Dockerfile, one can create a template Docker image and use this image as the base image for other application Docker images, implicitly including the following instructions:

```
FROM my-template-image
# The following two instructions are implicitly added
# COPY . /app
# RUN pip install -r /app/requirements.txt
```

By utilizing build hooks, `ARGs`, and the `ONBUILD` instruction, you can automate and customize the Docker image build process to fit your specific requirements. These features enhance efficiency, provide flexibility, and enable the creation of reusable base images that can be extended or customized by other Dockerfiles. Automating the build process streamlines development workflows and allows for easier maintenance and management of Docker images.

Here's an interactive lab exercise if you want to know more about the hooks defined here:

https://killercoda.com/meysam/course/mastering-docker/chapter3.4

Figure 3.4: *A group of people putting their hands on top of each other. source: https://unsplash.com/photos/Zyx1bK9mqmA*

Image Management and Distribution

In the world of Docker, effectively managing and distributing Docker images is crucial for seamless deployment, collaboration, and scalability. This section delves into the critical aspects of image management and distribution, providing you with the knowledge and techniques to handle Docker images efficiently. From saving and loading images for offline use to pushing and pulling images from Docker registries, this section equips you with the tools to manage, share, and distribute your images effectively. Let's explore the world of image management and distribution to unlock the full potential of your containerized applications.

Saving and Loading Docker Images for Offline Use

In Docker, saving and loading Docker images is invaluable, especially when working in offline or restricted environments. Saving Docker images allows you to create portable snapshots of your images, including all their layers and dependencies, which can then be loaded onto other Docker hosts. This capability enables you to share images with others or deploy them in environments without internet connectivity. Here are a few examples of how to save and load Docker images:

1. Saving Docker Images

Saving a Docker image is when you want to use SCP or other similar tools to ship an image to a remote machine by transferring an archive. To save a Docker image to a file, you can use the `docker save` command followed by the image's name or ID and specify the output file name. For instance:

```
docker save -o mynginx.tar nginx:alpine
```

This command saves the `nginx:alpine` image as a tar file named `mynginx.tar`.

2. Loading Docker Images

Once you have the saved Docker image file, you can load it onto another host using the `docker load` command.

```
docker load -i mynginx.tar
```

This command loads the Docker image from the `mynginx.tar` file into the local Docker environment.

3. Transferring Docker Images

You can also transfer Docker image files between machines using secure file transfer protocols (for example, SCP), USB drives, or network-shared folders. Once the image file is available on the target machine, you can load it using the `docker load` command.

4. Using Docker Save and Load with Compressed Files

You can compress the saved Docker image file to save disk space or transfer files more efficiently. For example, when saving the image, you can pipe the output to a compression tool like `gzip`:

```
docker save nginx:alpine | gzip > mynginx.tar.gz
```

Similarly, when loading a compressed Docker image file, you can use the appropriate decompression tool, such as `gunzip`, in the load command:

```
gunzip -c mynginx.tar.gz | docker load
```

By saving and loading Docker images, you can work with images offline, share them across different environments, or distribute them to remote Docker hosts. This capability ensures portability and facilitates the seamless deployment of containerized applications, regardless of internet connectivity constraints.

Pushing and Pulling Images to and from Docker Registries

Docker registries are critical in sharing and distributing Docker images among developers, teams, and deployment environments. Pushing images to a registry allows you to store and share your Docker images with others while pulling images from a registry enables you to obtain pre-built images from public or private repositories. Docker Hub is a popular public registry, but you can also set up private registries for internal use. Here's an explanation of pushing and pulling Docker images with examples:

1. Pushing Images to a Registry

To push a Docker image to a registry, you need to tag it with the registry's URL and repository name before pushing it. For example, if you have an image named `myimage` and want to push it to a Docker Hub repository called `myusername/myrepo`:

```
docker tag myimage:tag myusername/myrepo:tag
docker push myusername/myrepo:tag
```

The first command tags the image with the repository details, and the second command pushes the image to the Docker Hub registry under your specified repository.

2. Pulling Images from a Registry

To pull a Docker image from a registry, you can use the `docker pull` command followed by the image's repository and tag. For example, to pull an image from Docker Hub:

```
docker pull myusername/myrepo:tag
```

This command retrieves the specified image from the Docker Hub registry and stores it locally on your machine.

3. Using Private Registries

If you have a private Docker registry, the process is similar. You need to authenticate with the registry before pushing or pulling images. Docker provides authentication mechanisms, such as username, password, or token. The exact authentication steps depend on the registry implementation.

For example, you can set up your private registry using the official Docker registry image and then push your local image to the private registry.

```
docker run -d -p 5000:5000 --name private-registry registry
docker tag myimage:tag localhost:5000/myrepository:tag
docker push localhost:5000/myrepository:tag
```

4. Docker Registry URLs

Every Docker image has at least three sections (four in case of non-official images):

1. **Registry**: The server that holds the Docker image, for example, `docker.io`, `ghcr.io`, and more.
2. **Repository**: The name of the image, for example, `postgres`, `mongo`, `nginx`, and more.
3. **Image name/username**: This is usually the name of the publisher/owner of the image and is a required part of non-official images.
4. **Tag**: The version of the Docker image, for example, `latest`.

These three sections are represented as follows:

```
# <registry>/<repository>:<tag>
# Example 1
docker.io/nginx:latest
# Example 2
nginx:latest
# Example 3
nginx
# Example 4: non-official images
docker.io/myuser/myimage:v1
```

The aforementioned three examples are identical. The reason is that `docker.io` is implicit if no other registry is specified. The same goes for the `latest` if no other tag is set.

That's why you would usually use the last example and implicitly use all the defaults without knowing.

If the registry URL is omitted, Docker assumes the image belongs to Docker Hub. Other private registries may have different URLs; specify them accordingly.

Pushing your Docker images to a registry makes them accessible to others in your team or community, facilitating collaboration and sharing of containerized applications. Similarly, pulling images from a registry allows you to leverage pre-built images, saving time and effort by not having to build everything from scratch. Docker registries streamline the image distribution process and serve as a centralized hub for sharing containerized software artifacts.

Tagging and Versioning Docker Images Effectively

Tagging and versioning Docker images is crucial for managing and organizing your image repository. Effective tagging helps identify different versions of an image, associate images with specific releases or environments, and ensure proper version control.

When tagging a Docker image, using the format `<image-name>:<tag>` is common. The tag can be any alphanumeric string representing a specific version, release, or other meaningful identifier. It's recommended to use a systematic approach to versioning, such as semantic versioning, to accurately convey the image's significance.

For example, let's consider a scenario where you have a web application image named `myapp` that has undergone multiple updates and releases. You can use versioning to tag the image with different versions:

```
docker build -t myapp:1.0 .
```

In this case, the tag "1.0" represents the initial release of the `myapp` image. As you make updates and improvements, you can increment the version accordingly:

```
docker build -t myapp:1.1 .
```

The `myapp` image is now tagged with version "1.1" to reflect the changes made since the initial release.

You can also use additional tags to provide context or associate images with specific environments or branches. For example:

```
docker build -t myapp:latest .
docker build -t myapp:development .
docker build -t myapp:feature-branch .
```

In this case, the `latest` tag represents the most recent version of the image, `development` indicates an image for development purposes, and the `feature-branch` associates the image with a specific feature branch in your version control system.

By effectively tagging and versioning your Docker images, you can quickly identify and manage different versions, releases, and variations of your containerized applications. This enables better organization, tracking, and control of images throughout their lifecycle, facilitating smooth deployment and maintenance processes.

Managing Image Repositories and Repository Automation

Managing image repositories is a critical aspect of Docker image management. It involves organizing, categorizing, and maintaining collections of Docker images in a structured manner. Repository automation refers to streamlining and automating the processes related to image repository management, including image uploads, metadata management, access control, and versioning. Here's a brief explanation:

Image repositories are centralized storage for Docker images, allowing teams to store, access, and share containerized applications. Organizing repositories effectively involves structuring images based on projects, teams, or applications and applying appropriate access controls to ensure proper security and governance.

Repository automation involves leveraging tools, scripts, or CI/CD pipelines to automate repository-related tasks. This can include automated builds and uploads of new images, versioning, metadata management, and integration with continuous integration and deployment systems. Automation reduces manual effort, improves consistency, and enables seamless integration with other parts of the development and deployment workflows.

For example, you can use a continuous integration tool like Jenkins or a container registry service like Docker Hub, Amazon Elastic Container Registry (ECR), or Google Container Registry (GCR) to automate the build and upload processes. These tools can be configured to trigger builds on code changes, automatically build Docker images, and push them to the appropriate repositories.

Additionally, repository automation can involve using version control systems (for example, Git) to manage Dockerfiles and track changes to image configurations. Integration with version control enables versioning, rollbacks, and image development and maintenance collaboration.

Figure 3.5: *A sleeping cat.*
source: https://unsplash.com/photos/eNXZvDGqGbM

Advanced Techniques

In the realm of Docker, there are advanced techniques that can elevate your containerization expertise to new heights. These techniques go beyond the basics and delve into more sophisticated strategies and practices to optimize performance, enhance security, and streamline workflows.

This section explores advanced techniques to expand your Docker knowledge and confidently empower you to tackle complex containerization scenarios. From orchestration and scaling to networking and advanced image management, we dive deep into these topics to unlock the full potential of Docker in your development and deployment workflows. Let's embark on this journey of advanced techniques and unlock the power of Docker's advanced capabilities.

Utilizing Multi-Stage Docker Builds for Optimized Images

Multi-stage builds in Docker allow you to create optimized and efficient images by separating the build environment from the final runtime environment. This technique helps reduce image size, eliminates unnecessary dependencies, and enhances security while maintaining the application's functionality. In this approach, you can have one stage for building the application and another stage for running it, discarding any build-time artifacts and dependencies not required during runtime.

To illustrate the utilization of multi-stage builds, let's consider a web application built with Node.js and bundled with Webpack. Here are the steps involved in creating an optimized Docker image using multi-stage builds:

1. Building Stage

In the first stage, we built an environment to compile and package the application. We can use a base image with Node.js and the necessary build tools, such as npm or Yarn. Here's an example Dockerfile snippet for the building stage:

```
FROM node:14 as builder
WORKDIR /app
COPY package*.json ./
RUN npm ci # Install dependencies
COPY . . # Copy application code
RUN npm run build
```

In this stage, we copy the package files, install the dependencies, and build the application using Webpack or any other tool specific to your application.

2. Runtime Stage

After the build stage, we move to the runtime environment. Here, we can use a lightweight base image like `nginx` or `node:14-alpine`, which only contains the necessary components to run the application. We copy the built artifacts from the previous stage into the runtime stage and configure the required runtime settings. Here's an example continuation of the Dockerfile for the runtime stage:

```
FROM nginx:latest
# Copy the built artifacts from the builder stage
COPY --from=builder /app/dist /usr/share/nginx/html
# Optionally, copy any additional configuration files
COPY nginx.conf /etc/nginx/conf.d/default.conf
# Expose the port
EXPOSE 80
# Start the nginx server
CMD ["nginx", "-g", "daemon off;"]
```

In this stage, we copy the built application code from the previous stage's `/app/dist` directory into the appropriate location for the runtime environment. We also copy any necessary configuration files, such as a `nginx.conf` file for custom NGINX settings. Finally, we expose the required port (for example, port 80) and define the command to start the NGINX server.

Using multi-stage builds, the final image only includes the compiled and optimized code required for runtime. The build-time dependencies and artifacts are discarded, resulting in a smaller and more efficient image.

To build the Docker image using the aforementioned Dockerfile, execute the following command in the project directory:

```
docker build -t myapp .
```

This command builds the Docker image with the name `myapp`. During the build process, Docker will execute both stages sequentially, and the resulting image will be optimized for runtime without any unnecessary build-time artifacts.

Utilizing multi-stage Docker builds reduces the image size and enhances security by excluding potentially sensitive build-time files and dependencies. Additionally, it improves performance during image builds and enables faster deployment and scaling of containers.

Here's the complete Dockerfile for reference:

```
# Building Stage
FROM node:14 as builder
WORKDIR /app
COPY package*.json ./
RUN npm ci
COPY . .
RUN npm run build
# Runtime Stage
FROM nginx:alpine
COPY --from=builder /app/dist /usr/share/nginx/html
COPY nginx.conf /etc/nginx/conf.d/default.conf
EXPOSE 80
CMD [“nginx”, “-g”, “daemon off;”]
```

Designing and Implementing Multi-Container Applications

Multi-container applications in Docker involve orchestrating multiple containers to work together as a cohesive system. This approach allows you to decompose complex applications into more minor, manageable services that can be scaled, updated, and deployed independently. Designing and implementing multi-container applications requires careful planning of container interactions, network configurations, and service dependencies. Here's an explanation of critical considerations and practices when designing and implementing multi-container applications:

Microservices Architecture

Multi-container applications often follow the microservices architectural pattern, where different components of an application are divided into separate services. Each service performs a specific function and communicates with other services via APIs or message queues. This decoupling of services enables independent development, scaling, and deployment, promoting flexibility and maintainability.

Container Orchestration

Tools like Docker Swarm or Kubernetes are commonly used to manage multi-container applications. These tools provide features such as service discovery, load balancing, automatic scaling, and container scheduling. They simplify the deployment and management of containerized applications across multiple hosts, ensuring high availability and efficient resource utilization.

Networking and Communication

Containers within a multi-container application need to communicate with each other. Docker provides networking options like bridge, overlay, and host networks to facilitate container communication. It's essential to design and configure appropriate network architectures to enable seamless container interaction while ensuring security and isolation.

Service Dependencies and Discovery

Multi-container applications often have interdependencies between services. It's crucial to identify and manage these dependencies effectively. Tools like service discovery (for example, Consul, and etcd) or container registries (for example, Docker Hub, private registries) can help register and discover services dynamically, allowing containers to locate and interact with dependent services.

Environment Configuration

Multi-container applications may require different configuration values for each service, such as database connection strings or API keys. Utilizing environment variables or configuration management tools allows you to provide specific settings to each container based on its role or environment. This ensures flexibility and maintainability when deploying the application across different environments.

You can build scalable, modular, resilient systems by designing and implementing multi-container applications. Proper consideration of container interactions, networking, service dependencies, and configuration management leads to flexible architectures that can be easily scaled and maintained. Leveraging container orchestration tools enhances the manageability of the application, providing features for load balancing, scaling, and high availability. Adopting these practices enables efficient development, deployment, and management of complex applications in Docker.

Understanding Image Vulnerabilities and Security Considerations

When working with Docker images, you must be aware of potential vulnerabilities and adopt security measures to protect your containerized applications. Understanding image vulnerabilities involves identifying potential risks and vulnerabilities in the images you use, such as outdated software, insecure configurations, or known vulnerabilities in the underlying base images or dependencies. Security considerations encompass best practices for securing your Docker images and containers to prevent unauthorized access, data breaches, or malicious activities. Here are vital aspects to consider when it comes to image vulnerabilities and security:

Image Scanning and Vulnerability Assessment

Regularly scan Docker images for vulnerabilities using security scanning tools like Official Docker Scout, or third-party tools like Clair, Trivy, or Anchore. These tools analyze images and their dependencies, reporting known vulnerabilities, outdated packages, and configuration weaknesses. You can identify and address security issues before deploying images into production environments by performing image vulnerability assessments.

There are automated, pre-made, and off-the-shelf tools you can scan for you in different CI tools. You wouldn't need to do all these yourself.

For example, Trivy is one of the leading tools to find vulnerabilities in the Docker image, and it has a GitHub Action to check your Docker image on every code change.

To get a hands-on experience, consider trying the following lab exercise:

https://killercoda.com/meysam/course/mastering-docker/chapter3.5

Base Image Security

Choose base images from trusted sources and maintain their security. Base images should be regularly updated to include security patches and bug fixes. Popular base images like those from Docker Official Images or trusted repositories are generally more reliable regarding security. Periodically check for base image updates and rebuild your images to incorporate the latest security fixes.

Secure Configuration and Runtime Isolation

Implement secure configurations for your Docker images and containers. Avoid running containers with unnecessary privileges and restrict capabilities to minimize potential attack vectors. Leverage Docker's security features, such as user namespaces and seccomp profiles, to isolate containers and reduce the impact of security breaches.

Secrets and Sensitive Data Management

Carefully handle secrets and sensitive data, such as passwords or API keys. Avoid hardcoding secrets in Dockerfiles or images. Instead, utilize Docker's secret management features or external secret management tools like HashiCorp Vault to store and retrieve sensitive information at runtime securely.

Access Control and Least Privilege Principle

Implement strict access controls and follow the principle of least privilege. Use separate user accounts for different containers and ensure proper user and group permissions are set within the images. Limit unnecessary network access, container capabilities, and filesystem access to reduce the attack surface.

Image Integrity and Authentication

Ensure image integrity by digitally signing your Docker images. Docker Content Trust provides image signing and verification mechanisms, allowing only trusted images to be deployed. Additionally, consider implementing image authentication mechanisms using private registries, image signing certificates, or image verification tools to ensure the authenticity and integrity of your images.

By understanding image vulnerabilities and following security considerations, you can strengthen the security posture of your Docker images and containers. Regular vulnerability assessments, secure configurations, secrets management, access controls, and image integrity measures contribute to building a robust and secure containerized environment. Prioritizing security protects your applications and data and maintains the trust and integrity of your containerized infrastructure.

Best Practices for Image Update and Maintenance

Properly updating and maintaining Docker images is crucial for ensuring your containerized applications' security, stability, and reliability. Best image update and maintenance practices involve adopting automated processes and leveraging continuous integration and continuous deployment (CI/CD) pipelines to streamline the update and release cycles. These practices help you stay up-to-date with security patches, bug fixes, and feature updates while minimizing downtime and ensuring consistent deployment. Here's an explanation of essential best practices, including the value of automation and CI/CD, along with a practical example:

Automated Image Builds

Implement automated image builds to ensure consistent and reproducible creation of Docker images. Automation tools like Jenkins, GitLab CI/CD, or GitHub Actions can trigger image builds whenever changes are pushed to the source code repository. Automated builds minimize human error, promote consistency, and enable faster image updates.

Version Control for Dockerfiles

Utilize version control systems (for example, Git) to manage and track changes to Dockerfiles. Keeping Dockerfiles in version control allows you to quickly review and roll back changes, maintain a history of image configurations, and collaborate effectively with team members.

Regular Security Scanning and Updates

Incorporate regular security scanning into your CI/CD pipeline to identify vulnerabilities and outdated dependencies in your Docker images. Tools like Official Docker Scout, or third-party tools like Trivy, Anchore, or Clair can automatically be integrated into the pipeline to scan images for security issues. Automate the process of applying security patches and updates to keep your images up-to-date and protected against known vulnerabilities.

Immutable Image Tags

Follow the practice of using immutable tags for your Docker images. Immutable tags, such as version numbers or commit hashes, ensure that images remain consistent and reproducible. Avoid using mutable tags like "latest" as they can lead to unpredictability and potential inconsistencies in the deployment process.

Retire and Remove Unused Images

Regularly review and retire unused or outdated Docker images to avoid unnecessary accumulation of image versions. Removing unused images reduces storage requirements and simplifies image management. Automation can be employed to periodically clean up and remove images that are no longer in use or meet predefined criteria.

Practical Example

Consider a scenario where you have a CI/CD pipeline for your application and want to incorporate best practices for image update and maintenance. Here's how the pipeline can be structured:

1. **Code Changes**: Developers push changes to the version-controlled source code repository.
2. **Automated Build**: The CI/CD pipeline is triggered, automatically building a new Docker image based on the updated code. The Dockerfile is retrieved from the version control system, and the image is built using the latest code and dependencies.
3. **Security Scanning**: The CI/CD pipeline integrates security scanning tools to automatically scan the newly built image for vulnerabilities and outdated packages.
4. **Tagging and Pushing**: Upon successful scanning, the image is tagged with a version number or commit hash and pushed to a private registry or Docker Hub.
5. **Deployment**: The updated image is then deployed to the desired environment using an automated deployment process, such as Kubernetes or Docker Swarm.

6. **Regular Updates**: The CI/CD pipeline is scheduled to run regularly or triggered by predefined events to ensure continuous monitoring and updating of Docker images as new code changes are introduced.

By following these best practices, you ensure that your Docker images are regularly updated, scanned for vulnerabilities, and deployed consistently. Automation through the CI/CD pipeline streamlines the update and maintenance process, enabling you to deliver secure and up-to-date containerized applications with reduced downtime and improved overall quality.

Figure 3.6: *A bike on a mountain during sunset.*
source: https://unsplash.com/photos/1ow9zrlldJU

Conclusion

In this chapter, we delved into the world of Docker image building and management. We explored various topics to help you master creating and optimizing Docker images. Key areas covered include understanding Docker image basics, exploring image layers and their significance, leveraging Docker image cache for faster builds, optimizing image size and reducing complexity, creating Docker images using Dockerfiles, incorporating best practices for image creation, automating the build process with build hooks and ARGs, and managing image repositories and distribution. We also discussed advanced techniques, such as multi-stage Docker builds, designing and implementing multi-container applications, understanding image vulnerabilities and security considerations, and best image update and maintenance practices.

Throughout this chapter, we emphasized the importance of understanding Docker image concepts, optimizing image size and build times, ensuring image security, and adopting automation and CI/CD practices. You can build efficient, secure, scalable containerized applications by mastering these concepts and implementing best practices. With this knowledge, you'll be well-equipped to harness the power of Docker and effectively manage your Docker images in various development and deployment scenarios.

In the next chapter, "*Docker Networking*," we will dive into the fascinating world of networking in Docker containers. Networking plays a vital role in orchestrating communication between containers, connecting them with the outside world, and enabling seamless interaction between services. We will explore various Docker networking options, including bridge networks, overlay networks, and host networks, and understand their unique use cases. Additionally, we will cover advanced networking topics such as container-to-container communication, service discovery, and load balancing.

References

1. **Docker Documentation**: Official documentation provided by Docker, covering various aspects of Docker, including image management, containerization, and best practices: https://docs.docker.com/
2. **Dockerfile Best Practices**: A comprehensive guide on Dockerfile best practices, offering recommendations for creating efficient and secure Docker images: https://docs.docker.com/develop/develop-images/dockerfile_best-practices/
3. **Docker Security**: Official Docker documentation on security, providing guidelines and best practices for securing Docker images and containers: https://docs.docker.com/engine/security/

Useful Links

- **Docker Hub**: A central repository of Docker images, offering a wide range of pre-built images for various software and services: https://hub.docker.com/
- **Docker Blog**: Official Docker blog featuring articles, tutorials, and updates on Docker technologies, best practices, and use cases: https://www.docker.com/blog/
- **Awesome Docker**: A curated list of Docker resources, tools, and tutorials on GitHub, providing an extensive collection of community-driven Docker-related content: https://github.com/veggiemonk/awesome-docker
- **Docker Questions on Stack Overflow**: A dedicated section on Stack Overflow for Docker-related questions, where you can find answers to common queries or ask your own: https://stackoverflow.com/questions/tagged/docker
- The lab exercise for this book is accessible online from this link: https://killercoda.com/meysam/course/mastering-docker/
- The repository for this book is accessible from this link: https://github.com/ava-orange-education/Ultimate Docker for Cloud Native Applications.

CHAPTER 4
Docker Networking

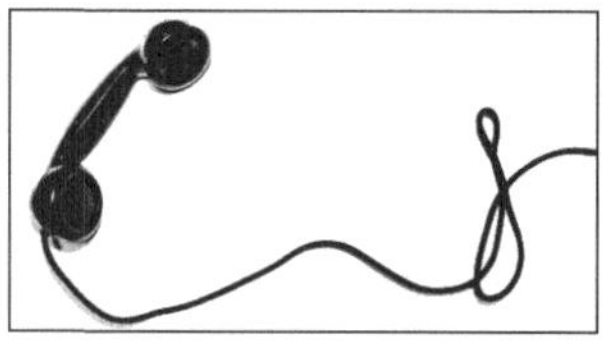

Figure 4.1: *Black corded telephone.*
source: https://unsplash.com/photos/4SNUcHPiC8c

Introduction

In the world of containerization, Docker has revolutionized how applications are deployed and managed. At the heart of Docker lies its powerful networking capabilities, which form the backbone of communication between containers and the external world. Docker networking allows containers to seamlessly connect with each other, enabling the creation of distributed applications and microservices architectures. This chapter is a definitive exploration of Docker's networking aspect, encompassing its primary objective of providing robust connectivity, isolation, and scalability. From fundamental networking concepts to advanced configuration options, we embark on a journey to unveil the full potential of Docker's networking architecture.

Structure

In this chapter, we will cover the following topics:

- Understanding Docker Networking Fundamentals
- Docker DNS and Service Discovery
- Container-to-Container Communication
- Managing Network Security
- Advanced Network Configuration

Understanding Docker Networking Fundamentals

Before we plunge into the intricate world of Docker's networking capabilities, let us first lay a solid foundation by exploring the fundamental principles that govern container connectivity. Docker networking is the backbone of inter-container communication, enabling containers to communicate with external systems. To comprehend this dynamic landscape, we unravel Docker's default networking behavior, which governs container communication within a single host. Delving into network namespaces, we discover how each container exists in its isolated networking environment, providing a sense of separation and security. From there, we embark on a journey through different networking modes, including Bridged, Host, Overlay, MACVLAN, and Null networking, each catering to specific use cases and addressing distinct connectivity requirements.

Docker Default Networking

When you deploy a Docker container without explicitly specifying a network, it automatically becomes part of the default bridge network created by Docker. This default behavior facilitates communication between containers running on the same Docker host, ensuring they can discover and interact with one another.

The default bridge network allows containers to access the external world through the host's network interface. By default, Docker assigns an IP address from the bridge subnet to each container, allowing them to communicate over the bridge network interface.

Here's the document from the docker documentation [source: https://docs.docker.com/engine/reference/run/#network-settings]:

> *By default, all containers have networking enabled and can make any outgoing connections. [...]*

The default bridge network works using a private address space, and containers can communicate using their respective IP addresses (if communication via container name is needed, the `--link` needs to be specified as explained later). This private address space is not routable from outside the host, which means containers in the default bridge network cannot be accessed directly from external systems. Docker uses Network Address Translation (NAT) to provide external container connectivity by mapping container ports to the host's ports. This process is known as port forwarding.

To see all these in practice, try the following lab exercise:

https://killercoda.com/meysam/course/mastering-docker/chapter4.1

While the default bridge network is straightforward, it may not be suitable for some use cases, especially those requiring more advanced networking configurations, such as cross-host communication or network isolation.

As we progress through this chapter, we will explore other networking modes and their use cases, offering more control and flexibility in managing container connectivity.

Network Namespaces

In containerization, isolation is a crucial aspect of ensuring that applications and their dependencies can run independently without interfering with one another. Network namespaces are a core feature of the Linux kernel that is pivotal in achieving this isolation within containers.

A network namespace is **a virtualized environment that encapsulates network-related resources**, such as network interfaces, routing tables, and IP addresses. When a container is created, Docker leverages the Linux kernel's network namespace feature to create a separate and isolated network namespace for each container. This means that each container has its own networking stack, which includes its *network interfaces*, *IP addresses*, and *routing rules*.

The network namespace isolation ensures containers can operate with distinct network configurations independent of the host and other containers. As a result, it prevents conflicts and enables seamless communication between containers on the same host without interfering with other containers or the host's network.

Containers within their isolated network namespaces can communicate over virtual network bridges provided by the Docker daemon, allowing for easy and secure communication within a host. Docker will also enable you to create user-defined networks, which provide more fine-grained control over container connectivity and facilitate cross-container communication across multiple hosts.

The Linux kernel's support for network namespaces is a crucial foundation for Docker's networking capabilities, enabling the creation of isolated environments for containers to operate effectively without interfering with each other or the host's networking stack. This network namespace feature, along with other kernel features, empowers Docker to provide a seamless networking experience and enables developers to build distributed applications quickly.

Bridge Networking Mode

In Docker networking, the bridge networking mode is a default and commonly used option that allows containers to communicate with each other and the external network. When a container is launched in bridge mode, it is connected to a virtual bridge network on the host. This bridge acts as a software switch, enabling communication between containers on the same bridge network. Unique subnets are created for different bridges and if otherwise not specified, the `172.16.0.0/16` subnet is used as the default subnet.

Key characteristics of the bridge networking mode include:

- **Isolation**: Each container connected to the bridge network has its own network namespace, providing a level of isolation. This means containers on the same bridge can communicate, but by default, they are isolated from containers on other bridges.
- **Automatic IP Assignment**: Containers in bridge mode can automatically receive an IP address from the built-in DHCP server of the bridge network. Alternatively, you can manually assign static IP addresses.
- **External Connectivity**: Containers in bridge mode can connect to the external network using the host's network stack. They can also be accessed from outside the host by mapping ports from the container to the host.
- **Name Resolution**: Containers on the same bridge network can communicate using container names as hostnames, facilitating easier service discovery within the Docker network.

To try out the bridge network, run the following commands in your Linux terminal:

```
docker network create demo

docker run --hostname nginx -d --rm --network demo nginx:alpine

docker run --rm --network demo curlimages/curl curl nginx
```

Host Networking Mode

This configuration option allows a container to **share the network namespace with the host system.** Unlike bridged networking, where containers get their own unique IP addresses, in host networking mode, containers use the network stack of the underlying host directly. This means that a container in host networking mode shares the same IP address and network interfaces as the host, effectively becoming a part of the host's network.

By leveraging host networking mode, containers can achieve a higher network performance and efficiency as they bypass the overhead of virtualized network interfaces and network address translation. This mode is handy for applications that require low-latency and high-throughput communication with the host or other devices on the network. Containers running in host networking mode can directly access services and applications running on the host system without additional network setup, just as easily as talking to `localhost`.

While host networking can provide performance benefits, it's essential to consider security implications. Containers in host networking mode are no longer isolated from the host's network and can interfere with or access services on the host system. This is unsuitable for scenarios where strong network isolation is required between containers and the host. It's recommended not to run the containers in this mode unless there's no other way!

Host networking mode is often used for specific use cases, such as when a containerized application must bind to particular network ports on the host or requires access to a network interface unavailable within the container's isolated network namespace. However, for most applications, the default bridged networking or user-defined networks are more appropriate, as they balance performance and security well.

Overlay Networking Mode

Overlay networking mode in Docker is a crucial feature designed to facilitate communication between containers running on different hosts within a Docker Swarm cluster or a Kubernetes cluster. When containers are deployed in a distributed environment **across multiple hosts**, traditional networking approaches like bridged or host networking become inadequate due to the need for seamless **cross-host communication**. Overlay networking mode addresses this challenge by enabling containers to communicate with each other transparently, regardless of the physical host they are running on.

Docker creates a virtual overlay network in overlay networking mode that spans all the cluster hosts. This overlay network forms a logical network fabric, allowing containers to communicate as if they were on the same local network, even though they might be located on different physical hosts in geographically dispersed data centers. The containers use a distributed key-value store, such as etcd or Consul, to maintain the network state and facilitate service discovery across the cluster.

Overlay networking mode is necessary to enable container orchestration platforms like Docker Swarm or Kubernetes to build and manage highly scalable, fault-tolerant distributed applications. With overlay networking, these platforms can deploy containers across a cluster of hosts without worrying about the underlying network infrastructure. Containers can be scheduled and rescheduled to different hosts without requiring manual network configuration, making the process seamless and efficient.

MACVLAN Networking Mode

MACVLAN networking mode in Docker is a unique approach to networking that allows containers to have their own separate MAC addresses on the host's physical network. Unlike other networking modes, where containers share the host's network stack or use a virtual bridge, MACVLAN creates a one-to-one mapping between container MAC addresses and the host's physical network interfaces.

In MACVLAN mode, each container appears to the physical network as an individual device with its own unique MAC address, just like a regular physical machine. This enables containers to operate in "bridge" mode, which means they can communicate directly with other devices **on the same physical network**, including the host and other containers. MACVLAN is particularly useful for scenarios where containers must be fully integrated into the existing network infrastructure and require direct access to physical network resources.

While MACVLAN provides great network integration, it does come with some limitations. Because each container has its own MAC address, there may be restrictions on how many MAC addresses can be assigned by the network hardware. Additionally, some network configurations may not be compatible with MACVLAN mode due to network switch-level conditions.

MACVLAN networking mode in Docker is essential because it provides a way to integrate containers directly into the physical network, allowing seamless communication with other devices on the same network. By leveraging MACVLAN, users can create highly integrated and flexible networking setups for their containers, making Docker an even more versatile tool for various networking use cases. However, it's essential to carefully consider the networking requirements and limitations when choosing MACVLAN mode, as it may not be suitable for every scenario.

ipvlan Networking Mode

In Docker networking, IPVLAN is a mode that allows containers to share the same IP address as the host system or other containers. IPVLAN creates multiple virtual network interfaces associated with the same physical interface, each with its own unique MAC address. This enables containers to be directly connected to the host's network, behaving as if they are physical devices on the same subnet.

With IPVLAN, containers can communicate with the external network and each other efficiently, using the host system's networking capabilities. This mode is particularly useful in scenarios where you want containers to have direct access to the underlying network, bypassing the typical NAT (Network Address Translation) used in bridge networking. However, it's essential to note that IPVLAN might not be suitable for all use cases, as it exposes containers to the host's network configuration and requires careful management to avoid IP conflicts.

Null Networking Mode

Null networking mode, or the "none" network driver, is a unique and minimalistic approach to networking in Docker. A container running in null networking mode has no network access or network interfaces. Essentially, the container is isolated from the network entirely, making it unable to communicate with the host or any external resources.

The null networking mode is helpful in scenarios where you want to run a container wholly isolated from the network without any network connectivity or exposure. This mode is often employed for specialized use cases, such as running containers in a restricted environment for security reasons or when a container's primary purpose is computation or processing tasks that do not require network access.

Using null networking mode, you can ensure that a container is entirely disconnected from the network, reducing its attack surface and minimizing the risk of network-related security vulnerabilities. This can be particularly valuable for running untrusted or potentially vulnerable applications in a sandboxed environment.

However, it's essential to be cautious when using null networking mode, as the container cannot access resources such as package repositories, external databases, or APIs. If a container requires specific network interactions, null networking mode is not suitable, and other network configurations, like the default bridge networking or custom user-defined networks, should be considered.

Third-party Network Drivers

While Docker provides a set of built-in network drivers, it's important to note that Docker's network plugin architecture is proprietary and currently not compliant with the Container Network Interface (CNI) specification. Developers exploring network customization in Docker should be aware that the community maintains third-party network drivers designed to extend Docker's networking capabilities. Although not currently CNI-compliant drivers within Docker, these drivers aim to offer specialized networking solutions tailored to specific use cases and requirements.

It's worth noting that there's an ongoing proposal within the Docker community to replace the legacy libcontainer implementation with a CNI-compliant alternative.. This potential shift aligns with the broader industry trend towards standardization and interoperability among container runtimes.

The CNI specification, while not currently supported by Docker's built-in drivers, is a standard followed by third-party network drivers. These drivers adhere to the CNI specification, ensuring interoperability and compatibility with various container runtimes beyond Docker. By embracing the CNI standard, these third-party drivers can seamlessly integrate with Docker, providing additional networking features and functionalities. Despite the ongoing discussions and potential changes to Docker's internal implementation, third-party network drivers offer capabilities such as advanced networking overlays, software-defined networking (SDN), improved performance, security enhancements, and support for multiple network plugins and backends.

To use a third-party network driver, install it on the Docker host and configure it to work with Docker. Once the driver is set up, you can create Docker networks using the third-party driver and deploy containers using those custom networks, gaining access to the specific networking features provided by the driver.

The availability of third-party network drivers adds significant flexibility and extensibility to Docker's networking ecosystem. It allows developers to tailor container networking solutions to their unique requirements, making Docker an even more powerful platform for building complex and diverse distributed applications.

To get a hands-on experience, head over to the lab exercise of this section, accessible from the following URL:

https://killercoda.com/meysam/course/mastering-docker/chapter4.2

Figure 4.2: *Customer service operators.*
source: https://unsplash.com/photos/mHusyBu4bxM

Docker DNS and Service Discovery

In the dynamic world of containerized applications, seamless service discovery and reliable DNS resolution are essential for efficient container communication. Docker DNS and Service Discovery are vital in enabling containers to locate and interact with one another, regardless of their IP addresses or host locations. In this section, we will delve into the intricacies of Docker's embedded DNS server, the mechanisms behind DNS resolution for container names, and how to customize DNS configurations. Additionally, we'll explore service discovery solutions, both internal to Docker and external, empowering you to build scalable and interconnected containerized applications effortlessly. Let's dive into the world of Docker DNS and Service Discovery and explore the tools that ensure smooth communication in distributed container environments.

Docker's Approach to DNS Resolution

When containers are connected to a Docker network, Docker sets up a built-in DNS server within the network. This embedded DNS server is a central component for DNS resolution within the Docker environment.

When one container needs to communicate with another container using its name, it sends a DNS query to the Docker DNS server, requesting the IP address associated with the container's name. The Docker DNS server, in turn, resolves the container name to its corresponding IP address and returns it to the requesting container.

For example, let's consider two containers, "`web_server`" and "`database_server`," both connected to the same Docker network:

```
docker network create demo



docker run -d --name database_client --network demo postgres:latest
sleep 300
docker run -d --name database_server --network demo postgres:latest
```

If the `database_client` container needs to communicate with the "`database_server`," it can simply use the container name "`database_server`" in its requests, and Docker's DNS resolution will handle the rest. The DNS server will resolve "`database_server`" to the correct IP address, allowing seamless communication between the two containers.

Docker's built-in DNS resolution mechanism simplifies container communication and service discovery, as it abstracts the underlying IP addresses and network configurations. Containers can refer to each other using their logical names, making the networking setup more dynamic and resilient to changes in IP addresses or host locations.

To get a hands-on experience, head over to the lab exercise of this section, accessible from the following URL:

https://killercoda.com/meysam/course/mastering-docker/chapter4.4

Customizing DNS Configuration

Docker allows users to customize DNS configuration for containers, enabling more flexible DNS resolution options and better integration with existing DNS infrastructure. By default, Docker uses its embedded DNS server for DNS resolution within the container environment. However, you can override this default behavior and specify your custom DNS settings for individual containers or the entire Docker daemon.

To customize the DNS configuration for a specific container, you can use the `--dns` option when running the container. For example:

```
docker run -d --name custom_dns_container --dns 8.8.8.8 nginx:latest
```

In this example, the `custom_dns_container` will use Google's public DNS server (8.8.8.8) for DNS resolution instead of Docker's default embedded DNS server.

Alternatively, you can customize DNS settings for the entire Docker daemon by editing the configuration file (usually located at `/etc/docker/daemon.json`). Here's an example of how to configure custom DNS settings in the Docker daemon configuration:

```
{
  "dns": ["8.8.8.8", "8.8.4.4"]
}
```

After such a change, you will need a restart of the docker daemon.

```
systemctl restart docker.service
```

In this case, Docker will use Google's public DNS servers (8.8.8.8 and 8.8.4.4) for DNS resolution **across all containers**.

Customizing DNS configuration is valuable when integrating Docker containers with specific DNS servers, such as your organization's internal DNS infrastructure or third-party DNS services. It allows containers to communicate with the desired DNS servers, ensuring proper name resolution for the applications within the containers.

Service Discovery with Docker's Embedded DNS Server

Docker's embedded DNS server facilitates service discovery within the container environment. Service discovery enables containers to locate and communicate with each other using their logical names, promoting dynamic and resilient communication without relying on specific IP addresses.

When running a container, you can influence how Docker's DNS resolver handles the container's name resolution by using the `--hostname` or `--name options`.

The `--hostname` option allows you to set a custom hostname for the container. When you use this option, Docker sets the specified hostname as the container's hostname, affecting how it identifies itself to other containers and the Docker DNS server. Other containers within the same Docker network can resolve this custom hostname to the container's IP address using Docker's DNS server.

For example:

```
docker run -d --name my_container --hostname my_custom_host nginx:latest
```

In this case, the container will be known as `my_container` and `my_custom_host`. Other containers in the same network can resolve `my_custom_host` to this container's IP address, simplifying service discovery.

The `--name` option allows you to give a friendly name to the container. By default, Docker uses the specified name as the container's hostname, influencing how other containers in the same network can discover it through DNS resolution.

For example:

```
docker run -d --name my_container nginx:latest
```

In this case, the container will be known as `my_container`, and other containers in the same network can resolve this name to its IP address using Docker's DNS server.

Now, head over to the lab exercise for this section to get a hands-on experience of this topic, accessible from the following URL:

https://killercoda.com/meysam/course/mastering-docker/chapter4.3

Using External Service Discovery Solutions

While Docker's embedded DNS server is effective for service discovery within a single Docker network, more complex containerized environments and microservices architectures often require external service discovery solutions to handle service registration, discovery, and load balancing across multiple Docker hosts and networks.

Several external service discovery solutions offer advanced features to address the challenges of dynamic container environments. These solutions typically provide centralized service registries and querying mechanisms, allowing containers to discover and connect services across distributed networks.

Some popular external service discovery tools and platforms include:

- Hashicorp **Consul** is a powerful service mesh solution that provides service discovery, health checking, and key-value store capabilities. It enables containers to register themselves with Consul agents and discover services using DNS or HTTP-based APIs.
- **etcd** is a distributed key-value store Kubernetes uses for service discovery and configuration management. Containers can use etcd's API to register and discover services within a Kubernetes cluster.

- Apache **ZooKeeper** is a centralized service for maintaining configuration information, naming, and providing distributed synchronization. It is commonly used in distributed systems, including Docker Swarm and Apache Kafka.
- **Eureka** is a service registry and discovery server used in Spring Cloud and microservices architectures. Containers can register with Eureka to make themselves discoverable to other services.
- **Kubernetes** provides built-in service discovery features through its DNS-based service discovery and Ingress controllers. It allows containers to discover services within the Kubernetes cluster using DNS or Ingress resources.

These external service discovery solutions offer health checks, load balancing, and failover mechanisms, making them suitable for large-scale, production-ready container deployments.

Container-to-Container Communication

This section focuses on the intricacies of container-to-container communication within Docker environments. Containers are designed to work together and often need to interact with each other to form complex distributed applications. We will explore various communication methods, from the simplest case of containers on the same network to more advanced scenarios involving communication across different networks or even between Docker Swarm services. Understanding how containers communicate with each other is crucial for building interconnected microservices architectures and leveraging the full potential of Docker's networking capabilities.

Communicating Between Linked Containers

In Docker, **linking** is a legacy method of enabling communication between containers. It allows one container to access the exposed network ports of another container. Docker creates a secure tunnel when containers are linked, allowing them to communicate over the network.

You can use the `--link` option when running the second container to create a link between the two containers. The syntax is as follows:

```
docker run -d --name server nginx
docker run -d --name client --link server curlimages/curl http://nginx
```

In this example, the `client` is linked to the `server`. The linked container's network ports are available to the other container, allowing them to communicate via the exposed ports.

However, it's important to note that linking has been deprecated in favor of more robust and flexible networking options, such as user-defined bridge networks or overlay networks. These modern networking methods offer better isolation, performance, and scalability than linking.

While linking can still be used in older Docker environments, it is recommended to use user-defined networks or other advanced networking solutions for new applications to ensure more resilient and scalable communication between containers.

Utilizing Container Aliases

Container aliases are more modern and flexible to facilitate container-to-container communication than the deprecated "linking" method. Aliases allow containers to refer to each other using custom names, making communication more intuitive and independent of container names.

When containers are connected to a user-defined bridge network, Docker automatically assigns a default alias to each container. This alias is the container's name by default, but you can customize it using the `--network-alias` option when running the container.

```
docker run -d --name nginx1 --hostname nginx2 --network-alias nginx3 nginx
```

In this example, the nginx container is accessible in its network with all three names `nginx1`, `nginx2`, and `nginx3`.

Container aliases make communication between containers more explicit and independent of container names. Other containers in the same network can now communicate with their aliases instead of their container name. This decouples the communication logic from specific container names, making the network configuration more dynamic and scalable.

Connecting Containers with User-defined Networks

User-defined networks in Docker offer a more flexible and powerful way to connect containers, promoting improved isolation, scalability, and easier management than using the default bridge network or the deprecated "linking" method.

You can create custom networks isolated from the host's default network and other networks with user-defined networks. Containers connected to the same user-defined network can communicate with each other seamlessly, using either container names or aliases.

You have seen examples of creating and using a user-defined network named `demo`.

To create a user-defined network, you can use the `docker network create` command:

```
docker network create my_network
```

Next, you can run containers and connect them to the custom network using the `--network` option:

```
docker run -d --name server1 --network my_network nginx
docker run -d --name server2 --network my_network nginx
```

Both `server1` and `server2` are now connected to the `my_network` user-defined network. They can communicate using their container names (or aliases assigned to them) within the network.

User-defined networks offer numerous advantages over the default bridge network, such as:

- **Enhanced Isolation**: Containers on a user-defined network are isolated from other networks, reducing potential interference and improving security.
- **Simplified Service Discovery**: Containers can communicate using their logical names or aliases, making service discovery more intuitive and less dependent on IP addresses or specific container names.
- **Easier Network Management**: User-defined networks allow you to organize and manage containers more effectively, especially when deploying complex microservices architectures.

Interacting Across Different Network Types

In Docker environments, you may encounter scenarios where containers must communicate across different network types. Docker provides various networking options, such as the default bridge network, user-defined bridge networks, overlay networks, and host networking mode. Each network type has its unique characteristics, and containers connected to different network types might face challenges when interacting with each other.

When containers are connected to different network types, they operate in isolated network namespaces, which means they have separate networking configurations and IP address spaces. By default, containers on various networks cannot communicate directly with each other using their container names or aliases.

To enable communication between containers on different network types, you can use additional networking solutions or workarounds, such as:

- **Exposing Ports**: Containers can communicate with each other through exposed ports. By publishing container ports using the `-p` or `--publish` option, you can make them accessible from different network types, allowing external containers to access specific services.
- **Overlay Networks**: If containers run in a Docker Swarm cluster, you can leverage overlay networks to enable cross-host communication. Overlay networks provide seamless communication between containers across different nodes in the Swarm.
- **External DNS**: For more complex scenarios involving containers on different networks or hosts, you can rely on external DNS servers or service discovery solutions to enable communication using domain names instead of IP addresses.

One crucial piece of information is that when running containers on the same machine while exposing ports on the host using the `--add-host` flag, you will need to add the DNS entry of the host machine into the docker container to be able to communicate to the other container through the host machine.

Here's an example:

```
docker run -p 1001:80 -d nginx:alpine

docker run --add-host=host.docker.internal:host-gateway \

  curlimages/curl http://host.docker.internal:1001
```

The `--add-host` flag will add a DNS entry for the current docker container, as you would typically do by manually modifying the `/etc/hosts` file.

The string `host.docker.internal` is not a special name and can be anything you prefer; the `host-gateway`, however, is a special name, and you can't customize it to something else.

Figure 4.3: *Security depicted as a lock.*
source: https://unsplash.com/photos/mT7lXZPjk7U

Managing Network Security

This section delves into the critical aspect of network security within Docker environments. We will explore techniques and best practices for securing Docker networks, including container isolation, network segmentation, restricting container access, and implementing firewalls.

Docker's Built-in Security Features

Docker provides several built-in security features that contribute to maintaining the integrity and safety of containerized applications. These features help protect the host system, the containers, and the overall Docker environment. Some of the key built-in security features provided by Docker include:

- **Namespace Isolation**: Docker uses Linux namespaces to isolate containers from each other and the host system. Each container has its own process, network, and file system namespace, preventing interference and unauthorized access between containers and the host.
- **Control Groups (cgroups)**: Docker utilizes cgroups to limit and manage container resource consumption. This ensures that one container cannot monopolize system resources, which enhances stability and prevents denial-of-service attacks.
- **Read-only File Systems**: You can configure Docker containers to have read-only file systems, minimizing the risk of unauthorized modifications and reducing the impact of potential security breaches.

- **Docker Content Trust**: Docker Content Trust (DCT) ensures the integrity and authenticity of container images by using digital signatures. This feature helps prevent malicious image tampering and ensures that only trusted images are deployed.
- **Seccomp Profiles**: Docker allows you to apply Seccomp profiles to restrict the system calls that a container can make. This mitigates the risk of containers exploiting system vulnerabilities and strengthens overall container security.
- **AppArmor and SELinux**: Docker supports security profiles such as AppArmor and SELinux to enforce fine-grained access controls on containers, limiting their capabilities and reducing potential attack surfaces.
- **Network Security**: Docker provides network segmentation through user-defined bridge networks and overlay networks. You can control container network access and isolate sensitive services by carefully designing your network topology.

Implementing Network Policies and Firewall Rules

Network policies and firewall rules are essential tools for controlling and managing traffic flow within Docker networks. They allow administrators to define granular access controls, restrict container communication, and enforce security policies to protect sensitive services and data.

Docker provides different ways to implement network policies and firewall rules, such as:

- **User-defined Bridge Networks**: When creating user-defined bridge networks, you can specify the `--internal` option to make the network internal-only. This prevents external access to containers within the network, providing an additional isolation layer.
- **iptables**: Docker uses iptables rules to manage packet filtering and network address translation. You can manually manipulate iptables rules on the host system to enforce custom firewall policies for Docker containers.
- **Third-party Networking Plugins**: Some third-party networking plugins offer advanced network policy features, such as Calico, Weave, or Cilium. These plugins provide more sophisticated security controls, including network segmentation and network-level access policies.

- **Cloud Provider Firewalls**: If you are running Docker in a cloud environment, you can use cloud provider firewalls to regulate incoming and outgoing traffic to and from Docker containers.

When implementing network policies and firewall rules, consider the principle of least privilege, allowing only the necessary network connections for each container. This reduces the attack surface and limits the potential impact of security breaches. Regularly review and audit your network policies to ensure they align with your security requirements and to promptly detect any potential misconfigurations.

Security Best Practices for Docker Networking

When deploying Docker containers and managing their networks, following security best practices is essential to ensure a robust and secure environment. Here are some indispensable security best practices for Docker networking:

- **Use User-defined Bridge Networks**: Create and use user-defined bridge networks to isolate containers and prevent unnecessary exposure to the host's default network.
- **Limit Exposed Ports**: Only expose the necessary ports for container services to minimize the attack surface.
- **Avoid Using Deprecated Features**: Avoid deprecated networking features like container linking and prioritize modern networking methods like user-defined bridge networks or overlay networks.
- **Implement Network Segmentation**: Segment your Docker networks to separate different components or services to reduce the risk of lateral movement in case of a security breach.
- **Enable Docker Content Trust**: Enable Docker Content Trust (DCT) to ensure the integrity and authenticity of container images, preventing the deployment of tampered or unauthorized images [official doc].
- **Apply Network-level Access Controls**: Use network policies, firewall rules, or third-party networking plugins to enforce access controls and restrict container communication.
- **Monitor Network Traffic**: Implement network monitoring and logging to detect potential security threats or unusual network activity.
- **Secure Host Network Interfaces**: Secure host network interfaces to prevent unauthorized access to Docker daemon ports and API endpoints.

- **Regularly Update and Patch**: Keep Docker and container images up to date with the latest security patches to address known vulnerabilities.
- **Use Network Security Tools**: Consider using additional security tools and services, such as intrusion detection systems (IDS), to enhance network security within Docker environments.

By adhering to these security best practices, Docker users can significantly reduce the risk of security breaches, unauthorized access, and data exposure in their containerized applications. Secure Docker networking practices contribute to a robust and reliable container environment that fosters trust in the safety and confidentiality of the deployed services.

Figure 4.4: *Craftsmanship takes expertise.*
source: https://unsplash.com/photos/qe0BpiHhIM0

Advanced Network Configuration

In this section, we will explore advanced network configuration options in Docker, delving into more intricate networking setups to meet the demands of complex container environments. We will delve into multi-host networking with overlay networks, the integration of external load balancers, and advanced network plugins. Additionally, we will discuss strategies for integrating Docker with existing network infrastructure, such as connecting containers to external networks and leveraging software-defined networks.

Multi-host Networking with Docker Swarm

Docker Swarm is a built-in orchestration tool in Docker that enables the management and scaling of containerized applications across multiple hosts. When running a Docker Swarm cluster, you can leverage multi-host networking to facilitate communication between containers running on different nodes of the Swarm.

Docker Swarm uses overlay networks to achieve multi-host networking. Overlay networks allow containers to communicate with each other across different hosts, creating a seamless and highly available network fabric for distributed applications. Containers within the same overlay network can communicate using their container names, making service discovery more intuitive and eliminating the need to deal with individual IP addresses.

When deploying services on a Docker Swarm, you can specify which network to use for each service. Swarm manager nodes handle the networking routing and ensure that traffic is efficiently routed between containers, regardless of their location within the Swarm.

Multi-host networking with Docker Swarm enables the creation of resilient and scalable containerized applications. As new nodes are added to the Swarm or existing nodes are removed, the overlay network dynamically adapts, ensuring containers can continue communicating without interruption.

Creating a Docker Swarm

We will discuss Docker Swarm in detail in *Chapter 7, Scaling Applications with Docker Swarm*, but this section will provide you with the information you need to set up a Swarm cluster.

You need at least one "manager" node and zero or more "worker" nodes to create a simple orchestration using a docker swarm.

Here are the steps to create a docker swarm.

In the manager node, run the following command:

```
docker swarm init --advertise-addr $MANAGER_IP
```

The variable `MANAGER_IP` is defined per host, and you should check the node's IP address using `ifconfig` or `ip addr` command-line tools.

The preceding command will give you the token you can use on any worker nodes in the same subnet as the manager node, as shown:

```
docker swarm join --token $JOIN_TOKEN $MANAGER_IP:2377
```

The manager and worker nodes must be in the same subnet and accessible for the join command to work correctly.

After the successful execution of both commands, the following command will show you all the nodes in the swarm:

```
docker node ls
```

Having the swarm in place, we can run a "stack." To do so, we only need a `compose.yml` file with defined services. We will talk about docker-compose in *Chapter 6, Docker Compose for Simplified Application Deployment*.

Here are the contents of our docker-compose file:

```
# compose.yml
services:
  nginx:
    image: nginx:alpine
  curl:
    image: curlimages/curl
    entrypoint: sleep infinity
```

With the preceding contents saved in a file named `docker-compose.yml`, we can run the stack as follow:

```
docker stack deploy -c docker-compose.yml nginx
```

This will give us the stack, running the `services` defined in the docker-compose file across all the nodes.

To check the services of our stack, we can run the following command:

```
docker stack ps nginx
```

This command will also give us the node where any number of our containers is running.

We can see the connectivity and service discovery in action by jumping into any nodes running our `curl` service and executing curl `http://nginx`.

If we want to increase the number of instances in one of the services, we can easily use the `docker service scale` command as follows:

```
docker service scale nginx_nginx=3
```

In the pair `nginx_nginx`, the first is the stack name we used in the `docker stack deploy`, and the other is the service name defined in the docker-compose file.

Using IPv6 in Docker Networks

Docker supports IPv6 networking, allowing containers to communicate over IPv4 and IPv6 addresses. By default, Docker uses IPv4 for container networking. Still, you can enable and configure IPv6 to take advantage of the expanded address space and support the transition to the next-generation Internet protocol.

To enable IPv6 in Docker, perform the following steps:

1. **Check IPv6 Availability**: Ensure your host system and network infrastructure support IPv6. Verify that your network router is configured to handle IPv6 traffic and that IPv6 addresses are available on the network.
2. **Enable IPv6 on Docker Daemon**: Edit or create the Docker daemon configuration file (usually located at `/etc/docker/daemon.json`) and add the following configuration to enable IPv6:

```
{
  "ipv6": true,
  "fixed-cidr-v6": "2001:db8:1::/64"
}
```

Replace `2001:db8:1::/64` with the desired IPv6 subnet range for the Docker containers. The subnet range should be allocated from your network's available IPv6 address space.

3. **Restart Docker Daemon**: After making changes to the Docker daemon configuration, restart the Docker daemon to apply the IPv6 settings: `sudo systemctl restart docker`
4. **Create IPv6-enabled Networks**: With IPv6 enabled on the Docker daemon, you can now create networks that support both IPv4 and IPv6 addresses. When creating a network, you can specify the IPv6 subnet using the `--ipv6` and `--subnet` options:

```
docker network create --ipv6 --subnet=2001:db8:2::/64 my_network
```

5. **Assign IPv6 Addresses to Containers**: When running containers, you can specify IPv6 addresses using the `--ipv6` option:

```
docker run -d --name my_container --network my_network \

  --ip6 2001:db8:2::100 nginx
```

With these steps, you can enable and utilize IPv6 networking in your Docker environment.

Custom Bridge Networks and Subnet Configuration

In Docker, custom bridge networks offer a powerful way to create isolated and self-contained container networks. Unlike the default bridge network, custom bridge networks allow you to define custom subnet configurations, enabling more precise control over IP address allocation and routing within the network.

To create a custom bridge network and configure the subnet, you can use the following steps:

1. **Create a Custom Bridge Network**: Use the `docker network create` command to create a custom bridge network:

   ```
   docker network create --driver bridge my_network
   ```

2. **Custom Subnet Configuration**: Docker will automatically assign a subnet to the custom bridge network by default. However, if you want to use a specific subnet, you can specify it during network creation using the `--subnet` option:

   ```
   docker network create --driver bridge --subnet 172.20.0.0/24 my_
   network
   ```

3. **Container Connectivity**: Containers connected to the custom bridge network can communicate with each other using their container names. Docker's built-in DNS server allows containers to resolve each other's names within the network.

4. **Port Publishing**: If you need to access services running inside containers on the custom bridge network from outside the network, you can publish specific container ports to the host using the `-p` or `--publish` option when running the container.

Custom bridge networks and subnet configuration are valuable features in Docker, especially when you require more fine-grained control over container networking. They facilitate the creation of isolated environments for applications, microservices, or specific components within your Docker setup. By configuring custom subnets, you can ensure that containers have predictable IP addresses and routing, which can be helpful for network troubleshooting and security purposes.

Network Scopes and External Connectivity

In Docker, network scopes refer to the accessibility of networks from outside the Docker host. Docker provides two network scopes: **local and swarm.**

- Local Scope: Networks with a local scope are isolated to the Docker host, where they are created. Containers running on the same host can communicate with each other using the network. However, containers on different hosts or outside the Docker host cannot access the network directly.
- Swarm Scope: When using Docker Swarm mode, specific built-in networks have a "swarm" scope, available only to the Swarm's internal components and services. These networks facilitate communication among Swarm components, such as managers and workers, and are not intended for general container communication.

While local scope networks are isolated to a single host, there are methods to enable external connectivity for containers running in these networks:

- **Port Publishing**: By publishing specific container ports to the host using the `-p` or `--publish` option, you can make services running inside containers accessible from outside the Docker host.
- **Host Networking Mode**: Containers can be run in **host** networking mode, sharing the network namespace with the host. In this mode, containers use the host's network stack directly, making them accessible on the host's IP address and all its network interfaces.

  Exposing Ports from Local Scope Networks: Containers running in local scope networks can access the host's network interface IP address (usually 127.0.0.1 or localhost) to communicate with services running on the host.

  Network scopes and external connectivity options in Docker allow you to manage how containers communicate within the host and with external systems.

Conclusion

In this comprehensive guide to Docker networking, we have explored the intricacies of container communication and connectivity within Docker environments. From the fundamentals of Docker networking, understanding the default networking behavior, and diving into various networking modes, to exploring advanced configurations and security best practices, we have covered a wide range of essential topics.

Docker's networking capabilities offer versatility and flexibility, allowing developers and administrators to design networks tailored to their specific application needs. Whether it's bridged networking for straightforward connectivity, overlay networking for multi-host setups, or using custom bridge networks for more fine-grained control, Docker provides a solution for various scenarios.

Furthermore, we delved into the significance of security in Docker networking, emphasizing the importance of isolating containers, implementing access controls, and leveraging Docker Content Trust for image integrity. By adhering to best practices and staying informed about potential security vulnerabilities, users can safeguard their containerized applications effectively.

Additionally, we explored service discovery mechanisms with Docker's embedded DNS server and highlighted external solutions for seamless communication between containers and microservices.

With the knowledge gained from this chapter, readers are now equipped to build, manage, and secure Docker networks, empowering them to create efficient, resilient, and scalable containerized environments. Docker's networking capabilities serve as a foundation for architecting modern distributed applications, fostering innovation, and driving the adoption of containerization technology.

As Docker and containerization continue to evolve, staying up-to-date with the latest developments and best practices is essential. By remaining well-informed and continuously honing our Docker networking skills, we can harness the full potential of containerization and shape the future of application deployment and management.

In the next chapter, we will see how to persist our data when running Docker containers, ensuring we won't lose data in case of restarts or system crashes. Since every processing needs to persist its data for subsequent access, the next chapter is crucial for understanding how to ensure that data's safety.

References

Throughout the writing of this chapter, the following resources have been used to gather information and ensure accuracy:

- **Docker Documentation:** https://docs.docker.com - The official documentation for Docker, providing comprehensive information on Docker networking and related topics.

- **Docker GitHub Repository:** https://github.com/docker/docker - The GitHub repository of Docker, containing the source code and issue tracking for the Docker project.
- **Docker Blog:** https://www.docker.com/blog - The official Docker blog featuring articles and updates on Docker networking features, best practices, and use cases.
- **Kubernetes Documentation:** https://kubernetes.io/docs - The official documentation for Kubernetes includes information on container networking and Kubernetes' Container Network Interface (CNI).
- **Calico Documentation:** https://docs.projectcalico.org - Documentation for Project Calico, an open-source container networking and network security solution for containers.
- **Weave Documentation:** https://www.weave.works/docs - Documentation for Weave, a network plugin for Docker that simplifies networking across containers.
- **Cilium Documentation:** https://cilium.io/docs - Documentation for Cilium, a networking and security project for Kubernetes and Docker environments.

These references have been invaluable in providing accurate and reliable information for creating this chapter on Docker networking. Readers seeking further details and an in-depth understanding of Docker networking concepts are encouraged to explore these resources for additional insights.

Useful Links

- The lab exercise for this book is accessible online from this link: https://killercoda.com/meysam/course/mastering-docker/
- The repository for this book is accessible from this link: https://github.com/ava-orange-education/Ultimate Docker for Cloud Native Applications.

Chapter 5
Persistent Data Management with Docker

Figure 5.1: *A hand is holding a bunch of keys in front of a metal locker.*
source: https://unsplash.com/photos/RcvQHQB9zgA

Introduction

Welcome to the world of Docker volumes! In this chapter, we'll focus on one key aspect: durability. Docker volumes ensure your data remains safe, reliable, and easily accessible within containers. We'll explore the different types of volumes, how to create and manage them effortlessly, and practical use cases in real-world applications.

Structure

In this chapter, we will cover these topics:

- Docker volumes and their importance
- Types of Docker volumes
- Types of Docker storage drivers
- Data management strategies
- Managing Docker volume lifecycle
- Docker volume plugins and extensions
- Security considerations

Importance and Benefits of Docker Volumes

In this section, we'll learn why Docker volumes are crucial in containerization and the advantages they bring. Docker volumes are vital in enhancing your applications, from data persistence to efficient container workflows. Let's see why they are crucial in today's containerization world.

Importance of Docker Volumes

In traditional bare-metal deployments, applications store data directly on the server's filesystem. However, this approach can lead to data loss or inaccessibility during updates, server failures, or if you need to move the application to another host along with all the stored data on the host machine.

Enter Docker volumes! They come to the rescue by decoupling data storage from the containers themselves. Instead of storing data inside the container, Docker volumes act as virtual USB drives for containers. This means the data remains safe, movable and isolated from the container.

This straightforward yet powerful feature enhances data management, making it more reliable and efficient in containerized environments. With Docker volumes, you can ensure that data persists even if containers are replaced or removed, providing peace of mind for your critical information.

Importance of Docker Volumes in Containerization

Docker volumes are paramount as they address a crucial challenge in containerization: managing data within containers. Unlike traditional virtual machines, containers are lightweight and stateless, posing a problem for data persistence.

To tackle this challenge, Docker volumes provide a dedicated mechanism for data storage that remains independent of the container lifecycle. This ensures that essential data persists even when containers are destroyed, updated, or replaced, offering a reliable foundation for running and managing applications.

By providing data durability and consistency across containerized environments, Docker volumes bridge the gap between the ephemeral nature of containers and the need for long-term data storage. They create a cohesive and robust data management solution, empowering you to run applications confidently.

Moreover, Docker volumes enhance application portability by decoupling data from the container. This allows you to seamlessly move containers between different environments without data loss or compatibility concerns.

Regardless of the containerized workload, whether microservices, web applications, or databases, Docker volumes play a vital role in ensuring your data remains secure, available, and persistent. This pivotal aspect unleashes the full potential of containerization, enabling scalable, efficient, and dependable application deployments.

Figure 5.2: *Shows multi-colored pen lot on a black background. source: https://unsplash.com/photos/sbE9zbcuiZs*

Types of Docker Volumes

The upcoming section will explore the different kinds of Docker volumes. These volume types offer various approaches to managing container data, ranging from named volumes and host bind mounts to anonymous volumes. Understanding each type's strengths and use cases will empower you to choose the most suitable data storage method for your specific containerized applications.

Named Volumes

Named volumes are a type of Docker volume that provides a convenient and structured way to manage container data. Unlike anonymous volumes, named volumes have user-defined names, making them easily identifiable and reusable across containers.

When you create a named volume, Docker automatically manages its lifecycle, ensuring the data persists even if the container is removed. This is especially useful when updating or replacing containers without losing critical data.

Imagine a web application running inside a Docker container, and you want to store user-generated content, such as uploaded images or files. Using a named volume ensures this data remains safe and available, even if you update the application or replace the container.

Creating a named volume is straightforward. When launching your container, you can use the Docker CLI or docker-compose to define a named volume. For example, with the Docker CLI, you can run the following command:

```
docker run -v postgres-data:/var/lib/postgresql/data postgres:15
```

In this example, we create a named volume named and mount it to the data directory of the Postgres container. This allows the container to read and write data to that location, persisting even after the container is stopped or removed.

Named volumes also support data sharing between multiple containers. You can attach the same named volume to different containers, enabling seamless data communication and consistency across your application's components.

```
docker run -v postgres-data:/pgdata alpine ls /pgdata
```

In summary, named volumes are a powerful and user-friendly way to manage data in Docker containers. They ensure data persistence, enable easy updates and replacements of containers without data loss, and promote data sharing between containers.

Host Bind Mounts

They are another type of Docker volume that allows you to directly mount a directory from the host machine into the container. This means you can access and manipulate files on the host machine from within the container, blurring the lines between the container and the host system.

Let's consider an example where you are developing a web application using Docker. Using your favorite text editor or IDE, you can edit the application's source code on your host machine with host bind mounts. The changes you make will instantly reflect inside the container without needing to rebuild or restart the container. This enables a smooth and efficient development workflow where you can quickly iterate and see the results in real time.

```
docker run -v $PWD:/app:ro --detach myapp
```

Someone might prefer using host bind mounts over named volumes mainly because of the flexibility and control it provides. While Docker manages named volumes and resides within the Docker engine, **host bind mounts give you direct access to files on the host system**. This means you can leverage your host's file system features, such as symbolic links, file permissions, and file system tools.

Additionally, host bind mounts allow you to share data between the host and the container bidirectionally. Any changes you make inside the container will be reflected on the host and vice versa. This makes it easy to test, inspect, and modify files on the host system, making host bind mounts an excellent choice for development and debugging scenarios.

However, it's essential to be cautious when using host bind mounts in production environments, as they tightly couple the container to the host system. This can lead to portability and versioning issues, making it harder to move the application to different environments without dependencies on the host system.

Host bind mounts are a powerful tool for development and testing, enabling seamless sharing of files between the host and the container. They offer flexibility and immediate feedback during development, making it more efficient. However, in production environments, it's crucial to carefully weigh the advantages against the potential downsides and consider the long-term implications of tightly coupling the container to the host system.

Anonymous Volumes

Anonymous volumes are a type of Docker volume that provides a simple and ephemeral solution for managing container data. Unlike named volumes, Docker automatically creates anonymous volumes when a container is launched and does not have user-defined names. Instead, Docker assigns a random and unique identifier to each anonymous volume, making them less recognizable and not directly reusable.

Anonymous volumes are handy when you need temporary and disposable storage for a container. For example, consider a container running a database server. You might want to ensure the database's data is persisted, but you don't need to access or reuse that data outside the container. In this case, an anonymous volume is ideal. It is created on-the-fly when the container starts, and when the container is removed, the anonymous volume is automatically deleted, ensuring there are no remnants of unused data cluttering your system.

Anonymous volumes provide a hassle-free way to manage data you don't need to preserve between container runs or share across different containers. They offer the convenience of data persistence without requiring extra effort or management from the user.

However, the downside of anonymous volumes is that they can become challenging to manage and identify over time. Since Docker generates unique identifiers for each anonymous volume, it's challenging to know what data is stored in each volume without inspecting the container configuration.

Let's consider a practical example to illustrate the usage of anonymous volumes.

Imagine you are developing a web application that requires a containerized database server using Docker. An anonymous volume can persist the database's data between container runs. When you start the database container, Docker automatically creates an anonymous volume to store the database data.

```
docker run -v /var/lib/mysql mysql:8
```

In this case, we launch the MySQL database container with a flag to specify the location where we want Docker to store the container's data. This tells Docker to use an anonymous volume to store the database files. This volume will be automatically managed and deleted when the container is removed.

Anonymous volumes are ideal for scenarios where you need temporary data persistence for a container. For instance, you might use anonymous volumes in testing environments or short-lived development containers, where you only require data storage while the container is running.

While anonymous volumes are suitable for ephemeral use cases, it's essential to be cautious in production environments where data retention and sharing between containers are crucial. In such cases, named volumes or host bind mounts provide more control and long-term stability.

Comparing Different Volume Types

When managing data within Docker containers, various volume types are available, each serving specific purposes. Let's compare the volume types to understand their strengths and use cases.

- **Volumes (aka named volumes)**: These volumes provide user-defined and identifiable storage for data. Docker manages them and offers data persistence even when containers are removed or replaced. Named volumes are well-suited for long-term data storage and sharing between multiple containers, ensuring data consistency across your application.
- **Host Bind Mounts**: Host bind mounts directly link a directory on the host machine to the container. This type of volume allows seamless sharing of files between the host and container, enabling quick development iterations and real-time updates. Host bind mounts are advantageous during development and debugging, offering access to the host's file system features.
- **tmpfs (aka Anonymous Volumes)**: Docker automatically creates Anonymous volumes during container startup and has randomly assigned identifiers. They are perfect for temporary data storage within the container's lifecycle. Anonymous volumes are ideal when data persistence is needed only during the container's runtime and don't require long-term retention or sharing.

Choosing the appropriate volume type depends on the nature of your application, data requirements, and the desired level of control over data management. Understanding the differences between these volume types empowers you to make informed decisions, effectively managing data within your containerized applications.

To try the following lab exercise for hands-on experience with different Docker volumes, please visit:

https://killercoda.com/meysam/course/mastering-docker/chapter5.1

Figure 5.3: *Brown powder in a clear glass jar.*
source: https://unsplash.com/photos/bA1r4unkXAQ

Docker Storage Drivers

A Docker storage driver is a crucial component that manages storing and accessing data within containers. It acts as a bridge between the container and the underlying storage system, handling the reading and writing of data to and from volumes. Each storage driver has its mechanisms and optimizations for data handling, influencing Docker volumes' performance, portability, and behavior. In this section, we will describe the storage drivers supported by Docker.

Role and Importance of Storage Drivers

The significance of understanding storage drivers transcends mere technicalities; it underpins the foundation of successful containerized architectures. The choice of a storage driver can influence container startup times, storage efficiency, compatibility with specific filesystems, and even data resilience in the face of failures.

Moreover, the emergence of various storage drivers reflects the dynamic nature of the Docker ecosystem, catering to diverse use cases and deployment scenarios. Whether it's the speed and efficiency of overlay2, the advanced features of ZFS and Btrfs, or the simplicity of VFS, each driver provides an opportunity to optimize container operations based on unique requirements.

We'll explain more about each driver in a bit.

Handling Data in Containers with Storage Drivers

When a container starts, a storage driver determines how the container's filesystem layers are created and connected. This involves employing techniques such as copy-on-write, where only the changes made to a container's filesystem are stored, resulting in efficient use of disk space. Storage drivers also handle the crucial process of image layering, allowing containers to share read-only layers while maintaining individualized write layers.

As containers modify data during runtime, storage drivers manage the changes using various mechanisms like snapshots. These snapshots capture the state of a filesystem at a specific time, enabling quick rollbacks or reproducing past states when needed. This becomes particularly valuable when dealing with updates, debugging, or ensuring data consistency.

Furthermore, storage drivers play a crucial role in handling data volumes, which are used to persist data independently of the container's lifecycle. These volumes can be seamlessly connected to containers, ensuring data remains intact even if the container is removed or replaced. Storage drivers oversee the interaction between the host filesystem and these volumes, allowing data to be shared, synchronized, and protected.

Different storage drivers offer distinct advantages and considerations. Overlay2, for instance, excels in efficient image layering, while ZFS provides advanced features like snapshots and data integrity checks. The choice of storage driver depends on the application's requirements, the host environment, and the desired balance between performance and features.

Overlay2 Storage Driver

Designed for efficiency and performance, Overlay2 revolutionizes how Docker handles images, layers, and data, contributing to faster container startup times, reduced disk space consumption, and improved overall system responsiveness.

At its core, Overlay2 employs a technique known as "overlay filesystem" or "overlayFS." This technique enables Docker to create a layered filesystem where multiple layers stack upon each other, forming a unified view of the container. Each layer represents a discrete piece of the container, such as the base image, application code, and runtime modifications.

The brilliance of Overlay2 lies in its copy-on-write mechanism. When a container needs to modify a file, Overlay2 creates a copy of the file in the uppermost writable layer. This approach eliminates duplicating entire layers, saving valuable disk space. It also enhances performance by only writing the changes made, minimizing I/O operations.

Overlay2 optimizes image layering. Docker images consist of multiple read-only layers that can be shared among containers. Overlay2's efficiency shines here by allowing containers to share common layers, significantly reducing the storage footprint. This is particularly advantageous in scenarios where multiple containers are based on the same image.

Furthermore, Overlay2 addresses the limitations of its predecessor, the original "overlay" driver. Overlay2 provides better stability, support for more advanced filesystem features, and improved performance. It's recommended for most use cases, especially when efficiency, speed, and compatibility are paramount.

However, it's important to note that Overlay2 is closely tied to the Linux kernel's capabilities. While it's a powerful choice for Linux-based containers, it might not suit every environment. The host kernel's compatibility and configuration should be considered when selecting Overlay2 as the storage driver.

AUFS Storage Driver

AUFS, short for Advanced Multi-Layered Unification Filesystem, represents a pioneering storage driver within the Docker ecosystem. Initially one of the earliest storage options, AUFS laid the groundwork for layered filesystems in containerization. While it's been largely superseded by more modern drivers like Overlay2, understanding AUFS remains valuable in tracing the evolution of container storage mechanisms.

At its core, AUFS revolutionized how Docker manages container images and filesystem layers. It introduced the concept of union mounts, which allow multiple filesystems to be mounted in a single unified view. This union mount approach enabled Docker to create layered filesystems, where each layer represents a specific container component, such as the base image and application modifications.

One of AUFS's key features is its ability to overlay multiple read-only filesystems, effectively creating a writable layer on top. When a container modifies a file, AUFS employs a copy-on-write mechanism. Instead of modifying the original file, AUFS creates a copy in the writable layer, preserving the integrity of the underlying layers. This approach has the advantage of isolating changes within the container without affecting the shared layers.

AUFS's layered approach also allows Docker to manage disk space efficiently. The storage footprint is significantly reduced since common layers can be shared among multiple containers. This efficiency is particularly evident when multiple containers are based on the same image, as they can utilize the same read-only layers while maintaining their writable layers.

However, as Docker and the container landscape evolved, certain limitations of AUFS became apparent. Compatibility with newer Linux kernels and concerns about stability led to the development of alternative storage drivers like Overlay2. While AUFS was historically a popular choice, its usage has waned in favor of drivers offering enhanced features, performance, and compatibility.

Device Mapper Storage Driver

Device Mapper is a crucial storage driver within the Docker ecosystem, offering robust block-level storage management capabilities. Rooted in its ability to create thin-provisioned snapshots and manage device mappings, Device Mapper contributes to Docker's versatility in handling data persistence and containerized applications.

At its core, Device Mapper operates by abstracting and virtualizing storage devices on the Linux system. It facilitates the creation of logical volumes that span multiple physical disks, allowing administrators to manage storage resources more flexibly and efficiently. This feature becomes particularly valuable in dynamic container environments where resource allocation and scaling are essential.

One of Device Mapper's notable features is its support for thin provisioning. Thin provisioning enables the creation of logical volumes that consume only the space required by actual data instead of allocating the full amount upfront. This efficiency ensures optimal disk utilization, primarily when containers must be provisioned quickly and storage consumption is a concern.

Device Mapper's support for snapshots is a powerful tool for data management. Snapshots allow the creation of point-in-time copies of a filesystem, preserving the state of the data at a specific moment. Docker leverages this feature to facilitate rapid container cloning, backup, and rollback processes. The ability to capture and reproduce specific filesystem states enhances data integrity and accelerates container lifecycle management.

In the context of Docker, the Device Mapper storage driver leverages these underlying features to manage container data. It creates a thin-provisioned logical volume for each container, which can be snapshotted for backup or replication. However, Device Mapper's design complexity might lead to potential overhead and performance considerations, especially when compared to more streamlined drivers like Overlay2.

Device Mapper is an excellent choice for enterprise environments and scenarios where advanced storage features are critical. It's particularly suitable for situations where granular control over storage resources, snapshot capabilities, and compatibility with existing infrastructure are significant concerns.

Btrfs Storage Driver

Short for the B-Tree filesystem, it represents a cutting-edge filesystem technology that has garnered attention for its advanced features and versatility, especially in modern containerization, such as Docker. Designed to address the evolving demands of data storage, Btrfs introduces innovative concepts that enhance data integrity, scalability, and flexibility.

At its core, Btrfs is built upon the principles of a B-tree data structure, allowing for efficient indexing and managing files and metadata. This foundation grants Btrfs exceptional capabilities, making it well-suited for scenarios requiring rapid data access, snapshot functionality, and the ability to handle vast amounts of data.

One of Btrfs's standout features is its support for copy-on-write snapshots. This mechanism enables Btrfs to create instantaneous point-in-time copies of entire filesystems or individual files. In a Docker context, this feature becomes highly relevant for quickly replicating containerized applications, performing backups, and ensuring data consistency across different development and deployment stages.

Moreover, Btrfs integrates advanced features like data deduplication and transparent compression. Deduplication identifies and eliminates duplicate data blocks, effectively optimizing storage utilization. Conversely, compression reduces the disk space required to store data, enhancing storage efficiency. These features align with Docker's goal of minimizing resource consumption while maintaining data integrity.

Btrfs's scalability is noteworthy, as it can handle vast filesystems and many files without significant performance degradation. This scalability makes it suitable for environments where Docker orchestrates numerous containers and relies on efficient data management at scale.

However, it's essential to recognize that while Btrfs offers remarkable capabilities, its adoption is less widespread than other filesystems due to specific considerations. It's considered relatively complex and might require careful configuration and management. Additionally, compatibility with various Linux distributions and kernel versions might impact its adoption in different environments.

ZFS Storage Driver

ZFS, which stands for Zettabyte File System, represents a groundbreaking advancement in storage technology with applications that extend to the world of Docker and containerization. Developed by Sun Microsystems, ZFS embodies a holistic approach to data management, offering a wealth of features designed to ensure data integrity, scalability, and flexibility.

It employs a 128-bit address space allowing virtually unlimited storage capacity, making it well-suited for environments dealing with massive datasets. ZFS's innovative checksumming mechanism detects and corrects data corruption, ensuring that the stored data remains intact and trustworthy.

One of ZFS's standout features is its support for "copy-on-write" snapshots. This technology enables the rapid creation of snapshots and point-in-time copies of datasets. This feature is invaluable for quickly duplicating container images, applications, and Docker context environments. Snapshots can be used for backup, testing, and rolling back to previous states, offering agility and resilience to containerized applications.

ZFS's "data deduplication" capability addresses the challenge of duplicate data. It identifies identical data blocks across the storage system and stores them only once, significantly reducing storage requirements. This is particularly beneficial in container environments where similar data must be present in multiple instances.

The "self-healing" nature of ZFS is another advantage. It continuously scrubs data to detect and correct errors, minimizing the risk of data corruption. This feature aligns well with Docker's focus on maintaining the integrity of containerized applications and their associated data.

Nevertheless, it's essential to consider that while ZFS offers exceptional capabilities, its adoption might involve complexities and considerations. Licensing and compatibility issues can impact its use in specific environments, and its memory requirements can be substantial.

VFS Storage Driver

VFS, which stands for Virtual File System, represents a foundational approach to managing files and data within Docker containers. While less intricate than other storage drivers like Overlay2 or ZFS, VFS is a straightforward and pragmatic solution for containers that prioritize simplicity and compatibility.

At its core, VFS is a simple storage driver directly interacting with the host's filesystem. Unlike more complex drivers implementing layered filesystems or block-level storage, VFS creates a one-to-one mapping between the container and the host filesystem. Changes made within a container are directly reflected on the host, and vice versa.

VFS's straightforward approach can be particularly suitable for specific use cases. It's often used in environments where Docker is employed for development, testing, or educational purposes. Since it doesn't involve the complexities of layered filesystems or device mapping, VFS can be more accessible to those new to containerization or those who prioritize ease of setup.

However, it's essential to acknowledge that VFS comes with trade-offs. While it's simple to use, it lacks more advanced storage drivers' efficiency and performance benefits. Containers using VFS might experience slower startup times and potentially higher disk I/O than drivers like Overlay2. Additionally, due to the direct interaction with the host filesystem, VFS might face limitations in scenarios where isolation and resource separation are critical.

In Docker's continuous pursuit of flexibility, VFS is a pragmatic choice for specific scenarios. Its approach offers a precise mapping between containers and the host filesystem, making it easy to understand and deploy, particularly in educational or entry-level Docker environments.

For further information, please visit https://killercoda.com/meysam/course/mastering-docker/chapter5.2

Data Management Strategies

In the fast-paced world of Docker, safeguarding your data with effective backup and restore practices is paramount. Here, we'll walk through practical CLI examples to showcase how to create backups and restore data within Docker volumes.

Backup

Creating a backup involves capturing the contents of a Docker volume and preserving it for future restoration. Let's say you have a container named `myapp` with a volume named `data_volume`. To back up the contents of this volume, you can use the following command:

```
docker run --rm \
  -v data_volume:/data:ro \
  -v /tmp:/backup \
  alpine \
  tar -czf /backup/data_backup.tar.gz -C /data .
```

In this example:

- `--rm` ensures that the temporary backup container is removed after the backup operation.
- `-v data_volume:/data` mounts the `data_volume` to the `/data` directory within the backup container.
- `-v /tmp:/backup` mounts the host's `/tmp` directory to the `/backup` directory within the backup container.
- `tar -czf /backup/data_backup.tar.gz -C /data` creates a compressed backup file of the volume's content.

Ultimately, there will be the backup file in the host operating system located at `/tmp/data_backup.tar.gz`.

Restore

Restoring a Docker volume involves recreating the volume's content from a backup. Let's assume you have the `/tmp/data_backup.tar.gz` backup file in your host machine. To restore the volume contents, you can use this command:

```
docker run --rm \
  -v data_volume:/data \
  -v /tmp:/backup:ro \
  alpine \
  tar -xzf /backup/data_backup.tar.gz -C /data
```

In this example, the options are similar to the backup command, but now the `tar` command extracts the contents from the backup file into the `data_volume`.

Real-World Example

Consider a scenario where you're updating your application container and want to ensure you can quickly restore data if needed. Before updating, perform a backup using the first command. Then, after the update, if any issues arise, restore the data using the second command to roll back to a stable state.

Automating backups using scripts or scheduling can streamline this process and ensure regular backups of critical data.

Figure 5.4: *Assorted-color leaves hanging decor.*
source: https://unsplash.com/photos/5IHz5WhosQE

Managing Volume Data Lifecycle

Managing the lifecycle of data stored within volumes is a critical aspect of maintaining order, data integrity, and efficient containerized workflows. This process involves orchestrating the evolution of data across various stages, from versioning to archiving, and ensuring seamless integration during container updates.

Versioning Data

Versioning data within Docker volumes entails preserving historical data snapshots as it evolve. This approach enables you to access previous states of your data, track changes, and roll back to specific points in the past. Docker doesn't inherently manage data versioning, but you can leverage version control systems or backup strategies to achieve this. By consistently tagging and documenting versioned data, you enhance traceability and improve your ability to troubleshoot issues that arise.

Having the data tracked in a version-controlled way lets you track the changes that occurred over time. One of the popular tools in the data-science community is DVC. Consider checking their documentation at https://dvc.org/ if you want to learn more.

Archiving Old Volumes

As containers and applications evolve, data might become obsolete. Archiving old volumes involves identifying and safely storing ones that are no longer used. Archiving helps free up storage resources and keeps the active environment clutter-free. Before archiving, ensure you've properly backed up the data and documented its purpose, as some data might need to be retrieved later for reference or compliance purposes.

Ensuring Data Integrity Across Container Updates

Container updates are a natural part of the software development lifecycle. However, ensuring data integrity when containers are updated is crucial to avoid data corruption or loss. Consider techniques such as blue-green deployments or rolling updates to maintain data consistency during updates. These methods ensure that data within volumes remains intact while transitioning to new container versions. Additionally, perform thorough testing to identify potential compatibility issues affecting data integrity during updates.

Advanced Consideration

Consider integrating your volume management strategy with continuous integration/deployment (CI/CD) pipelines for more advanced scenarios. This approach automates container updates' testing, deployment, and rollback, tightly aligning data lifecycle management with your application's evolution.

Volume Plugins and Extensibility

Docker's extensibility empowers users to tailor their container environments to specific needs, and one area where this extensibility shines is in volume plugins. Volume plugins provide the means to seamlessly integrate Docker with various storage solutions, cloud platforms, and specialized storage backends, enhancing the flexibility and compatibility of Docker's volume management.

Docker's volume system is designed to be pluggable, meaning that users can extend its capabilities by integrating third-party volume plugins. These plugins act as intermediaries between Docker and external storage systems, bridging the gap between the containerized application and diverse storage backends.

Examples of Docker Volume Plugins

We will introduce some of the current examples of such plugins as follows:

Docker Volume Driver for Amazon EBS

This plugin integrates Docker with Amazon Elastic Block Store (EBS), allowing containers to use EBS volumes as persistent storage. This is particularly useful when running Docker on Amazon Web Services (AWS) and requiring scalable and durable block storage.

Rex-Ray

Rex-Ray is a powerful open-source volume plugin supporting multiple cloud providers and storage systems, including AWS, Azure, and Google Cloud. It offers a unified interface for managing storage across various platforms, enhancing portability and flexibility. Consider checking their repository at https://github.com/rexray/rexray if you want to learn more.

Portworx

Portworx is a Kubernetes-native storage solution that can also be used as a volume plugin in Docker. It provides advanced features like data replication, backup, and disaster recovery, suitable for stateful applications requiring high availability. To learn more, take a look at their documentation at https://portworx.com.

NetApp Trident

NetApp Trident integrates Docker with NetApp storage systems, enabling efficient and optimized storage provisioning, management, and snapshot capabilities. You can learn more about Trident in its GitHub repository, accessible at https://github.com/NetApp/trident.

Advantages and Disadvantages

If you want to consider whether you should be using Docker volume plugins, here are some of the advantages:

- **Integration with Specialized Storage**: Volume plugins enable Docker to seamlessly interact with storage solutions tailored to specific use cases, such as distributed storage systems, cloud-based storage, or enterprise-grade storage arrays.
- **Simplified Management**: Volume plugins often provide abstraction layers that simplify the management and provisioning of complex storage systems, freeing users from dealing with low-level storage details.
- **Enhanced Portability**: With the right volume plugin, applications can be designed to use familiar Docker volume APIs while running on diverse storage platforms, promoting application portability.
- **Scalability and Performance**: Some volume plugins offer optimized performance and scalability features that might not be present in Docker's default volume drivers.

And to have a complete picture, here is a list of the disadvantages of Docker volume plugins:

- **Complexity and Learning Curve**: Implementing and configuring volume plugins can introduce complexity, especially for users unfamiliar with the plugin's setup and management. Setting up and managing plugins correctly requires additional time and effort.
- **Dependency on Third-Party Solutions**: Relying on third-party volume plugins means introducing dependencies on external software. If a plugin's development slows down or becomes obsolete, it could impact your ability to manage storage for your containerized applications effectively.
- **Compatibility and Maintenance**: Volume plugins must remain compatible with the evolving Docker ecosystem. Docker updates, changes in the storage backend, or the plugin itself might require continuous maintenance and updates to ensure compatibility and stability.
- **Limited Portability**: While volume plugins can enhance application portability, they can lead to vendor lock-in. If you heavily rely on a specific plugin and want to switch to a different storage solution, migrating your data and adapting your application could be challenging.
- **Performance Overhead**: Some volume plugins might introduce performance overhead due to the additional layers of abstraction they introduce between Docker and the underlying storage. This could impact I/O operations and overall application performance.
- **Security and Isolation Concerns**: Introducing external volume plugins might raise security and isolation concerns. Users need to ensure that the plugin and the storage backend are secure and do not compromise the container environment.

- **Lack of Standardization**: Docker volume plugins are not standardized across storage solutions. Each plugin might have a unique configuration, management process, and feature set, making it harder to switch between different plugins.
- **Documentation and Support**: The quality of documentation and community support for specific volume plugins can vary widely. Some plugins lack comprehensive documentation, making it challenging for users to troubleshoot issues or implement best practices.
- **Limited Features**: While some volume plugins offer advanced features, others might have limitations compared to native Docker volumes. Users need to evaluate whether the features provided by a plugin meet their specific requirements.
- **Performance Variability**: Performance variability can be an issue depending on the plugin and storage backend. Users must thoroughly test and benchmark the plugin's performance to meet their application's needs.

Although they bring a lot to the table, Docker volumes are not a silver bullet and have disadvantages. It's important to carefully assess your needs, thoroughly research available plugins, and consider the long-term implications before integrating volume plugins into your containerized workflows.

Security and Considerations

Ensuring data security stored within Docker volumes is crucial. Addressing security considerations related to user permissions, encryption, and data protection within volumes contributes to maintaining data integrity and protecting sensitive information.

User and Group, Permissions

Containerized applications interact with data within volumes, and it's crucial to manage user and group permissions effectively to prevent unauthorized access and maintain data segregation. Docker volumes can inherit permissions from the host system, potentially leading to issues if not appropriately managed. To mitigate this, Docker allows you to specify user and group IDs within the container. By using appropriate IDs that align with the host system's users and groups, you ensure consistent and secure access to volume data.

Encryption and Data Protection

Encryption is pivotal in safeguarding data privacy and security. Docker does not inherently provide data encryption within volumes, but you can utilize encryption techniques within the container itself or rely on external encryption mechanisms. For sensitive data, consider encrypting the data within the container before it's stored in a volume. Additionally, if your storage backend supports encryption, you can leverage encryption-at-rest solutions to protect data stored in volumes on the disk.

Securing Data with Third-Party Tools

Several third-party tools can enhance the security of data stored in Docker volumes.

Several third-party tools offer user-friendly solutions for enhancing security, encryption, and data management within Docker volumes. Here are some notable options:

Docker Volume Crypt

Docker Volume Crypt is a tool designed specifically for encrypting Docker volumes. It wraps volumes in encrypted filesystems, ensuring that data stored within volumes is encrypted at rest.

- **Features**: Provides strong encryption for Docker volumes, adding a layer of security to sensitive data. Supports encryption using industry-standard encryption algorithms.
- **Ease of Use**: The tool simplifies encrypting and decrypting volumes, making it more user-friendly for those looking to secure their data.

HashiCorp Vault

HashiCorp Vault is a comprehensive secrets management tool that can also manage sensitive configuration data and secrets used within Docker containers.

- **Features**: Provides a centralized platform for managing secrets, encryption keys, and sensitive information. Offers advanced access controls and auditing capabilities.
- **Ease of Use**: HashiCorp Vault has a user-friendly interface and comprehensive documentation to guide users through securing and managing secrets.

SOPS (Secrets OPerationS)

SOPS is a tool for managing and encrypting configuration files and secrets in various applications, including Docker containers.

- **Features**: Integrates with various systems and tools, including Docker Compose, and allows you to encrypt sensitive data using PGP or AWS KMS.
- **Ease of Use**: SOPS is known for its simplicity and integration capabilities, making securing sensitive configuration data within Docker volumes easier.

Bitnami's Sealed Secrets

Sealed Secrets is an open-source project that provides a way to encrypt secrets in a GitOps-friendly manner, making it suitable for use in containerized environments.

- **Features**: Offers a secure and GitOps-compatible method of managing secrets and sensitive data. Uses asymmetric cryptography for encryption.
- **Ease of Use**: Sealed Secrets integrates seamlessly with Kubernetes, commonly used with Docker. It simplifies the process of securing and managing secrets within containerized applications.

Docker Secrets Management Tools

Various tools, such as `docker-secret` and `docker-secrets-manager`, aim to simplify the management of Docker secrets and sensitive data by providing user-friendly interfaces and automation.

It's important to note that the ease of use and user-friendliness of these tools can vary based on your familiarity with encryption concepts and the specific requirements of your environment. Before adopting any third-party tool, take the time to evaluate its features, compatibility with your existing setup, and documentation and community support. Additionally, always ensure the tool aligns with your security and compliance requirements.

Figure 5.5: *A black and white checkered flag flying in the sky.*
source: https://unsplash.com/photos/a-black-and-white-checkered-flag-flying-in-the-sky-
65oNjZMX5NY

Conclusion

In the journey of mastering Docker volumes, you have navigated through a range of essential concepts that empower you to wield containerized data with finesse. We've explored the significance of Docker volumes as vital vessels for data persistence, providing a lifeline to maintain the integrity of our applications. Understanding the types of volumes and the drivers that underpin their functionality has equipped you to tailor storage solutions that align with your needs.

We delved into the strategies for managing data within Docker volumes, encompassing versioning, archiving, and preserving data integrity during container updates. This knowledge bestows the ability to gracefully manage the ebb and flow of data in a dynamic container world. We've also dived into security and permissions, reinforcing the importance of safeguarding your data through user permissions, encryption, and security tools. This guardianship ensures your data remains resilient against potential threats.

Throughout this chapter, we've encountered the power of extensibility through third-party volume plugins, expanding your container toolkit with integration possibilities into diverse storage realms. As you continue your journey with Docker volumes, remember that each piece of knowledge gained contributes to your mastery of containerized data, enabling you to orchestrate storage with confidence, agility, and security.

In the next chapter, we will cover a powerful tool that simplifies the deployment and management of multi-container applications. Docker Compose streamlines the process of defining, configuring, and orchestrating complex application stacks, enabling you to replicate development environments and deploy applications easily. If you have done everything through the use of ad-hoc CLI commands, get ready for the declarative approach to deploy your applications using Docker Compose in the next chapter.

References

- **Docker Documentation**: To explore official Docker documentation for comprehensive insights into Docker volumes and related concepts, please visit https://docs.docker.com/
- **Docker Volume Overview**: To learn more about Docker volumes, their types, and usage from the official Docker documentation, please visit https://docs.docker.com/storage/volumes/

Useful Links

- Data Version Control: https://dvc.org
- Rex-Ray Storage Driver: https://github.com/rexray/rexray
- Portworx: https://portworx.com
- NetApp Trident: https://github.com/NetApp/trident
- Lab exercise for this book: https://killercoda.com/meysam/course/mastering-docker/

CHAPTER 6

Docker Compose for Simplified Application Deployment

Figure 6.1: *A conductor orchestrating musicians.*
source: https://unsplash.com/photos/yUJVHiYZCGQ

Introduction

In modern software deployment, achieving simplicity and efficiency is paramount. This chapter immerses us in the power of this tool. Discover how Docker Compose streamlines intricate service orchestration and configuration, transforming deployment into a seamless and efficient experience.

The most significant selling point for Docker Compose is its ability to orchestrate and manage multiple deployments and containers. That is why it is crucial to know its ins and outs to launch various services using its syntax and definition, which is this chapter's purpose.

Structure

In this chapter, we will cover these topics:

- Understanding Docker Compose Essentials
- Streamlining Services with Docker Compose
- Syntax and Definition of Docker Compose
- Advanced Tips and Techniques

Understanding Docker Compose Essentials

Imagine you have many separate parts that need to work together to create a complete application - like the building blocks of a puzzle. Docker Compose acts like the glue that brings these pieces together. It lets you describe all the parts your application needs in a simple file, then starts and stops them correctly. This is super useful because you don't have to remember complex commands to launch each piece individually; Docker Compose handles the orchestration for you. It is like telling Docker Compose your application's setup blueprint, turning it into an actual working application.

In this section, we will explore the core ideas behind Docker Compose, including how to define services, manage networks, and set up volumes. By the end, you will have a solid grasp of the essential concepts that underpin Docker Compose, setting the stage for smoother and more efficient application deployments.

Streamlining Services with Docker Compose

Suppose you have a complex application with multiple services, like a web server, a database, and other components. Each of these services needs to communicate and work together seamlessly. Without Docker Compose, you might have to start each service individually, configure them to talk to each other and ensure they're running in the proper order. It's like trying to conduct an orchestra without a conductor.

Docker Compose is like the conductor that orchestrates the services for you. With a simple configuration file, you can define all the services your application needs, their dependencies, and how they should interact. Docker Compose then handles starting, stopping, and managing these services as a cohesive unit. This saves you time and effort and reduces the chances of errors when managing services manually.

Figure 6.2: *A pen and a notebook on a desk.*
source: https://unsplash.com/photos/xG8IQMqMITM

Syntax and Definition of Docker Compose

In this section, we will go through some examples of how to write Docker Compose while explaining different aspects of each attribute defined and the reason behind such definition. These examples are meant to be practical guidance on how different attributes play a role in the overall stability of your Docker Compose definition.

To use Docker Compose, you need two pieces in place:

1. `docker-compose` plugin installed in your system; this step is optional if you have Docker Desktop v1.13 or greater.
2. Definition of your compose in a file named `compose.yml`.

If you prefer having the standalone docker-compose binary, you can download a compiled version from the latest GitHub release for your platform from the following URL:

https://github.com/docker/compose/releases/latest

Downloading one of the binaries can look something like this in a Linux machine with an AMD CPU.

```
curl -sSfLo docker compose \

"https://github.com/docker/compose/releases/latest/download/docker-
compose-linux-x86_64"
chmod +x docker compose
mkdir -p ~/.docker/cli-plugins
mv docker-compose ~/.docker/cli-plugins
```

Example 1: Web App and Database

After downloading the binary, we can write the compose file definition.

Let's create two services to provide an example of a real-world application. One web application written by us (in an arbitrary programming language) and a PostgreSQL database.

The requirement for such a definition is as follows:

- Both services must be on the same network so that the web application can communicate with the database.
- The database must have a volume attached so the container can restart without data loss; remember, docker containers are ephemeral unless a volume is explicitly attached to them.
- Create a one-direction dependency from the web application to the database so the database can start and the web application next.
- We want to expose the web application to all the network interfaces, for example, on port 8000.
- We want the database port to only be exposed on the localhost on port 5432.
- We want auto-reload functionality in the container, so we must define a read-only mount from our src directory to the running container in the web application.

With all those requirements, here is what the definition will look like:

```
# docker compose.yml
version: "3.9" # Version is now obsolete and not recommended to specify

services:
  web:
    build: web
    command: ./main.py
    ports:
```

```
      - "8000:8000"
    volumes:
      - ./web:/app:ro
    environment:
      - PORT=8000
      - DSN=postgres://demo:demo@db:5432/demo?sslmode=disable
    depends_on:
      db:
        condition: service_healthy
  db:
    image: postgres:15
    volumes:
      - postgres_data:/var/lib/postgresql/data/
    ports:
      - "127.0.0.1:5432:5432"
    environment:
      - POSTGRES_USER=demo
      - POSTGRES_PASSWORD=demo
      - POSTGRES_DB=demo
    healthcheck:
      test: ["CMD", "pg_isready", "-U", "demo"]
      interval: 10s
      timeout: 5s
      retries: 10
      start_period: 10s
      start_interval: 5s

volumes:
  postgres_data:
```

The full code is accessible from the following URL:

https://github.com/ava-orange-education/Ultimate Docker for Cloud Native Applications/tree/main/chapter6/web-database

A couple of things are important to mention in this Docker Compose definition.

The `build` attribute specifies where to look for a `Dockerfile` like a `docker build -t sample.` will specify the same with a dot (the current working directory).

With `ports` for both services, you can notice that the web application is exposed on all interfaces (implicitly `0.0.0.0`), but the database is only on the localhost machine. Avoiding exposing services that wouldn't need to takes us one step closer to ensuring we're not at risk; the alternative is to expose PostgreSQL on all interfaces and have a firewall rule defined to limit the number of hosts that can access such ports.

Placing every line of the `ports` attribute in quotations is highly recommended, especially in the official documentation. The reason is that YAML might do its parsing on numbers before passing it to the Docker engine and you might see unexpected behaviors.

For each service, a `volumes` attribute is defined for the web application to have the same tree structure as the host machine (to have auto-reload in the container) and for the database to persist its data files. This way, when the database is restarted, we will not lose our data (as discussed in the previous chapter).

Passing environment variables to the containers is done with either of the following:

- `environment`: for specifying a few key-value pairs.
- `env_file`: for passing a filename of many key-value pairs that cannot be put in the compose file and not harm the readability and shortness.

As a rule of thumb, if you have more than 10 values to pass to the compose file, it is better to write them in a separate file and pass the filename to `env_file`.

The last vital attribute to mention here is the `depends_on`. The Docker Compose will create and run the dependency services according to dependency ordering.

As seen in the definition, dependency is having a condition that will wait for the database service to become healthy before running the web application. This is powerful if you don't want to see surprises in your application deployment, and it makes sure that all the different pieces are running and healthy before announcing the entire stack as successful.

Running the services inside this Docker Compose definition file is as simple as running the following command in the same directory as the `compose.yml` file.

```
docker compose up -d
```

The logs will be similar to the following:

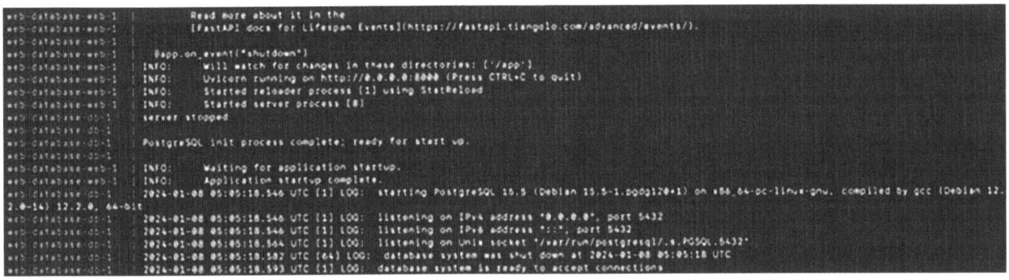

And the output if sending an HTTP request will be as follows:

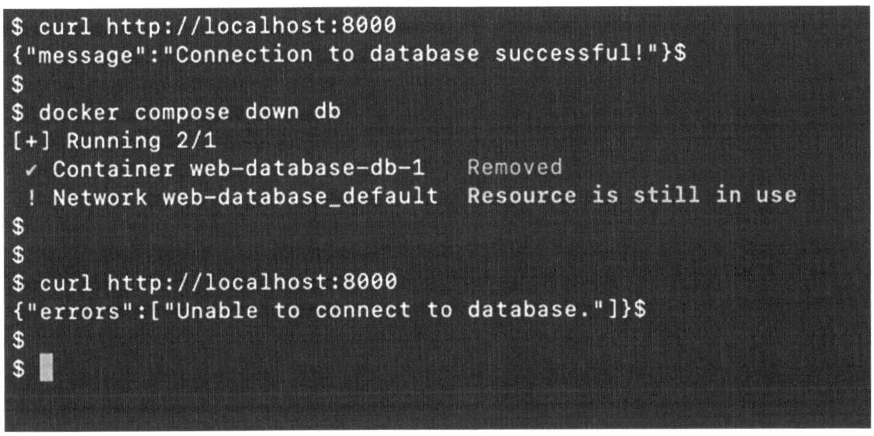

Example 2: Background Worker and Message Broker

This example will illustrate a use case where we will deploy an application that subscribes to a message queue topic. After processing the message, it will persist the reports in an external database (that we do not self-host).

Suppose we have a Python application using Celery with Redis as a message broker to process some data. The data's nature is optional since we only try to demonstrate the Docker Compose definition file in this chapter.

The requirement for this example is as follows:

- The background worker process and the Redis must be on the same network.
- The redis should be exposed on the internal network and password-protected.
- The background worker needs to have some environment variables defined, two of the most important ones being the message queue broker URL and the external database connection string.

- For the sake of simplicity, we do not care about Redis' persistence, and we can afford to lose some of the messages if the broker goes down and the message has not been processed.

With such requirements, here is what the Docker Compose definition will look like:

```
services:
  worker:
    build:
      context: ./app
      dockerfile: ../docker/Dockerfile.dev
    image: worker
    pull_policy: build
    cap_drop:
      - ALL
    depends_on:
      - redis
    # the order matters in the following env_file list if there are
    dependencies
    env_file:
      - .env.redis
      - .env.worker
    environment:
      - PYTHONUNBUFFERED=1
      - DSN=mongodb+srv://demo:demo@frankfurt.abcdefg.mongodb.net/?w=ma-
      jority
    healthcheck:
      interval: 30s
      retries: 5
      start_period: 1s
      test: ["CMD", "sh", "-c", "celery -A tasks:app status"]
      timeout: 3s
    networks:
      - worker
    volumes:
      - ./app:/app:ro
  redis:
    command: /entrypoint/start-server.sh
    env_file:
      - .env.redis
```

```
    image: redis:7-alpine
    networks:
      - worker
    # redis is exposed in a private network
    ports:
      - "10.20.30.40:6379:6379"
    volumes:
      - ./redis:/entrypoint/:ro
networks:
  worker:
    driver: bridge
```

The complete code for this example is accessible from the following URL:

https://github.com/ava-orange-education/Ultimate Docker for Cloud Native Applications/tree/main/chapter6/celery-redis

NOTE: You will have to replace the IP address `10.20.30.40` with the address of your host machine (most likely a private IP address inside your access point).

Let's explain the attributes and the way they have been initialized.

As you can see from the first service, the `build` is capable of more than just receiving one string value (as in the previous example). You can specify the context for building the Docker image and where to find the definition for a `Dockerfile`.

The `build` directive in this definition is equivalent to the following terminal command:

```
docker build -t worker -f ../docker/Dockerfile.dev ./app
```

This allows for multiple things to happen:

- You can separate the `Dockerfile` definitions and your application code to decouple the operational and development aspects.
- You can define multiple `Dockerfile` for different environments, though having one `Dockerfile` with various stages for different deployment environments is also possible (as explained in previous chapters).
- You can rename your `Dockerfile` to represent its purpose and then explicitly pass the name to the Docker Compose definition.
- The `context` is a compelling attribute as it will indicate the root where the Docker engine will start building the image. This means you can create

a boundary for the application source code and all the other generated binaries to avoid making the context heavier and the build process slower.

The `image` attribute allows you to define a name for the built image, which may help deploy the same app elsewhere or push to some container registry in the public or private offerings.

The `pull_policy` will specify the intended behavior for the image, whether we want to pull from a registry, build the image locally, and so on. If not specified, the default behavior is different whether or not the context is set.

The next attribute, optional but can enhance your operational security, is `cap_drop` (or `cap_add`), which tells the Docker Daemon which Linux capabilities you would like to give to the underlying containers. Unless required for the container's functionality, a best practice is to drop all privileges to isolate the impact of the running container on the host machine to avoid exposure.

Dependency and its limitations have been explained here and will not need repetition.

The environments, however, deserve further elaboration. As you can see, we can provide hard-coded values to the `environment` or pass some file names to the `env_file`.

The behavior of the Compose file is that, at the time of invocation and before creating any service, any variable in the form of `$PORT` or `${PORT}` will try and get its value from either the current shell's environment variables (for example, `export PORT=8000`) or will use the contents of the `.env` file in the current directory as a last resort to fill in those values. If none have a value for that variable, an empty string will be replaced. This act of replacing a variable with its environment variable value is called shell expansion.

The critical thing to mention is that if such a shell expansion is used in the `environment`, those variables must be present by the time they get parsed, that is, the value should be either exported in the shell or present in the `.env` file.

On the other hand, if the number of variables we want to pass to the application is more than a handful, we better put all of them in a specific env file and pass the filename to the `env_file` attribute.

The two options available are exporting the variable before running the stack using `export PORT=8000` or putting the key-value pair in a file named `.env` in the same directory as the `docker compose.yml`.

The other alternative that also supports shell expansion is `env_file`. You can place an environment variable in the file as a value and feed those values by prior `env_file` elements in the list, exporting them on the shell or putting them in `.env` as before.

We have used this powerful feature in the first service, where two environment variable files are passed to the worker service. In the first file, the Redis password is defined, and in the second one, the placeholder is used to have the same value and to adhere to DRY!

Here are the contents of both files:

```
# .env.redis
REDIS_PASSWORD=mastering-docker

# .env.worker
REDIS_BROKER_URL=redis://:${REDIS_PASSWORD}@redis:6379/0
REDIS_BACKEND_URL=redis://:${REDIS_PASSWORD}@redis:6379/1
```

This is only possible because the `env_file` elements are order-sensitive, and the first ones are parsed first, which means by the time the Docker engine reaches the element `.env.worker`, the `${REDIS_PASSWORD}` will already have its value.

This shell expansion is mighty when we want to avoid repeating the same value in multiple places; we just need to ensure the order of the env files is correct since the top ones are evaluated first.

The next attribute is `healthcheck`. As you can see in the value of the `test`, this is just another one of the `Dockerfile` syntaxes. Since Docker Compose and `Dockerfile` are basically from the same foundations, having the same syntax language streamlines the integration process.

The health checks are also optional, but the thing that makes them very useful is the visual you get when you want to see whether the service is healthy after booting up.

They are also used when you define a dependency between services, as seen in the current and the previous example.

Here is what will happen if we get that info from Docker Compose.

```
$ docker compose ps --format json | jq | grep -E 'Status|Health'
    "Status": "Up 3 seconds (health: starting)",
    "Health": "starting",
```

```
$ # A few moments later
$ docker compose ps --format json | jq | grep -E ‘Status|Health’
    “Status”: “Up 44 seconds (healthy)”,
    “Health”: “healthy”,
```

This information is handy in operations to know if your services behave as they should.

Note that the same information can be retrieved from a simple `docker ps` command.

The next attribute you see in the file is networks. These are one or more strings you specify that the container should be connected to and receive an IP address on each of those network bridges (networking has been discussed in the last chapter).

Make sure each entry you specify in any one of the `services.[*].networks` are also defined in the networks at the root of the Compose definition.

You can also use other network drivers, which you can specify accordingly in the definition section.

The critical thing to mention here is that if you do not set any network in your service or the network at the root of the file, the default action is to create one bridge network and place all the services inside that.

One may occasionally want to separate different services, where you can define various networks and attach different services to each as desired.

Figure 6.3: *Variety of ice creams.*
source: https://unsplash.com/photos/Wpg3QmOzaGk

Example 3: Load Balancer with HAProxy

In this example, we will try to create two upstream servers hosting a sample static file, load balancing the incoming traffic between them using the popular HAProxy load balancer.

The requirements for this example are as follows:

- The services need to be on the same network to communicate seamlessly.
- There is a dependency between the load balancer and the upstream services to ensure traffic is routed to the healthy service, but the dependency is not required since the load balancer has its health check.
- We need a health check on both upstream services to define a correct dependency between services.
- We must mount the config to the load balancer and upstream services.
- We want the container to run in a read-only filesystem for further security enhancement.
- We want to mount some ephemeral volume to the upstream backend to write the logs and the PID file.
- We want to drop all the Linux capabilities for the load balancer service.
- We want to explicitly allow the load-balancer container to open ports 80 and 443.
- We want to put CPU constraints on the load balancer container.
- We want the containers always to restart unless explicitly stopped.
- Finally, since the requirements for this example are getting too big, we want to separate the definitions of the load balancer and the upstream services in different compose files and include them in the root file. This feature was introduced in Docker Compose v2.20.

The final compose file will look like this to satisfy the long list of these requirements.

```
include:
  - ./upstream-compose.yml

services:
  haproxy:
    configs:
      - gid: haproxy
        mode: 0440
```

```
        source: haproxy.cfg
        target: /usr/local/etc/haproxy/haproxy.cfg
        uid: haproxy
    cpu_count: 2
    depends_on:
      nginx1:
        condition: service_healthy
        required: false
      nginx2:
        condition: service_healthy
        required: false
    image: haproxy:2.8
    ports:
      - "8080:80"
      - "8443:443"
    read_only: true
    restart: unless-stopped
    secrets:
      - gid: haproxy
        mode: 0440
        source: haproxy-certs
        target: /usr/local/etc/haproxy/certs/
        uid: haproxy
    sysctls:
      - net.ipv4.ip_unprivileged_port_start=0
    ulimits:
      nofile:
        soft: 65536
        hard: 65536

configs:
  haproxy.cfg:
    file: ./haproxy/haproxy.cfg

secrets:
  haproxy-certs:
    file: ./haproxy/certs/
```

The complete code is accessible from the following URL:

https://github.com/ava-orange-education/Ultimate Docker for Cloud Native Applications/tree/main/chapter6/load-balancer

Some directives are explained before, but some are new and need clarification.

The latest update from Docker Compose allows for defining upstream services in another file and then including them in the current `docker compose.yml` to have better readability and maintainability of the definitions.

In this case, we have defined the `nginx1` and `nginx2` in the `upstream-compose.yml` file in the same directory as the `docker compose.yml` file, and that is why the Docker engine can bring the definitions from that file as well. This is a recent version; you must upgrade your Docker to use it.

The `services.haproxy.configs` must already be defined in the root `configs` directive, or you will see an error. It acts as a volume mount like before, but it is more explicit in that no file or directory is created by the container in such a path, but rather a read-only mapping of some configuration.

The same goes for `services.haproxy.secrets` that map the configuration as a sensitive into the container. It allows defining passwords and other credentials into the container without exposure. The root `secrets` must also be defined before mounting into the container.

When we want to limit the amount of usage our container can use, we can use the relevant directives. In this case, `cpu_count` tells the Docker engine that our container cannot use more than two CPU cores.

Dependency has been explained, but since in our `haproxy.cfg` file, we have enabled health checks for the upstream servers; we would not mind if the Docker fails to bring those services up. Instead, we would only send traffic to them if the load balancer decides they are healthy to receive traffic.

In this definition, we expose the two `ports` directive to all network interfaces in the current host, `0.0.0.0`.

The `read_only` directive tells the Docker engine that the container is not allowed to create anything in the filesystem it is running on. To test this, we can easily try to `exec` into the container and run `touch /file`, which will complain with the following error:

```
touch: cannot touch '/file': Read-only file system
```

If we want the container to have a read-only filesystem but be able to create some files on specific directories, we would have to mount such a path explicitly in the `volumes` directive, either as an ephemeral volume or persisting Docker volumes. You will see an example of this behavior in the `upstream-compose.yml` file coming up next.

The default behavior of Docker is to restart all the containers all the time, with or without an exit code of zero. We are being explicit here and specifying that if we stop the container manually, we would not want it to be restarted again, that is, `docker stop haproxy`.

The `sysctl` directive is to specify kernel parameters when running the containers. In this case, we want to allow the running processes inside the container to open ports 80 & 443. Without this directive, our processes will terminate with a non-zero exit code complaining about not being able to open the port.

It is important to mention that the default behavior of not letting the container open ports lower than 1024 has been changed since Docker v20.03, as explained in the following link:

https://medium.com/@olivier.gaumond/why-am-i-able-to-bind-a-privileged-port-in-my-container-without-the-net-bind-service-capability-60972a4d5496

The `ulimits` directive is where we can tune our applications' user limits. This is useful when there is a specific requirement for increasing the container's limit, for example, the number of open files for the MongoDB container.

In the case of our example, every network connection, as in every single client connecting to the HAProxy server, will consume one file descriptor, and that is why we have increased the maximum amount of file descriptors the HAProxy container can create in its filesystem.

For every connection in HAProxy and for every queued connection in the backlog, there will be a need to create a file descriptor in the filesystem. If the file descriptor is exhausted, the connections are dropped. As a general rule of thumb, doing performance benchmarks per server to know the limitations and fine-tuning you need to have the optimal value for these directives is good.

Now that we have seen the root compose file, it's time to see the definitions for the upstream servers. But, before seeing the content of the file, you have to know that to avoid duplication, we're separating the common attributes into another file and reuse that for our services.

The following is the contents of the common file named `nginx.yml`.

```
services:
  nginx:
    healthcheck:
      interval: 5s
      retries: 3
      start_interval: 5s
      start_period: 5s
      test: ["CMD", "curl", "-f", "http://localhost:80"]
      timeout: 1s
    image: nginx:1-alpine
    read_only: true
    restart: unless-stopped
```

With this common setup, let's write our Compose file as follows, leveraging the extends attribute in Compose definition.

```
services:
  nginx1:
    extends:
      file: nginx.yml
      service: nginx
    pull_policy: missing
    volumes:
      - ./nginx1:/usr/share/nginx/html/:ro
      - /var/cache/nginx
      - /var/run/
    configs:
      - nginx1.conf

  nginx2:
    extends:
      file: nginx.yml
      service: nginx
    volumes:
      - ./nginx2:/usr/share/nginx/html/:ro
      - /var/cache/nginx
      - /var/run/
    configs:
      - nginx2.conf
```

```
configs:
  nginx1.conf:
    file: ./nginx1/nginx.conf
  nginx2.conf:
    file: ./nginx2/nginx.conf
```

The two upstream services have health-check definitions, so the load balancer can use that in its dependency directive. However, the load balancer won't require the upstream services to be healthy since its health check is defined in the HAProxy config file. Other than that, the health checks are similar to what we have discussed in the previous examples.

The `pull_policy` directive specifies to the Docker engine whether to download the image from the registry or to use the existing image on the host machine. This can save you incoming traffic and speed up the time for the container to start.

One crucial information to mention here is that it is a best practice to treat the Docker images as immutable and not to push to the same tag to overwrite the image; otherwise, the `pull_policy: missing` will not receive the latest changes and use the old image. Instead, try to use different tags for your images; that way, even a `pull_policy: missing` will download the latest version of your image.

The `volumes` directive requires an essential explanation here; since we have `read_only: true` explicitly defined, the running container will not be allowed to create anything in the filesystem other than the paths specified in the `volumes` directive. It is a good idea to mount a read-only filesystem into your container and only allow specific directories to have write access, as it will enhance the security measures of your deployment.

This example included some of the good directives of the Docker compose definition file. We will wrap the syntax section with one final example as follows.

Example 4: Batch Jobs

This example will include one `service` for processing a sample batch job and the other one that may aggregate it, but in this simple example, it will only print it to the console. The idea is to share some volume between the containers of the two services in a declarative way that follows DRY (Don't Repeat Yourself).

Here is the short list of requirements for this example:

- Since one of the services is a batch job, we expect it to exit with a zero code at the end of processing and `restart: always` is not always fit for this service. Instead, we want it to restart if it fails with a non-zero code.
- We want the batch job to have an `init` process to handle signals since the application itself is not handling the signals internally, and good supervision on top of the app can help a lot in managing the child process.
- Finally, we want the two containers, the batch job, and the aggregator, to share the same volume, but we want to avoid repeating ourselves throughout the file.

These requirements will map to the following implementation:

```
version: "3.9"

services:
  batch:
    build: processing
    init: true
    restart: on-failure
    environment:
      - DATA_DIR=/data
      - NUM_SIMULATIONS=10000
    volumes:
      - /data

  aggregator:
    image: alpine
    init: true
    working_dir: /app
    restart: unless-stopped
    volumes_from:
      - batch:ro
    volumes:
      - ./aggregator:/app:ro
    command: /app/entrypoint.sh
```

Let us explain some of the remaining attributes we still need to discuss.

The `init: true` indicates that we want the Docker engine to spin up a parent process at PID 1 to handle the signals we send to the running process in the container.

This is an excellent choice if the application is not handling signals within the app. Having such a parent process inside the container allows for quickly restarting and killing the container, which would otherwise take a long time.

The result of not having the **init** is shown here.

```
$ docker compose top
batch-jobs-aggregator-1
UID    PID       PPID      C     STIME    TTY    TIME          CMD
Root   716361    716330    0     16:26    ?      00:00:00      /bin/sh -ex .
/entrypoint.sh
root   716363    716361    0     16:26    ?      00:00:00      sleep 10

batch-jobs-batch-1
UID     PID        PPID       C     STIME    TTY    TIME          CMD
root    715775     715742     99    16:26    ?      00:00:39      python main.py
```

As you can see, both containers have their first process to be precisely what the application logic is. This means the process has to be responsible for `SIGTERM`, `SIGKILL`, and all the other signals.

But this is our application, and we did not manage any signals, so we are using the `init: true` instead. In effect, it will result in the following.

```
$ docker compose top
batch-jobs-aggregator-1
UID     PID        PPID       C     STIME    TTY    TIME          CMD
root    716330     716309     0     16:26    ?      00:00:00      /sbin/docker-init
-- /app/entrypoint.sh
root    716361     716330     0     16:26    ?      00:00:00      /bin/sh -ex /app/
entrypoint.sh
root    716363     716361     0     16:26    ?      00:00:00      sleep 10

batch-jobs-batch-1
UID     PID        PPID       C     STIME    TTY    TIME          CMD
root    715742     715723     0     16:26    ?      00:00:00      /sbin/docker-init
-- python main.py
root    715775     715742     99    16:26    ?      00:00:39      python main.py
```

The official Docker documentation mentions that the init is OS-specific and can spawn different processes across different platforms. The `/sbin/docker-init` is for a container running on a Linux machine.

The difference between whether or not to have such an init process is best visible when trying to stop or restart the container. When there is no signal handling, either inside the application code or using the Docker built-in init process, it will take a longer time for restart or stop to happen.

Here is an example of the time it takes to restart without the init process.

```
$ time docker compose restart
[+] Restarting 2/2
✓ Container batch-jobs-aggregator-1  Started
0.8s
✓ Container batch-jobs-batch-1       Started
0.5s

real    0m0.849s
user    0m0.037s
sys     0m0.009s
```

It is taking less than one second to restart both containers, which is acceptable.

Here is the example of restarting the same two containers without the init process.

```
$ time docker compose restart
[+] Restarting 2/2
✓ Container batch-jobs-aggregator-1  Started  11.0s
✓ Container batch-jobs-batch-1       Started  11.2s

real    0m11.174s
user    0m0.033s
sys     0m0.010s
```

It is ten times more than the last time, and it is unacceptable this time. That is why having that **`init: true`** in your Docker Compose service definition is a good idea if you do not handle the signals in your app.

Using Docker's built-in init process is one of many ways to have the parent process for your container.

We can also use third-party open-source tools such as **`dumb-init`**. Yelp developed it, and it is accessible through the following public URL:

https://github.com/Yelp/dumb-init.

Such a tool requires downloading their binary for your platform-specific container and putting it as the parent PID. Here is an example of how that is done.

```
# Dockerfile

RUN curl -sSfLo dumb-init \
    "https://github.com/Yelp/dumb-init/releases/download/v1.2.5/dumb-
init_1.2.5_x86_64" && \
    chmod +x dumb-init && \
    mv dumb-init /usr/local/bin/dumb-init

ENTRYPOINT ["/usr/local/bin/dumb-init", "--"]
```

This will delegate the task of signal handling to the `dumb-init` binary, which is specifically designed to do just that. Perfect for situations where you don't want to rely on Docker's internal mechanisms.

The `working_dir` is when you want to override the service's working directory. It is the extension of `WORKDIR` in a `Dockerfile` definition. If none is specified, the default is the root of the filesystem.

The last piece of information worth mentioning in this final example is `volumes_from`.

This will allow us to mount one or more volumes into one container and use the exact definition to mount the same volumes into other containers.

Imagine you want to share volumes between the containers; this directive will allow for not specifying the same volumes repeatedly.

It keeps your Docker Compose definition clean, readable, and short.

To elaborate the directive further, it will mount all the volumes with the same source and target definition to the other containers. In our example, the `/data` ephemeral volume will be mounted to the same `/data` in the target container.

This will wrap up our examples, and if you want to get a hands-on lab exercise, head over to the following link.

https://killercoda.com/meysam/course/mastering-docker/chapter6.1

Advanced Tips and Techniques

This section of the book will cover the advanced usage of the Docker Compose and how to use it to your advantage.

You have seen multiple examples so far of how to use different configurations. Still, this section will zoom in on the details of each directive in the Docker Compose file to give a better understanding of its capabilities.

Environment Variables

To use environment variables in the services running in Docker Compose, you have three ways available to you.

The first approach allows you to pass them directly as key-value pairs to the Compose file, such as the following.

```
app:
  image: busybox
  environment:
    - KEY=VALUE
  command: printenv KEY
  restart: no
```

The second approach is to pass the key only so that the Docker engine would take the value from your terminal.

```
app:
  image: busybox
  environment:
    - KEY
  command: printenv KEY
  restart: no
```

Which will require two steps to run as follows.

```
export KEY=VALUE
docker compose up -d
```

It doesn't have to be necessarily an `expose` for the `KEY` to be passed to the running application. You can even put the key-value pair in the `.env` file, and Docker Compose will pick that up automatically.

The last, more flexible approach is to put them in a file and pass the file name to the Compose, as shown here.

```
app:
  image: busybox
  env_file:
    - my-app-env.txt
  command: printenv KEY
  restart: no
```

This will require to have the file present at the specified location.

The best part about putting your variables in another file is that you can use bash interpolation. To give a concrete example, imagine having an environment variable file such as the following:

```
# my-app-env.txt
KEY=VALUE
ANOTHER_KEY=${KEY}-my-suffix
```

Now, we can mount this file as an environment variable as follows:

```
version: "3.9"

services:
  app:
    image: busybox
    env_file:
      - my-app-env.txt
    command: printenv KEY ANOTHER_KEY
    restart: no
```

But whichever approach you use, the preceding three steps will be identical.

Volumes

You can have custom-defined volumes in your Docker Compose file. This includes passing additional flags to the underlying driver storage, sharing volumes between multiple containers, or using externally defined volumes in your Compose definition.

Let's see how to create a volume of type `tmpfs`.

```
version: "3.9"

services:
  app:
    image: busybox
    command: sh -c 'mount | grep /app/data && df -h /app/data'
    restart: no
    volumes:
      - app-volume:/app/data

  another-app:
    image: busybox
```

```
    command: sh -c 'mount | grep /app/data && df -h /app/data'
    restart: no
    volumes:
      - app-volume:/app/data

volumes:
  app-volume:
    driver: local
    driver_opts:
      type: tmpfs
      device: tmpfs
      o: size=100m,uid=1000
```

The `driver_opts` allows us to specify to the underlying storage driver what the volume type will be. If you are wondering how to retrieve this information, look at the `mount` command's manual page.

Now that you've seen this let's share a volume between two containers.

```
version: "3.9"

services:
  app1:
    image: busybox
    command:
      - sh
      - -c
      - |
        sleep 1
        touch /app/data/file1.txt
        ls -lh /app/data
    restart: no
    volumes:
      - app-volume:/app/data

  app2:
    image: busybox
    command:
      - sh
      - -c
      - |
        while [ ! -f /app/data/file1.txt ]; do
```

```
          echo "Waiting for file1.txt to be created..."
          sleep 1;
        done;

        touch /app/data/file2.txt
        ls -lh /app/data
    restart: no
    volumes:
      - app-volume:/app/data

volumes:
  app-volume:
```

This can be useful in some contexts where you want to share data volumes between containerized applications.

We are allowed to use the `volumes_from` directive, but that will mount all the volumes from a container, which may differ from what we want since adding volumes explicitly gives us better control.

Another use case for volumes is when we want to mount an external volume into the container. A volume is called external if the definition/creation of the volume was done outside the `docker compose.yml` file.

Here is what such a definition file would look like.

```
version: "3.9"

services:
  app:
    image: busybox
    command:
      - sh
      - -c
      - |
        ls -lh /app/data
        touch /app/data/file1.txt
        ls -lh /app/data
    restart: no
    volumes:
      - app-volume:/app/data
```

```
volumes:
  app-volume:
    external: true
```

Since the volume definition specifies that it will be external, running the `docker compose up` command will fail with the following error:

```
external volume "app-volume" not found
```

Instead, we can create the volume outside the compose file as follows.

```
docker volume create app-volume
```

And then create the services in the Compose file.

Working with Multiple Compose File

One thing that we haven't yet mentioned until now is the ability to use multiple compose files from a single workspace. This, in essence, means that you can define services and definitions in multiple Compose files and combine the results of them all to get what you want.

To provide a concrete example, imagine we have an application requiring an SQL-compatible database connection.

We'll define the application in one Compose file, the database definition, and its connection string in their corresponding Compose file.

Let's write the definition of our [simple] application without further ado.

```
# app-compose.yml
version: "3.9"

services:
  app:
    image: busybox
    command: printenv DSN
    restart: no
```

Let's write two other compose files for two of the most popular SQL databases.

```
# postgresql-compose.yml
version: "3.9"

services:
  app:
```

```
    environment:
      - DSN=postgres://docker:docker@postgres:5432/docker?sslmode=disable

  postgres:
    image: postgres:15
    environment:
      - POSTGRES_PASSWORD=docker
      - POSTGRES_USER=docker
      - POSTGRES_DB=docker
```

And another one.

```
# mysql-compose.yml
version: "3.9"

services:
  app:
    environment:
      - DSN=mysql://docker:docker@mysql:3306/docker

  mysql:
    image: mysql:8
    environment:
      - MYSQL_DATABASE=docker
      - MYSQL_USER=docker
      - MYSQL_PASSWORD=docker
      - MYSQL_ROOT_PASSWORD=docker
```

Having these files in the directory, we can run the services in one of the following forms.

```
# Either this:
docker compose -f app-compose.yml -f postgresql-compose.yml up -d

# Or this
docker compose -f app-compose.yml -f mysql-compose.yml up -d
```

Since this command will need a `-f` flag for every compose file we need, it may get hectic if there are many Compose files (There is a third way which we'll get to in a moment).

That is where environment variables can help simplify the workflow for all the current and future Compose runs.

Docker Compose supports the use of `.env` files in the working directory. Therefore, I'll add my environment variable in there.

```
# .env
COMPOSE_FILE=app-compose.yml:postgresql-compose.yml
```

And then, once again, we can run `docker compose up -d`, and it will have the same effect as when we explicitly provided both `app-compose.yml` and `postgresql-compose.yml` in the command line.

In case you're in doubt, there is an excellent command to help you realize which Compose files will get picked up by Docker Compose.

Having the same .env file as above, if we run docker compose config in the working directory, we will get all the configs and definitions Docker will receive to create my services.

```
$ docker compose config
name: multi-compose
services:
  app:
    command:
    - printenv
    - DSN
    environment:
      DSN: postgres://docker:docker@postgres:5432/docker?sslmode=disable
    image: busybox
    networks:
      default: null
    restart: "no"
  postgres:
    environment:
      POSTGRES_DB: docker
      POSTGRES_PASSWORD: docker
      POSTGRES_USER: docker
    image: postgres:15
    networks:
      default: null
networks:
  default:
    name: multi-compose_default
```

This command can be convenient even outside the multi-compose situation where you must see the interpolated environment variables inside the docker compose.yml file.

Imagine having a `.env` file with the following content.

```
# .env
NAME=John
```

And having a Compose file definition such as the following:

```
# docker compose.yml
version: "3.9"

services:
  app:
    image: busybox
    command: echo Hello ${NAME:-World}
    restart: no
```

Running docker compose up -d command with or without .env present in the directory will give me different results. Because the Docker engine will try to interpolate all those variables from the current environment variables and pass it to the compose file.

Let's walk through three examples to provide a concrete context.

```
$ # first, with .env present and without any export
$ cat .env
NAME=John
$ docker compose up
[+] Running 2/2
✓ Network bash-interpolation_default  Created
✓ Container bash-interpolation-app-1  Created
Attaching to bash-interpolation-app-1
bash-interpolation-app-1  | Hello John
bash-interpolation-app-1 exited with code 0
$ # second, removing .env and still no export
$ rm .env
$ docker compose up
[+] Running 1/0
✓ Container bash-interpolation-app-1  Recreated
Attaching to bash-interpolation-app-1
bash-interpolation-app-1  | Hello world
```

```
bash-interpolation-app-1 exited with code 0
$ # Finally, export the variable in the shell, overriding all the others
$ export NAME=Alex
$ docker compose up
[+] Running 1/0
✓ Container bash-interpolation-app-1  Recreated
Attaching to bash-interpolation-app-1
bash-interpolation-app-1  | Hello Alex
bash-interpolation-app-1 exited with code 0
```

Compose Profiles

You have seen how crazy it can get to have multiple compose files and then pass every filename to the `-f` flag. As promised earlier, there is a better way, a third way. In this approach you won't have to maintain more than one compose files, but rather one, specifying a "profile" for each of the services as a list of strings that the service belongs to.

Let's clear things up with an example.

Imagine having the following `compose.yml` in a directory.

```
services:
  app:
...
    profiles:
      - mysql
      - postgres
  mysql:
...
    profiles:
      - mysql
  postgres:
...
    profiles:
      - postgres
```

With this file, we have the option to run the app in the following ways.

```
# Just the services with mysql
docker compose --profile mysql up -d

# Just postgres
docker compose --profile postgres up -d
```

```
# Both
docker compose --profile postgres --profile mysql up -d
```

Now that you have seen how to work with multiple Compose files, let's jump into scaling the applications inside Compose files.

Scaling Applications

It may be a requirement for an application to scale to more than one instance, whether to handle more load, to increase availability, and so on.

In that case, one of the many options is to use the command line to increase the number of instances.

Imagine having the following Compose file definition.

```
version: "3.9"

services:
  app:
    image: busybox
    init: true
    command: sh -c "printenv HOSTNAME; sleep 5"
    restart: no
```

We will get the following output if this Compose file is run with four instances.

```
$ docker compose up --scale app=4
[+] Running 5/1
✓ Network scaling_default  Created
✓ Container scaling-app-4  Created
✓ Container scaling-app-2  Created
✓ Container scaling-app-1  Created
✓ Container scaling-app-3  Created
Attaching to scaling-app-1, scaling-app-2, scaling-app-3, scaling-app-4
scaling-app-4  | 05169e11fc06
scaling-app-2  | 7b38743b3f3e
scaling-app-1  | d0ea0b82b6a6
scaling-app-3  | a7bcbdd51717
scaling-app-4 exited with code 0
scaling-app-2 exited with code 0
scaling-app-1 exited with code 0
scaling-app-3 exited with code 0
```

Live Update

One of the best features of Docker for local development is live update, using which you can develop your application while Docker will take care of syncing the updated files to the container, or rebuilding the image entirely if that is what you need.

Let's go through an example to see this in action.

```
services:
  watcher:
    build: ./app
    command: sh -c "watch -n 1 'ls -l /watch'"
    volumes:
      - /watch
    develop:
      watch:
        - action: sync
          path: ./src
          target: /watch
        - action: rebuild
          path: ./another/path
          target: /rebuild
          ignore:
            - dont/watch/this
```

The build context in this definition is quite rudimental, with the following content in its Dockerfile.

```
FROM busybox
```

With this setup, if we run `docker compose watch`, the Docker engine will take hold of the terminal and sync all the files in the specified path to the container, syncing some of them and rebuilding the image for some others.

This is a very potent feature if you want to get live updates from your host machine reflected in the Docker image.

Figure 6.4: *Finish line.*
source: https://unsplash.com/photos/bssA-XRpH3s

Conclusion

In summary, this chapter has thoroughly explored Docker Compose, aiming to give you a solid grasp of its core concepts and practical applications. We started by discussing the fundamental principles behind Docker Compose and how it simplifies the deployment of multi-container applications. Throughout the chapter, we have broken down the most commonly used directives and attributes in a Docker Compose file, offering practical examples for better understanding.

The explanation was done with practical and real-world examples of each directive's meaning and how to use it. With this knowledge, you should feel comfortable navigating Docker Compose, whether creating your `docker compose.yml` files or deciphering configurations from others. Docker Compose is a valuable tool for streamlining the management and scaling of applications in containerized environments.

As you continue mastering Docker, remember that Docker Compose is a powerful ally in designing resilient and efficient containerized solutions. By embracing the principles discussed in this chapter, you are well on your way to becoming proficient in orchestrating containers and effectively deploying applications to meet the challenges of today's dynamic software landscape.

In the next chapter, you can expect a comprehensive exploration of Docker Swarm, covering its essential concepts, cluster setup, service deployment, scaling strategies, and critical CLI commands. This chapter will equip you with the knowledge and skills to effectively orchestrate and manage containerized applications at scale using Docker Swarm on one or multiple nodes.

Test Your Knowledge

Now that we have covered Docker Compose in this chapter, it's a good time for you to test how much you have gained following along.

The following questions are not an exhaustive list of the things covered here but can be a good starting point to assess your understanding of the key concepts in this chapter on Docker Compose.

Multiple Choice Questions

1. Which of the following statements about Docker Compose is true?
    A. Docker Compose is primarily designed for production deployments.
    B. Docker Compose allows you to define services, networks, and volumes in a single YAML file.
    C. Docker Compose provides a built-in web-based UI for managing containers.
    D. Docker Compose is a container orchestration platform similar to Kubernetes.
2. When defining services in a `docker compose.yml` file, you can specify (mark all that apply):
    A. The number of container replicas.
    B. Container image names.
    C. Environment variables.
    D. Network policies.
3. What is the purpose of a named volume in Docker Compose?
    A. To define a network for containers.
    B. To specify the number of replicas for a service.
    C. To persist data across container restarts or removals.
    D. To set environment variables for services.

4. Which Docker Compose command starts containers defined in a `docker compose.yml` file?

    A. `docker compose down`

    B. `docker compose create`

    C. `docker compose run`

    D. `docker compose up`

5. In Docker Compose, how can you scale a specific service to have multiple replicas?

    A. Specify the desired number of replicas within the `docker compose.yml` file.

    B. Use the `docker compose scale` command.

    C. Manually create additional containers using `docker run`.

    D. Use the `docker compose up -d --scale SERVICE_NAME=NUMBER` command.

Answers

1. B
2. B and C
3. C
4. D
5. B

References

Here are some official sources and references for readers who want to explore Docker Compose further:

Docker Official Documentation - Compose: The official Docker documentation provides comprehensive guides, tutorials, and reference materials on Docker Compose. It covers everything from primary usage to advanced configurations. Docker Compose Documentation. https://docs.docker.com/compose/

Docker Compose GitHub Repository: Docker Compose is an open-source project, and its source code and issue tracker can be found on its GitHub repository. This resource is valuable for staying up-to-date with the latest developments and reporting issues. Docker Compose GitHub Repository. https://github.com/docker/compose]

Docker Community Forums: The Docker Community Forums are a great place to seek help, share knowledge, and participate in discussions about Docker Compose and general containerization. Docker Community Forums. https://forums.docker.com/

Docker Blog: Docker's official blog often features articles, tutorials, and updates related to Docker Compose and other Docker-related topics. It's a good source for staying informed about the latest developments. Docker Blog. https://www.docker.com/blog/

Docker YouTube Channel: Docker's official YouTube channel hosts webinars, tutorials, and talks related to Docker Compose and containerization. Video content can complement your learning experience. Docker YouTube Channel. https://www.youtube.com/user/dockerrun

GitHub - Awesome Docker: The *Awesome Docker* GitHub repository curates a list of valuable resources, tools, and projects related to Docker and Docker Compose. It's a community-driven collection of helpful references. Awesome Docker on GitHubAwesome Docker on GitHub. Awesome Docker on GitHub. https://github.com/veggiemonk/awesome-docker

The source codes for every piece of code you see in this book are publicly accessible in the GitHub repository. Mastering Docker Github Repository. https://github.com/ava-orange-education/Ultimate Docker for Cloud Native Applications

The lab exercises for this and all the book's other chapters are accessible on the Killercoda platform. Mastering Docker Killercoda Lab Exercises. https://killercoda.com/meysam/course/mastering-docker/

These official sources provide information and community support to help readers deepen their understanding of Docker Compose and enhance their container orchestration skills.

CHAPTER 7

Scaling Applications with Docker Swarm

Figure 7.1: *A conductor orchestrating musicians.*
source: https://unsplash.com/photos/yUJVHiYZCGQ

Introduction

So far, we have covered how to deploy Docker applications on one node. This chapter will walk you through the ins and outs of scaling the applications across multiple nodes, allowing for scalability and the availability of your application in case one host goes down or there's an upgrade window that the host needs to restart.

By the end of this chapter, you will have a solid understanding of running a group of Docker applications on multiple host machines, scaling them on demand, and ensuring their availability.

Structure

In this chapter, we will cover the following topics:

- Introduction to Docker Swarm
- Setting Up Docker Swarm
- Service Deployment and Scaling
- CLI Reference
- Load Balancing and Service Discovery

Introducing Docker Swarm

In today's world of running applications, adjusting their size, such as making them bigger or smaller, as needed is essential. We'll learn about Docker Swarm, a tool that helps you quickly make your container-based applications scale when necessary. Before diving in, we'll discuss why scaling is so important, how Docker Swarm fits into the picture, and what we'll cover in this chapter. So, let's get started and explore how to scale with Docker Swarm, a skill that's very useful for DevOps professionals and anyone involved with containers.

Importance of Scaling

Scaling is the secret sauce that enables your applications to adapt and perform in the ever-changing landscape of today's digital world. Imagine you're running a popular website, and suddenly, it goes viral. A flood of users rushes in, and your server struggles under the load. This is where scaling comes into play. It's the ability to seamlessly and automatically adjust resources to meet your application's demands. Scaling ensures your website doesn't crash under heavy traffic, your e-commerce platform continues to process orders smoothly during a holiday rush, and your microservices-based application remains responsive as your user base grows.

With scaling, you can avoid performance bottlenecks, downtime, and frustrated users. With effective scaling strategies, you can maintain a responsive, reliable, and cost-efficient infrastructure, ensuring your applications deliver a top-notch experience regardless of their challenges.

Docker Swarm in the Scaling Landscape

Now that we have established why scaling is crucial, let's take a closer look at where Docker Swarm fits into the larger picture of scaling solutions.

Docker Swarm is part of the broader ecosystem of container orchestration tools designed to simplify the management of containerized applications. This section will explore what Docker Swarm brings and how it compares to other popular orchestration solutions like Kubernetes.

Docker Swarm is an integral part of the Docker ecosystem, designed to provide native container orchestration capabilities. Docker itself revolutionized application packaging and delivery with its container technology. Containers offer a consistent, lightweight, and portable way to package and run applications and their dependencies. Docker Swarm extends this by providing built-in orchestration, making managing and scaling containerized applications easier. For those familiar with Docker, the transition to Docker Swarm is often smoother, as it leverages existing Docker knowledge and tools.

Docker Swarm vs Kubernetes

While Docker Swarm is a solid choice for container orchestration, it's essential to understand how it compares to Kubernetes, another leading orchestration platform. Here's a comparison of their key features:

- **Ease of Use**: Docker Swarm is known for its simplicity and minimal learning curve. It's easier to set up and configure, making it an excellent choice for teams looking for a quick start. On the other hand, Kubernetes has a steeper learning curve due to its complexity and extensive feature set.
- **Use Cases**: Docker Swarm is well-suited for more minor to medium-sized projects or teams looking for straightforward orchestration. It's ideal for cases where rapid deployment and scaling are required without extensive complexity. Kubernetes shines in large-scale, complex environments with advanced requirements such as auto-scaling, advanced networking, and comprehensive support for stateful applications.
- **Ecosystem Integration**: Docker Swarm integrates with the Docker ecosystem, including Docker Compose, for defining multi-container applications. Kubernetes has a broader ecosystem and a larger community, offering various extensions and plugins for different use cases.
- **Scalability**: Kubernetes is designed for massive scalability and is known for managing thousands of containers across clusters. Docker Swarm is more straightforward to scale and operate, making it a good choice for smaller to medium-sized deployments.

Ultimately, the choice between Docker Swarm and Kubernetes depends on your specific project requirements, team expertise, and scalability needs. Each team should decide, based on their requirements, which is more suitable for their project.

Figure 7.2: *A pen and paper for note-taking.*
source: https://unsplash.com/photos/5bYxXawHOQg

Definitions and Terminologies

Before we dive into the practical part of this chapter, we will first need to understand some of the terminologies we'll use throughout the rest of the chapter.

Cluster

A Docker Swarm cluster is a group of Docker nodes (managers and workers) that work together to manage and run containerized applications.

The cluster provides a unified interface for deploying and scaling applications, ensuring high availability and handling load balancing.

Manager

A Docker Swarm manager node is responsible for orchestrating the cluster's activities. It's the central control point that manages the overall state of the Swarm.

Managers maintain the desired state of services, handle service scheduling, and distribute tasks to worker nodes. They also coordinate cluster management tasks like adding or removing nodes.

Worker

Worker nodes are responsible for running the containers that make up your services. They execute tasks assigned by manager nodes.

Workers do not participate in the decision-making process regarding service placement but are essential for the execution of tasks.

The Docker CLI and every command related to the Docker Swarm will only be allowed in the manager node.

Service

In Docker Swarm, a service defines a task or set of tasks that should be executed on the cluster. It specifies the container image, desired replicas, ports, and other settings.

Services are the primary building blocks of applications in Docker Swarm, ensuring that the defined containers are running as expected.

Task

A task is an individual unit of work in Docker Swarm. Managers schedule tasks to run on worker nodes.

Each service has one or more tasks associated with it, and these tasks represent the running instances of the service's containers.

Overlay Network

An overlay network in Docker Swarm is a virtual network that spans all nodes in the cluster, allowing containers to communicate with each other regardless of their physical host.

Overlay networks facilitate seamless connectivity between containers running on different nodes within the cluster.

Stack

A stack is a way to deploy a collection of services (and networks) that compose an application. Stacks are defined using a Docker Compose file and can be deployed as a single unit.

Global Service

A global service is a type of service in Docker Swarm where a single replica of the service runs on every available worker node in the cluster.

It's typically used for services that must be present on every node, such as monitoring agents.

As we have a basic understanding of the terminologies, let's explore the practical, hands-on part of this chapter.

Setting Up Docker Swarm

To set up a Docker Swarm, the minimum requirement is to have one host machine capable of running applications with Docker installed. You can quickly run a single-node Docker Swarm on your local machine without dependency other than Docker.

Suppose you'd like to try this out with multiple nodes. In that case, you can use one of the available options online, including but not limited to Docker in Docker, Vagrant, multiple physical machines, VMWare ESXi, and so on.

For the sake of simplicity, we won't introduce new technology in this book and will only rely on the knowledge we have gained to set up our Docker Swarm cluster.

The idea is to use Docker in Docker, allowing us to run containers inside containers.

To do that, we can use all the knowledge we have gathered to write a `docker-compose.yml` file, which will run three services, as follows:

- One manager node is capable of initializing the cluster.
- One worker node that is capable of running application workloads.
- One one-off job that will set up the cluster and exit with zero.

To help with the book's readability, we'll provide the file's content in two sections.

Docker Nodes Common Attributes

We need definitions for all the containers in this file, and to adhere to DRY, we'll define them only once, as follows:

```
x-common: &common
  image: docker:24
  pull_policy: missing
  read_only: true
```

Since there are some common attributes we want for multiple containers, we will use YAML merge functionality as specified in the following documentation:

https://yaml.org/type/merge.html

The gist of this approach is that all the child attributes of `x-common` will be populated to `bootstrap`, `manager`, and `worker`. The same goes for `x-swarm-common` (coming up next), which will apply only to the Docker Swarm cluster nodes.

First and foremost, we will use the official image named docker. Docker published and maintained this, making it a reliable source for our task and many others. At the time of writing this book, 24 is the latest tag available with docker image on Docker Hub.

The pull policy is to avoid pulling the image for a second time if it is already on the host machine.

We want the Docker container to run in read-only mode, hence the directive.

Docker Swarm Common Attributes

This is the common definition used for the manager and worker to spin up a Docker container with a Docker engine as its primary process:

```
x-swarm-common: &swarm-common
  command:
    - dockerd
    - "--host"
    - tcp://0.0.0.0:2375
    - "--tls=false"
    - "-H"
    - unix:///var/run/docker.sock
  healthcheck:
    interval: 3s
    retries: 3
    start_interval: 1s
    start_period: 1s
    test:
      - CMD
      - docker
      - info
    timeout: 1s
  privileged: true
```

```
  volumes:
    - /var/lib/docker
    - /var/run/
```

There are a couple of important information that need elaboration.

This image must run in a privileged mode to run the Docker engine process and bind it to a socket inside the container. Hence, `privileged: true` must be set on every service to run the Docker engine.

The health check is vital for our use case since the third container in this definition will need a healthy manager and worker to bootstrap the Docker Swarm cluster. For the sake of simplicity, if the docker info is responding correctly, we know that the Docker engine is running without problem.

Finally, we need to override the default command because otherwise, it will try to start the Docker engine with TLS enabled, and for the sake of our simple demo project, that is not required. However, you may need to add a layer(s) of security if your use case is beyond a demo.

Bootstrapper

This service will run only after the manager and the worker nodes are running and healthy.

Here's what the definition of this service will look like:

```
bootstrap:
    <<: *common
    command:
      - sh
      - "-c"
      - |
        docker -H tcp://manager:2375 swarm init
        docker -H tcp://manager:2375 swarm join-token worker -q \
          > /swarm-data/worker-token

        docker -H tcp://worker:2375 swarm join --token \
          $(cat /swarm-data/worker-token) manager:2377
    depends_on:
      manager:
        condition: service_healthy
      worker:
        condition: service_healthy
```

```
    restart: on-failure
    volumes:
      - /swarm-data
```

The image of this service is exactly as before because we need access to the Docker CLI.

The volumes have an ephemeral volume defined, and we only want this volume to be accessible for the current session. Losing the data would not have a significant impact on our operations.

The two crucial pieces of information are the `command` and the `depends_on` definition.

In the dependency, we have conditioned this service to run only after the manager and the worker are healthy. If they haven't become healthy, this container will be created but will not start running.

The `command` has three of the most essential Docker Swarm commands, which we elaborate on here:

The command `docker swarm init` will initialize a new cluster on the current host. It will complain if the node is already part of another cluster.

Running this command will give the following output:

```
Swarm initialized: current node (SOME_RANDOM_STRING) is now a manager.


To add a worker to this swarm, run the following command:


    docker swarm join --token LONG_RANDOM_STRING HOST_IP_ADDRESS:2377


To add a manager to this swarm, run 'docker swarm join-token manager'
and follow the instructions.
```

Some of the actual values have been replaced with placeholders for readability.

The instruction on the output is explicit for the operator of the cluster. For every new node that will join our cluster, we need to specify whether it is joining as a manager or worker.

Based on the earlier definitions, if the host does not need to coordinate and orchestrate the cluster, it is sufficient to add it as a worker. We can always promote or demote a node.

The command `docker swarm join-token worker` will print the command needed to run on the worker nodes to join the cluster. There is also a similar command to join as a manager.

The command `docker swarm join --token TOKEN manager:2377` will run against the worker node's Docker engine, resulting in two nodes in the Docker Swarm cluster - one manager and one worker.

A crucial piece of information to mention here is the use of the `-H` flag. This will tell the Docker CLI where to send the requests, that is, the server address of the Docker engine.

The same can be achieved by setting the `DOCKER_HOST` environment variable. The shell script in the command can also be written as follows:

```
export DOCKER_HOST=tcp://manager:2375

docker swarm init
docker swarm join-token worker -q > /swarm-data/worker-token

export DOCKER_HOST=tcp://worker:2375
docker swarm join --token $(cat /swarm-data/worker-token) manager:2377
```

This method may be preferred considering that the commands are shorter and the repeatable `-H` flag will not need to be provided for every command. Note that the code snippet we're working with here is using `-H` flag and `DOCKER_HOST` environment variable interchangeably for demonstration purpose.

The entire definition of the manager, the worker, and the bootstrapper can be written in a `docker-compose.yml` file, as shown in the following code:

```
version: "3.9"

x-common: &common
  image: docker:24
  pull_policy: missing
  read_only: true

x-swarm-common: &swarm-common
  command:
    - dockerd
    - "--host"
    - tcp://0.0.0.0:2375
```

```
      - "--tls=false"
      - "-H"
      - unix:///var/run/docker.sock
    healthcheck:
      interval: 3s
      retries: 3
      start_interval: 1s
      start_period: 1s
      test:
        - CMD
        - docker
        - info
      timeout: 1s
    privileged: true
    volumes:
      - /var/lib/docker
      - /var/run/

services:
  bootstrap:
    <<: *common
    command:
      - sh
      - "-c"
      - |
        export DOCKER_HOST=tcp://manager:2375

        docker swarm init
        docker swarm join-token worker -q > /swarm-data/worker-token

        export DOCKER_HOST=tcp://worker:2375

        docker swarm join --token $(cat /swarm-data/worker-token)
manager:2377
    depends_on:
      manager:
        condition: service_healthy
      worker:
        condition: service_healthy
    restart: on-failure
```

```
    volumes:
      - /swarm-data

  manager:
    <<: [*common, *swarm-common]
    hostname: manager

  worker:
    <<: [*common, *swarm-common]
    hostname: worker
```

It goes without saying that to create the Dockèr Swarm cluster, our nodes need to be on the same network, irrespective of the method we choose for our cluster creation. Docker Compose takes care of that by placing them all in the same network if not otherwise specified.

Running this `docker-compose.yml`, as usual, will give us two nodes inside a Docker Swarm cluster - one manager and one worker.

We can check the bootstrap logs to see the manager node's IP address to interact with the cluster:

```
docker-compose logs bootstrap
```

Among the logs, we will see the IP address of the Docker manager node.

Since the Docker Compose definition explicitly exposes the advertised address of the Docker engine on `tcp://0.0.0.0:2375`, we can easily replace the value of the IP in the placeholder and get the currently running nodes in the cluster using the following command (from inside our host machine).

Let's first get the IP address of our container:

```
docker inspect -f \
  '{{.Name}} - {{range
.NetworkSettings.Networks}}{{.IPAddress}}/{{.IPPrefixLen}}{{end}}' \
  $( docker ps | awk 'NR>1 {print $1}' )
```

As complicated as it may look, this command is only querying the name and the IP address of all the running containers in the host machine using the Go template specified in the documentation:

https://docs.docker.com/config/formatting/

After running this command, we will get an output as follows:

```
/single-manager-swarm-manager-1 - 192.168.160.2/20
/single-manager-swarm-worker-1 - 192.168.160.3/20
```

Now that we know the manager node's IP address, let's use the address and get the list of all the nodes in the Swarm cluster.

The crucial point is that these IP addresses are obtained from a virtual bridge created by the Docker engine. The Docker engine creates these bridges on-demand for every `docker network create` command.

Since the network inside the Docker Compose definition is new, all these steps are executed by the Docker engine.

When a bridge is created, the machine that is hosting that bridge also gets an IP address on the bridge. This means that we can communicate with the Docker container directly using the IP address it has been assigned.

The following command is running from the host machine that spun the Swarm cluster.

```
DOCKER_HOST=tcp://192.168.160.2:2375 docker node ls
```

This command runs on the same host machine that created the Docker Compose containers.

With that, we will get an output as follows:

```
ID                            HOSTNAME    STATUS     AVAILABILITY    MANAGER
                                                                     STATUS
ENGINE VERSION
iqsw140a3pch3m6k5ei4grc7g *    manager    Ready      Active          Leader
24.0.6
ydfdfrkbz6tid0h7uvnyvskbj      worker      Ready      Active
24.0.6
```

We now have access to the Swarm cluster and can see the information of the nodes inside the cluster. Knowing this, we can now use this Swarm cluster and create services and tasks inside the cluster.

However, before doing that, it's worth mentioning that having this cluster with single or multiple managers would not make much difference. The commands you can run in one manager are no different than those you run on any other manager.

The Docker Swarm works in a leader-follower model, which means only one manager is the leader at any time. And if the leader goes down, there will be an election for a new manager, that is, in case `--autolock` has not been provided to `docker swarm init`, so when the manager goes down, the election will appoint a new leader. Otherwise, the old manager will need to start again, get unlocked, and then the cluster can proceed with its orchestration.

Hence, another demo to run a Swarm with multiple managers is redundant, not as informative, and, therefore, skipped for brevity.

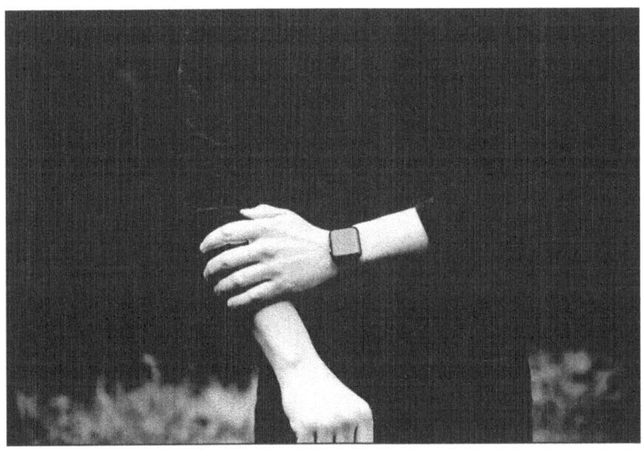

Figure 7.3: *Rolling up sleeves.*
source: https://unsplash.com/photos/KKa0WwIg1Ig

Creating and Running Services

With the cluster we created in the last step, we can now start using the cluster and create services.

In this section, we will provide some practical examples and include the relevant topics from CLI, Docker engine, and Swarm cluster to familiarize you with everything related to cluster.

Run a Simple Web Server

The simplest way to create a service is to run an Nginx container:

```
docker -H tcp://192.168.160.2:2375 \
  service create --name web --publish 8080:80 nginx:1-alpine
```

Here's what happens: for every node inside our Docker Swarm cluster, port `8080` is forwarded to the container running inside the cluster, whether or not that container is running on the same node.

This is crucial information and may be a bit confusing, so let's elaborate.

Docker Swarm services can publish their port on the host machine in two ways, as follows:

- **Routing mesh**: In this mode, the published port (for example, 8080) is published in all the nodes running inside the cluster and will forward the traffic to any one of the running containers, whether hosted on their own or in another node.
- **Swarm mode**: In this mode, the published port is only exposed on the host that is running the container. It is more concrete and flexible, but the downside is that the operator is responsible for ensuring the traffic is routed to the correct node when load-balancing traffic.

The second mode is more complicated, may be needed only for specific environments, and requires special considerations. Our demo will cover the first method - the default way of running a service and publishing its port.

The routing mesh method gives us the ability to run a `curl` command against any one of the nodes running inside the cluster and still get a response from the upstream server because the Docker engine (also known as the Docker daemon) is responsible for load balancing the traffic to the correct node and container.

This is very powerful and can give us much flexibility regarding load balancing and traffic redirection. If we ever want to scale our applications, we won't have to worry about service discovery and updating the IP addresses. Instead, the Docker engine will take care of that automatically behind the scenes.

The following two curl commands will result in the same outcome, that is, sending the traffic to the only container hosting the Nginx container, wherever that container is hosted.

The following command are running in the host machine that spun the Swarm cluster.

```
curl 192.168.160.2:8080
curl 192.168.160.3:8080
```

This is great for us; we can always send traffic to the containers publishing a port if we talk to the nodes.

There is, however, a limitation to this method. We cannot have multiple services publishing ports on the same host target. This makes sense since by explicitly specifying the target port on the host, we are reserving that port for our container in all the cluster nodes, whether they host the container or not makes no difference.

The workaround for this is to publish ports into different numbers to avoid conflicts. Alternatively, we can leave the host port unspecified, so that the Docker engine can choose an open port based on the system's availability. This type of port publishing is called an ephemeral port and may change when restarting or rolling out upgrades.

If we get curious and wonder where our container is hosted, we can run the following command:

```
DOCKER_HOST=tcp://192.168.160.2:2375 docker service ps web
```

The output information will display the node hosting the container(s).

We can replace `ps` with `logs` in the preceding command to check the logs.

Running WordPress Stack

Stacks are supersets of services where we can group multiple related services, define their characteristics in a Docker Compose format, and deploy that stack with the definition of the compose file.

One crucial piece of information is that although compose and stack specification have a lot of similarities, some attributes are parsed by one and ignored or failed by the other.

For example, the `deploy` directive only applies to Swarm stacks and will be ignored if Docker Compose runs.

That's why it is essential to refer to the documentation if in doubt.

As for our demo, we want to have a WordPress and a MySQL container in the same network. WordPress will scale to more than one instance, while MySQL is a single instance that ensures the durability of our data.

Let's first provide the definition for MySQL and explain the new directives:

```
db:
  image: mysql:8
  volumes:
    - db_data:/var/lib/mysql
  environment:
    MYSQL_DATABASE: wordpress
    MYSQL_USER: wordpress
    MYSQL_ROOT_PASSWORD: wordpress
    MYSQL_PASSWORD: wordpress
```

```
  healthcheck:
    test: ["CMD", "mysqladmin", "ping", "-h", "localhost"]
    interval: 10s
    timeout: 2s
    retries: 5
    start_period: 3s
  deploy:
    replicas: 1
    placement:
      constraints:
        - node.role == worker
```

The new directive, `deploy`, has two attributes: one for specifying the number of replicas we want to create for this container and the other to specify that we want this container to run only on a worker node. The manager node is already occupied with orchestration, and we don't want a critical system like the database to have a resource consumption problem. This is the rationale behind the decision.

All the other directives are self-explanatory and were explained in the previous chapter.

Next, we'll define our WordPress app as follows:

```
wordpress:
  depends_on:
    - db
  image: wordpress:6
  ports:
    - "80"
  volumes:
    - /var/www/html/
  environment:
    WORDPRESS_DB_HOST: db:3306
    WORDPRESS_DB_USER: wordpress
    WORDPRESS_DB_PASSWORD: wordpress
    WORDPRESS_DB_NAME: wordpress
  deploy:
    replicas: 3
    placement:
      preferences:
        - spread: node
    restart_policy:
```

```
      condition: on-failure
      delay: 5s
      max_attempts: 10
      window: 30s
    rollback_config:
      parallelism: 1
      delay: 10s
      failure_action: pause
      monitor: 5s
      max_failure_ratio: 0.3
      order: start-first
```

Before explaining the deploy directive and its child attributes, it's important to mention another difference between Docker Compose and Swarm specifications. While in the Docker Compose definition, we can place conditions for dependencies, for example, when the application is healthy, this capability is not yet supported in Swarm stacks.

To explain the child attributes of the `deploy` directive, we can see that the placement strategy can also have `preferences` instead of `constraints`. In the case of the former, the app will be deployed if the condition is not satisfied; the condition is treated as nice-to-have.

However, in case of `constraints`, the container will not be created if the Docker engine cannot satisfy the condition.

As seen in the `restart_policy`, this version is more verbose and allows richer flexibility than the Compose specification. We can customize how we want the app to restart and how long and often that should occur.

The `rollback_config` directive is exclusively for the Swarm stack. As it may happen that a new rollout might fail, and we might need to rollback to an earlier version. However, if the rollback also fails, we can define what actions should be taken in such a case.

We can create our Swarm stack by having the definition of these two services in a file. It's important to note that the file's name doesn't matter and shouldn't be as strict as Docker Compose requires. To keep things transparent, we'll name the file `docker-compose.yml` and deploy it using that file name.

With that said, we can proceed and create our stack as follows:

```
DOCKER_HOST=tcp://192.168.160.2:2375 docker stack deploy \
  -c docker-compose.yml ecommerce
```

It will take some time for the stack to pull the image and create the containers, but we can check the result using the following command:

```
DOCKER_HOST=tcp://192.168.160.2:2375 docker stack services ecommerce
```

This command will give the following output:

```
ID            NAME                MODE       REPLICAS IMAGE        PORTS
ii1vz0z5xt03 ecommerce_db        replicated 1/1      mysql:8
ixg6s1w8fpgc ecommerce_wordpress replicated 3/3     wordpress:6 *:30001-
                                                                  >80/tcp
```

Since we didn't specify a host port in the compose definition, the Docker engine assigned an ephemeral port of `30001`. This is still the same behavior as before; all nodes in the cluster will forward all the traffic from `30001` to container `80`.

If we want to scale our WordPress application to more or less containers, we can execute the following command in the terminal:

```
DOCKER_HOST=tcp://192.168.160.2:2375 docker service scale ecommerce_
wordpress=6
```

It's also possible to modify the `docker-compose.yml` file with any desired behavior, such as the image, and deploy the stack using the same command. If there has been any change, the Docker engine will reconcile. If not, the stack will remain as it is.

If we want to update one of our stack's services and don't want that change to be reflected by the `docker-compose.yml` file, we can easily run an ad-hoc command as follows:

```
DOCKER_HOST=tcp://192.168.160.2:2375 docker service update \

  ecommerce_wordpress --image wordpress:5
```

And if we're unhappy with the change, we can always roll back to the previous version of the deployment as follows:

```
DOCKER_HOST=tcp://192.168.160.2:2375 docker service rollback ecommerce_
wordpress
```

We have covered some of the commands so far, but to have it all in one place for reference, we'll provide a full explanation of maintaining a Docker Swarm cluster from the CLI.

Figure 7.4: *Gear of a manual car.*
source: https://unsplash.com/photos/D19rXKDUPYM

CLI Reference

This section will cover CLI commands you can use when working with Docker binary to maintain your Docker Swarm cluster.

Without further ado, let's learn about it.

docker swarm

This sub-command is used for creating or joining a cluster. Optionally, you can add a PEM-format certificate and private key to your cluster, which is possible through `docker swarm ca`.

For example, if none was provided initially, the following command will rotate the cluster's certificate or generate a new one:

```
DOCKER_HOST=tcp://192.168.160.2:2375 docker swarm ca --rotate
```

After the command succeeds, we can check to see if the certificate of the nodes in our cluster is ready using the following command:

```
docker node ls --format '{{.ID}} {{.Hostname}} {{.Status}}
{{.TLSStatus}}'
```

The same can also be retrieved with `docker node inspect --pretty NODE_ID`, or simply with `DOCKER_HOST=tcp://192.168.160.2:2375 docker node inspect self`.

Next, to initialize a new cluster, we use `docker swarm init`, and the most crucial flag for this command is the `--advertise-addr`. Still, you can specify some of the others, including but not limited to, the manager listen-to address, the network interface to bind the manager server, and more.

Then, to join such a cluster, we will use `docker swarm join`, which requires a value for the flag `--token` and a required positional argument for the host and port of the manager.

When adding new nodes to the cluster, we can use the `docker swarm join-token`, specifying whether we want this token to have a manager role or just a worker.

If we no longer want to have a node in the cluster, we can either run `docker node rm NODE` from one of the manager nodes of the cluster or execute the command `docker swarm leave` from the worker who wants to leave.

The second method will take some time for the manager(s) of the cluster before realizing the node has left the cluster. It also requires the manager to remove the node from the cluster anyway since the node info will still be kept in the cluster. Only a manual removal (or an automated script) will delete that information; otherwise, the node will be shown as `Down` but still be a part of the cluster.

Two commands are helpful for **when auto-lock has been set on the Swarm cluster**.

As explained earlier, auto-lock is used when we don't want the cluster to auto-elect the new manager in case the old one goes down. It can become a bottleneck but won't make the cluster's data inconsistent. If auto-lock is not set, the following two commands are useless.

One of these commands is `docker swarm unlock-key`, and the other is `docker swarm unlock`. The former will print out a token to be used later on by the unlock command when the manager restarts and needs to be **unlocked** with such a token.

It may happen on rare occasions; if it does, Docker supports that.

The last available sub-command is docker swarm update, which helps update the cluster's configuration for specific attributes, including the auto-lock mentioned earlier.

docker config and docker secret

These two are similar but different in practice. A brief explanation is required here to specify the differences and how they can be used.

In Docker Swarm clusters, both Docker configs and Docker secrets are designed to be secure, but they differ in how containers manage and access them.

Docker configs store configuration files or data needed by services running in Docker Swarm, for example, application configuration. They are only encrypted at rest but **not in transit** and are stored in an encrypted form on the manager nodes but can be retrieved in plaintext by containers.

When a service uses a Docker config, the container can access the config's contents in plaintext.

On the other hand, Docker secrets store sensitive data, such as passwords or private keys, that should remain confidential. They are designed to be more secure and are encrypted **both at rest and in transit** between manager and worker nodes.

Containers can access Docker secrets, but the secrets are presented as files in the `/run/secrets` directory inside the container. The contents of the secret files are accessible in plaintext within the container.

Knowing this, we can create, inspect, list, and remove both from the Docker Swarm manager node. We can mount either or both into a container using attributes in the Docker Compose file or the flags when creating a service from the command line.

Here's an example snippet to showcase the use of secret:

```
$ cat mysecret.yml
hello: world
$ export DOCKER_HOST=tcp://192.168.160.2:2375
$ docker secret create mysecret mysecret.yml
$ docker service create \
> --name myservice --secret mysecret alpine \
> sh -c "cat /run/secrets/mysecret; sleep infinity"
$ docker service logs myservice
myservice.1.3ofz9tvc9p0s@manager    | hello: world
myservice.1.3ofz9tvc9p0s@manager    |
```

In this example, we first create a secret named `mysecret` from a file in the current directory. Then, when creating the service, we pass the appropriate flag to mount the secret to the container. The proof is that the container will see the plaintext value inside the file while, at the same time, the cluster encrypts the secret at rest and in transit to ensure it is kept safe.

docker node

This sub-command allows the control of the nodes inside the cluster, though this command can only run in the manager nodes because of the required access level.

You can try running `docker --help` in a worker node to see that the Swarm sub-commands are fewer than you could see in a manager node.

The most commonly used sub-command is the `docker node ls`, which will list all the nodes in the cluster, the version of the Docker they are running, and their role in the cluster.

You can filter this command or get a different output than the default table, such as JSON.

The next most helpful sub-command is the `docker node ps`, which will let you see which node each container is running. This one also can be filtered or formatted with anything other than the default table.

There are two sub-commands for changing a node's role in the cluster: `docker node promote` and `docker node demote`, which will change the role of the target node. Any manager can demote the other manager in the cluster at any point in time or promote a worker node to a manager.

The crucial information is that you can't remove a node from the cluster before demoting it to a worker node.

If you need detailed information about a node, `docker node inspect` is your friend. You can either get the information about the current node with the keyword `self` or specify another node's name or ID.

Last but not least, one useful sub-command in this section is the `docker node update`, which, at its basic functionality, provides the option to pause or drain a node if we want to do patches or upgrades on the host machine. After doing so, we can use the same command to restore it to active mode.

Here's an example snippet:

```
$ export DOCKER_HOST=tcp://192.168.160.4:2375
$ export MANAGER_ID=$(docker node ls --format '{{.ID}}' --filter
role=manager)
$ docker node update ${MANAGER_ID}--availability drain
$ # doing some upgrades
$ docker node update ${MANAGER_ID} --availability active
```

docker service

With this command, you can create ad-hoc services. It is flexible because you wouldn't need a written docker-compose file to run your application in the Swarm cluster.

At the same time, this may be a disadvantage since having a written docker-compose file is a self-documented version of the operation and deployment and can easily be replicated, for example, in a CI/CD pipeline.

However, for a demo and a learning experience, it gives a lot of value. So, let's find out what each of its sub-commands is doing.

To create a service, we have the `create` sub-command with many proper flags and options, some of which are shown in the following code:

```
docker service create \
 --name mastering-docker \
 --detach \
 --config source=app-config,uid=1000,gid=1000,mode=0440,target=/app-config.
   txt \
 --secret source=app-secret,uid=1000,gid=1000,mode=0440,target=/app
   -secret.txt \
 --user 1000:1000 \
 --restart-condition none \
 busybox sh -c "hostname && cat /app-config.txt /app-secret.txt"
```

The flags and options are the same as those you would specify in a docker-compose file.

To see detailed information about the service in JSON format, use the `inspect` command:

```
docker service inspect mastering-docker
```

We can also check the logs with the following command:

```
docker service logs mastering-docker
```

To list the running services:

```
docker service ls
```

Or to see the running tasks in a created service:

```
docker service ps mastering-docker
```

If we ever need to change some of the attributes of the running service, we can use the `update` sub-command. Note that only some things can be changed, and you may have to recreate the service:

```
docker service update --detach --image busybox:1.36 mastering-docker
```

If we're unhappy with the update, we can easily roll back:

```
docker service rollback --detach mastering-docker
```

And if we want to increase or decrease the number of running instances:

```
docker service scale -d mastering-docker=3
```

Finally, when we want to remove the service:

```
docker service rm mastering-docker
```

docker stack

This last command is one of the most important. You have seen examples when trying to run some applications using the definitions in a `docker-compose.yml` file.

Stack is the most potent command, whether running locally on your machine or used in a CI/CD pipeline to automate the process of deployments.

Let's see how we can use this command.

To see the final YAML definition of the stack passed to the Docker engine server right before getting created, we can use the `docker stack config`, which prints the YAML-encoded in the `stdout`.

Here's the result of running that command against our sample WordPress application:

```
docker stack config -c docker-compose.yml
version: "3.9"
services:
  db:
    deploy:
      replicas: 1
      placement:
        constraints:
        - node.role == worker

...truncated…


  wordpress:
    depends_on:
```

```
    - db
    deploy:
      replicas: 3
      rollback_config:
        parallelism: 1
        delay: 10s
        failure_action: pause
        monitor: 5s
        max_failure_ratio: 0.3
        order: start-first

...truncated...
```

The output of this command will include all the keys and directives, even those not directly written by us in the `docker-compose.yml` file. This is because right before the Docker engine creates the stack, it needs to have all the information, whether explicitly defined by us or implicitly valued by the defaults.

If you are ever curious how the application behaves the way it does, `config` is an excellent source of information to realize the currently set values per each entry.

Next, the `docker stack deploy` is used to create a new stack or update a previously deployed stack. We've seen examples of this command earlier.

The essence of what makes this command so powerful is that it has a very similar API to what `docker-compose` has. They share some common attributes in the `docker-compose.yml` file, allowing us to reuse our current files.

There are also some minor differences here and there, but they are not troublesome, and you can quickly catch up. To understand which directives are specific to Docker Swarm and which are only used in Docker Compose, you can always check the documentation. As a general rule of thumb, the `deploy` directive in the `docker-compose.yml` file is solely used for Docker Swarm, and some other directives may be ignored when deploying with Docker Swarm.

In the official documentation, you will find notes for any directives on whether Docker Swarm accepts that parameter.

Another highlight that needs to be mentioned is that `docker stack deploy` can receive the YAML definition either from a file path passed via the `-c` flag, or you can pass the definition from the Linux pipe command as follows:

```
cat docker-compose.yml | docker stack deploy -c -
```

There are also three other useful flags you can pass to this command:

1. `--prune` removes any service from the stack if the new definition doesn't contain a definition. Docker calls these services orphans, as the current service no longer owns them.

This means we can deploy our stack with three services with the name `foo`, and then later, when we decide that one of the services is no longer required, we can remove that service entry from our YAML definition and redeploy with the following command:

```
docker stack deploy -c docker-compose.yml --prune foo
```

2. The next helpful flag is `--resolve-image`, which allows us to specify whether we want to redeploy our application even if the Docker image hasn't changed (the default behavior), redeploy when the image **has** changed, or not at all.

Imagine having a service with two services in the definition.

If the `deploy` command is executed again, the following will happen per each flag option:

a. `docker stack deploy --resolve-image=always` will try to recreate the container even if the image hasn't changed.

b. `docker stack deploy --resolve-image=changed` will only recreate the containers if the images have changed, or else leave them be as they are.

c. Finally, `docker stack deploy --resolve-image=never` will update the stack if it is already deployed, even if the image has changed.

In real-world scenarios, you will likely need to use the `changed` option, as it is the closest to the continuous delivery process, rolling out new updates frequently and not touching the deployment when nothing changes.

3. Lastly, the `--with-registry-auth` flag will pass the Docker credentials in the host machine to the Docker engine when creating or updating the stack. Imagine having Docker credentials defined in the manager node but not the worker node. This flag enables you to use the credentials in the manager for pulling from [private] Docker registries.

Note that it doesn't necessarily have to be a private registry to need a credential. For example, Docker Hub has a rate limit on the number of pulls an anonymous request can do. That's why it can be helpful to pass the credentials so your application won't have trouble pulling the images.

Now that we have learned about deployment, let's explore some of the other valuable sub-commands in this category.

- `docker stack ls` is very useful to list your currently running stacks. It can give table-formatted information (default behavior), JSON, or template. One of the first things you can do when getting the management control of a Docker Swarm is to list your currently running stacks to see what applications are deployed.
- The next command in this category is `docker stack ps STACK_NAME`. It has a handy output showing on which node each container is created, the currently deployed version of the container, the image it is running on, and its previous deployments. It gives you an excellent picture if you want to see the history of the rollouts the stack and its services have had.
- In the `ps` command, you can specify if you want to see node ID instead of resolved hostnames with `--no-resolve`. You can also see the non-truncated output with `--no-trunc`. The default behavior is truncating the output to make it readable and fit on the screen, but you may want to change it.
- As we've seen before, we can also remove a stack with `docker stack rm STACK_NAME`. This can rarely happen in a production environment, where you only update the stack and roll out new versions of the same application, but the option is available if needed.
- Another command similar to the earlier `ps` command is the `docker stack services STACK_NAME`, which will print only the currently running containers and their hosting nodes, but not the earlier versions of the services. It is helpful if you only want to see the live version of the stack.

As we have seen so far, the stack sub-command is a very useful category in the day-to-day management of the Docker Swarm cluster. It can be used to create a new stack or update an already deployed one.

You have seen a brief overview of all the sub-commands related to Docker Swarm. These have some similarities with regular Docker container creation and include specific features available only in Swarm mode. Be sure to explore the documentation for a comprehensive overview of the available flags and options, not only to see the available flags but also as a reference for any future work.

Now, let's wrap this chapter up with some theories.

Figure 7.5: *A farmer sowing seeds on the farm.*
source: https://unsplash.com/photos/ppE5mjUS8t0

Load Balancing and Service Discovery

Load balancing in Docker Swarm is crucial for distributing incoming network traffic across multiple containers or nodes. This ensures optimal resource utilization and high availability for your containerized applications.

Load balancing involves efficiently routing incoming requests to various service replicas. Docker Swarm accomplishes this by intelligently distributing traffic among these replicas, ensuring a balanced workload.

In Docker Swarm, you define the desired number of service replicas. The Swarm manager automatically balances the load by evenly distributing incoming requests among these replicas. This automated process simplifies the management of containerized services.

Docker Swarm supports a round-robin load-balancing algorithm, evenly distributing requests between the upstream servers.

Service Discovery in Docker Swarm

Service discovery simplifies locating and connecting to services within a Docker Swarm network. It's a fundamental aspect of managing containerized applications.

In the context of Docker Swarm, service discovery refers to the automatic detection and connection to services within the swarm. Docker Swarm achieves this by providing a built-in DNS service, which allows containers to find each other using service names rather than hardcoded IP addresses.

Docker Swarm assigns unique service names to each service. It also enables DNS resolution within the swarm network, making it effortless for services to communicate with each other using these names. This abstraction simplifies the inter-container communication process.

Service discovery adjusts dynamically as you scale services up or down within Docker Swarm. New replicas are seamlessly integrated into the network, and DNS resolution updates automatically. This flexibility ensures that your services can scale without disruptions.

In some scenarios, you may need to interact with services outside the Docker Swarm network. Docker Swarm facilitates external service discovery and integration with external systems through various networking configurations.

Practical Example

As promised, we'll deploy a service with three replicas, publish a port from the container to the hosting node, and send a request to see if the load balancing is working correctly.

First, let's create an echo server that simply replies with the contents of our HTTP request:

```
docker service create \
  --name echo-server \
  -d \
  --publish=80:80 \
  --replicas=3 \
  ealen/echo-server:0.8.2
```

Running the preceding command will give us a service in the current Docker Swarm cluster. Now, let's try and send a request to this container in the following format:

```
curl NODE_IP:80
```

The node IP can be either the IP address of the manager node or the worker node. When you send a request to the node, the Docker Swarm will route the traffic to the container, even if the target host does not have any of those containers running locally.

So, here's the result of running the curl command that sends traffic to the manager of the Swarm.


```
{
  "host": {
    "hostname": "192.168.160.2",
    "ip": "::ffff:10.0.0.2",
    "ips": []
```

```
  },
  "http": {
    "method": "GET",
    "baseUrl": "",
    "originalUrl": "/",
    "protocol": "http"
  },
  "request": {
    "params": {
      "0": "/"
    },
    "query": {},
    "cookies": {},
    "body": {},
    "headers": {
      "host": "192.168.160.2",
      "user-agent": "curl/7.81.0",
      "accept": "*/*"
    }
  },
  "environment": {
    "PATH": "/usr/local/sbin:/usr/local/bin:/usr/sbin:/usr/bin:/sbin:/bin",
    "HOSTNAME": "21cbe17efc5f",
    "NODE_VERSION": "18.17.1",
    "YARN_VERSION": "1.22.19",
    "HOME": "/root"
  }
}
```


If we send the request multiple times, the environment will have different `HOSTNAME` values. This is the power of load balancing inside a Docker Swarm cluster. We didn't have to add or modify anything; it is present out-of-the-box, and we can safely use it to our advantage.

Running the preceding `curl` command will give us responses from different upstream servers. We can apply the knowledge we have gained to prove this further.

Let's try to get the Swarm server logs to identify the responding service:

```
docker service logs echo-server --tail=10 -t
```

Output:

```
2023-09-23T06:24:25.471417392Z echo-server.2.klhmoqexr0mk@manager |
...truncated...
2023-09-23T06:24:35.051467441Z echo-server.2.klhmoqexr0mk@manager |
...truncated...
2023-09-23T06:24:35.702425688Z echo-server.2.klhmoqexr0mk@manager |
...truncated...
2023-09-23T06:24:36.356095731Z echo-server.2.klhmoqexr0mk@manager |
...truncated...
2023-09-23T06:24:25.863639417Z echo-server.3.qnak50nmz1aq@worker  |
...truncated...
2023-09-23T06:24:25.892625594Z echo-server.1.1azkrkdl9n7g@worker  |
...truncated...
2023-09-23T06:24:34.835696672Z echo-server.3.qnak50nmz1aq@worker  |
...truncated...
2023-09-23T06:24:35.484584220Z echo-server.3.qnak50nmz1aq@worker  |
...truncated...
2023-09-23T06:24:34.609227863Z echo-server.1.1azkrkdl9n7g@worker  |
...truncated...
2023-09-23T06:24:36.141358630Z echo-server.3.qnak50nmz1aq@worker  |
...truncated...
2023-09-23T06:24:35.270628574Z echo-server.1.1azkrkdl9n7g@worker  |
...truncated...
2023-09-23T06:24:35.921117802Z echo-server.1.1azkrkdl9n7g@worker  |
...truncated...
2023-09-23T06:24:36.569057796Z echo-server.1.1azkrkdl9n7g@worker  |
...truncated...
```

You can see that requests are distributed among the upstream servers, which is advantageous because we don't have to worry about overloading a single application.

Pro tip: If you don't want to overload your Swarm nodes, consider placing a load balancer in front of these nodes, such as HAProxy. This ensures that all the requests are distributed among the nodes by the load balancer and between the services by the Docker Swarm cluster.

While we have covered load balancing, the question remains: where is service discovery?

To answer this question, we first need to elaborate on a topic we haven't covered yet for good reason - to keep things simple and build the knowledge incrementally.

Now that you have a solid foundation, let's explain Network Overlay in Docker Swarm: what it is, why it is crucial to the workings of Docker Swarm, and how it plays a role in the big picture.

Docker Swarm Network Overlay

Docker Swarm overlay networks allow containers to communicate with each other across multiple Docker hosts. This is essential for running distributed applications with Docker Swarm.

Overlay networks are created using the `overlay` network driver. When you create an overlay network, you specify a subnet range. Docker then creates a virtual network interface (VNI) on each Docker host in the swarm. The VNI is used to encapsulate traffic to and from the overlay network.

When you create a Docker service and attach it to an overlay network, Docker will automatically assign an IP address to each container in the service from the overlay network subnet. This allows containers in the service to communicate with each other directly, regardless of which Docker host they are running on.

Overlay networks also **support service discovery**. This means containers on the overlay network can automatically discover each other by name. This is essential for running microservices-based applications, where each service comprises multiple containers.

Overlay networking is crucial to Docker Swarm because it allows containers to communicate with each other across multiple Docker hosts. This is essential for running distributed applications with Docker Swarm.

Without overlay networking, containers on different Docker hosts would need to be manually configured to communicate with each other. This would be complex and error-prone.

Overlay networking also provides several benefits for running distributed applications, including:

- **Scalability**: Overlay networks are scalable to large numbers of Docker hosts. This makes them ideal for running large-scale distributed applications.

- **Resilience**: Overlay networks are resilient to node failures. If a Docker host fails, the overlay network will automatically reconfigure itself to route traffic around the failed host.
- **Performance**: Overlay networks can provide high performance for container-to-container communication.

In our example, if we want to run a container that can access the earlier echo server, we will need to put both services in the same network overlay.

One way of achieving this is to find out the network to which the service is attached, easily retrievable by running `docker service inspect echo-server`.

Another approach is to create an overlay network, attach it to the echo server, and use that network when running other services to place all services in the same network.

Since this book is about Docker, we will proceed with the second approach to learn how to create an overlay network, attach it to the currently running Swarm service, and spin up new services inside the same network.

To create the new network, we can use the following command:

```
docker network create --driver overlay mastering-docker
```

Now that we have the new network, we can attach it to the echo server using the following command:

```
docker service update --network-add mastering-docker --detach echo-server
```

Finally, we can create a new service, place it in the same network, and use the name `echo-server` to check for the service discovery capability of Docker Swarm.

To achieve this, we will create a service that runs the `sleep` command, so that we can use it as a shell by executing inside the container:

```
docker service create \
  --detach \
  --name curl \
  --network mastering-docker \
  curlimages/curl:8.3.0 sleep infinity
```

Now, let's run a command inside the `curl` container to see how service discovery plays a role in Docker Swarm.

There is currently one limitation of what we want to achieve. We would like to `exec` into the container and run commands from inside the container. However, we cannot simply run `docker service exec SERVICE_NAME` because Docker Swarm doesn't [yet] have that functionality.

To overcome this limitation, it is essential to understand the node hosting the container and run the `docker exec` from that specific node.

To get that information, we will run the `ps` command:

```
docker service ps curl
```

The output will contain the hosting node under the `NODE` column. The Docker Swarm nodes are all Docker containers (as set up at the beginning of this chapter).

There is a need to modify the `DOCKER_HOST` to communicate with the host's Docker engine.

At the moment, our `curl` container is running inside the worker node. As such, the following command we will use to get an interactive shell from it:

```
export DOCKER_HOST=192.168.160.3
container_id=$(docker ps -aqf “name=curl”)
docker exec -it $container_id curl echo-server
```

Certainly, this command will return a response from the echo server in the same network.

As discussed earlier on the load balancer, running this command multiple times will result in the request reaching different upstream servers, effectively distributing the total number of requests between the servers.

Load Balancer Algorithm

We have discussed the Docker Swarm load balancer so far and mentioned that it supports a round-robin algorithm for traffic distribution. This simple but effective algorithm distributes traffic evenly across all available containers in a service.

However, other load-balancing algorithms may be more suitable for specific applications. For example, use a least connections algorithm to distribute traffic to the containers with the fewest active connections. Alternatively, you could use a weighted round-robin algorithm to distribute traffic to containers based on their capacity.

Unfortunately, it is not currently possible to modify the load-balancing algorithm of Docker Swarm. However, there are a few ways to work around this limitation:

- **Use an external load balancer**: You can use an external load balancer, such as NGINX or HAProxy, to distribute traffic to your Docker Swarm cluster. This will give you more control over the load-balancing algorithm.
- **Use a service mesh**: A service mesh is a software layer between your applications and the underlying infrastructure. Service meshes can provide various features, including load balancing, service discovery, and fault tolerance. Famous examples around the industry include Hashicorp Consul, Istio, and Linkerd.
- **Use a custom swarm orchestrator**: A few custom swarm orchestrators support different load-balancing algorithms. For example, the Kubernetes-Swarm orchestrator supports a variety of load-balancing algorithms, including least connections, weighted round-robin, and random.

Which option is right for you?

The best way to modify the load balancing algorithm of Docker Swarm depends on your specific needs and requirements. Consider using an external load balancer or a service mesh if you need fine-grained control over the load-balancing algorithm. Or, using a custom swarm orchestrator if you want a more complete solution.

Here are some additional things to consider when choosing a load-balancing algorithm:

- **The type of application you are running**: Some applications are more sensitive to latency than others. For example, a web application may be more latency-sensitive than a batch-processing application.
- **The traffic patterns of your application**: Some applications have predictable traffic patterns, while others have unpredictable traffic patterns.
- **The number of containers in your service**: Use a load-balancing algorithm that scales well if you have many containers in your service.

There is no silver bullet, and you'll have to consider your workload and requirements to find the best tool for the job. However, you have gained enough knowledge to make an informed decision after reading this chapter.

Figure 7.6: *A person meditating in a mountain view.*
source: https://unsplash.com/photos/38BhHXOMC6M

Conclusion

Docker Swarm is a powerful tool for managing and deploying containerized applications. It provides several features that make it ideal for running distributed applications, including:

- **Scalability**: Docker Swarm can scale to large numbers of nodes, making it ideal for running large-scale distributed applications.
- **Resilience**: Docker Swarm is resilient to node failures. If a node fails, the other nodes in the swarm will automatically take over the work being done by the failed node.
- **Performance**: Docker Swarm can provide high performance for container-to-container communication.
- **Ease of use**: Docker Swarm is relatively easy to use. It can be managed using the Docker CLI or the Docker Swarm GUI.

Docker Swarm is still under development, but some companies have already adopted it to run their production applications. It is a good choice for companies looking for a scalable and reliable way to run containerized applications.

In this chapter, we have covered the fundamentals and the ins and outs of Docker Swarm. We have also discussed the benefits of using Docker Swarm and why it is a good choice for running distributed applications.

If you want to manage and deploy containerized applications, then Docker Swarm is an excellent option. It is a powerful and scalable tool that can be used to run large-scale distributed applications.

Please learn more about Docker Swarm and try it out yourself. You can find more information about Docker Swarm on the Docker website.

In the next chapter, we will cover the security aspect of Docker in more detail and shed some light on the best practices to secure your workload when delivering your operations using the Docker tooling.

References

For further reading and to dive deeper into Docker Swarm and related topics, you can explore the following official sources and references:

- **Docker Official Documentation - Docker Swarm**: The official Docker documentation provides comprehensive guides, tutorials, and reference materials on Docker Swarm. You can find information on Swarm mode, service management, and more. [Docker Swarm Documentation] (https://docs.docker.com/swarm/)
- **Docker GitHub Repository**: Docker's official GitHub repository is a valuable resource for exploring the source code, issue tracker, and discussions related to Docker Swarm and other Docker projects. [Docker GitHub Repository] (https://github.com/docker)
- **Docker Blog**: Docker's blog often features in-depth articles, case studies, and updates on Docker Swarm, container orchestration, and related technologies. It's a great source for staying up-to-date with the latest developments. [Docker Blog] (https://www.docker.com/blog/)
- **Docker YouTube Channel**: Docker's official YouTube channel hosts webinars, tutorials, and talks related to Docker Swarm, containerization, and container orchestration. You can find video content that complements your learning. [Docker YouTube Channel] (https://www.youtube.com/user/dockerrun)
- **GitHub - Awesome Docker**: The "Awesome Docker" GitHub repository curates a list of valuable resources, tools, and projects related to Docker and Docker Swarm. It's a community-driven collection of helpful references. [Awesome Docker on GitHub] (https://github.com/veggiemonk/awesome-docker)
- **Stack Overflow - Docker Questions**: Stack Overflow is a popular platform for asking and answering technical questions. You can find a wealth of knowledge related to Docker Swarm by exploring questions and answers from the Docker community. [Docker Questions on Stack Overflow] (https://stackoverflow.com/questions/tagged/docker)
- **Docker Community Forums**: Docker's official community forums are a great place to seek help, share knowledge, and participate in discussions related to Docker Swarm and containerization. [Docker Community Forums] (https://forums.docker.com/)

- The lab exercises and source codes for everything in this book are placed in the GitHub repository, publicly accessible to everyone. https://github.com/ava-orange-education/Ultimate Docker for Cloud Native Applications

These official sources and references provide a wealth of information and community support to help you deepen your understanding of Docker Swarm and enhance your container orchestration skills.

CHAPTER 8

Securing Docker Deployments

Figure 8.1: *Two people wearing safety at work.*
source: https://unsplash.com/photos/80zZ1s24Nag

Introduction

In this chapter, we embark on a journey to fortify your understanding of Docker security. Security is a cornerstone of any containerized environment, and it's essential to grasp the best practices for safeguarding your Docker deployments.

Throughout this chapter, we'll explore best practices to secure Docker, the measures to secure the Docker daemon, and discuss strategies for controlling access to Docker resources. We'll also shine a light on image security and vulnerability scanning, ensuring you're well-prepared to keep your containers safe. Moreover, we'll touch upon securing container communication and dive into the intricacies of hardening Docker hosts and the applications running within containers. By the end of this chapter, you'll have a comprehensive toolkit to bolster the security of your Docker ecosystem.

Structure

In this chapter, we will cover the following topics:

- Best Practices to Secure Docker
- Securing the Docker Daemon
- Access Control for Docker Resources
- Image Security and Vulnerability Scanning
- Hardening Docker Hosts and Containerized Applications

Best Practices to Secure Docker

Securing Docker containers is crucial. Here are some recommended industry best practices for securing Docker containers:

- **Use Official Images**: Start by using official Docker images from trusted sources like Docker Hub, Amazon Container Registry, GitHub Container Registry, and so on. These images are regularly updated and maintained with security patches. They are interval-checked for security vulnerabilities, and remedies are patched constantly to keep the community safe and the internet secure.
- **Regularly Update Images**: Keep your base images and application dependencies up-to-date to ensure you're not using versions with known vulnerabilities. Having a cronjob to check your Docker images for vulnerabilities and other types of scanners can help you identify what is outdated and needs a remedy.
- **Least Privilege Principle**: Follow the principle of least privilege. Limit the capabilities and permissions given to containers. Only provide what's necessary for the application to function. Try to run your containers as non-root so that the footprint of its exposure is limited as much as possible.
- **Use Multi-Stage Builds**: Utilize multi-stage builds to minimize the size of your final container image. It will help remove non-essential files and directories from your final image and reduce the attack surface.
- **Implement Image Scanning**: Use container image scanning tools like Docker Scout, Clair, Trivy, or Anchore to identify vulnerabilities in your images. They will give you a good report on the latest CVEs and whether or not you're advised to update your image.
- **Secure Your Docker Daemon**: Restrict access to the Docker daemon. Use Unix socket permissions and avoid exposing the Docker daemon over the

network whenever possible. A good practice is not to expose the server on all the network interfaces, or if you do, secure the authentication using TLS certificates.

- **Use Docker Bench Security**: Docker Bench Security is a tool that checks for standard best practices around deploying Docker containers securely. It can help you identify areas where your setup might need improvement.
- **Network Segmentation**: Segment your network to isolate containers, especially if you're running containers with different security levels or from different untrusted sources. This entails physically partitioning your worker nodes in private and public networks and putting groups of related containers into one network on the virtual layer.
- **Resource Limits**: Enforce resource limits on containers to prevent resource exhaustion attacks. Docker provides options to limit CPU, memory, and other resources. If you don't, you will be at the risk of resource exhaustion and Out-of-Memory (OOM) kill, which the operating system will kill the processes using too many resources just to keep the system alive.
- **Apparmor/SELinux Profiles**: Consider using AppArmor or SELinux to create profiles restricting container processes' access to the host system. These are advanced topics and require a complete guide, and therefore out of scope, but we're introducing them here so that you know your options.
- **Secrets Management**: Manage secrets and sensitive configuration data outside the container image. Use tools like Docker Secrets or Kubernetes Secrets. Encrypt your secrets at rest and in transit, and only decrypt them when running your containers.
- **Monitoring and Logging**: Implement thorough monitoring and centralized logging to quickly detect and respond to security incidents. Remember, you wouldn't know how to boost your application runtime and secure its environment without monitoring. As the popular Google SRE book mentions, Hope is not a strategy"!
- **Container Orchestration Security**: If you're using Kubernetes or another container orchestration platform, follow the best practices for securing the orchestration layer. There are significant security pieces of advice around the industry you can follow to secure your environment.
- **Regular Audits and Penetration Testing**: Periodically perform security and penetration testing to identify vulnerabilities and weaknesses in your containerized applications.
- **Education and Training**: Continuously educate your team about container security best practices and keep up-to-date with security news and developments in the Docker ecosystem.

Official Images

One fundamental practice when securing your Docker deployments is using official Docker images from trusted sources. Official images are provided and maintained by reputable organizations and are a reliable foundation for building your containers. These images undergo rigorous security checks, receive regular updates, and are promptly patched to address any discovered vulnerabilities. By incorporating official images into your containerization workflow, you benefit from a strong security posture from the outset.

Defining Official Images

Official images are typically provided by the organizations or communities responsible for containerizing software or technology. For instance, Docker Hub hosts a vast repository of official images, including those for popular software like Ubuntu, Nginx, and PostgreSQL. These images are considered official because the official maintainers or owners of the respective software maintain them. Other container registries, such as **Amazon Container Registry** (ACR), **Google Container Registry** (GCR), and **GitHub Container Registry** (GHCR), also offer their official images for various technologies.

Verifying Official Status

To verify whether an image is official, you can look for a special **official** badge or label associated with it on container registries like Docker Hub. Additionally, you can check the image description, where maintainers usually provide information about the image's official status.

Another interesting factor is the number of downloads of an image. Suppose you see a Docker image with a high number of downloads. That can indicate being a trusted source for the community. However, it is not the determining factor because a malicious actor can upload an image and download it many times personally to increase the number of downloads. Still, it is a number that can give some credit to the author of the image.

Integrating Official Images into Your Workflow

To improve the software delivery process of your organization, you can use Container Registry Policy.

Container Registry Policy allows you to define a policy that enforces official images for your organization's projects. Many container registry platforms, including Docker Hub, provide policy management features that allow you to set rules for image selection. Some of the well-known registry policies are the Docker Trusted Registry (DTR), Amazon Elastic Container Registry (ECR), Google Container Registry (GCR), Azure Container Registry (ACR), Harbor, Artifactory, Open Policy Agent (OPA), Kubernetes Admission Controllers.

Regularly Update Images

Keeping your container images up to date is fundamental to maintaining a secure and reliable Docker environment. As software developers release updates and patches to address security vulnerabilities and improve functionality, container images need periodic updates to stay secure and efficient. Here's why regularly updating your Docker images is crucial, along with best practices, to implement this process effectively.

Reasons for Updating Docker Images

Some of the reasons for updating Docker images are:

- **Security Patches**: The primary reason to update Docker images is to apply security patches and fixes. Over time, vulnerabilities may be discovered in the software components within your images. Regular updates ensure that your containers are protected against known vulnerabilities.
- **New Features and Improvements**: Updates often include new features, optimizations, and performance improvements. By keeping your images current, you can use these enhancements to maintain or improve your containerized applications' functionality and efficiency.
- **Dependency Management**: Container images may include dependencies like libraries, frameworks, or middleware. As these dependencies evolve, updating your images helps you manage compatibility and ensures your application remains functional.

Best Practices for Updating Docker Images

Some of the best practices are as follows:

- **Regular Scans**: Use container scanning tools to regularly check your images for known vulnerabilities. Automated scans can help you identify outdated components and prioritize updates based on severity.
- **Image Versioning**: Implement a clear versioning strategy for your images. This makes tracking changes easier and ensures you deploy your containers' latest, patched versions.

- **Automated Builds**: Set up automated image builds triggered by source code changes or upstream updates. CI/CD pipelines can automate the process of building and pushing updated images to your container registry.
- **Scheduled Updates**: Create a schedule for image updates based on the software's release cycles, security announcements, or your organization's policies. Regularly review and update images accordingly.
- **Testing**: Before deploying updated images to production, thoroughly test them in a staging environment to ensure they work correctly with your application. Automated testing can help catch potential issues early.
- **Rollback Plan**: Always have a rollback plan if an updated image introduces unexpected problems. This plan should include a procedure to revert to the previous version quickly.
- **Monitoring and Alerts**: Implement monitoring and alerting systems to detect any issues that may arise after image updates in production. This allows you to respond promptly to anomalies.

Least Privilege Principle

The Least Privilege Principle is a fundamental security concept in the Docker ecosystem. It involves granting the minimum access and permissions required for a process or user to perform their tasks, reducing the attack surface and potential security risks. Implementing this principle helps ensure that, in the event of a security breach or misconfiguration, the impact is minimized. Here's how you can apply the Least Privilege Principle in Docker:

Use Non-Root Users

Running Docker containers as the root user can be risky, as it grants extensive privileges within the container. Instead, create and use non-root users with limited permissions. Here's how to do it:

In your `Dockerfile`, add a `USER` instruction to specify a non-root user. For example:

```
FROM ubuntu
RUN useradd -m myuser
USER myuser
```

The same can be achieved at runtime using the `-u` flag with docker run to specify a non-root user. For example:

```
docker run -u myuser myimage
```

Limit Capabilities

Docker containers can be further isolated by restricting Linux capabilities within the container. Capabilities determine the specific privileges a process or container has.

To limit the capabilities of a Docker container, use the `--cap-drop` and `--cap-add` flags with docker run to drop or add capabilities explicitly. For example:

```
docker run --cap-drop=ALL --cap-add=NET_ADMIN myimage
```

By default, Docker containers start with fewer capabilities than a typical Linux host, which is considered relatively safe. Still, they are not as minimal as having no capabilities (`--cap-drop=ALL`).

While it is not strictly necessary to use `--cap-drop=ALL` in every Docker container, dropping unnecessary capabilities to limit the potential attack surface is a good security practice. Docker's default capabilities allow many system-level actions that most applications might not need. Therefore, dropping capabilities your container does not require is a sensible approach to enhance security.

When you start a Docker container without specifying additional capabilities using the `--cap-add` or `--cap-drop` flags, it inherits the default set of capabilities. This default set includes `CAP_DAC_READ_SEARCH` (read access to file system objects) and CAP_NET_BIND_SERVICE (binding to privileged ports).

As a general rule of thumb, dropping all container capabilities and only granting the required capabilities needed to run the container is recommended.

Isolate Containers

Apply network and file system isolation between containers to limit communication and access.

To control container connectivity, utilize Docker's network modes like bridge, host, and none. Choose the appropriate mode based on your application's needs.

Use Docker volumes or bind mounts to limit access to the host file system. Only mount the necessary directories as read-only or read-write.

Figure 8.2: *The root of an old tree on the ground.*
source: https://unsplash.com/photos/MskbR8VLNrA

Securing the Docker Daemon

Securing the Docker Daemon is a critical aspect of ensuring the overall security of your Docker environment. The Docker daemon, or the Docker engine, manages Docker containers and handles container-related operations on the host system. Securing it is crucial because unauthorized access or vulnerabilities in the daemon can lead to potentially serious security breaches.

Here are some available options to secure the Docker Daemon:

- **Use TLS for Communication**: Enabling **Transport Layer Security** (TLS) for Docker communication is essential. This involves configuring the Docker daemon to use TLS certificates, encrypting communication between Docker clients and the daemon, and preventing eavesdropping and unauthorized access.
- **Implement Authentication and Authorization**: Set up authentication and authorization mechanisms to control who can interact with the Docker daemon. Docker supports different authentication methods, including user-based access control, role-based access control (RBAC), and integration with identity providers like LDAP or other tools.
- **Network Firewall Rules**: Restrict network access to the Docker daemon by configuring firewall rules. You can use tools like `iptables or firewalld to limit incoming connections to only trusted sources.`
- **Audit Docker Daemon Activity**: Enable Docker daemon logging and auditing to monitor and track activities related to the daemon. This can help you detect and respond to any suspicious or unauthorized actions.
- **Use Docker Bench for Security**: As mentioned earlier, Docker Bench for Security is an open-source tool that provides a set of best practices and security checks specifically for Docker. Running Docker Bench periodically can help identify and address security issues.

- **Update and Patch**: Regularly update the Docker daemon to apply security patches and updates. Keeping the Docker software up to date is crucial to address known vulnerabilities.

Enforce Docker Daemon TLS Authentication

In this section, to give you a good overview of the processes involved, we'll protect the Docker Daemon behind TLS authentication.

To give context, the Docker Daemon does not enforce TLS authentication by default, which means any user on the system who has access to the Docker socket, `unix:///var/run/docker.sock`, will be able to send their request, and the Daemon will gladly serve them. It's important to mention that upon installation, the Docker socket is only accessible to the root user, and if anyone needs access to the socket, the command to give such permission is as follows:

```
sudo usermod -aG docker <username>
```

Every socket in the Linux operating system is owned by a user and a group. You will be granted permission to talk to the socket if you're either the user or in the group of the socket owner. This grants permission to any user in the group docker in the Linux filesystem.

Although the preceding claim holds, it's essential to note a couple of things:

- **Local Access**: This is primarily a concern for local access to the Docker Daemon on the machine where Docker is installed. This may be a minor issue in a typical development or single-user environment. However, securing access to the Docker Daemon is crucial in a multi-user or production environment.
- **Security Best Practices**: Docker allows you to configure authentication and authorization mechanisms to improve security. You can restrict access to the Docker Daemon by configuring it to use TLS certificates or controlling access to the socket using file permissions. Implementing these security practices is essential to prevent unauthorized access.

This design decision made it easier for users on a local machine to interact with the Docker Daemon.

At the same time, this has some implications if you install Docker on a machine and allow external access to that Daemon, for example, opening a port on a network interface card (NIC).

Therefore, if you ever need to install the Daemon on a host machine and require authentication on top of the Daemon, one of the secure ways is to use TLS authentication.

The way it works is that you will create a self-signed certificate to act as your **Certificate Authority** (CA) and use the private key of the CA to generate more certificates for the server as well as any client that will send a request to the Docker Daemon.

With that explanation, let's first generate a self-signed certificate. There are many ways, and using the step-cli is preferred for its intuitive interface, but since OpenSSL is more popular and well-known, we'll cover both.

```
# Generate the private key first
openssl genrsa -out ca.key 4096
# Using that private key, create a self-signed certificate for the CA
openssl req -x509 -new -nodes -key ca.key -sha256 -days 3650 -out ca.crt
-subj "/CN=ca"
```

The next step is to create one certificate for the server and another for the client.

```
# Certificate and key for the Docker Daemon (the server)
openssl genrsa -out server.key 4096
openssl req -new -key server.key -out server.csr -subj "/CN=docker-daemon"
openssl x509 -req -in server.csr -CA ca.crt -CAkey ca.key -CAcreateserial
-out server.crt -days 3650 -sha256
# Certificate for one of the clients
openssl genrsa -out client.key 4096
openssl req -new -key client.key -out client.csr -subj "/CN=docker-client"
openssl x509 -req -in client.csr -CA ca.crt -CAkey ca.key -CAcreateserial
-out client.crt -days 3650 -sha256
```

With these certificates in place, all left for running our Daemon is a configuration file, setting the certificate path for the Daemon to pick up.

Here's what such a file would look like if you intend to modify the main Docker Daemon on the system.

```
{
  "tls": true,
  "tlscacert": "/etc/docker/ca.crt",
  "tlscert": "/etc/docker/server.crt",
```

```
  "tlskey": "/etc/docker/server.key",
  "hosts": ["tcp://0.0.0.0:2376", "unix:///var/run/docker.sock"]
}
```

This forces Docker to respond to client requests if only they provide a valid certificate issued by the CA.

To test things out, we can either configure the main Docker Daemon running on the machine or run another Docker Daemon process to avoid using `sudo` privileges to modify any file or directory.

For the purpose of demonstration, we will spin up another process to avoid contaminating the main Daemon or its configuration.

That said, we will place all the certificates under the current directory's `certs` path.

In the end, here's the tree structure of that directory.

```
certs/
├── ca.crt
├── ca.key
├── client.crt
├── client.key
├── server.crt
└── server.key
```

And the Daemon configuration file is modified to look as follows:

```
{
  "tls": true,
  "tlscacert": "./certs/ca.crt",
  "tlscert": "./certs/server.crt",
  "tlskey": "./certs/server.key",
  "pidfile": "/tmp/docker.pid",
  "data-root": "/tmp/docker",
  "hosts": ["tcp://0.0.0.0:10000", "unix:///tmp/docker.sock"]
}
```

As you can see, we're modifying some of the default behavior of the Docker Daemon so that it won't need to interfere with the main Daemon of the host machine.

Here is the command to run the Docker Daemon.

```
sudo dockerd --config-file daemon.json
```

Let's keep this terminal open, and from another terminal, run the following command:

```
DOCKER_HOST=localhost:10000 docker ps
```

This command will fail in error with the following output:

```
Error response from daemon: Client sent an HTTP request to an HTTPS
server.
```

This is the expected behavior since the server is running in TLS mode, and any requests in plain text will not be processed.

If you're ever tempted to see if sending a random certificate will be authenticated by the server, we got you covered. Let's try sending a certificate that the CA did not sign.

```
DOCKER_HOST=localhost:10000 docker --tls \
  --tlscacert /tmp/random-ca.crt \
  --tlscert /tmp/random-cert.crt \
  --tlskey /tmp/random-cert.key \
  ps
```

The output will look like the following:

```
the server probably has client authentication (--tlsverify) enabled;
check your TLS client certification settings: Get
"https://localhost:10000/v1.24/containers/json": remote error: tls: bad
certificate
```

As you can see, the Daemon rightfully rejects the certificate because it hasn't been signed by the trusted CA that was passed to the Docker Daemon.

As such, it rejects the request and demands that the CA sign the client certificate that the Daemon has.

Finally, let's try to pass in the certificate of our trusted client in the command line.

```
DOCKER_HOST=localhost:10000 docker --tls \
  --tlscacert ./certs/ca.crt \
  --tlscert ./certs/client.crt \
```

```
  --tlskey ./certs/client.key \
  ps
```

This time, the command executes successfully, and we get a response from the server.

```
CONTAINER ID   IMAGE     COMMAND   CREATED   STATUS    PORTS     NAMES
```

Before jumping into the next section, and as promised, here are the equivalent commands to create certificates using step-cli. You can see that it's much easier to work with, especially if you're not an expert on certificates and their intricacies.

```
step certificate create ca \
  ca.crt ca.key \
  --profile root-ca \
  --insecure \
  --no-password

step certificate create docker-daemon \
  server.crt server.key \
  --ca ./ca.crt --ca-key ./ca.key
```

Now that you have seen the initial security guardrail, let's talk about firewalls and why adding this layer of security is necessary as an extra measure.

Restricting Docker Daemon Access Using Firewalls

Firewalls are crucial gatekeepers, controlling network traffic and regulating access to your Docker daemon. By implementing firewall rules, you can further enhance the security of your Docker host and protect against unauthorized access and potential threats.

The Role of Firewalls

Firewalls act as a protective barrier between your Docker daemon and the external network, ensuring that only trusted sources can communicate with the Docker daemon's API. By restricting access through firewall rules, you can:

- **Limit Exposure**: Firewalls allow you to specify which IP addresses or networks are permitted to access the Docker daemon. This reduces the exposure of your Docker daemon to potentially malicious actors.

- **Prevent Unauthorized Access**: Unauthorized users or systems are blocked from requesting the Docker daemon's API. This safeguards your Docker host from unauthorized control.
- **Control Docker API Traffic**: Firewall rules enable you to define the specific ports and protocols to access the Docker daemon. This fine-grained control ensures that only essential traffic is allowed.

Implementing Firewall Rules

Here are steps to implement firewall rules effectively to restrict Docker daemon access:

1. **Identify Trusted Networks**: Determine which IP addresses or networks are trusted and need access to the Docker daemon. This typically includes your internal network, trusted systems, and authorized users.
2. **Allowlist Authorized IPs**: Configure your firewall to allow traffic only from the identified trusted sources. Use firewall rules to permit incoming connections to the Docker daemon's API port (e.g., port 2375 for HTTP or port 2376 for HTTPS) from these trusted IPs.
3. **Deny by Default**: Adopt a deny by default policy, where all incoming connections are blocked unless explicitly allowed. This ensures that any traffic that does not match your defined rules is automatically denied.
4. **Enable Logging**: Enable logging for your firewall rules to monitor and track any denied or allowed connections. This can help in auditing and detecting potential security incidents.
5. **Regularly Review and Update Rules**: Periodically review and update your firewall rules to accommodate changes in your network infrastructure and access requirements. Ensure that the rules remain aligned with your security policies.
6. **Use Docker's Built-in Protections**: Docker provides built-in protections like authentication and encryption. Continue to use these features in conjunction with firewall rules for comprehensive security.

Necessity of Firewall

We have discussed securing the Docker Daemon by enforcing TLS authentication so that no unauthenticated request is allowed and processed on the server.

But you might wonder, why is a firewall necessary when we already have TLS authentication?

A firewall is necessary even when TLS authentication is set up in the Docker Daemon for several reasons, including:

- **Defense in Depth**: Security best practices often follow the principle of defense in depth, which means using multiple layers of security controls. While TLS authentication is a robust method for securing communications between Docker clients and the daemon, adding a firewall provides an additional layer of protection. It is a barrier to unauthorized access before traffic reaches the Docker daemon.
- **Network Segmentation**: Firewalls allow you to segment your network effectively. By defining firewall rules, you can restrict access to specific IP addresses or networks, creating isolated communication pathways for Docker traffic. This segmentation helps contain potential security breaches and limits lateral movement within your network.
- **Protection against Misconfigurations**: Misconfigurations can happen, even with strong authentication. A firewall acts as a safety net, preventing unintended exposure of the Docker daemon to the external network or unauthorized users in case of misconfigurations.
- **Preventing Unauthorized Discovery**: Even if TLS authentication is enforced, an open Docker daemon port can still be discovered by attackers scanning for open ports on your server. A firewall ensures that the Docker daemon's port is only accessible to trusted entities with proper authorization.
- **Additional Access Control**: Firewalls offer granular control over which IP addresses or networks are allowed to access the Docker daemon. This level of access control complements TLS authentication, allowing you to define specific access policies based on your organization's requirements.
- **Logging and Monitoring**: Firewalls provide logging capabilities, allowing you to monitor and audit traffic. This visibility helps identify and investigate potential security incidents, enhancing your ability to respond to threats effectively.
- **DDoS Attack Mitigation**: Firewalls can be configured to detect and mitigate DDoS attacks by applying rate limiting and traffic filtering rules. During a DDoS attack, the firewall can identify and block traffic from malicious sources, helping to absorb and deflect the attack traffic before it reaches the Docker daemon. This proactive DDoS protection ensures that legitimate requests can still access your Docker services while minimizing the attack's impact. It complements TLS authentication and access control mechanisms to maintain service availability during DDoS threats.

Using the firewall, here are two methods to apply a rate limit on the Docker Daemon's port.

The following rule would allow the first ten connections to match the rule without being limited but would then limit the rate to 100 per second:

```
iptables -A INPUT -p tcp --dport 2375 -m limit --limit 100/s --lim-
it-burst 10 -j ACCEPT
```

Once you have added the rate-limiting rule to iptables, you must save the changes and restart the iptables service. You can do this using the following commands:

```
iptables-save
service iptables restart
```

If you know nothing of iptables, you can check out the following article, which goes in-depth on what the tool is and how to use it (written by the author of this book).

https://medium.com/skilluped/what-is-iptables-and-how-to-use-it-781818422e52

It is important to note that rate-limiting can harm legitimate traffic, so it is important to test your rules carefully before deploying them in a production environment.

You can also use a firewall GUI tool to apply rate-limiting to the Docker Daemon's port. For example, the UFW firewall GUI tool has a built-in option for limiting the rate of connections to a specific port.

To apply rate-limiting to the Docker Daemon's port using UFW, you would use the following command:

```
ufw limit tcp 2375 100/s
```

This command would limit the rate of incoming TCP connections to port 2375 (Docker Daemon) to 100 connections per second.

Once you have applied the rate-limiting rule, you must reload the UFW firewall. You can do this using the following command:

```
ufw reload
```

You can also use other firewall GUI tools to apply rate-limiting to the Docker Daemon's port. Please consult the documentation for your firewall GUI tool for more information.

Now that you have seen the authentication part of securing your Docker Daemon let's jump into the authorization section to see how to allow certain roles and users to access specific resources.

Figure 8.3: *The red light.*
source: https://unsplash.com/photos/ErpVemXm5wc

Access Control for Docker Resources

Access control for Docker resources refers to implementing security measures that regulate and restrict the actions and permissions granted to users, applications, or systems within a Docker environment.

It involves defining and enforcing policies determining who can perform specific operations on Docker containers, images, volumes, networks, and other resources. By configuring access control, administrators can ensure that only authorized entities have the necessary privileges to interact with Docker resources, enhancing the security and integrity of containerized applications and infrastructure.

Role-based access control (RBAC) for Docker

Enforcing Role-Based Access Control (RBAC) for the Docker Daemon involves defining and managing user roles, permissions, and access policies to control who can perform specific actions within the Docker environment.

While Docker itself does not provide native RBAC support, several third-party tools and solutions can help you implement RBAC for Docker Daemon. Here are some options:

- **Portainer**: Portainer is an open-source management UI for Docker that offers RBAC capabilities. It allows you to define user roles and permissions, control access to Docker resources, and manage containers, images, and volumes through a web-based interface.

- **Kubernetes with RBAC**: If you use Kubernetes to manage Docker containers, Kubernetes provides a robust RBAC system. You can use Kubernetes RBAC to control access to your containerized applications and manage Docker containers running within Kubernetes pods. Kubernetes is discussed in *Chapter 11 - Introduction to Kubernetes.*
- **Authz Plugin for Docker**: Docker provides an authorization plugin framework that allows you to integrate external authorization systems. You can develop custom authorization plugins that enforce RBAC policies. Tools like **Open Policy Agent** (OPA) can be used to create custom RBAC policies for Docker.
- **Docker Security Tools**: Some container security tools, like Aqua Security and Sysdig Secure, offer RBAC features as part of their container security solutions. These tools can help you define and enforce RBAC policies for Docker containers.
- **IAM and LDAP Integration**: You can integrate Docker with Identity and Access Management (IAM) systems or Lightweight Directory Access Protocol (LDAP) services. This allows you to leverage existing user management and RBAC capabilities provided by IAM or LDAP systems.
- **Custom Solutions**: For more advanced RBAC requirements, you can build custom RBAC solutions tailored to your organization's needs. This might involve scripting and automation to manage access control policies based on user roles and groups.

Auditing and Monitoring Docker Resource Access

Auditing and monitoring Docker resource access involves tracking and recording activities related to using Docker resources, such as containers, images, networks, and volumes, to gain insights into the behavior of your containerized environment and ensure security, compliance, and operational efficiency. This process typically includes:

- **Logging Docker Events**: Docker provides an event-logging mechanism that records key events and actions within the Docker. These events include container start and stop, image pulls, network configurations, and more. Collecting and analyzing these logs allows you to monitor the activities of containers and Docker daemons.
- **Centralized Logging**: Aggregating Docker event logs from multiple hosts and containers into a centralized logging system (for example, Loki, ELK Stack, Splunk, and Fluentd) allows efficient monitoring, analysis,

and alerting. Centralized logging simplifies the process of tracking and responding to security incidents or operational issues.

- **Alerting and Notifications**: Implement alerting mechanisms that trigger notifications when specific events or conditions occur. For example, you can set up alerts to notify administrators when containers are terminated unexpectedly or when resource usage exceeds predefined thresholds.
- **Access Control and Authentication**: Enforce user authentication and access controls to ensure only authorized personnel can interact with Docker resources. Track user access and actions to monitor for any suspicious or unauthorized activities.
- **Container Security Tools**: Utilize container security solutions and tools like Sysdig, Aqua Security, or Twistlock. These tools often include auditing and monitoring features that help you track and analyze container activities, detect vulnerabilities, and identify potential security threats.
- **Compliance and Auditing Tools**: In regulated industries or environments with strict requirements, consider using compliance and auditing tools specializing in container security and compliance checks. These tools help ensure your Docker environment adheres to industry standards and regulations.
- **Real-time Monitoring**: Implement real-time monitoring to detect anomalies or security breaches promptly. Continuous monitoring allows you to respond quickly to potential threats and minimize their impact.
- **Log Retention and Analysis**: Retain Docker logs for an appropriate duration to comply with regulatory requirements and for historical analysis. Log analysis can help identify trends, patterns, and potential security incidents.
- **Integration with SIEM**: Integrate Docker log data into your Security Information and Event Management (SIEM) system to correlate Docker-related events with broader security incidents across your infrastructure. This provides a holistic view of security across your organization.

So far, you have seen how to secure and audit Docker Daemon. Now, let's see how to secure your images and containers via Docker Daemon.

Image Security and Vulnerability Scanning

Image security and vulnerability scanning are crucial processes in containerized environments to identify and mitigate security risks associated with container images. These practices ensure that the images used to create containers are free from known vulnerabilities, malware, and other security issues.

Image Security

Here are some steps you can take to ensure the images you use are safe and come from a trusted party:

- **Image Sources**: Ensure you obtain container images from trusted and reputable sources, such as official repositories, known vendors, or internal registries. Avoid using images from unverified or untrusted sources.
- **Image Signing**: Consider digitally signing your container images using tools like Docker Content Trust or Notary. Image signing provides a way to verify the integrity and authenticity of images before deployment.
- **Base Image Security**: Pay special attention to the security of base images, as they are the foundation for your application images. Regularly update and patch base images to include the latest security fixes.
- **Static Analysis**: Use static analysis tools to scan container images for known vulnerabilities, misconfigurations, and insecure software components. Tools like Trivy, Clair, and Anchore can help identify image security issues.

Vulnerability Scanning

Here are the items for checking for any vulnerability in the Docker images:

- **Docker Scout**: Docker Scout is a software supply chain security solution that helps developers find and fix vulnerabilities in container images by analyzing images to create a software bill of materials (SBOM), a list of all the components and dependencies in the image. It then correlates the SBOM with a continuously updated vulnerability database to identify known vulnerabilities in the image. Docker Scout can be used during development to help developers identify and fix vulnerabilities early on, in production to scan images before they are deployed, and for compliance to help organizations comply with regulations that require them to identify and manage vulnerabilities in their software supply chain.
- **Regular Scanning**: Implement regular vulnerability scans of container images throughout their lifecycle, from development to deployment. Automated scanning can detect vulnerabilities in both the OS packages and application dependencies.

- **CVE Databases**: Vulnerability scanners rely on Common Vulnerabilities and Exposures (CVE) databases to match known vulnerabilities with image components. Keep these databases up to date to ensure accurate scans.
- **Severity Assessment**: Vulnerability scanners typically assign severity levels to identified vulnerabilities. Prioritize remediation efforts based on the severity of vulnerabilities to address the most critical issues first.
- **Integration with CI/CD**: Integrate vulnerability scanning into your CI/CD pipeline to catch vulnerabilities early in development. Automated scans can prevent vulnerable images from reaching production.
- **Policy Enforcement**: Establish policies that define how to handle images with vulnerabilities. Policies may include rejecting or quarantining images with critical vulnerabilities, initiating remediation workflows, or notifying relevant teams.
- **Continuous Monitoring**: Continuously monitor container images in production for newly discovered vulnerabilities. Vulnerabilities can emerge after an image is initially scanned, so ongoing monitoring is essential.
- **Patch Management**: Develop a patch management process to address vulnerabilities promptly. Patching should be part of your regular maintenance and update schedule.

Continuous Vulnerability Scanning in CI/CD Pipelines

Continuous vulnerability scanning in CI/CD (Continuous Integration/Continuous Deployment) pipelines is a security practice that automatically scans container images and application code for vulnerabilities at every stage of the software development and deployment lifecycle.

This proactive approach ensures that security checks are integrated seamlessly into the development and delivery process, helping to identify and address vulnerabilities early.

Here's an overview of continuous vulnerability scanning in CI/CD pipelines.

Integration with CI/CD

To have continuous scanning inside a CI/CD pipeline, you can take the following steps in no order:

- **Pre-Build Scanning**: Vulnerability scanning can start as early as the code commit stage. CI/CD systems can trigger scans before the build process begins to catch vulnerabilities in the application code and dependencies.
- **Image Scanning**: As container images are built-in CI/CD pipelines, vulnerability scans are performed to identify any vulnerabilities in the base images, OS packages, and application dependencies.
- **Policy Enforcement**: Define policies that specify how vulnerabilities should be handled. Policies can dictate whether an image can be promoted to the next pipeline stage, require vulnerabilities to be fixed within a specific timeframe, or automatically block images with critical vulnerabilities.

Key Practices

Here are the general guidelines and practices to achieve CI/CD integration security:

- **Automated Scanning**: Use automated vulnerability scanning tools like Trivy, Clair, Anchore, or commercial solutions integrated into your CI/CD pipeline. These tools can detect known vulnerabilities in the application code and container images.
- **Severity Assessment**: Vulnerability scanners often assign severity levels to identified vulnerabilities. Prioritize remediation efforts based on severity, focusing on critical and high-severity vulnerabilities first.
- **Fail Build on Vulnerabilities**: Consider configuring your CI/CD pipeline to fail the build process if critical vulnerabilities are detected. This ensures that vulnerable code or images do not progress to further stages.
- **Integration with Container Registries**: Integrate vulnerability scanning tools with your container registry. This allows you to automatically scan images as they are pushed to the registry, ensuring that only secure images are available for deployment.
- **Continuous Monitoring**: Implement continuous monitoring for vulnerabilities even after deployment. Vulnerabilities can emerge after an image is initially scanned, so ongoing monitoring is essential to detect new threats.
- **Reporting and Feedback**: Provide actionable feedback to developers about identified vulnerabilities, including guidance on how to remediate them. Collaboration between development and security teams is crucial for effective vulnerability management.

Benefits

Continuous vulnerability scanning in CI/CD pipelines includes, but is not limited to, the following benefits:

- **Early Detection**: Vulnerabilities are identified early in the development process, reducing the cost and effort required for remediation.
- **Security by Design**: Security becomes an integral part of the development lifecycle, fostering a culture of *security by design*.
- **Reduced Risk**: By blocking vulnerable code and images from progressing in the pipeline, the risk of deploying insecure applications is minimized.
- **Compliance**: Helps organizations meet compliance requirements by proactively addressing security vulnerabilities.
- **Improved Response Time**: Swift remediation of vulnerabilities improves response time to potential threats.

Hardening Docker Hosts

This book section will delve into essential security practices and techniques to fortify the underlying Docker hosts and the containerized applications they run. These measures are critical for safeguarding against potential threats, ensuring the isolation and integrity of containers, and maintaining a robust and secure container environment.

Host OS Security Best Practices

Securing the host operating system (OS) is fundamental to Docker container security. A compromised host OS can lead to container vulnerabilities and expose your entire infrastructure to risks. Here are fundamental host OS security best practices:

- **Regular Updates**: Keep the host OS updated with security patches and updates. Unpatched vulnerabilities in the OS can be exploited to gain access to containers.
- **Minimal Installation**: Install only the necessary components on the host OS. Minimize the attack surface by removing unnecessary software, services, and daemons.
- **Use Trusted Images**: Start with a minimal, trusted OS image for your Docker hosts. Images like Alpine Linux are designed for security and can be a good choice for the host OS.

- **Least Privilege**: Run the Docker daemon with the least privilege necessary. Avoid running it as the root user; configure it to use a non-root user or utilize user namespaces.
- **SELinux or AppArmor**: Implement security-enhanced Linux (SELinux) or AppArmor profiles to further isolate Docker containers from the host OS. These mandatory access control systems can limit the actions containers can perform.
- **Limit Kernel Capabilities**: Drop unnecessary Linux capabilities when starting Docker containers. Use `--cap-drop` and `--cap-add` options judiciously to restrict container capabilities.
- **Resource Constraints**: Enforce resource constraints on containers to prevent resource exhaustion attacks. Configure limits for CPU, memory, and other resources to ensure fair container allocation.
- **Container Runtime Hardening**: Choose a container runtime that emphasizes security, like containerd or cri-o, and regularly update it. Ensure the runtime itself is adequately secured against vulnerabilities.
- **Logging and Monitoring**: Set up centralized logging and monitoring for the host OS. Monitor logs for unusual activities and configure alerts for security incidents.
- **Network Segmentation**: Use segmentation techniques like firewall rules and network policies to isolate Docker hosts from other parts of your infrastructure. Limit external access to Docker daemon ports.
- **Container Image Trust**: Verify the trustworthiness of container images you run on the host. Implement image signing and verification mechanisms to ensure image integrity.
- **Filesystem Protections**: Use file system protections like Read-Only Root Filesystem or mount options to protect critical host directories from unauthorized modifications.
- **User Management**: Manage user accounts and access control on the host OS diligently. Remove unnecessary users and grant permissions only to trusted personnel.
- **Regular Auditing**: Implement security and vulnerability assessments on the host OS. Identify and remediate security weaknesses promptly.
- **Backups and Disaster Recovery**: Regularly back up your Docker host configurations and data. Establish a disaster recovery plan to respond to security incidents effectively.

Isolating Containers from the Host

Isolating containers from the host is a fundamental security practice in Docker and other containerization platforms. This isolation ensures that containers operate independently and securely, minimizing the risk of security breaches and protecting the host system.

Here are vital methods to achieve container isolation from the host:

- **Namespaces**: Docker uses Linux namespaces to provide process-level isolation. Each container runs in its namespaces for processes, networks, mount points, and more. This prevents containers from seeing or interacting with processes and resources outside their namespace.
- **Cgroups (Control Groups)**: Control groups manage and limit container resource usage. They prevent one container from consuming all available CPU, memory, or other resources, ensuring fair resource sharing.
- **Read-Only Root Filesystem**: Set the root filesystem of containers to read-only whenever possible. This prevents containers from changing the host's filesystem and enhances security.
- **User Namespaces**: User namespaces allow mapping container user IDs to different user IDs on the host. This mitigates potential privilege escalation attacks, as containers operate with reduced privileges compared to the host.
- **Seccomp Profiles**: Seccomp (Secure Computing Mode) filters system calls that containers can make. By configuring Seccomp profiles, you can restrict which system call containers are allowed to use, reducing the attack surface.
- **AppArmor and SELinux**: Use security-enhanced Linux (SELinux) or AppArmor to create mandatory access controls. These tools restrict the actions containers can perform, adding an extra layer of security.
- **Docker Security Profiles**: Docker offers various security profiles, such as "seccomp" and "apparmor," that you can apply to containers. These profiles restrict container capabilities and system calls.
- **Host Firewall Rules**: Implement firewall rules on the host to control network traffic to and from containers. Limit container access to specific ports and IP ranges as needed.
- **Network Policies**: Use network policies within container orchestration platforms like Kubernetes to define and enforce communication rules between containers and external services.

- **Use of Trusted Images**: Only deploy containers with images from trusted sources. Avoid running unverified or untrusted container images to minimize the risk of malicious code.
- **Runtime Protection**: Employ runtime protection solutions that continuously monitor and secure container behavior during execution, detecting anomalies and security threats.
- **Regular Security Audits**: Conduct regular security audits and vulnerability assessments of the host and container images. Address identified weaknesses promptly to maintain a secure environment.

Kernel Hardening and Security Patches

Kernel hardening and security patch management are critical components of ensuring the security and stability of a Docker host system. The kernel is the operating system's core and pivotal in container isolation and resource management.

The following is an in-depth look at these practices.

Kernel Hardening

- **Minimize Kernel Modules**: Remove or turn off unnecessary kernel modules to reduce the potential attack surface. Only load modules that are required for your specific use case.
- **Kernel Parameters**: Review and configure kernel parameters (`sysctl`) to enhance security. Adjust settings related to network security, file system permissions, and memory management for better protection.
- **GRSecurity/PaX**: Consider using security enhancements like GRSecurity and PaX to harden the kernel further. These patches provide additional security features such as exploit mitigations and access controls.
- **AppArmor and SELinux**: Implement AppArmor or SELinux security modules to enforce mandatory access controls (MAC) on kernel resources. These modules help confine processes, including container runtimes.
- **Kernel Runtime Security**: Use runtime security tools like Runtime Security Instrumentation (RSI) and eBPF (extended Berkeley Packet Filter) to monitor and protect the kernel at runtime. These tools can detect and respond to kernel-level security incidents.
- **Secure Boot**: Enable Secure Boot on your host system to ensure the kernel and boot components are cryptographically verified during boot, protecting against boot-time attacks.

Security Patch Management

Security patch management systematically applies updates and fixes to software and systems to protect them from known vulnerabilities and security threats.

Here is the list of items to remember:

- **Regular Updates**: Keep the kernel updated with security patches and updates. Vulnerabilities in the kernel can be exploited to gain access to the host system and containers.
- **Live Kernel Patching**: Explore live kernel patching solutions like `kpatch` and `kGraft`, which allow you to apply security patches without rebooting the system. This minimizes downtime and enhances security.
- **KernelCare**: Consider using KernelCare, a commercial live patching service, to apply kernel security patches automatically and without interruptions.
- **Subscription Services**: If you're using a Linux distribution, subscribe to vendor support services like Red Hat or Ubuntu's Extended Security Maintenance (ESM) to receive timely security updates for the kernel.
- **Vulnerability Scanning**: Integrate vulnerability scanning tools into your host system to identify and prioritize kernel vulnerabilities. Regularly scan for weaknesses and apply patches promptly.
- **Testing**: Before applying kernel updates in production, test them in a non-production environment to ensure they don't introduce compatibility issues with your applications or containers.
- **Automated Patching**: Consider automating the process of applying kernel security patches to ensure timely and consistent updates.

Figure 8.4: *The view of small boats by the beach.*
source: https://unsplash.com/photos/iJaFrm7Z9m4

Conclusion

Securing Docker environments is paramount in today's containerized world. By implementing the best practices discussed in this chapter, such as kernel hardening, container isolation, and regular security patch management, you can significantly enhance the security posture of your Docker infrastructure.

These measures safeguard your host systems and protect the integrity and isolation of containerized applications. Emphasizing security throughout the entire container lifecycle, from image creation to deployment, is essential to proactively address vulnerabilities and potential threats.

The next chapter will focus on integrating Docker containers into the CI/CD pipeline. You can expect to explore how Docker simplifies and streamlines the development and deployment processes, enabling agile and efficient software delivery.

We will delve into the practices, tools, and strategies that empower organizations to leverage Docker containers seamlessly within their CI/CD workflows, promoting rapid development, testing, and deployment cycles while maintaining security and consistency.

References

Here are some official sources and useful links for further reading on Docker security, including kernel hardening, container isolation, and best practices:

Docker Official Documentation

- Docker Security Overview: https://docs.docker.com/engine/security/
- Docker Security Best Practices: https://docs.docker.com/develop/security-best-practices/

Linux Kernel Hardening

- The Linux Kernel Self-Protection Project: https://kernsec.org/
- GRSecurity: https://grsecurity.net/
- PaX: https://pax.grsecurity.net/

SELinux and AppArmor

- SELinux Official Documentation: https://selinuxproject.org/page/Main_Page

- AppArmor Official Documentation: https://gitlab.com/apparmor/apparmor/-/wikis/home

Container Orchestration Platforms

- Kubernetes Security Documentation: https://kubernetes.io/docs/concepts/security/
- Docker Swarm Official Documentation: https://docs.docker.com/engine/swarm/secrets/
- Amazon ECS Security: https://docs.aws.amazon.com/AmazonECS/latest/developerguide/security.html

Linux Kernel Patch Management

- KernelCare: https://www.kernelcare.com/
- kpatch: https://github.com/dynup/kpatch
- kGraft: https://documentation.suse.com/sles/12-SP5/html/SLES-kgraft/index.html

Container Security Scanning

- Trivy Scanner: https://github.com/aquasecurity/trivy
- Clair Vulnerability Scanner: https://github.com/quay/clair
- Anchore: https://anchore.com/

This Book's Codes and Lab Exercises

- Public GitHub repository for the book: https://github.com/ava-orange-education/Mastering-Docker
- Lab exercises of the book: https://killercoda.com/meysam/course/mastering-docker/

Miscellaneous

- Public GitHub repository of the famous Udemy course: https://github.com/BretFisher/udemy-docker-mastery

These official resources and links provide comprehensive information on Docker security practices, kernel hardening, and related topics. Exploring these sources can help you deepen your understanding of container security and keep your Docker environment secure and well-protected.

CHAPTER 9

Docker in Continuous Integration and Deployment

Figure 9.1: *Wall-E in wonder.*
source: https://unsplash.com/photos/wall-e-photo-OI1ToozsKBw

Introduction

This chapter covers Docker in Continuous Integration and Deployment (CI/CD). It marks a pivotal juncture in your journey through the world of Docker, bridging the gap between containerization and the seamless, automated delivery of your applications. We will explore the dynamic landscape of CI/CD and how Docker can serve as a linchpin in streamlining your software development and deployment processes.

We aim to equip you with the knowledge and tools to fully embrace modern software development practices. We will begin by understanding the fundamental concepts of CI/CD and why it's crucial in today's fast-paced software industry. From there, we will embark on a comprehensive exploration of integrating Docker into your CI/CD pipeline. You can expect detailed discussions on best practices, practical examples, and real-world scenarios to illustrate the power of Docker in automating your deployment workflows.

Structure

In this chapter, we will discuss the following topics:

- Understanding CI/CD Fundamentals
- Integrating Docker into CI/CD Pipeline
- Building a Docker-Centric CI/CD Workflow
- Optimizing CI/CD with Docker Using Best Practices
- Real-world CI/CD Scenarios with Docker
- Docker's Role in Modern CI/CD

Understanding CI/CD Fundamentals

Continuous Integration and Continuous Deployment, commonly called CI/CD, form the backbone of modern software development. CI/CD is a set of practices and principles that aim to streamline the software delivery process. At its core, CI/CD is about **automating and optimizing the steps from code development to deployment.**

Importance of CI/CD

CI/CD is crucial because it addresses the challenges of delivering software in a fast-paced, ever-changing landscape. It allows development teams to collaborate, regularly delivering incremental updates and fixes. CI/CD minimizes manual errors and accelerates the release cycle by automating testing, building, and deployment tasks.

Advantages of CI/CD

Among the many benefits one can gain by leveraging the power of CI/CD in their software delivery process, these are a few to name:

- **Rapid Delivery**: CI/CD enables the rapid release of new features, bug fixes, and updates, ensuring your software remains competitive and relevant in the market.
- **Quality Assurance**: Automated testing at every stage of the pipeline guarantees that only thoroughly tested and reliable code reaches production, minimizing the risk of defects.
- **Efficiency**: Automation reduces the manual overhead in the development process, allowing your team to focus on innovation and code quality.
- **Continuous Feedback**: CI/CD provides continuous feedback, helping teams to identify and address issues early in the development cycle, ultimately saving time and resources.
- **Reliability**: By automating deployment, CI/CD promotes consistency and reliability in the release process, reducing the chances of deployment-related failures.
- **Long-term Stability**: Once stabilized, CI/CD practices are repeatable and reliable over the long run, ensuring that your software development and deployment processes remain robust and adaptable to evolving requirements.

By embracing CI/CD, you can streamline your development and deployment processes, ensuring that your software is delivered faster and with greater reliability and quality. In the upcoming sections, we will explore how Docker seamlessly integrates with CI/CD, enhancing the benefits and efficiency of this essential practice.

Creating Your First CI/CD Pipeline

This section explores the essential concepts of building and versioning Docker images, a fundamental step in incorporating Docker into your CI/CD pipeline.

GitHub Actions

If you're among the many people who keep their source codes in GitHub, then one of the most advanced yet developer-friendly CI/CD pipelines is at your disposal.

GitHub Actions is the name of the CI/CD pipelines hosted and managed by GitHub. Using it will allow you to define numerous tasks that can be performed on different triggers. It will make many of your automation efforts easier because it works!

That said, let's try to write the YAML definition of a CI process that will perform the following task:

On every push to the default branch (main), build the Docker image and push it to the Docker Hub.

To satisfy this requirement, we'll need a YAML file, not very different from the following:

```
name: ci

on:
  push:
    branches:
      - main

permissions:
  contents: read

jobs:
  build:
    runs-on: ubuntu-latest
    env:
      IMAGE_NAME: mastering-docker
    steps:
      - name: Checkout
        uses: actions/checkout@v4
      - name: Set up QEMU
        uses: docker/setup-qemu-action@v3
      - name: Set up Docker Buildx
        uses: docker/setup-buildx-action@v3
      - name: Login to Docker Hub
        uses: docker/login-action@v3
        with:
          username: ${{ secrets.DOCKERHUB_USERNAME }}
          password: ${{ secrets.DOCKERHUB_TOKEN }}
      - name: Calculate short SHA
        id: sha
        run: echo “sha=${GITHUB_SHA::7}” >> $GITHUB_OUTPUT
      - name: Build and push
        uses: docker/build-push-action@v5
        with:
```

```
        tags: |
          ${{ env.IMAGE_NAME }}:${{ steps.sha.outputs.sha }}
        context: .
        push: true
```

The definition of this file is very intuitive, thanks to the friendly API spec of GitHub Actions. Nevertheless, let's try to explain things step by step.

At the top of the file, we define the name of the CI. It is recommended to choose a name that is intuitive to your workflow and the task you're assigning it.

Figure 9.2 shows the CI name on the GitHub Actions page:

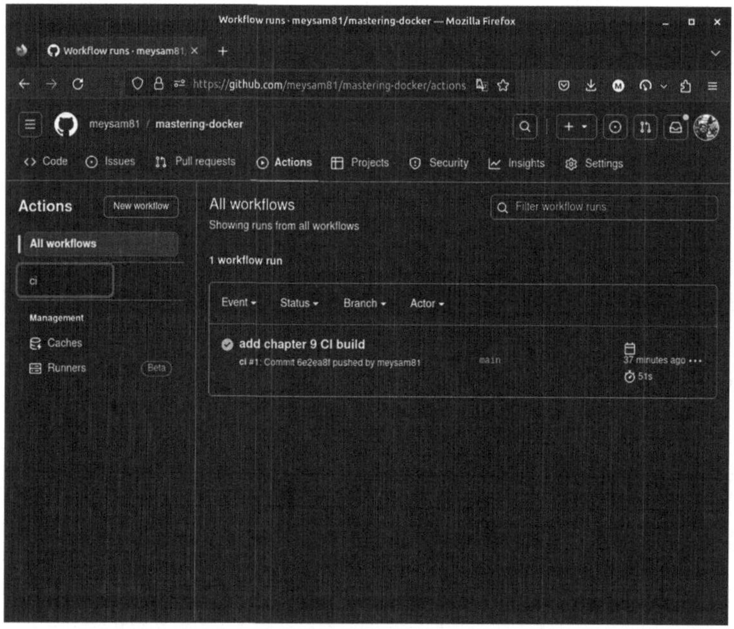

Figure 9.2: *GitHub Actions run for the repository of this book*

After defining the CI name at the top of the file, we specify the trigger. The trigger specifies when this CI will run, that is, which actions will trigger the CI.

```
on:
  push:
    branches:
      - main
```

Next, the permissions attribute specifies what resources this CI has access to and at what level. Since we need to clone the repository to see its content, reading the contents is the most basic permission we should give to the CI.

```
permissions:
  contents: read
```

The last attribute, and the most important one, specifies how many jobs you want to run and what you want each to do. You can have more than one job definition in this section. It's a good idea to have jobs that are small in size and complexity so that they are manageable and do not run for an extended time.

The default timeout for GitHub Actions is 10 hours, which is unlikely you will meet with small tasks. However, it's important to be mindful that if your CI gets bigger in size and complexity, you may need to either tune the timeout yourself or break the job into smaller ones.

Returning to our CI definition file. After specifying the name of the job, for example, `build`, we should also specify the operating system on which we want our CI to run. This ensures that the underlying build system is what your code requires to perform its tasks.

```
jobs:
  build: # <- This is the name of the job
    runs-on: ubuntu-latest
```

For our use case, we are running on the latest Ubuntu machine, which, at the time of writing this book, is Ubuntu 22.04. Unless you have a particular reason, you are advised to use the latest operating system version, for example, macos-latest, to have all the patches and avoid exposing yourself to vulnerabilities and unpatched security holes.

After specifying the operating system, we set one environment variable shared for all the tasks in this job. We can also define per-task environment variables if we don't want to share some values with other steps.

```
jobs:
  build: # <- This is the name of the job
...
...
    env:
      IMAGE_NAME: mastering-docker
```

In each job, we can define one or more steps to perform some actions. These steps can be as simple as running a shell script, or it can use a ready-made and off-the-shelf GitHub Action.

```
jobs:
  build:
...
...
    steps: # <- an array of jobs
```

In our preceding CI definition, we have six tasks, with only one being an inline shell script. The remaining tasks are either community-maintained or official GitHub actions.

The key point here is that off-the-shelf Actions may or may not require input to perform their job, and we use the keyword to pass specific values to them. It accepts one or more key-value pairs that will be passed to the underlying action.

For example, consider the following definition for the final build step:

```
      - name: Build and push
        uses: docker/build-push-action@v5
        with:
          tags: |
            ${{ env.IMAGE_NAME }}:${{ steps.sha.outputs.sha }}
          context: .

          push: true
```

You can see that there are three inputs to this action. The first input specifies the tag of the image.

This is similar to building the Docker image on the CLI using the following command:

```
docker build --tag myimage .
```

The keyword context specifies where the working directory of the Docker is when building the image. While we can also pass the dockerfile as another input, specifying context is enough if the context and the Dockerfile are in the same path.

The final input determines whether or not we want to push the image after the build is complete.

One critical information to point out here is the use of GitHub Secrets in the CI definition file with the syntax `${{ secrets.DOCKERHUB_TOKEN }}`. This key will be replaced by its value, as specified in the GitHub Secrets tab within the Settings of each repository, as shown in *Figure* 9.3.

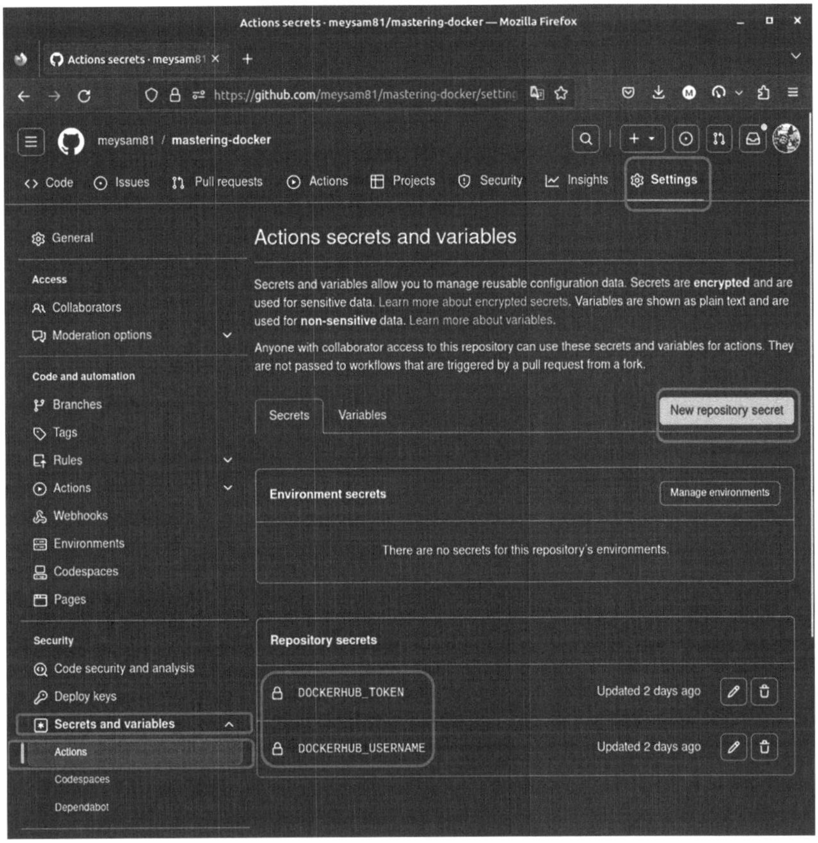

***Figure 9.3:** GitHub Secrets settings page for the repository of this book*

How can a simple docker build on the CLI become complex with multiple steps?

You will see multiple steps in a GitHub Actions workflow for building and pushing a Docker image to provide a well-structured and extensible approach to containerization and CI/CD. While this definition may seem to have many steps, each step serves a specific purpose, offering flexibility and robustness to the workflow:

1. **Set up QEMU**: This step sets up QEMU (Quick EMUlator), which is necessary for multi-architecture builds. It ensures compatibility and support for various CPU architectures.

2. **Set up Docker Buildx**: This action sets up Docker Buildx, an extension to the standard Docker CLI that provides features for building multi-platform images. It's beneficial when you want to build images for multiple CPU architectures or platforms.

3. **Log in to Docker Hub**: This step logs into Docker Hub to authenticate before you can push images to it. It uses your Docker Hub credentials stored as secrets.
4. **Build and push**: The workflow's core step is to build the Docker image and push it to the Docker Hub. This Action is versatile, allowing you to specify various parameters like image tags and build arguments.

Overall, each step ensures a smooth and well-orchestrated process, even in more complex scenarios. It's important to note that you can customize these steps based on your project's requirements. Suppose your use case is straightforward and doesn't require multi-architecture builds. In that case, you can simplify the workflow by omitting the QEMU and Buildx setup steps, as long as your Dockerfile is compatible with the default architecture of your GitHub runner (typically `amd64` on GitHub-hosted runners). The level of complexity in a GitHub Actions workflow depends on the specific needs of your project.

That said, a simple GitHub Action that builds only for amd64 CPU architecture can be as simple as shown in the following code snippet:

```
name: ci

on:
  push:
    branches:
      - main

jobs:
  build:
    runs-on: ubuntu-latest
    steps:
      - name: Checkout code
        uses: actions/checkout@v4
      - name: Build and Push Docker Image
        env:
          DOCKER_USERNAME: ${{ secrets.DOCKERHUB_USERNAME }}
          DOCKER_PASSWORD: ${{ secrets.DOCKERHUB_TOKEN }}
        run: |
          docker build -t user/app:latest .
          echo $DOCKER_PASSWORD | docker login -u $DOCKER_USERNAME
--password-stdin
          docker push user/app:latest
```

As you can see, building and pushing a Docker image can be as simple as this last example.

Once again, every project has specific needs, and some may not even need a multi-platform build. For those cases, you can quickly drop QEMU and Buildx for the sake of simplicity.

Now that you have seen an example in GitHub Action, let's write another CI for GitLab.

GitLab CI

GitLab is a robust DevOps platform integrating automation and **CI/CD** seamlessly into the software development lifecycle. It offers a single, unified environment for source code management, continuous integration, and continuous deployment. One of its primary benefits is that it simplifies the DevOps process by providing a single interface for various stages of development, from version control and issue tracking to building, testing, and deploying applications. GitLab's top features include built-in **CI/CD** pipelines that are easily configured using a `.gitlab-ci.yml` file, a container registry for storing Docker images, integrated security scanning, and extensive project and team collaboration tools, making it an all-in-one solution for modern software development teams.

With that introduction out of the way, let's write a CI definition with the exact requirement to build a Docker image and push it to Docker Hub:

```
docker-build:
  image: docker:cli
  stage: build
  services:
    - docker:dind
  variables:
    DOCKER_IMAGE_NAME: meysam81/mastering-docker-chapter9-nginx-gitlab
  before_script:
    - docker login -u "$DOCKERHUB_USERNAME" -p "$DOCKERHUB_TOKEN"
  script:
    - cd chapter9/github-actions/
    - docker build -t "$DOCKER_IMAGE_NAME:$CI_COMMIT_SHORT_SHA" .
    - docker push "$DOCKER_IMAGE_NAME:$CI_COMMIT_SHORT_SHA"
    - |
      if [[ "$CI_COMMIT_BRANCH" == "$CI_DEFAULT_BRANCH" ]]; then
        docker tag "$DOCKER_IMAGE_NAME:$CI_COMMIT_SHORT_SHA"
```

```
“$DOCKER_IMAGE_NAME:latest”
        docker push “$DOCKER_IMAGE_NAME:latest”
      fi
  rules:
    - if: $CI_COMMIT_BRANCH
      exists:
        - chapter9/github-actions/Dockerfile
```

While the YAML file definitions have some GitLab-specific syntax and specifications, the idea remains the same, so the final implementation is similar.

The same variables that we passed as “secrets” in the GitHub workflow definition are used as environment variables in the GitLab counterpart. They serve the same idea and purpose but in different ways. *Figure* 9.4 shows how a GitLab secret is defined.

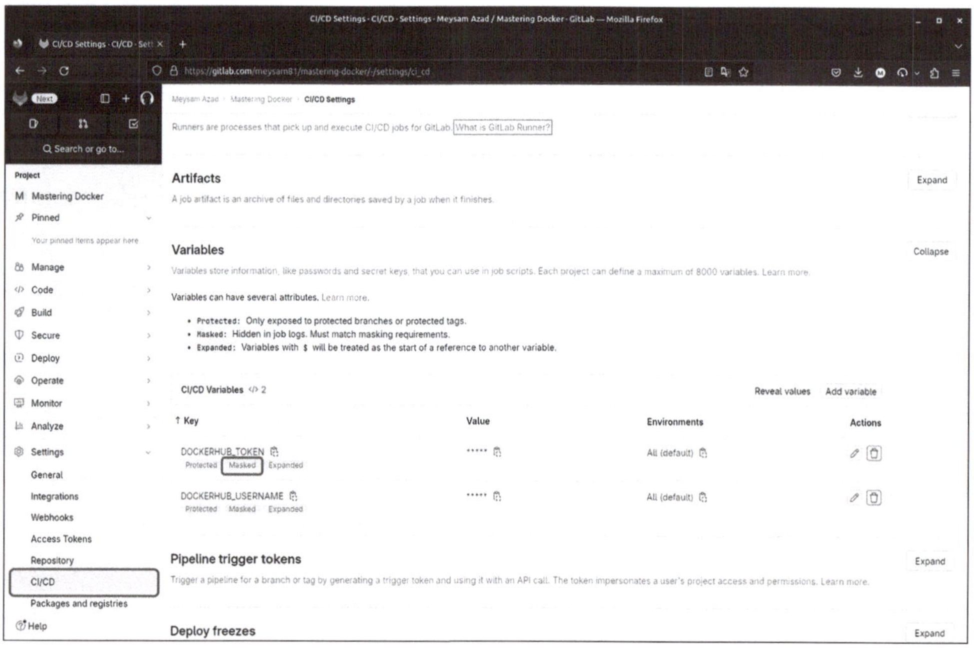

Figure 9.4: *GitLab Masked Variables for the repository of this book*

The property that makes a variable a “secret” in the GitLab pipeline is masked. It will modify the output of the pipeline logs so that the secure variable won’t be printed in the output as plaintext. You can see an example run of a pipeline in *Figure* 9.5.

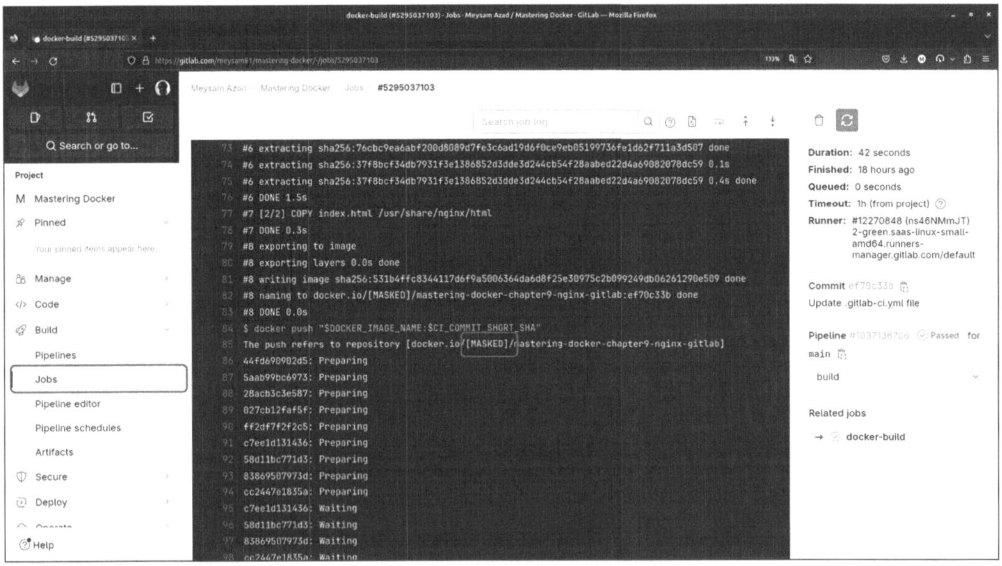

Figure 9.5: *GitLab masked variables not printed on the screen*

To provide some context, GitHub also masks the secret variables with an asterisk (*) character; essentially, it's the same idea implemented differently.

The similarities between these two CI definitions might make you wonder; once you have learned to work with one **CI/CD** stack, picking up others will be quite easy.

So far, both CI definitions are triggered when a new commit is pushed to the default branch (usually `main` or `master`). This is a potent behavior when you want continuous integration, that is, when a code change occurs, the CI gets triggered, and a new image is built.

You may add additional steps to the CI, such as deploying the built image into some environments. As an additional tip, just know that the last step (deployment) is called Continuous Deployment (CD), whereas the first part (building the image) is called Continuous Integration (CI).

In modern software development, one thing that can improve the software delivery processes is isolating the CI and CD steps. This way, you can build and create your application and save it to an artifact repository, for example, Nexus Repository Manager or Artifactory, and then using one of the available CD tools, deploy the said build into production, for example, using ArgoCD or FluxCD. This is out of the scope of this book, but it's good for you to have a clear picture of where each tool takes a stance.

Docker CI/CD Integration Best Practices

You have seen two concrete examples of building Docker images in two of the most famous git repositories. It's time to provide some tips on how to optimize your build and your pipelines as follows:

- **Use Multi-Stage Builds**: Employ multi-stage builds in your Dockerfiles to minimize image sizes and optimize build times. Separate the build and runtime environments to reduce unnecessary dependencies. *Chapter 3: Building and Managing Docker Images* provided an in-depth guide on optimizing your builds with multi-stage.
- **Automate Testing**: Implement automated testing of Docker images in your `CI/CD` pipeline. Include unit, integration, and security tests to ensure image reliability.
- **Leverage Caching**: Use Docker image caching to speed up builds. Cache dependencies and layers to avoid rebuilding from scratch. You will see an example later in this chapter on how to use caching in `CI/CD`.
- **Version Control for Dockerfiles**: Place Dockerfiles and other `CI/CD` configuration files under version control. This ensures reproducibility and traceability.
- **Immutable Images**: Treat Docker images as immutable artifacts. Avoid making changes directly within containers; create new images with updates.
- **Secret Management**: Securely safeguard sensitive data like API keys and credentials using Docker secrets or environment variables. Other alternatives in cloud providers include but are not limited to AWS Secrets Manager, Azure Vault, and GCP Secret Manager.
- **Continuous Monitoring**: Implement continuous monitoring and logging of Docker containers to identify and resolve issues promptly.
- **Image Scanning**: Integrate image scanning tools to identify vulnerabilities in Docker images and ensure security compliance. You will see an example of image scanning integrated into the CI later in this chapter.
- **Documentation**: Document your Docker-centric `CI/CD` pipelines. Describe image build processes, dependencies, and deployment strategies for better collaboration among team members.
- **Pipeline as Code**: Define your `CI/CD` pipeline as code using tools like `Jenkinsfile` (for Jenkins), `.gitlab-ci.yml` (for GitLab), or GitHub Actions. This ensures that pipeline configurations are versioned and easily replicable.

- **Artifact Repositories**: Store and manage Docker images in artifact repositories like Docker Hub, AWS ECR, or Google Container Registry. This simplifies image sharing and distribution.
- **Retain Historical Images**: Keep a version history of Docker images to enable rollbacks and troubleshooting.
- **Custom Base Images**: Build and use custom base images with only essential dependencies, which can help maintain consistency and security.

Multi-Platform Builds

Multi-platform builds in Docker and `CI/CD` context involve building and running container images for various CPU architectures and platforms within a single pipeline –for example, AMD, ARM, and more.

This allows you to create versatile, cross-compatible images that cater to a broader range of infrastructure requirements, enhancing the portability and flexibility of your containerized applications. In the upcoming sections, we'll delve into the intricacies of multi-platform support and its significant advantages in modern software development and deployment pipelines.

Necessity of Multi-Platform Builds

The need for multi-platform support in containerization and CI/CD arises from the diversity of hardware and operating system architectures in today's computing landscape. Different devices and cloud providers often require containers built for specific CPU architectures, such as ARM, x86, or AMD64, and distinct platforms like Linux, Windows, and macOS.

Multi-platform support ensures that your containerized applications can seamlessly run on a wide range of infrastructure without modification. For instance, a single Docker image could run on an x86-based server and an ARM-based IoT device, simplifying deployment across heterogeneous environments.

With multi-platform support, managing multiple image variants for different platforms would be simpler, time-consuming, and prone to errors. This flexibility enhances the adaptability of your applications to diverse deployment scenarios, making multi-platform builds a crucial aspect of modern containerization. In the following sections, we'll explore how to implement multi-platform support effectively within your CI/CD pipelines.

Multi-Platform Build in Action

Using GitHub Actions, we will provide an example of building a Docker image for multiple platforms and CPU architectures. Hence, the title - pun intended.

The mission in this example is to build our Docker image for both MacOS and Linux machines and two CPU architectures: AMD64 and ARM64.

To go through this example, we'll use our first snippet, which is compatible with our requirements.

Apart from other steps in the job to build and push the image to the container registry, here are the changes that will be added to the earlier GitHub Action:

```
- name: Build and push
  uses: docker/build-push-action@v5
  with:
    tags: |
      ${{ env.IMAGE_NAME }}:${{ steps.sha.outputs.sha }}
    platforms: linux/amd64,linux/arm64,darwin/amd64,darwin/arm64
    context: .
    push: true
```

The only difference from the last snippet is the added `platforms` keyword. There are three ways Docker documentation recommends when building a Docker image for multiple platforms as follows:

1. The first one is QEMU, the easiest to use if the builder supports it and has the smallest overhead from an operation perspective. We're using this method in our examples.
2. The second one is to use a native Docker build on every node that requires the image. This one will be more expensive since we must have a compatible node for every build.
3. Lastly, and if the base image supports this, you can build the image using the cross-compile method, in which the host node can differ from the target Docker image OS and CPU architecture, but Docker Buildx will take care of all the details.

The method you choose to use can heavily depend on your application and its dependencies and libraries. However, for our demo application, using QEMU is sufficient.

Triggering the CI above will give us a Docker image with four architectures, as seen in the specification.

The end Docker image will have the following tags and architectures, as shown in *Figure* 9.6.

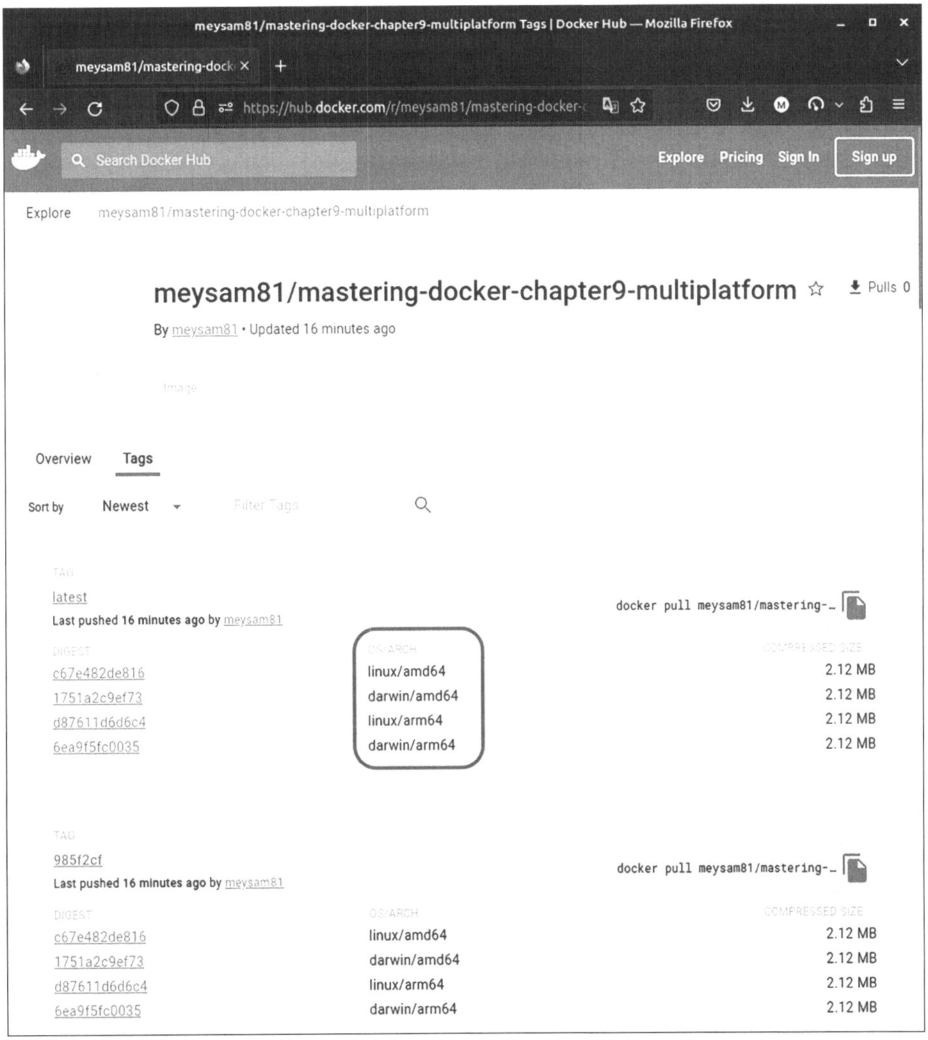

Figure 9.6: *DockerHub repository for the Docker image of this book*

This is a powerful outcome if we aim to deploy the application to different machines and environments with varied underlying CPU architectures.

With this functionality within Docker, we can deploy our app to a full-blown AMD machine and a minimal IOT with an ARM CPU. This is only one example of many possibilities. The sky is the limit!

Now that you know about multi-platform build, it's time to discuss the integration of Docker Compose and CI/CD pipeline.

Docker Compose in CI/CD

You have seen the powers of Docker Compose in *Chapter 6: Docker Compose for Simplified Application Deployment.*

On the other hand, you have seen a small glimpse of possibilities when you leverage the CI/CD in your development and delivery processes.

It's time to combine the two and provide the extreme power you can have when using the best of both.

Managing multi-container applications in CI/CD pipelines using Docker Compose provides several key features and advantages. Here's a non-exhaustive list of features and capabilities:

- **Application Definition**: Docker Compose allows you to define your entire multi-container application stack in a single, version-controlled YAML file. This file specifies the services, networks, volumes, and their configurations. This is a significant advantage in CI/CD as it ensures consistency and reproducibility.
- **Service Dependencies**: Docker Compose handles service dependencies, ensuring that services are started in the correct order. This is crucial in CI/CD pipelines, where components may rely on one another. You can specify dependencies explicitly, ensuring that services are only started when their dependencies are ready.
- **Parallel Testing**: In CI/CD, testing is a critical step. Docker Compose enables parallel testing of services. Multiple test containers can be run simultaneously, speeding up the overall testing process and providing faster feedback to developers.
- **Isolation**: Docker Compose creates isolated environments for multi-container applications, preventing service conflicts. In CI/CD, this isolation is valuable as it ensures that changes in one service don't affect others during testing and deployment.
- **Scalability**: Docker Compose allows you to scale services horizontally by specifying the desired number of containers for a service. This feature is beneficial in CI/CD to simulate different usage scenarios and ensure that the application can scale efficiently when deployed to production.
- **Volume Mounting**: You can define volumes in Docker Compose to persist data between runs. In CI/CD, this is crucial for database services

or services that must retain the state between tests. Volumes ensure that data isn't lost when containers are destroyed and recreated.

- **Environment Variables**: Docker Compose allows you to manage environment variables for each service, making it easy to configure services differently in various CI/CD stages (for example, development, testing, production).
- **Testing and Deployment Consistency**: Docker Compose ensures that the same application stack used in testing is deployed in production, reducing the risk of issues caused by differences in configurations. This consistency is vital in CI/CD pipelines to guarantee that what's tested matches what's deployed.
- **Integration with CI Tools**: Docker Compose integrates seamlessly with popular CI/CD platforms and tools, such as Jenkins, GitLab CI/CD, and GitHub Actions. You can include Docker Compose commands in your CI/CD scripts to define, build, and manage your application stack.
- **Easy Tear Down**: Docker Compose makes it simple to tear down the entire application stack when testing is complete. This benefits CI/CD by ensuring that resources are efficiently released, and environments are clean for subsequent runs.
- **Custom Network Configuration**: You can define custom networks in Docker Compose, allowing services to communicate over isolated networks. This feature is helpful for more complex applications and microservices architectures.

Now that you have seen why they can be so powerful together, let's provide an example:

```
version: "3"
services:
  web:
    image: my-web-app:latest
    ports:
      - "80:80"
  database:
    image: postgres:16
    environment:
      POSTGRES_USER: user
      POSTGRES_PASSWORD: password
  tests:
    build:
```

```
      context: .
      dockerfile: Dockerfile.tests
    depends_on:
      - web
      - database
```

In this Docker Compose YAML file, we can see the following definitions:

- **Application Definition**: We define three services: a web application, a PostgreSQL database, and a testing service.
- **Service Dependencies**: The test service depends on the web and database services. This ensures that tests are only run when the required services are up and running.
- **Parallel Testing**: The tests service is configured to build from a Dockerfile (Dockerfile.tests) that contains the testing code. Multiple test containers based on this Dockerfile can be run simultaneously, enabling parallel testing of the web application's functionality.

In an example CI/CD pipeline, the following can be one of the many desired processes:

- The pipeline will spin up the defined services using this Docker Compose file.
- Tests can be executed in parallel, improving the overall testing speed.
- Dependencies are managed, ensuring that services start in the correct order.
- Environment variables and network configurations can be tailored for different stages of the CI/CD pipeline (for example, development, testing, production).
- Once testing is complete, Docker Compose allows easy tear-down of the entire application stack, ensuring that resources are efficiently released.

Let's see what the CI/CD would look like for this specification:

```
name: CI/CD Pipeline

on:
  push:
    branches:
      - main

jobs:
  build:
```

```
    runs-on: ubuntu-latest
    steps:
    - name: Checkout code
      uses: actions/checkout@v4
    - name: Build Docker Images
      run: docker-compose -f docker-compose.yml --push build

  test:
    runs-on: ubuntu-latest
    needs: build
    steps:
    - name: Checkout code
      uses: actions/checkout@v4
    - name: Set up Docker Compose
      run: docker-compose -f docker-compose.yml up -d
    - name: Run Tests
      run: docker-compose -f docker-compose.yml run tests

    - name: Tear down Docker Compose
      run: docker-compose -f docker-compose.yml down
```

In this CI/CD pipeline, we have the following jobs:

Build Stage: The pipeline is triggered when the code is pushed to the main branch.

The first job is to build the Docker images for the defined services in `docker-compose.yml`.

The test job runs after the build job completes (notice the keyword needs). It then sets up Docker Compose to start the application stack and runs tests within the tests service.

Security and Docker in CI/CD

Security is a paramount concern when integrating Docker into CI/CD pipelines. In today's fast-paced development and deployment landscape, ensuring the security of containerized applications is crucial.

Docker's unique architecture and the dynamic nature of CI/CD workflows introduce specific security considerations. In the upcoming sections, we will delve into various security aspects, covering topics such as image scanning, vulnerability management, access control, and best practices to bolster security in your Docker-based CI/CD processes.

Security Considerations

When using Docker in CI/CD pipelines, addressing various security considerations is essential to safeguard your containerized applications and the overall development and deployment process. Here are some key aspects to consider:

- **Image Scanning and Vulnerability Management**: Perform image scanning to identify and mitigate vulnerabilities in container images. Utilize tools like Clair, Trivy, or Docker Security Scanning to identify potential security risks in your Docker images. Regularly update base images and third-party dependencies to patch known vulnerabilities.
- **Access Control and Permissions**: Enforce access control and permissions to ensure only authorized personnel can interact with Docker and Docker-related resources. Implement role-based access control (RBAC) to restrict who can create, modify, and deploy Docker images and containers.
- **Securing Docker Daemon**: The Docker daemon should run with least-privilege access rights. Limit who can access the Docker daemon and restrict its capabilities using Linux namespaces and cgroups. Use Docker's built-in authentication mechanisms and TLS encryption for secure communication with the Docker daemon.
- **Content Trust and Image Signing**: Enable Docker Content Trust to ensure the integrity and authenticity of container images. Digital signatures provide trust in image sources, preventing the execution of unauthorized or tampered images.
- **Least-Privilege Principle**: Follow the principle of least privilege by defining minimal capabilities for your containers. Remove unnecessary privileges and any capabilities that allow privilege escalation.
- **Security Best Practices**: Adhere to security best practices when creating Dockerfiles. Avoid running containers as the root user, drop unnecessary privileges, use the HEALTHCHECK instruction, and minimize the attack surface by only installing essential packages.
- **Network Security**: Isolate containers and network traffic as needed. Use Docker's network modes to control container networking. Employ network segmentation and firewall rules to control traffic between containers and external resources.

- **Monitoring and Logging**: Implement real-time monitoring and logging to detect and respond to security incidents promptly. Use Docker's logging drivers and consider container security solutions for deeper insights into container behavior.
- **Orchestration Security**: If using container orchestration platforms such as Kubernetes or Docker Swarm, secure these platforms as well. Follow best practices for securing orchestrators and the entire CI/CD ecosystem.
- **Compliance and Auditing**: Establish policies and practices to comply with industry standards and regulatory requirements (for example, GDPR, HIPAA). Regularly audit and assess the security of your Docker images and containers.
- **Container Runtime Security**: Consider runtime security solutions that provide runtime protection and anomaly detection for containers. Tools like Falco can help monitor and alert on suspicious container behavior.
- **Automated Security Testing**: Integrate security testing into your CI/CD pipeline. This includes static analysis, dynamic analysis, and runtime security testing to catch vulnerabilities early in development.

In the subsequent sections, we will explore these security aspects in more detail and provide practical guidance on addressing them effectively in your Docker-based CI/CD pipelines.

Image Scanning and Vulnerability Management

Securing Docker images in CI/CD pipelines involves image scanning, vulnerability management, and best practices. Here's a comprehensive overview of these aspects:

- **Image Scanning**: Image scanning tools like Trivy, Clair, or Docker Security Scanning are essential for identifying vulnerabilities in container images. These tools assess images for known security issues and provide reports with severity levels.
- **Continuous Scanning**: Integrate image scanning into your CI/CD pipeline to scan images at each stage, from development to production. Automated scanning ensures that vulnerabilities are identified and addressed early in the process.
- **Dependency Updates**: Regularly update your base images and dependencies to include security patches and updates. Tools like Renovate can help automate this process by checking for new versions of packages and dependencies.

Best Practices

To follow the industry's best practices and standards, the following is a guideline to help you enhance the security aspect of your application before it's too late:

- **Minimalistic Base Images**: Start with minimalistic base images to reduce the attack surface. Alpine Linux and distroless images are popular choices that contain only essential components.
- **Non-Root User**: Run containers with a non-root user whenever possible. Limit the privileges granted to containers to reduce the risk of privilege escalation.
- **Health Checks**: Include `HEALTHCHECK` instructions in Dockerfiles to ensure containers are running as expected. Define custom health checks based on your application's requirements.
- **Multi-Stage Builds**: Use multi-stage builds to create lean production images. Build artifacts in one stage and copy only necessary files to the final image. This reduces image size and potential vulnerabilities.
- **Container Security Best Practices**: Adhere to general container security best practices, such as not storing sensitive data in environment variables, not exposing unnecessary ports, and ensuring that you're only running required processes.

Image Scanning in CI

Now that you have seen some of the theories, let's provide a practical example: integrating image scanning as automation to the development process in a way that can be easy for us to track and remediate.

The following GitHub Action workflow is an example, scanning the built image (on another job) on every push to the default branch, every pull request against the default branch, and periodically (every midnight).

```
name: ci

on:
  pull_request:
    branches:
      - main
  push:
    branches:
      - main
  schedule:
```

```
    - cron: 0 0 * * *

permissions:
  contents: read
  security-events: write
  pull-requests: write

jobs:
  trivy-scan:
    runs-on: ubuntu-latest
    steps:
      - name: Login to Docker Hub
        uses: docker/login-action@v3
        with:
          password: ${{ secrets.DOCKERHUB_TOKEN }}
          username: ${{ secrets.DOCKERHUB_USERNAME }}
      - id: docker-scout
        name: Docker Scout
        uses: docker/scout-action@v1
        with:
          command: compare
          github-token: ${{ secrets.GITHUB_TOKEN }}
          ignore-unchanged: true
          image: my-user/my-image:latest
          only-severities: critical,high
          write-comment: ${{ github.event_name == 'pull_request' }}
      - id: docker-scout-cves
        name: Analyze for critical and high CVEs
        uses: docker/scout-action@v1
        with:
          command: cves
          image: ${{ matrix.image }}:${{ env.IMAGE_TAG }}
          sarif-file: sarif.output.json
          summary: true
      - id: upload-sarif
        if: ${{ github.ref == 'refs/heads/main' }}
        name: Upload SARIF result
        uses: github/codeql-action/upload-sarif@v2
        with:
          sarif_file: sarif.output.json
```

Configuring the scan to run intervals and automatically without an external trigger is recommended since packages go outdated frequently, and you wouldn't want to miss out on some security patch upgrades to expose your application(s) and your users.

When the preceding CI is committed to the source code, you can see any vulnerability in the GitHub Security Tab, as shown in *Figure* 9.7. However, you wouldn't see anything now since this app didn't have any!

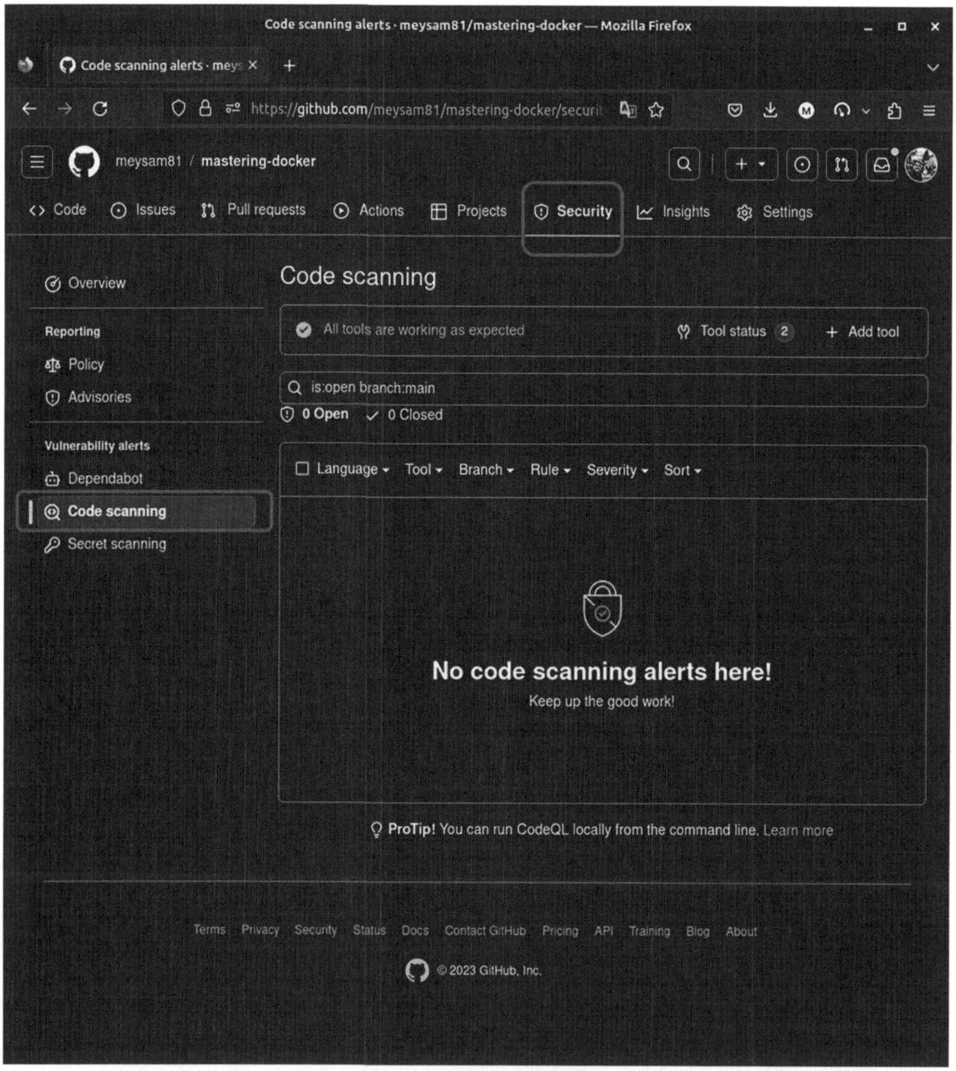

***Figure* 9.7:** *GitHub Security tab*

Monitoring

Monitoring and logging are critical in ensuring your containerized applications' health, performance, and security within CI/CD pipelines. We will cover the specifics of monitoring containerized services, aggregating logs, and using these insights to proactively identify and address issues in your Docker-based CI/CD workflows.

Tooling Available for Monitoring CI/CD

Monitoring Docker containers in CI/CD pipelines is essential for ensuring your containerized applications' health, performance, and security. Here are some of the available tools at your disposal:

- **Container Orchestration Tools**: If you're using container orchestration tools like Kubernetes or Docker Swarm in your CI/CD pipeline, leverage their built-in monitoring capabilities. These tools offer native support for monitoring and provide insights into container health, resource usage, and application performance.
- **Docker Stats and API**: Docker provides a variety of ways to access container metrics. The `docker stats` command offers a quick overview of container resource usage (CPU, memory, and more). You can also access container metrics programmatically using the Docker Remote API.
- **cAdvisor (Container Advisor)**: Google's cAdvisor is a lightweight container that collects and exports container metrics to various monitoring systems. You can run cAdvisor as a sidecar container to monitor other containers in your CI/CD pipeline.
- **Prometheus and Grafana**: Prometheus is a popular open-source monitoring system designed for containerized environments. It allows you to collect and query metrics from Docker containers and services. Grafana, when integrated with Prometheus, provides a visualization layer for monitoring dashboards.
- **Custom Monitoring Scripts**: You can create custom monitoring scripts or applications that interact with Docker's API to collect specific metrics. These scripts can be run as part of your CI/CD pipeline to gather container-related data.
- **Alerting and Thresholds**: Establish alerting thresholds based on the monitored metrics. For example, set alerts for high CPU usage, memory consumption, or container failures. Tools like Prometheus Alertmanager or third-party alerting services can be used.

- **Log Aggregation**: Log aggregation tools like the ELK Stack (Elasticsearch, Logstash, Kibana) or the EFK Stack (Elasticsearch, Fluentd, and Kibana) can centralize and analyze container logs. This provides insights into application behavior and can help identify issues.
- **Container Orchestration Metrics**: Container orchestration platforms often expose additional metrics related to the orchestration. For example, Kubernetes exposes pod and node health metrics, which can be monitored and alerted upon.
- **Security Monitoring**: Incorporate security monitoring into your CI/CD pipeline. Tools like Falco can help you detect and alert suspicious container behavior, potentially indicating security threats or vulnerabilities.
- **Continuous Integration and Deployment Monitoring**: Monitor the CI/CD pipeline to ensure that builds, tests, and deployments function as expected. Tools like Jenkins, GitLab CI/CD, and Travis CI offer built-in monitoring and reporting capabilities.
- **Historical Data and Trend Analysis**: Store historical monitoring data to analyze trends and make informed decisions about scaling, resource allocation, and overall application performance improvements.
- **Proactive Issue Resolution**: Use monitoring data to proactively address issues, scaling containers up or down as needed and ensuring that your CI/CD pipeline is responsive to application requirements.

Incorporating effective monitoring into your Docker-based CI/CD pipeline lets you gain insights into your containerized applications' behavior, identify performance bottlenecks, and promptly address security concerns. By combining the right tools and practices, you can ensure that your containers run smoothly in production and remain aligned with your application's quality and security standards.

Log Management

Introducing log management and analysis for Dockerized applications is crucial for gaining insights into your containerized environment's behavior, diagnosing issues, and ensuring the security and performance of your applications. The following is a non-exhaustive list of resources for the subject matter.

- **Centralized Log Collection**: Centralize log collection from Docker containers and services. Using tools like Fluentd, Logstash, or Filebeat, you can gather logs from multiple containers and send them to a centralized location for further analysis.

- **Structured Logging**: Implement structured logging to standardize log formats. Structured logs are more straightforward to parse and analyze, enabling more efficient log management and searching.
- **Log Drivers and Output**: Docker offers various log drivers, such as JSON-file, syslog, or journald. Choose a log driver that fits your needs and integrates well with your log management stack.
- **Elasticsearch, Logstash, and Kibana (ELK Stack)**: ELK Stack is a popular choice for log management. Elasticsearch stores logs using the Logstash processes and enriches them, and Kibana provides a user-friendly interface for searching and visualizing logs.
- **Fluentd and Fluent Bit**: Fluentd and Fluent Bit are lightweight log collectors and processors. They can gather logs from Docker containers and forward them to various output destinations, including Elasticsearch, databases, or cloud storage.
- **Container Log Tags**: Add tags to container logs to distinguish between services and environments. This helps in filtering and categorizing logs for analysis.
- **Log Rotation and Retention**: Implement log rotation and retention policies to manage log files efficiently. Configure how long logs should be retained and when old logs should be rotated or deleted.
- **Alerting and Monitoring**: Set up alerting rules to trigger notifications when specific log events or patterns occur. Tools like Prometheus Alertmanager can help with this.
- **Custom Log Analysis**: Create custom log analysis scripts or applications to extract meaningful insights from logs. These scripts can identify specific events, errors, or trends.
- **Security Event Monitoring**: Monitor logs for security events and anomalies. Tools like Splunk or SIEM (Security Information and Event Management) can provide real-time security monitoring.
- **Performance Monitoring**: Analyze logs to understand application performance. Look for patterns related to response times, resource consumption, and application errors that impact performance.
- **Real-Time Alerts**: Set up real-time alerts to be notified immediately when critical log events occur. This proactive approach helps in quickly addressing issues and minimizing downtime.
- **Historical Log Data Analysis**: Store log data for historical analysis and trend identification. Historical data is valuable for spotting recurring issues and planning improvements.

- **Compliance and Auditing**: Comply with industry standards and regulatory requirements by ensuring that log data is securely stored and accessible for auditing purposes.
- **User Access Control**: Implement access control for log data. Control who can access and analyze logs to maintain data privacy and security.

Introducing log management and analysis into your Dockerized CI/CD pipelines is essential for maintaining the health and security of your containerized applications. By collecting, analyzing, and acting upon log data, you can detect and resolve issues promptly, improve performance, and ensure compliance with security and regulatory standards.

Container Observability

Tools and practices for container observability are crucial for gaining real-time insights into your Dockerized applications, understanding their behavior, and efficiently troubleshooting issues. In the following two sections, you will see how to enhance visibility into your containerized application and the practices around the tooling.

Observability Tools

The tools available for monitoring are countless, and each application may need its specific monitoring for efficient observability. Nevertheless, the following are some of the top ones in the industry:

- **Prometheus**: An open-source monitoring and alerting toolkit designed for containerized environments. Prometheus allows you to collect and store metrics from Docker containers and services and set up custom alerting rules.
- **Grafana**: Often used with Prometheus, Grafana provides a visualization layer for creating dashboards and visualizing monitoring data. It's a powerful tool for analyzing metrics and trends.
- **Jaeger**: A distributed tracing system that allows you to trace requests as they flow through your containerized applications. It helps identify bottlenecks and troubleshoot performance issues.
- **Zipkin**: Another distributed tracing system that enables you to track and analyze the flow of requests across microservices within your container ecosystem.
- **OpenTelemetry**: A set of APIs, libraries, agents, and instrumentation to provide application observability. It supports tracing, metrics, and logging

to gain insights into the performance and behavior of your containerized applications.

- **Sysdig**: A container monitoring and security platform that offers visibility into container performance, security, and compliance. It includes features like anomaly detection and forensics.
- **Datadog**: A cloud-based monitoring and analytics platform that provides observability into containerized applications. It offers real-time performance metrics, logs, and traces.

Best Practices

Having the tools mentioned above in mind, here are some general recommendations you can apply to your workflows:

- **Instrumentation**: Instrument your applications with appropriate libraries to gather metrics, logs, and traces. Use open standards like OpenTelemetry for consistency.
- **Labels and Tags**: Apply labels or tags to your containers, services, and metrics to provide context and facilitate filtering and searching.
- **Custom Metrics**: Define custom metrics that align with your application's performance and business KPIs. These custom metrics provide insights unique to your application.
- **Structured Logging**: Implement structured logging to facilitate log analysis. Use a consistent and machine-readable log format.
- **Service Mesh**: Consider using a service mesh like Istio or Linkerd to gain additional observability features, including circuit breaking, load balancing, and end-to-end tracing.
- **Alerting Rules**: Establish alerting rules based on your monitoring data to receive notifications when specific conditions or thresholds are met.
- **Real-Time Dashboard**: Create real-time dashboards to visualize critical metrics, performance trends, and the status of your containerized services.
- **Anomaly Detection**: Implement anomaly detection to identify abnormal behavior in your containerized applications. This can help you discover issues before they impact performance or reliability.
- **Logs Aggregation**: Aggregate logs from various sources into a centralized system for more straightforward analysis. Tools like the ELK Stack (Elasticsearch, Logstash, Kibana) or cloud-based log management solutions can assist with log aggregation.

- **Documentation and Onboarding**: Ensure your team knows the observability tools and practices. Provide documentation and onboarding sessions to maximize the value of these tools.
- **Continuous Improvement**: Continuously analyze and improve observability practices. Review metrics, logs, and traces regularly to refine your monitoring and debugging strategies.

By incorporating these observability tools and best practices, you can gain an in-depth insight into your containerized applications and ensure their reliability, performance, and security throughout your CI/CD pipelines. Container observability plays a vital role in maintaining the health and robustness of your Dockerized ecosystem.

Figure 9.8: *A picture of a little girl and a robot.*
source: https://unsplash.com/photos/photo-of-girl-laying-left-hand-on-white-digital-robot-0E_vhMVqL9g

Conclusion

In our journey through this chapter, we've witnessed the transformative power of Docker within the realm of Continuous Integration and Continuous Deployment (CI/CD). Docker's containerization technology has truly revolutionized how we approach modern software delivery.

Docker's lightweight and portable containers have emerged as the linchpin of efficient CI/CD practices, addressing the age-old challenge of "it works on my machine." Packaging applications and their dependencies within containers have achieved reproducibility, consistency, and enhanced collaboration between development and operations teams. Docker ensures that what's developed in a developer's local environment reaches production – no more surprises or compatibility issues.

We've also explored the advantages of integrating Docker into CI/CD pipelines. Docker's role in speeding delivery, ensuring quality, and enhancing reliability cannot be overstated. It's not just about containerization; it's about forging a seamless path from development to production, underpinned by consistent and scalable deployments.

Security considerations have also come to the forefront of our journey. Image scanning and vulnerability management are critical to securing Docker containers. Access control and least-privilege principles ensure that your CI/CD pipeline remains safeguarded against unauthorized access and privilege escalation.

The pillars of monitoring and logging have been underscored for keeping a watchful eye on containerized applications. Real-time monitoring and log analysis enable us to quickly unearth performance bottlenecks and security vulnerabilities, offering a proactive edge in issue resolution.

Lastly, we've embraced the concept of observability. With tools like Prometheus and Grafana, we've gained unparalleled visibility into our Dockerized applications. Coupled with best practices, such as structured logging and anomaly detection, observability helps us steer our CI/CD ship with precision and confidence.

As we conclude this chapter, we encourage you to harness the insights garnered here to elevate your CI/CD workflows. Docker is a steadfast ally in this endeavor, fostering efficiency, uniformity, and dependability in software delivery.

In our next chapter, "*Docker on Cloud Platforms*," we'll traverse the path of taking your Dockerized applications to the cloud. Here, we'll unveil the dynamic realms of container orchestration, cloud-native solutions, and the bountiful advantages of cloud platforms for scalability, availability, and resilience. Stay tuned for a comprehensive exploration of Docker in the cloud.

References and Useful Links

Here are some useful links and official sources that you can use to continue your study on the subject matter further:

- Official Docker documentation offers comprehensive guides, tutorials, and reference materials. Website: https://docs.docker.com/
- Kubernetes documentation is a valuable resource for those interested in container orchestration. Website: https://kubernetes.io/docs/home/

- Prometheus documentation provides in-depth information on setting up and using Prometheus for monitoring. Website: https://prometheus.io/docs/
- Grafana's official documentation guides users on creating interactive and shareable dashboards. Website: https://grafana.com/docs/
- For log management, the ELK Stack is a popular choice. Elastic's official documentation covers Elasticsearch, Logstash, and Kibana. Website: https://www.elastic.co/guide/en/index.html
- Jaeger's documentation provides information on distributed tracing for containerized applications. Website: https://www.jaegertracing.io/docs/
- Zipkin's official documentation offers insights into distributed tracing in containerized environments. Website: https://zipkin.io/pages/quickstart
- Sysdig's documentation covers container monitoring and security aspects. Website: https://sysdig.com/learn/documentation/
- Datadog's documentation provides insights into container monitoring and analytics. Website: https://docs.datadoghq.com/
- OpenTelemetry's official documentation guides users in instrumenting applications for observability. Website: https://opentelemetry.io/docs/
- Falco's documentation explores runtime security for containerized applications. Website: https://falco.org/docs/
- Trivy is a popular image-scanning tool for Docker. You can find the source code and documentation on its GitHub repository. GitHub: https://github.com/aquasecurity/trivy
- Docker Content Trust's official documentation covers image signing and security. Website: https://docs.docker.com/engine/security/trust/
- For an extensive collection of observability tools and practices, refer to the CNCF Cloud Native Landscape. CNCF Landscape: https://landscape.cncf.io/

These resources offer a wealth of knowledge and guidance for readers who wish to explore further the topics covered in this chapter.

Chapter 10
Docker on Cloud Platforms

Figure 10.1: *The clouds in the sky.*
source: https://unsplash.com/photos/cloudy-sky-at-daytime-v9bnfMCyKbg

Introduction

In this chapter, we will demystify the Cloud Providers in the context of Docker, exploring the dynamic intersection of Docker and cloud computing. We'll begin by defining what it means to be "cloud-native" and explore the fundamental concepts of running Docker containers in the cloud, the major cloud service providers and their offerings for running Docker containers, and container orchestration.

We will also discuss deployment strategies, networking, and security, as well as monitoring and logging. Of course, using cloud providers entails considerations for cost optimizations. As such, we'll provide some guidelines that can help make your workload efficient.

Finally, we'll provide some of the best practices from around the industry, briefly discuss multi-cloud deployments, and wrap this chapter up with a prediction for future trends.

Structure

We will cover the following topics in this chapter:

- Understanding Cloud-Native Docker
- Cloud Service Providers
- Container Orchestration
- Deployment Strategies, Networking & Security
- Monitoring and Logging
- Cost Optimization
- Hybrid and Multi-Cloud Deployments
- Best Practices and Future Trends

Understanding Cloud-Native Docker

At its core, being "cloud-native" implies that an application, in this case, Docker containers, are designed, deployed, and managed with the cloud in mind from the outset. This design philosophy optimizes the containerized application's ability to exploit the dynamic and scalable nature of cloud platforms but also has some unique characteristics for an application to be counted as such.

Key Characteristics of Cloud-Native Docker

The following list is non-exhaustive but has some of the highlights of cloud-native applications.

- **Microservices Architecture**: Cloud-native Docker leverages a microservices architecture, breaking down applications into smaller, independently deployable units. This approach allows for greater flexibility, scalability, and fault isolation.
- **Container Orchestration**: A fundamental aspect of cloud-native Docker is container orchestration tools like Kubernetes. Orchestration simplifies container management, automates scaling, and ensures high availability.
- **Dynamic Scalability**: Cloud-native Docker adapts seamlessly to fluctuating workloads, automatically scaling containers up or down

to meet demand. This elasticity is a defining feature of cloud-native applications.

- **Self-Healing**: In the cloud-native paradigm, applications are designed to be self-healing. If a container fails, the system automatically replaces it, ensuring continuous availability.
- **Immutable Infrastructure**: Cloud-native Docker promotes immutable infrastructure, where containers are replaced rather than updated. This minimizes configuration drift and ensures consistency.
- **Graceful Shutdown and Startup**: Code should handle graceful shutdowns to ensure that services can be stopped and started without losing data or causing data corruption.
- **Statelessness and Persistence**: Emphasize statelessness by storing persistent data outside the container to prevent data loss in case of container restarts or failures.
- **Health Checks and Readiness Probes**: Implement health checks and readiness probes in your applications to inform the orchestrator of the container's status, ensuring only healthy containers receive traffic.
- **Externalized Configuration**: Store configurations outside the container to adjust to different environments without modifying code. This allows for easier reconfiguration upon restart or relocation.
- **Retry Mechanisms and Circuit Breakers**: Implement retry mechanisms and circuit breakers in your code to handle network reallocation or temporary resource offline scenarios, allowing services to gracefully recover from transient failures.
- **Idempotent Operations**: Design operations to be idempotent, allowing them to be repeated without changing the system's state. This is crucial for operations that might occur during container restart or scale.
- **Automated Recovery Strategies**: Consider implementing self-healing mechanisms that automatically recover the system from various failures, reducing the need for manual intervention.
- **Container-Agnostic Design**: Develop applications that aren't dependent on the specific characteristics of a container, allowing for portability and reducing the impact of changes in the underlying infrastructure.

Benefits of Cloud-Native Docker

Now that you know what makes up a cloud-native app let's see its benefit to the software delivery process.

- **Enhanced Resilience**: Cloud-native Docker applications are inherently more resilient due to their self-healing nature, making them well-suited for cloud environments where failures can occur.
- **Efficient Resource Utilization**: By automatically adjusting resources, cloud-native Docker optimizes resource utilization, leading to cost savings and improved performance.
- **Rapid Deployment**: Cloud-native applications can be deployed quickly, enabling faster time-to-market and agility in responding to changing business requirements.
- **Portability**: Cloud-native Docker containers are designed to be platform-agnostic, allowing them to run on various cloud providers or on-premises infrastructure with minimal modifications.

As we move forward in this chapter, it's essential to keep the principles of cloud-native Docker in mind. This understanding will be the foundation for exploring how cloud service providers and container orchestration platforms enable the realization of these principles in practice. From AWS and Azure to Kubernetes and beyond, we'll dig deeper into the technical intricacies of deploying and managing Docker in the cloud.

Figure 10.2: *A woman carrying a basket in a local market.*
source: https://unsplash.com/photos/woman-carrying-basket-with-vegetables-L5mvKk4vi8A

Cloud Service Providers

There are countless public and private cloud service providers, each offering the deployment model of a cloud-native app. These providers, including Amazon Web Services (AWS), Microsoft Azure, Google Cloud Platform (GCP), and others, play a pivotal role in the world of cloud-native Docker. We'll introduce their services briefly, showcasing how they integrate Docker into their platforms and understand how this integration optimizes operations and deployment.

Amazon Web Services (AWS)

AWS has been at the forefront of cloud computing, the first major public cloud provider in 2006. It offers a variety of services tailored for Docker users. AWS Elastic Container Service (ECS) and AWS Fargate provide scalable and managed environments for running Docker containers. ECS simplifies container management by handling cluster orchestration, while Fargate abstracts infrastructure management, allowing you to focus solely on your containers. Additionally, AWS also supports Kubernetes through Amazon EKS, enabling more flexibility for container orchestration.

Let's elaborate on each of their offerings to provide you with a better understanding when choosing the right technology for your requirements.

Amazon Elastic Container Service (ECS)

AWS Elastic Container Service (ECS) is a fully managed container orchestration service that helps you quickly deploy, manage, and scale containerized applications. AWS ECS provides several features and capabilities that make it a popular choice for deploying containerized applications in the cloud.

- **Container orchestration**: AWS ECS provides several features for orchestrating containerized applications, such as service scheduling, load balancing, and health checks. This helps you to ensure that your applications are always running and available.
- **Scalability**: AWS ECS can automatically scale your containerized applications up or down based on demand. This helps you to avoid overprovisioning resources and save costs.
- **Reliability**: AWS ECS is designed to be highly reliable and scalable. It provides some features for ensuring the reliability of your applications, such as container isolation, networking, and security.
- **Integration with other AWS services**: AWS ECS is tightly integrated with other AWS services, such as Amazon Elastic Compute Cloud (EC2), Amazon Elastic Container Registry (ECR), and Amazon Elastic Load Balancing (ELB). This makes it easy to deploy and manage your containerized applications on AWS.

AWS ECS is a good choice for deploying containerized applications in the following scenarios:

- When you need a fully managed container orchestration service.
- When you need to scale your containerized applications up or down based on demand.

- When you need to deploy containerized applications on multiple AWS services.
- When you must deploy containerized applications in a highly reliable and scalable environment.

Examples of use cases for AWS ECS are as follows:

- **Web applications**: AWS ECS can deploy and manage web applications, such as e-commerce websites and content management systems (CMSs).
- **Microservices**: AWS ECS can be used to deploy and manage microservices-based architectures.
- **Batch processing**: AWS ECS can deploy and manage batch processing workloads, such as data processing and machine learning jobs.
- **Mobile backends**: AWS ECS can be used to deploy and manage mobile backends.
- **Game servers**: AWS ECS can be used to deploy and manage game servers.

Amazon Elastic Kubernetes Service (EKS)

AWS Elastic Kubernetes Service (EKS) is a managed Kubernetes service that makes it easy to deploy, manage, and scale containerized applications. AWS EKS provides some features and capabilities that make it a popular choice for deploying containerized applications in the cloud.

Features and capabilities of AWS EKS include:

- **Managed Kubernetes**: AWS EKS manages the Kubernetes control plane for you, so you don't have to worry about the day-to-day operations of Kubernetes. This frees you up to focus on developing and deploying your applications.
- **High availability**: AWS EKS provides a highly available Kubernetes control plane. It runs across multiple Availability Zones in your AWS region, so your applications are always running and available, even in a failure.
- **Security**: AWS EKS provides several security features for your Kubernetes clusters, such as encryption at rest and in transit, network isolation, and role-based access control (RBAC).
- **Integration with other AWS services**: AWS EKS is tightly integrated with other AWS services, such as Amazon Elastic Compute Cloud (EC2), Amazon Elastic Container Registry (ECR), and Amazon Elastic Load Balancing (ELB). This makes it easy to deploy and manage your containerized applications on AWS.

AWS EKS is a good choice for deploying containerized applications in the following scenarios:

- When you need a managed Kubernetes service with high availability and security.
- When you need to deploy containerized applications on multiple AWS services.
- When you must deploy containerized applications in a hybrid environment, such as on-premises and AWS.
- When you need to deploy containerized applications at scale.

Examples of use cases for AWS EKS are as follows:

- **Web applications**: AWS EKS can deploy and manage web applications, such as e-commerce websites and content management systems (CMSs).
- **Microservices**: AWS EKS can be used to deploy and manage microservices-based architectures.
- **Batch processing**: AWS EKS can deploy and manage batch processing workloads, such as data processing and machine learning jobs.
- **Mobile backends**: AWS EKS can deploy and manage mobile backends.
- **Game servers**: AWS EKS can be used to deploy and manage game servers.

AWS Fargate

AWS Fargate is a serverless compute engine that lets you run containerized applications without provisioning or managing servers. Fargate eliminates the need to choose and manage server types, scale clusters of servers, or maintain application infrastructure.

Features and capabilities of AWS Fargate include:

- **Serverless compute**: Fargate is a serverless compute engine, meaning you don't have to worry about provisioning or managing servers. Fargate automatically scales your containers up or down based on demand, so you never overprovision resources.
- **Pay-as-you-go**: Fargate is billed by the second, with no upfront costs or long-term commitments. You only pay for the resources that your containers use.
- **Support for multiple container orchestration platforms**: Fargate supports both Amazon Elastic Container Service (Amazon ECS) and Amazon Elastic Kubernetes Service (Amazon EKS). This lets you choose the container orchestration platform that best meets your needs.

- **Integration with other AWS services**: Fargate is tightly integrated with other AWS services, such as Amazon Elastic Container Registry (ECR), Amazon Elastic Load Balancing (ELB), and Amazon Virtual Private Cloud (VPC). This makes it easy to deploy and manage your containerized applications on AWS.

AWS Fargate is a good choice for deploying containerized applications in the following scenarios:

- When you want to focus on developing and deploying your applications without worrying about managing servers.
- When you need to scale your containerized applications up or down quickly and easily.
- When you want to avoid the overhead of managing server infrastructure.
- When you want to pay for the resources that your containers use without worrying about upfront costs or long-term commitments.

Examples of use cases for AWS Fargate are as follows:

- **Web applications**: Fargate can deploy and manage web applications, such as e-commerce websites and content management systems (CMSs).
- **Microservices**: Fargate can be used to deploy and manage microservices-based architectures.
- **Batch processing**: Fargate can deploy and manage batch processing workloads, such as data processing and machine learning jobs.
- **Mobile backends**: Fargate can be used to deploy and manage mobile backends.
- **Game servers**: Fargate can be used to deploy and manage game servers.

Amazon Beanstalk

AWS Elastic Beanstalk is a platform as a service (PaaS) offering from Amazon Web Services (AWS) that enables developers to deploy and manage web applications and services without having to provision or manage servers. Elastic Beanstalk automatically handles the deployment, scaling, and load balancing of applications, making it easier for developers to focus on building and maintaining their applications.

Elastic Beanstalk supports Docker deployments, which enables developers to deploy their containerized applications to AWS Elastic Container Service (ECS) or AWS Fargate. To deploy a Dockerized application to Elastic Beanstalk, developers can create a file that specifies the Docker image and configuration for their application. Elastic Beanstalk will then use this file to deploy the application to ECS or Fargate.

Once your application is deployed, Elastic Beanstalk will automatically handle the scaling and load balancing of your application. You can also use Elastic Beanstalk to monitor your application's health and performance.

Here are some of the benefits of using AWS Elastic Beanstalk for Docker deployments:

- **Simplicity**: Elastic Beanstalk makes it easy to deploy and manage Dockerized applications. Developers can focus on building and maintaining their applications without worrying about provisioning or managing servers.
- **Scalability**: Elastic Beanstalk automatically scales applications up or down based on demand. This makes it easy to handle spikes in traffic without worrying about running out of resources.
- **Reliability**: Elastic Beanstalk provides a reliable platform for deploying and running Dockerized applications. AWS covers the underlying infrastructure so developers can focus on their applications.
- **Cost-effectiveness**: Elastic Beanstalk is a cost-effective way to deploy and run Dockerized applications. Developers are only charged for the resources that their applications use.

Overall, AWS Elastic Beanstalk is a good choice for deploying Dockerized applications to the cloud. It is simple to use, scalable, reliable, and cost-effective.

Microsoft Azure

Azure's container offerings include Azure Container Instances (ACI) for a serverless container deployment experience. Azure Kubernetes Service (AKS) provides managed Kubernetes clusters, simplifying orchestration. Azure also offers Azure Container Registry, facilitating Docker image storage and management. With these services, Azure presents a comprehensive ecosystem for Docker container users.

Let's explain each a little bit more.

Azure Container Instances (ACI)

Azure Container Instances (ACI) is a fully managed service for deploying and running containerized applications in Azure without provisioning or managing servers. ACI is serverless, so you only pay for the resources that your containers use, and there is no upfront cost or long-term commitment.

Features and capabilities of Azure Container Instances are:

- **Serverless computing**: ACI is a serverless computing service, so you don't have to worry about provisioning or managing servers. ACI automatically scales your containers up or down based on demand, so you permanently conserve resources.
- **Pay-as-you-go**: ACI is billed by the second, with no upfront costs or long-term commitments. You only pay for the resources that your containers use.
- **Support for multiple container orchestration platforms**: ACI supports both Docker and Kubernetes. This lets you choose the container orchestration platform that best meets your needs.
- **Integration with other Azure services**: ACI is tightly integrated with other Azure services, such as Azure Container Registry (ACR), Azure Virtual Network (VNET), and Azure Load Balancer. This makes it easy to deploy and manage your containerized applications on Azure.

Azure Container Instances is a good choice for deploying containerized applications in the following scenarios:

- When you want to focus on developing and deploying your applications without worrying about managing servers.
- When you need to scale your containerized applications up or down quickly and easily.
- When you want to avoid the overhead of managing server infrastructure.
- When you want to pay for the resources that your containers use without worrying about upfront costs or long-term commitments.

Examples of use cases for Azure Container Instances:

- **Web applications**: ACI can deploy and manage web applications, such as e-commerce websites and content management systems (CMSs).
- **Microservices**: ACI can be used to deploy and manage microservices-based architectures.
- **Batch processing**: ACI can deploy and manage batch processing workloads, such as data processing and machine learning jobs.
- **Mobile backends**: ACI can be used to deploy and manage mobile backends.
- **Game servers**: ACI can be used to deploy and manage game servers.

Azure Kubernetes Service (AKS)

Azure Kubernetes Service (AKS) is a managed Kubernetes service that makes it easy to deploy, manage, and scale containerized applications in Azure. AKS provides many features and capabilities that make it a popular choice for deploying containerized applications in the cloud.

Features and capabilities of Azure Kubernetes Service (AKS) are:

- **Managed Kubernetes**: AKS manages the Kubernetes control plane for you, so you don't have to worry about the day-to-day operations of Kubernetes. This frees you up to focus on developing and deploying your applications.
- **High availability**: AKS provides a highly available Kubernetes control plane. It runs across multiple Availability Zones in your Azure region, so your applications are always running and available, even in a failure.
- **Security**: AKS provides some security features for your Kubernetes clusters, such as encryption at rest and in transit, network isolation, and role-based access control (RBAC).
- **Integration with other Azure services**: AKS is tightly integrated with other Azure services, such as Azure Container Registry (ACR), Azure Load Balancer, and Azure Virtual Network (VNET). This makes it easy to deploy and manage your containerized applications on Azure.

AKS is a good choice for deploying containerized applications in the following scenarios:

- When you need a managed Kubernetes service with high availability and security.
- When you need to deploy containerized applications on multiple Azure services.
- When you need to deploy containerized applications at scale.
- When you must deploy containerized applications in a hybrid environment, such as on-premises and Azure.

Azure Service Fabric

Azure Service Fabric is a distributed systems platform that makes it easy to package, deploy, and manage scalable and reliable microservices and containers. Service Fabric addresses the significant challenges in developing and managing cloud-native applications.

Features and capabilities of Azure Service Fabric are:

- **Microservices development and lifecycle management**: Service Fabric provides a framework for developing and managing microservices, including support for service discovery, load balancing, and fault tolerance.
- **Container support**: Service Fabric can deploy and manage containers, including Docker containers and Azure Container Instances (ACI).
- **Scalability and reliability**: Service Fabric is designed to be highly scalable and reliable, even in the face of failures. It can automatically scale your applications up or down based on demand, and it can automatically restart failed services.
- **Integration with other Azure services**: Service Fabric is tightly integrated with other Azure services, such as Azure Container Registry (ACR), Azure Load Balancer, and Azure Monitor. This makes it easy to deploy and manage your microservices and containers on Azure.

Azure Service Fabric is a good choice for deploying applications in the following scenarios:

- When you need to develop and manage microservices-based architectures.
- When you need to deploy and manage containers at scale.
- When you need a highly scalable and reliable platform for your applications.
- When you need to integrate your applications with other Azure services.

Google Cloud Platform (GCP)

GCP, known for its Kubernetes expertise, offers Google Kubernetes Engine (GKE), a managed Kubernetes service. GKE integrates with other GCP services like Cloud Build for CI/CD and Stackdriver for monitoring and logging. GCP's strong support for Kubernetes makes it a powerful choice for running Docker containers in a cloud environment.

Now, let's explain each offering in further detail.

Google Kubernetes Engine (GKE)

Google Kubernetes Engine (GKE) is a managed Kubernetes service that makes it easy to deploy, manage, and scale containerized applications on the Google Cloud Platform (GCP). GKE provides several features and capabilities that make it a popular choice for deploying containerized applications in the cloud.

Features and capabilities of Google Kubernetes Engine (GKE) are:

- **Managed Kubernetes**: GKE manages the Kubernetes control plane for you, so you don't have to worry about the day-to-day operations of Kubernetes. This frees you up to focus on developing and deploying your applications.
- **High availability**: GKE provides a highly available Kubernetes control plane. It runs across multiple zones in your GCP region, so your applications are always running and available, even in a failure.
- **Security**: GKE provides some security features for your Kubernetes clusters, such as encryption at rest and in transit, network isolation, and role-based access control (RBAC).
- **Integration with other GCP services**: GKE is tightly integrated with other GCP services, such as Google Container Registry (GCR), Cloud Load Balancing, and Cloud Networking. This makes it easy to deploy and manage your containerized applications on GCP.

GKE is a good choice for deploying containerized applications in the following scenarios:

- When you need a managed Kubernetes service with high availability and security.
- When you need to deploy containerized applications on multiple GCP services.
- When you need to deploy containerized applications at scale.
- When you must deploy containerized applications in a hybrid environment, such as on-premises and GCP.

Google Compute Engine (GCE)

Google Compute Engine (GCE) is an Infrastructure as a Service (IaaS) offering that provides virtual machines (VMs) for running stateless and stateful workloads. GCE offers a variety of VM machine types and sizes to meet the needs of a wide range of applications.

During the creation of the instances, you can specify option to install Docker on the host and upon doing so, you will be able to run the containers using Docker.

Features and capabilities of Google Compute Engine (GCE):

- **Scalability**: GCE is highly scalable, allowing you to quickly and easily scale your workloads up or down based on demand.

- **Performance**: GCE offers a variety of high-performance machine types, including GPUs, TPUs, and custom VMs.
- **Reliability**: GCE is designed to be highly reliable, with features such as live migration and automatic failover.
- **Security**: GCE provides several security features, such as encryption at rest and in transit, network isolation, and role-based access control (RBAC).
- **Integration with other GCP services**: GCE is tightly integrated with other GCP services, such as Google Cloud Storage, Google Cloud Load Balancing, and Google Cloud Networking. This makes it easy to build and deploy scalable and reliable applications on GCP.

GCE is a good choice for deploying applications in the following scenarios:

- When you need a scalable and reliable platform for your applications.
- When you need to deploy high-performance applications, such as machine learning workloads.
- When you need to integrate your applications with other GCP services.

Cloud Run

Cloud Run is a fully managed serverless computing platform that enables developers to build and run stateless containerized applications without managing servers or infrastructure. Cloud Run provides some features and capabilities that make it a good choice for deploying a wide variety of applications in the cloud.

Features and capabilities of Cloud Run are:

- **Serverless computing**: Cloud Run is a serverless computing platform, meaning developers don't have to worry about managing servers or infrastructure. Cloud Run automatically scales applications up or down based on demand, so developers are only charged for the resources that their applications use.
- **Container support**: Cloud Run supports Docker and Kubernetes containers. This makes it easy for developers to deploy their containerized applications to Cloud Run.
- **Pay-as-you-go pricing**: Cloud Run is billed by the second, with no upfront costs or long-term commitments. Developers only pay for the resources that their applications use.
- **Integration with other GCP services**: Cloud Run is tightly integrated with other GCP services, such as Google Cloud Storage, Google Cloud

Load Balancing, and Google Cloud Networking. This makes it easy for developers to build and deploy scalable and reliable applications on GCP.

Cloud Run is a good choice for deploying applications in the following scenarios:

- When developers want to focus on building and running their applications without worrying about managing servers or infrastructure.
- When developers need to deploy stateless containerized applications.
- When developers want to pay for the resources that their applications use without having to worry about upfront costs or long-term commitments.
- When developers need to integrate their applications with other GCP services.

Figure 10.3: *People running in a marathon.*
source: https://unsplash.com/photos/grayscale-photo-of-people-during-marathon-ttbCwN_mWic

Other Cloud Providers

Beyond the big three, other cloud providers such as IBM Cloud, Oracle Cloud, and Alibaba Cloud also offer Docker container services. These providers have their unique features, pricing models, and integrations, catering to a diverse set of user requirements.

For other cloud providers and multi-cloud strategies, several solutions exist to deploy Docker containers in production. We will introduce some of the famous solutions available online.

IBM Cloud Kubernetes Service

IBM Cloud Kubernetes Service offers managed Kubernetes clusters with native Kubernetes tooling and features. It provides flexibility and scalability for running containerized applications while integrating with various IBM Cloud services. This service is suitable for deploying and managing applications that require Kubernetes orchestration.

DigitalOcean Kubernetes (DOKS)

DigitalOcean offers a managed Kubernetes service, allowing users to deploy, manage, and scale containerized applications using Kubernetes. DOKS provides a simplified Kubernetes experience, offering quick setup and easy management of clusters. It is a viable option for users looking for simplicity and ease of use with Kubernetes.

Alibaba Cloud Container Service for Kubernetes (ACK)

Alibaba Cloud provides a managed Kubernetes service that supports the orchestration and management of containerized applications. ACK integrates with other Alibaba Cloud services, providing scalability, reliability, and security for running applications in a Kubernetes environment. It is suitable for deploying and managing containers on Alibaba Cloud.

Oracle Cloud Infrastructure Container Engine for Kubernetes (OKE)

Oracle Cloud Infrastructure offers a managed Kubernetes service, OKE, which simplifies the deployment and management of containerized applications. It provides control and flexibility for running Kubernetes-based applications while integrating with other Oracle Cloud services.

Red Hat OpenShift

Red Hat OpenShift is a Kubernetes-based container platform that offers an enterprise-grade solution for container orchestration. It provides additional tooling and capabilities beyond a basic Kubernetes environment, supporting a DevOps-centric approach and enabling rapid application development and deployment.

Interweaving Docker and Cloud Providers

The integration of Docker and cloud service providers streamline container deployment and operations. These providers offer features such as load balancing, auto-scaling, and managed infrastructure, which are invaluable for ensuring the reliability and scalability of Docker applications. They also provide services for deploying containers from container registries, making it easy to manage images.

Furthermore, cloud providers often offer solutions for CI/CD pipelines, enabling the seamless integration of Docker containers into the development and deployment workflow. This not only accelerates the development cycle but also ensures consistency and reliability throughout the container lifecycle.

Understanding the offerings of various cloud service providers in the context of Docker is crucial for making informed decisions regarding the deployment and management of containerized applications.

Container Orchestration

Container orchestration platforms, particularly Kubernetes, play an integral role in managing Docker containers within the dynamic landscape of cloud environments. However, container orchestration extends beyond Kubernetes, encompassing several notable options, each with distinct advantages and considerations.

Kubernetes

As the predominant player in container orchestration, Kubernetes offers a robust set of features that streamline the deployment, scaling, and management of containerized applications. It provides advanced orchestration capabilities, facilitating self-healing, auto-scaling, and load balancing, ensuring high availability and resilience. Kubernetes' expansive ecosystem, with a vast array of tools and a thriving community, allows for extensibility and integration with various cloud services. However, the intricacies of managing Kubernetes can pose a steep learning curve for newcomers. The need for proficient operational expertise and potential complexities in setting up and managing the infrastructure are among the considerations when opting for Kubernetes.

Docker Swarm

Contrasting Kubernetes, Docker Swarm represents a simpler, more lightweight alternative for container orchestration. It seamlessly integrates with Docker, making it easier for users familiar with it to transition into orchestration. Docker Swarm's ease of setup and a more straightforward learning curve make it an attractive option for smaller-scale projects or those seeking a less complex orchestration solution. Nonetheless, it may need some of the advanced features and scalability Kubernetes offers, and its community support might be less vast and diverse.

Red Hat OpenShift

Red Hat OpenShift, built on Kubernetes, provides an enterprise-ready container platform with additional tooling for a comprehensive DevOps experience. It simplifies the deployment of applications, abstracting the complexities of Kubernetes while offering enhanced security and management capabilities. However, the added features and enterprise-grade support may come with increased costs, making it more suitable for larger enterprises with the resources and requirements for such robust functionalities.

Nomad by HashiCorp

Nomad, an alternative to Kubernetes, offers a simple and flexible orchestrator. It's designed to deploy and manage containerized and non-containerized applications. Its focus on simplicity and ease of use makes it an appealing choice for smaller organizations or those not requiring the extensive feature set provided by Kubernetes. Nonetheless, it might need more advanced capabilities found in more established orchestrators.

Each platform has its merits and potential drawbacks, and the choice largely hinges on the specific requirements, scale, and expertise of the organization or individuals utilizing container orchestration. Understanding the nuances of each option is crucial in selecting the most suitable solution for a particular use case within a cloud environment.

When choosing the technology stack for your team, you have to consider more than just the pros and cons of the tool itself but also the knowledge gap between the peers of your team, as it significantly influences the overall efficiency, collaboration, and success of the project.

Overall, the infrastructure of your organization has to be maintainable over the long run if you plan to succeed in software delivery. Stability, availability, and fault tolerance are just a few critical factors to mention here, and it is a non-exhaustive list of crucial factors when it comes to picking a technology.

Deployment Strategy

In deploying production-grade software leveraging Docker on the cloud, diverse deployment strategies offer unique approaches to minimize risks and ensure seamless delivery. These strategies aim to maintain application stability, minimize downtime, and enhance user experience while introducing new features or updates.

Blue-Green Deployments

Blue-Green deployment involves running two identical production environments: one active (blue) and one inactive (green). When new updates or changes are to be deployed, they are implemented in the "green" environment. Once the new environment is tested and ready, traffic switches from the "blue" environment to the "green" one. This approach allows for minimal downtime and swift rollback if issues arise.

Canary Releases

Canary releases involve rolling out updates or new features to a subset of users, allowing real-world testing in a controlled environment. It gradually expands the update to a broader audience. By monitoring performance and user feedback, any issues or regressions can be identified and resolved before full deployment. This strategy offers risk mitigation by limiting the impact of potential problems.

Rolling Updates

Rolling updates are executed by incrementally updating containers across the infrastructure, typically one at a time. This process maintains application availability while gradually replacing the old version with the new one. The rolling update strategy ensures continuous service availability, particularly in systems that require constant uptime.

A/B testing

This strategy involves deploying two different software versions to different subsets of users. The two versions of the software can be identical, except for a small change, such as a new feature or a different design. By comparing the performance of the two software versions, organizations can determine which version is performing better and decide whether to deploy it to all users.

Feature flags

This strategy involves using feature flags to turn features on or off in the software. This allows organizations to gradually roll out new features to users and monitor their performance before enabling them for all users. It also allows organizations to turn off features that are causing problems quickly.

Each deployment strategy has merits and intricacies, addressing specific use cases and risks. When deploying with Docker on the cloud, other considerations like the infrastructure's auto-scaling capabilities, environment isolation, and the container orchestration tool used (for example, Kubernetes and Docker Swarm) also influence the choice of strategy.

Furthermore, other approaches, such as A/B testing, feature toggles, and immutable infrastructure, enhance deployment strategies, offering versatility and adaptability in rolling out production-grade software on the cloud. The choice of strategy should align with the project's requirements, the risk tolerance of the organization, and the specific goals and priorities for the software release.

Networking and Security

Running Docker on cloud platforms entails comprehensive considerations regarding networking and security to ensure the safety and optimal functionality of containerized applications. Several key components and features within various cloud providers enable these crucial aspects:

Virtual Private Clouds (VPCs)

VPCs form the fundamental networking construct in cloud environments, allowing users to create isolated networks where Docker containers can operate. They offer granular control over IP addressing, routing, and access control, allowing the segmentation of resources.

Security Groups

Cloud providers employ security groups as a firewall mechanism to control inbound and outbound traffic for Docker containers. These act as virtual firewalls at the instance level and help manage access by defining rules that permit or deny traffic. Security groups are essential for controlling network access and strengthening the security posture of container deployments.

Network Isolation and Segmentation

Container networking solutions offered by cloud providers aim to ensure network isolation and segmentation. Techniques like Kubernetes Network Policies or AWS VPC peering enable the creation of secure and separate network segments for containerized applications, minimizing the attack surface and containing potential security breaches.

Encryption and Identity Management

Encryption mechanisms, such as TLS (Transport Layer Security), are imperative for securing communication between containers and external services. Cloud platforms often provide managed solutions for key and identity access management (IAM), offering secure and compliant methods for controlling access and authentication.

Comparing these aspects across cloud platforms, AWS, for instance, features VPCs that allow highly customizable network configurations and security groups that provide detailed control over traffic. Similarly, Azure's Virtual Network (VNet) offers similar capabilities, emphasizing network segmentation and secure container communication. Google Cloud Platform leverages Virtual Private Clouds and Identity and Access Management (IAM) for robust security controls.

When assessing these offerings, factors such as ease of setup, flexibility, and compliance with industry standards become pivotal. AWS, with its well-established services like VPC and security groups, caters to advanced networking and security needs. Azure emphasizes user-friendly configurations with its VNet and strong identity management. GCP, known for its robust network isolation and IAM, balances simplicity and control.

In pursuing the most suitable solution, considerations on ease of management, scalability, and integration with other cloud services should align with the specific security and networking requirements of the containerized applications. These offerings aim to fortify Docker deployments, and the choice often rests on the organization's specific needs, compliance standards, and the depth of network and security control required.

Monitoring and Logging

Monitoring and logging are integral components of managing Docker containers in the cloud, enabling effective troubleshooting, performance optimization, and ensuring the overall health and stability of applications. Multiple solutions and strategies are available to set up monitoring and logging, offering unique features and functionalities across different cloud platforms:

Cloud Provider Monitoring Services

Major cloud providers offer native monitoring solutions tailored to their platforms. AWS provides Amazon CloudWatch, which allows users to collect and track metrics, set alarms, and gain insights into resource utilization. Azure Monitor provides in-depth metrics, application insights, and integration with Azure services. Google Cloud offers Stackdriver Monitoring for resource visibility, logging, and diagnostics.

Third-Party Monitoring Tools

Various third-party tools provide comprehensive monitoring and logging capabilities for Docker containers. Prometheus, an open-source monitoring system combined with Grafana for visualization, is famous for Kubernetes-based environments. Datadog, Splunk, and New Relic are widely used for their extensive monitoring, alerting, and logging capabilities.

Container Orchestration Tool Integration

Container orchestration platforms like Kubernetes, Docker Swarm, and others offer built-in monitoring and logging features. Kubernetes integrates with tools like Prometheus and Fluentd for collecting metrics and logs. Docker Swarm provides built-in capabilities for logging and monitoring container performance.

When comparing these solutions, factors like ease of setup, granularity of metrics, alerting capabilities, and integration possibilities are crucial considerations. AWS CloudWatch, with its native integration with AWS services, offers a comprehensive monitoring solution but might lack flexibility in integrating with non-AWS environments. Azure Monitor excels in providing deep insights into Azure resources but might pose challenges when working with hybrid or multi-cloud environments. Google Cloud's Stackdriver provides a unified solution for monitoring across various GCP services.

Third-party tools like Prometheus, when paired with Grafana, are highly customizable and offer robust monitoring capabilities, but they require more configuration and expertise. Commercial tools like Datadog, Splunk, and New Relic provide comprehensive features and often support multi-cloud environments, but they might come with additional costs.

The choice among these solutions depends on the specific needs of the application, existing cloud infrastructure, desired level of granularity, and the organization's expertise in managing, interpreting, monitoring and logging data. Ensuring optimal performance and effective troubleshooting of Docker containers in the cloud demands a thoughtful evaluation of available tools and services to select the most suitable solution for the intended use case.

Figure 10.4: *Coins and dollars.*
source: https://unsplash.com/photos/three-round-gold-colored-coins-on-100-us-dollar-banknotes-eBWzFKahEaU

Cost Optimization

When deploying applications to one of the cloud providers, cost optimization is a necessary step, as it directly impacts the operational expenses of maintaining containerized workloads. Employing various strategies and best practices can significantly reduce costs without compromising performance or reliability. We provide guidelines and tips to optimize your workload to avoid overcharging your business.

Rightsizing Resources

Evaluating the resource allocation of containers and adjusting them to match actual application needs is vital. Refrain from over-provisioning resources, as this can lead to unnecessary costs. Employ tools for monitoring and analyzing resource utilization, such as AWS CloudWatch or Azure Monitor, to identify underused resources.

Reserved Instances and Savings Plans

Cloud providers often offer options like Reserved Instances (AWS) or Savings Plans (Azure and Google Cloud) to commit to specific resource configurations for a lower price. By committing to longer-term usage, users can obtain significant discounts compared to on-demand pricing.

Auto-Scaling and Elasticity

Implement auto-scaling based on actual demand–Configure Docker environments to scale automatically during peak times and scale down during periods of lower utilization. Cloud-native services like AWS Auto Scaling or

Azure Autoscale enable dynamically adjusting resources in response to traffic fluctuations.

Spot Instances and Preemptible VMs

Leveraging spot instances in AWS or preemptible VMs in Google Cloud can significantly reduce costs for non-mission-critical workloads. These instances offer substantial discounts but come with the risk of potential interruptions, making them suitable for fault-tolerant and batch-processing workloads.

Cost Allocation and Tagging

Properly tagging resources and containers allows for precise identification of cost sources. This enables cost allocation to specific projects or departments, facilitating better financial management and decision-making.

Practical guidelines for implementing cost optimization include performing regular audits of resource utilization, employing automation and scheduling to power off or terminate resources during non-peak hours, and adopting a **pay-as-you-go** approach to align expenses with actual usage.

Understanding the necessity of cost optimization is crucial, as it not only reduces operational expenses but also enables better financial planning and resource allocation. Efficiently managing the expenses associated with running Docker on the cloud allows businesses to achieve better cost control, allocate resources judiciously, and maximize the return on cloud investments. These strategies not only minimize costs but also contribute to a more sustainable and efficient cloud infrastructure, ensuring an optimal balance between performance and budget constraints.

Hybrid and Multi-Cloud Deployments

Hybrid and multi-cloud deployments involving Docker bring about a strategic approach that integrates resources and services from multiple cloud environments, on-premises infrastructure, or a combination of both. These deployment models offer a range of benefits, but navigating their complexities requires a comprehensive understanding of their implications and advantages:

Hybrid Deployments

Hybrid deployments typically involve integrating on-premises infrastructure with one or more cloud environments. Organizations may opt for a hybrid approach to leverage the advantages of both on-premises and cloud-based systems, ensuring flexibility, compliance, and data sovereignty. Docker enables consistent deployment across hybrid infrastructures, allowing applications to run seamlessly regardless of the underlying environment.

Multi-Cloud Deployments

Multi-cloud deployments span multiple cloud service providers, allowing the distribution of workloads or applications among different platforms. This strategy can mitigate vendor lock-in, enhance resilience, and provide optimized solutions for diverse needs. Docker's portability and compatibility facilitate the movement of applications across different cloud platforms, ensuring consistent deployment and management.

Benefits of Hybrid and Multi-Cloud Deployments

Maintaining such an environment is challenging, as we shall discuss shortly, but it has some bold advantages.

- **Flexibility and Redundancy**: Deploying across multiple environments or cloud providers offers redundancy, ensuring business continuity in case of failures in a specific region or service provider.
- **Compliance and Data Sovereignty**: Hybrid deployments enable the placement of sensitive workloads in on-premises environments while leveraging the scalability and agility of cloud resources for other non-sensitive workloads.
- **Optimized Performance and Cost Savings**: Leveraging multiple cloud providers allows organizations to select services that best suit specific workloads and optimize costs using varied pricing models.

Complexities and Considerations

There is no free lunch, even more so in software engineering. The cost of running multi-cloud or hybrid solutions is the following non-exhaustive list.

- **Data Integration and Interoperability**: Ensuring seamless communication and data integration across disparate environments requires robust networking and interoperability strategies.
- **Management and Governance**: Managing and governing multiple platforms, ensuring security, compliance, and unified policies across hybrid or multi-cloud environments necessitates meticulous planning and administration.

- **Vendor Lock-in and Portability**: Avoiding vendor lock-in while maintaining application portability across environments demands compatibility and standardization, which can be challenging.

Best Practices for Hybrid and Multi-Cloud Deployments

If you decide to opt in on this train, you have to make sure you're doing it right, including but not limited to asking your professional network, reading real-world case studies, testing the water yourself, etc. Here are some of the best practices that can help you better implement this task.

- **Standardized Containerization**: Leverage Docker's standardized containers to ensure consistent deployment across various environments.
- **Interoperability and Integration**: Prioritize interoperability and data integration among cloud providers and on-premises systems.
- **Security and Governance**: Implement robust security measures and standardized governance practices to ensure consistency across the deployment landscape.

Navigating the complexities and leveraging the benefits of hybrid and multi-cloud deployments requires a comprehensive understanding of the business requirements, careful planning, and a well-thought-out strategy. Docker's flexibility, portability, and standardized containerization play a significant role in achieving consistency and compatibility across disparate cloud environments, enabling organizations to optimize resources, enhance resilience, and maximize the benefits of multi-faceted deployment strategies.

Practical Examples

You have seen the theories and explanations. It's time to deploy an app in the cloud so that you can get a feeling of how it is done. If you haven't done this before, this will give you a good idea of the process involved.

Deploying a Containerized App in AWS

There are plenty of ways to deploy a containerized application to AWS, each with pros and cons and tailored to a specific use case. We can't provide all the examples in one book, so we'll settle for only one, the easiest to do and perfect for a demo application.

In this example, we'll use AWS Copilot CLI to deploy an application to AWS ECS, the managed container deployment solution AWS offers.

All we need is a Dockerfile that holds the application definition, and using this, we'll deploy a container to AWS with minimum effort, thanks to Copilot CLI.

To download the latest version, head to their GitHub repository, accessible from the following URL.

https://github.com/aws/copilot-cli/

The instructions on the README file should be enough to help you install it on your local machine. For us, we're using an Ubuntu-based machine and the command to install the CLI is as follows:

```
curl -Lo copilot \
  https://github.com/aws/copilot-cli/releases/latest/download/copi-
lot-linux
chmod +x copilot
sudo mv copilot /usr/local/bin/copilot
copilot --version # As of writing this book: v1.31.0
copilot --help
```

Next up, there is only one Dockerfile needed, which will be a simple Nginx server for our demo application as follows.

NOTE: The contents of the `index.html` can be a simple `Hello World` with no extra templates!

```
FROM nginx:1-alpine

COPY ./index.html /usr/share/nginx/html/index.html

EXPOSE 80

CMD ["nginx", "-g", "daemon off;"]
```

The file index.html holds a minimal Hello World and nothing else.

Finally, to deploy this application, we use the following command.

```
# Set your AWS account profile if you have more than one
AWS_PROFILE=my-aws-account

copilot init \
  --app mastering-docker \
  --name web \
  --env dev \
```

```
--type 'Load Balanced Web Service' \
--dockerfile ./Dockerfile \
--deploy
```

This command will take care of all the implementation details for every needed resource to deploy this app in an AWS account.

Using this approach will take a lot of details out of the way and is one of the fastest ways to deploy your app in a live environment.

Though, one piece of caution is needed here. This command will deploy as many resources needed in the target AWS account, so if you don't want to get charged, you better run this command in a sandboxed environment or where you have some AWS credit to spare; otherwise, you might get charged for something you didn't intend to.

If you don't know too much about AWS, don't fret, as this book does not cover AWS cloud providers, and we're only providing a demo deployment. The AWS cloud, or any other provider for that matter, will require its source and is out of the scope of this book.

The final result for the command above is the following AWS CloudFormation templates.

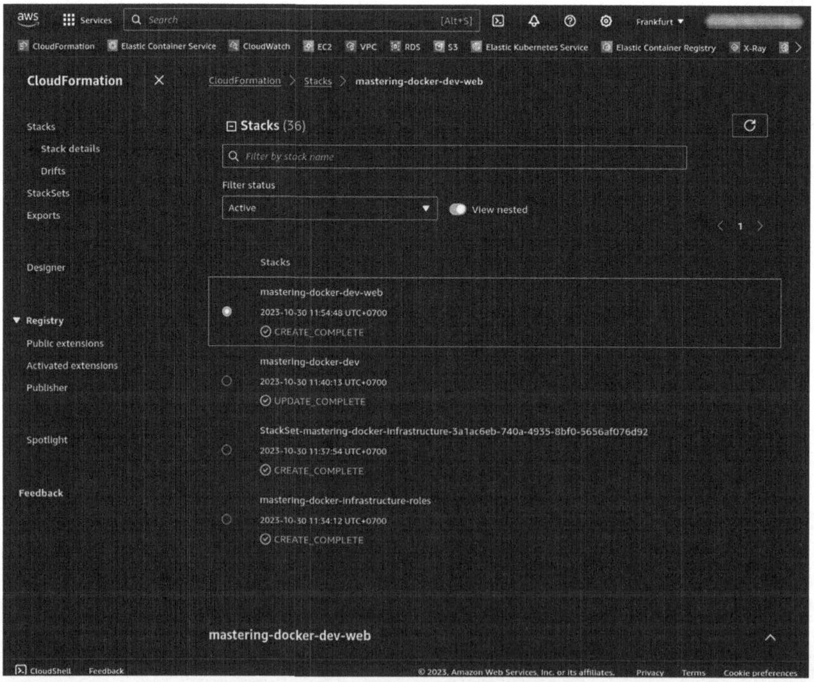

Figure 10.5: *Copilot CLI deployed CloudFormation stacks (image by author from AWS Console)*

And if we look at the ECS clusters, we can see our newly created cluster.

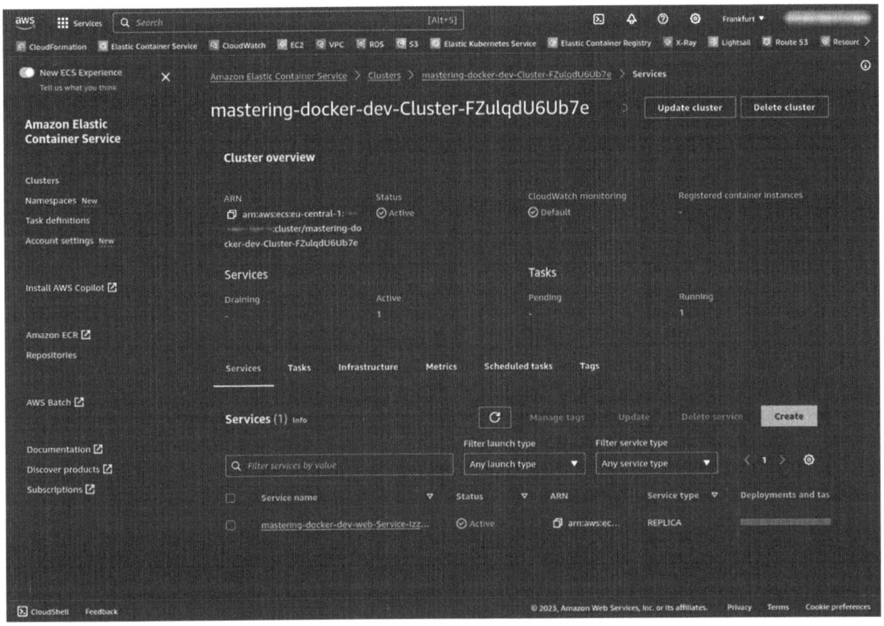

Figure 10.6: *ECS cluster deployed using Copilot CLI (image by author from AWS Console)*

Opening the service on the page above, we can see the application logs just as we would get when running `docker logs`.

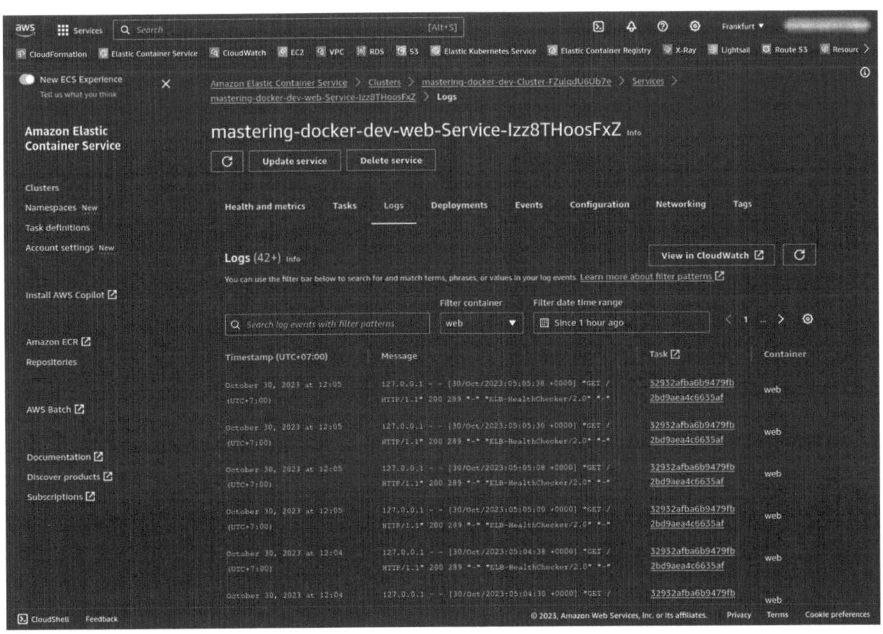

Figure 10.7: *ECS container logs (image by author from AWS Console)*

Lastly, the Copilot CLI also created a load balancer for our application, as in *Figure 10.8*.

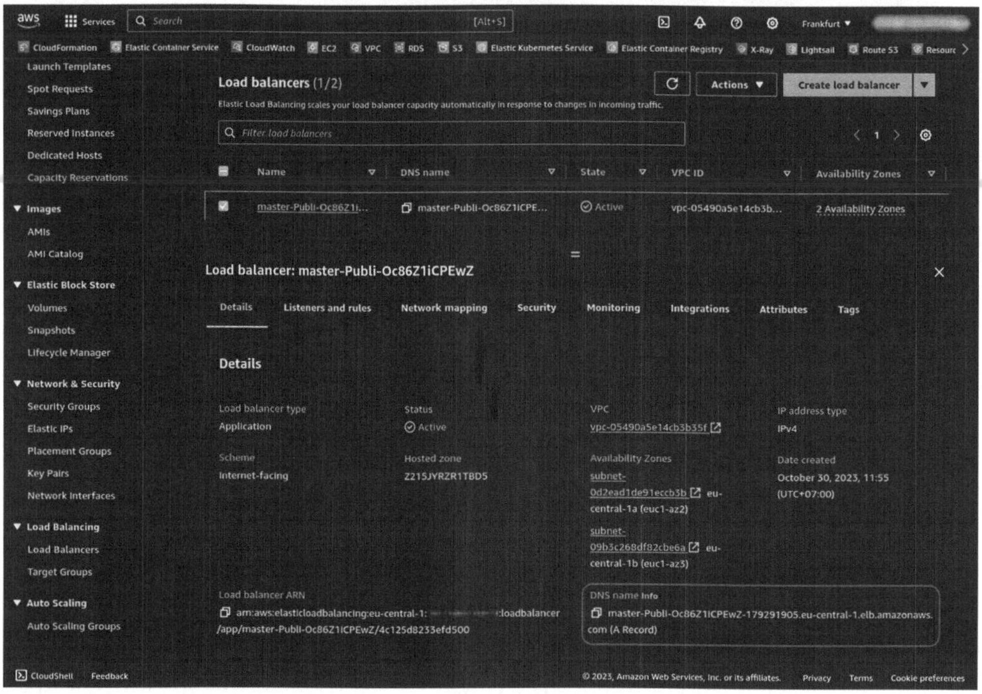

Figure 10.8: *AWS ALB deployed by Copilot CLI (image by author from AWS Console)*

The DNS name is the address we can use in a browser or with the `curl` command to get the response from our newly created container.

The HTML response will be the same as already defined in Dockerfile and index.html, the same behavior we would expect to get if running the container locally using the docker run command.

Case Studies

We have seen some theories and some practical examples. It's time to study a few real-world examples of using Docker to deploy application(s) in production using the cloud providers.

Ikea Retail uses Docker in production on AWS

Ikea Retail is a global furniture retailer with over 400 stores in 63 countries. In 2018, Ikea Retail began using Docker to deploy and manage its microservices-based architecture on AWS.

Ikea Retail chose Docker because it offered several benefits, including:

- **Portability**: Docker images can be run on any platform that supports Docker, which gave Ikea Retail the flexibility to deploy its applications on any cloud provider or on-premises.
- **Consistency**: Docker images provide a consistent runtime environment for applications, which helped Ikea Retail to reduce the risk of errors and improve the reliability of its applications.
- **Scalability**: Docker images are lightweight and easy to scale, which helped Ikea Retail to handle the high traffic volumes that it experiences during peak periods.

Ikea Retail initially deployed a small number of Docker images to production, but it quickly scaled up its Docker usage. Today, Ikea Retail runs over 100,000 Docker images in production on AWS.

Things Ikea Did Right

Ikea Retail did several things right when it adopted Docker in production:

- **It started small**: Ikea Retail tried to migrate only some of its applications to Docker at a time. Instead, it started by migrating a small number of applications to Docker. This allowed Ikea Retail to learn from its experience and identify any potential problems before it migrated its entire application portfolio to Docker.
- **It used a managed Kubernetes service**: Ikea Retail used Amazon Elastic Kubernetes Service (EKS) to manage Docker containers. This allowed Ikea Retail to focus on its applications and let AWS manage the underlying Kubernetes infrastructure.
- **It implemented a CI/CD pipeline**: Ikea Retail implemented a CI/CD pipeline to automate the process of building, testing, and deploying its Docker images to production. This helped Ikea Retail to deliver new features to its customers more quickly and reliably.

Things They Learned

Ikea Retail learned a few things by doing wrong when it adopted Docker in production:

It underestimated the importance of monitoring: Ikea Retail initially underestimated the importance of monitoring its Docker containers. This led to a few outages when Ikea Retail's containers became overloaded. Ikea Retail has since implemented a comprehensive monitoring solution to track the performance and health of its Docker containers.

It didn't have a clear rollback plan: Ikea Retail needed a clear one when it started deploying Docker images to production. This made it difficult to roll back to a previous version of an image if there was a problem with a new deployment. Ikea Retail has since implemented a rollback plan to ensure that it can quickly roll back to a previous version of an image if necessary.

Ikea Overall Experience

Overall, Ikea Retail's experience with Docker in production has been positive. Docker has helped Ikea Retail to improve the portability, consistency, and scalability of its applications. Ikea Retail has learned a few things along the way, but it has been able to overcome any challenges it has faced.

Ikea Retail's case study demonstrates that Docker can be used successfully in production on AWS. By starting small, using a managed Kubernetes service, and implementing a CI/CD pipeline, Ikea Retail has been able to reap the benefits of Docker while minimizing the risks.

Netflix Usage of Docker in Production

Netflix is a global streaming entertainment service with over 220 million subscribers in over 190 countries. In 2015, Netflix began using Docker to deploy and manage its microservices-based architecture on Azure.

Netflix chose Docker because it offered several benefits, including:

- **Speed**: Docker images are fast to deploy and start-up, which is essential for Netflix because it must quickly and reliably deliver streaming video to its customers.
- **Efficiency**: Docker images are efficient in terms of resource usage, which helps Netflix to reduce its costs.
- **Portability**: Docker images can be run on any platform that supports Docker, which gives Netflix the flexibility to deploy its applications on any cloud provider or on-premises.

Netflix runs over 500,000 Docker containers in production on Azure. Netflix uses a variety of tools and technologies to manage its Docker containers, including:

- **Docker Swarm**: Docker Swarm is a native tool for managing Docker clusters. Netflix uses Docker Swarm to orchestrate its Docker containers across its Azure infrastructure.
- **Netflix Conductor**: Netflix Conductor is a scheduling and orchestration system for microservices. Netflix uses Netflix Conductor to manage

the lifecycle of its Docker containers, including starting, stopping, and restarting them.

- **Spinnaker**: Spinnaker is a continuous delivery platform that Netflix uses to deploy its Docker containers to production.

Things Netflix Did Right

Netflix did several things right when it adopted Docker in production:

- **It invested in training**: Netflix invested in training its engineers on Docker. This helped to ensure that its engineers had the skills and knowledge to use Docker effectively.
- **It used a container orchestration platform**: Netflix used Docker Swarm to orchestrate its containers. This helped Netflix to manage its Docker containers at scale.
- **It built its tools and technologies**: Netflix built its tools and technologies, such as Netflix Conductor and Spinnaker, to manage Docker containers. This gave Netflix more control over its Docker environment and allowed it to customize its solutions to meet its specific needs.

Things They Learned

Netflix learned a few things by doing wrong when it adopted Docker in production:

It underestimated the importance of security: Netflix initially underestimated the importance of securing its Docker containers. This led to a few security breaches. Netflix has since implemented several security measures to protect its Docker containers, such as network isolation, encryption, and authentication.

It needed a clear disaster recovery plan: Netflix needed a clear disaster recovery plan when it first started deploying Docker images to production. This made it difficult to recover from a disaster if one occurred. Netflix has since implemented a disaster recovery plan to ensure that it can quickly recover from a disaster if it occurs.

Netflix Overall Experience

Overall, Netflix's experience with Docker in production has been positive. Docker has helped Netflix to improve the speed, efficiency, and portability of its applications. Netflix has learned a few things along the way, but it has been able to overcome any challenges it has faced.

Netflix's case study demonstrates that Docker can be used successfully in production on Azure. By investing in training, using a container orchestration platform, and building its tools and technologies, Netflix has been able to reap the benefits of Docker while minimizing the risks.

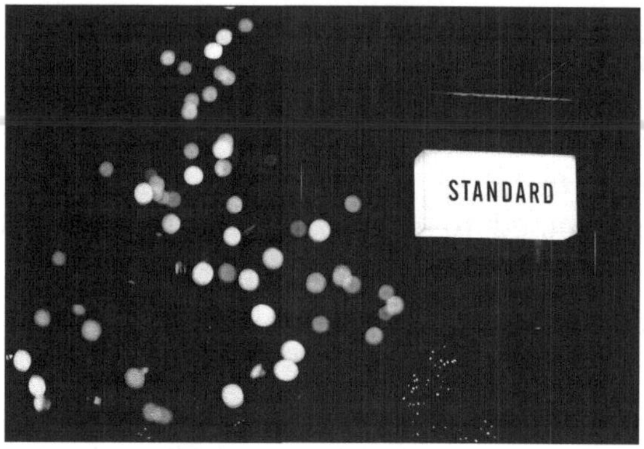

Figure 10.9: *Standard sign on the wall.*
source: https://unsplash.com/photos/white-standard-led-signage-mounted-on-wall-fJSRg-r7LuI

Use Cases and Best Practices

You have seen two real-world case studies. Here are three more.

- **Spotify**: Spotify uses Docker to deploy and manage its microservices-based architecture on Google Cloud Platform (GCP). Docker has helped Spotify to improve the scalability, reliability, and efficiency of its applications.
- **Airbnb**: Airbnb uses Docker to deploy and manage its microservices-based architecture on Amazon Elastic Kubernetes Service (EKS). Docker has helped Airbnb to improve the speed, scalability, and reliability of its applications.
- **Walmart**: Walmart uses Docker to deploy and manage its microservices-based architecture on Azure Kubernetes Service (AKS). Docker has helped Walmart to improve the speed, scalability, and efficiency of its applications.
- **Banco BV**: Banco BV, a leading financial institution, employs Kubernetes for enhanced scalability, reliability, and efficiency in its banking services. Through containerization and Kubernetes clusters, Banco BV achieves seamless orchestration, auto-scaling for varying workloads, and streamlined resource utilization. This ensures optimal performance, high availability, and continuous delivery of innovative financial products, all while optimizing infrastructure costs and maintaining a secure banking environment. [source: https://www.google.com/url?q=https://

cloud.google.com/blog/products/containers-kubernetes/banco-bv-migrates-from-openshift-to-gke-and-anthos&sa=D&source=docs&ust=1704471706890710&usg=AOvVaw1FIwIxY-ySrHcScKnp97J-]

Best Practices

Best practices for deploying Docker on various cloud platforms based on the data around the industry from professional and experienced engineers are as follows:

- **Use a managed container orchestration service**: Managed container orchestration services such as Amazon EKS, Google Kubernetes Engine (GKE), and Azure Kubernetes Service (AKS) provide some benefits, such as simplified deployment and management, scalability, and reliability.
- **Use a Docker registry**: Docker registries such as Docker Hub provide a central place to store and manage Docker images. Using a Docker registry can help you to improve the security and reliability of your Docker environment.
- **Implement a continuous integration and continuous delivery (CI/CD) pipeline**: A CI/CD pipeline can help you automate the process of building, testing, and deploying Docker images to production. This can help you to deliver new features to your customers more quickly and reliably.
- **Use a monitoring solution**: A monitoring solution can help you track the performance and health of your Docker containers. This can help you to identify and resolve problems before they cause outages.

Additionally, here is a list of more practices to enforce you for delivering your application using Docker:

- **Use small, focused Docker images**: Smaller Docker images are faster to deploy and start up, and they are also more efficient in resource usage.
- **Use a layering strategy for building Docker images**: Layering allows you to reuse common components in different Docker images. This can help you to reduce the size and complexity of your Docker images.
- **Use volumes to store persistent data**: Volumes allow you to store data outside your Docker containers. This makes it easier to manage and back up your data.
- **Use networks to isolate your Docker containers**: Networks can help you isolate your Docker containers from each other and the host machine. This can help to improve the security of your Docker environment.

By following these best practices, you can deploy Docker on various cloud platforms in a secure, reliable, and efficient way.

Future Trends

Docker is a popular containerization platform that organizations of all sizes use to deploy and manage their applications in the cloud. Docker offers several benefits, including portability, consistency, and scalability.

Here are some emerging trends and predictions for the future of Docker in the cloud:

- **Increased adoption of managed Kubernetes services**: Managed Kubernetes services such as Amazon EKS, Google Kubernetes Engine (GKE), and Azure Kubernetes Service (AKS) provide many benefits, such as simplified deployment and management, scalability, and reliability. As a result, we expect to see increased adoption of managed Kubernetes services.
- **Greater use of Docker containers in serverless computing**: Serverless computing is a cloud computing model in which the cloud provider manages the server infrastructure and automatically scales resources based on demand. Docker containers can be used to package and deploy serverless applications. We expect to see greater use of Docker containers in serverless computing.
- **More support for Docker on edge computing devices**: Edge computing is a distributed computing paradigm that brings computation and data storage closer to data sources, such as IoT devices. Docker containers can be used to package and deploy edge applications. We expect to see more support for Docker on edge computing devices.
- **Increased use of Docker for machine learning and artificial intelligence (AI) applications**: Docker containers can package and deploy machine learning and AI models. We expect to see increased use of Docker for machine learning and AI applications.

Solutions and offerings

Cloud providers such as Amazon Web Services (AWS), Microsoft Azure, and Google Cloud Platform (GCP) offer a variety of solutions and offerings for deploying and managing Docker in the cloud.

- **Amazon EKS**: Amazon EKS is a managed Kubernetes service that makes it easy to deploy, manage, and scale Kubernetes applications. Amazon EKS provides many features ideal for running Docker containers, such as support for multiple Kubernetes versions, networking and security features, and various Kubernetes add-ons.

- **Azure Kubernetes Service (AKS)**: Azure Kubernetes Service (AKS) is a managed Kubernetes service that makes it easy to deploy, manage, and scale Kubernetes applications. Azure Kubernetes Service provides many features ideal for running Docker containers, such as support for multiple Kubernetes versions, networking and security features, and various Kubernetes add-ons.
- **Google Kubernetes Engine (GKE)**: Google Kubernetes Engine (GKE) is a managed Kubernetes service that makes it easy to deploy, manage, and scale Kubernetes applications. Google Kubernetes Engine provides many features ideal for running Docker containers, such as support for multiple Kubernetes versions, networking and security features, and various Kubernetes add-ons.

In addition to cloud providers, some third-party vendors offer solutions and offerings for deploying and managing Docker in the cloud. Some of these vendors include Red Hat OpenShift and VMware Tanzu.

Docker is a popular containerization platform used by organizations of all sizes to deploy and manage their applications in the cloud. We expect to see continued growth in adopting Docker in the cloud in the future, as well as new and innovative ways to use Docker to deploy and manage applications in the cloud.

Figure 10.10: *A dock in a lake.*
source: https://unsplash.com/photos/gray-wooden-sea-dock-near-green-pine-trees-under-white-sky-at-daytime-1EYMue_AwDw

Conclusion

After an exhaustive exploration of the myriad facets of leveraging Docker in cloud-native environments, it's evident that the landscape of cloud computing and containerization is evolving rapidly. Understanding what it means to be "cloud-native" and the foundational concepts of running Docker containers in the cloud is a stepping stone toward building agile, scalable, and resilient systems.

From the comprehensive insights into major cloud service providers like AWS, Azure, and GCP to the pivotal role of container orchestration platforms such as Kubernetes in managing Docker containers, this journey has unveiled the significance of choosing the right tools and strategies for efficient deployment.

Delving into deployment strategies like blue-green deployments, canary releases, and rolling updates offered a rich understanding of the mechanisms crucial for maintaining application stability and minimizing downtime. Networking and security intricacies, including VPCs and security groups, form the bedrock of a secure and well-architected cloud environment for Docker containers.

Setting up monitoring and logging is pivotal to ensure optimal performance and to troubleshoot issues effectively. Strategies for cost optimization, such as reserved instances and auto-scaling, provide an avenue to achieve a delicate balance between operational costs and performance.

Exploring hybrid and multi-cloud deployments illuminated the complexities and benefits of leveraging diverse cloud environments. Real-world use cases and best practices provided valuable insights into how organizations effectively deploy Docker on various cloud platforms.

Finally, examining case studies of organizations leveraging Docker on cloud platforms showcased practical implementations. It demonstrated the diverse ways these concepts are implemented in the real world. Gazing into the future, the evolving trends and the growing role of Docker in the cloud promise continued innovation and evolution in the domain.

The quest to harness the full potential of Docker in cloud-native ecosystems requires a holistic understanding of these concepts, constant adaptation to emerging trends, and a relentless pursuit of best practices to utilize the dynamic capabilities offered by cloud-based containerization effectively. As Docker continues to advance with the evolution of cloud computing, staying informed and proactive will be pivotal for organizations seeking to maximize the benefits of cloud-native Docker deployments.

In the next chapter, we will briefly cover some of the main topics and components of Kubernetes, the go-to orchestrator for managing containers at scale. This will give you a friendly overview of what value yet another tool brings and why it came into existence in the first place. If you don't know much about Kubernetes, the next chapter can be a good head-start for your journey toward excellence.

References and Useful Links

The following is a list of references used to write this chapter, as well as links to helpful links that interested readers can use to solidify their study further.

Books

- "Kubernetes: Up & Running" by Kelsey Hightower, Brendan Burns, and Joe Beda
- "Docker Deep Dive" by Nigel Poulton
- "The DevOps Handbook: How to Create World-Class Agility, Reliability, & Security in Technology Organizations" by Gene Kim, Patrick Debois, John Willis, and Jez Humble

Online Resources

- Docker Documentation https://docs.docker.com/
- Kubernetes Documentation https://kubernetes.io/docs/
- AWS Official Documentation https://docs.aws.amazon.com/
- Amazon Elastic Container Service - AWS Observability Best Practices. https://aws-observability.github.io/observability-best-practices/recipes/ecs/
- Introduction | AWS Distro for OpenTelemetry. https://aws-otel.github.io/docs/introduction/?ref=ippon-it-consulting-from-discovery-to-delivery-advanced-aws-partner
- Discovering the Basics of Azure Cloud Services. https://www.tenthline.com/discovering-the-basics-of-azure-cloud-services/
- How to deploy Laravel apps - Elastic Beanstalk. https://blog.mallow-tech.com/2016/03/deploying-laravel-applications-using-aws-elastic-beanstalk/
- Azure Official Documentation https://docs.microsoft.com/en-us/azure/
- How To Create An AKS Cluster with Azure CLI: Step-by-Step Guide – Learn Azure, OpenAI, M365, Terraform, Cybersecurity. https://www.ntweekly.com/2022/03/01/how-to-create-an-aks-cluster-with-azure-cli-step-by-step-guide/
- Brief Introduction of Azure Kubernetes Service – SOS Group Limited. https://soshk.com/brief-introduction-of-azure-kubernetes-service/
- Google Cloud Platform Documentation https://cloud.google.com/docs

- Wikipedia Edge Computing en.wikipedia.org/wiki/Edge_computing
- The Evolution of Container Usage at Netflix https://netflixtechblog.com/the-evolution-of-container-usage-at-netflix-3abfc096781b
- Understanding design of microservices architecture at Netflix https://www.techaheadcorp.com/blog/design-of-microservices-architecture-at-netflix
- How IKEA Retail Standardizes Docker Images for Efficient Machine Learning Model Deployment https://www.docker.com/blog/how-ikea-retail-standardizes-docker-images-for-efficient-machine-learning-model-deployment/
- History of IKEA.com: Static files and Microfrontends https://medium.com/flat-pack-tech/history-of-ikea-com-static-files-and-microfrontends-6def9d7c4285

Training and Courses

Docker Mastery Course on Udemy https://www.udemy.com/course/docker-mastery/

Kubernetes for Developers on Pluralsight https://www.pluralsight.com/courses/kubernetes-developers-core-concepts

Articles and Blogs

The New Stack https://thenewstack.io/

CNCF Blog https://www.cncf.io/blog/

Kubernetes Blog https://kubernetes.io/blog/

Forums and Community Platforms

Docker Community Forums https://forums.docker.com/

Kubernetes Reddit Community https://www.reddit.com/r/kubernetes/

Stack Overflow - Docker Tag https://stackoverflow.com/questions/tagged/docker

Additional Resources

State of Kubernetes Report by CNCF https://www.cncf.io/

AWS Whitepapers https://aws.amazon.com/whitepapers/

These resources offer a wealth of knowledge and continuous updates in the rapidly evolving field of cloud-native deployments, containerization, and cloud computing. They provide diverse perspectives, practical tutorials, and a platform for discussions to deepen understanding and expertise in deploying Docker on cloud platforms.

CHAPTER 11
Introduction to Kubernetes

Figure 11.1: *Two divers in the deep water.*
source: https://unsplash.com/photos/a-scuba-diver-swims-through-an-underwater-cave-yx-7TJle8LhM

Introduction

In this chapter, you can anticipate a concise yet informative exploration of Kubernetes–a dominant force in container orchestration. The chapter will shed light on the fundamental essence of Kubernetes, delving into its inception, evolution, and the pivotal challenges it aims to address in modern cloud computing and containerized applications.

Through a brief yet insightful journey, the chapter outlines the key characteristics and unique features that propelled Kubernetes into its broad adoption across industries. It will highlight the essential problems it resolves, elucidating why it became the cornerstone of orchestrating containerized workloads and handling the complexities of modern distributed systems. The focus will be on encapsulating the core value that Kubernetes brings, setting the stage for a deeper understanding and appreciation of its significance in contemporary software development and deployment practices.

Structure

- Kubernetes Architecture
- Kubernetes Concepts
- Practical Examples

Origins and Evolution of Kubernetes

Kubernetes is an open-source container orchestration platform that automates the deployment, management, and scaling of containerized software applications (apps) and services. It was initially developed by Google, based on the Borg system that Google uses to run its large-scale infrastructure.

The name Kubernetes comes from the Greek word for "helmsman" or "pilot." It is a fitting name, as Kubernetes is responsible for steering the course of containerized applications.

Kubernetes was first released to the public in 2014, and it has quickly become the most popular container orchestration platform in the world. It is used by companies of all sizes, from startups to Fortune 500 companies, to run their containerized applications.

Key Characteristics

Kubernetes has evolved significantly since its initial release. Some of the critical changes that have been made over the years include:

- **Support for more container runtimes**: Kubernetes initially only supported Docker, but it now supports a variety of other container runtimes, including CRI-O and containerd. This gives users more flexibility in how they choose to run their containerized applications.
- **Improved scalability and performance**: Kubernetes has been optimized for scalability and performance, enabling it to handle large-scale workloads. It is also now more efficient in terms of resource usage.
- **More features and functionality**: Kubernetes has constantly added new features and functionality. For example, it now supports Kubernetes Network Policies (KNPs), which allow users to control network traffic between pods.

Importance of Kubernetes

Kubernetes is critical because it makes it easy to run containerized applications at scale reliably and efficiently.

Here are some of the critical reasons why Kubernetes is critical:

- **Scalability**: Kubernetes can scale horizontally to support large-scale workloads. This means you can easily add more resources to your cluster as your application grows.
- **Reliability**: Kubernetes is designed to be highly reliable, even during failures. If a node in your cluster fails, Kubernetes will automatically reschedule the workloads to other nodes. This helps to ensure that your application is always available.
- **Portability**: Kubernetes applications can be deployed in any infrastructure that supports Kubernetes, including on-premises, cloud, and hybrid environments. This allows you to choose the infrastructure that best meets your needs.
- **Cost savings**: Kubernetes can help you to save money on your infrastructure costs. By running your applications in containers, you can use fewer resources and reduce overall costs.
- **Increased agility**: Kubernetes can help you increase your development team's agility. By making it easy to deploy and manage containerized applications, Kubernetes can help you to get your applications to market faster.
- **Improved security**: Kubernetes can help you improve your applications' security. By isolating your applications in containers and using Kubernetes features like Kubernetes Network Policies, Kubernetes can help to protect your applications from attack.

Real-world Examples

Many companies are using Kubernetes to reap the benefits of running containerized applications at scale. Here are a few real-world examples:

- **Google**: Google utilizes Borg, its proprietary cluster management system, to operate its expansive infrastructure. Like the open-source Kubernetes, Borg enables Google to scale its applications horizontally and maintain their consistent availability effectively.
- **Netflix**: Netflix uses Kubernetes to run its streaming service. Kubernetes helps Netflix to scale its service up and down to meet demand and to ensure that its service is always available to its users.

- **Spotify**: Spotify uses Kubernetes to run its music streaming service. Kubernetes helps Spotify to scale its service horizontally and to ensure that its service is always available to its users.
- **Airbnb**: Airbnb uses Kubernetes to run its travel booking platform. Kubernetes helps Airbnb scale its platform horizontally and ensure it is always available to its users.

These are just a few examples of the many companies using Kubernetes to reap the benefits of running large-scale containerized applications.

Kubernetes Architectures

Kubernetes architecture comprises two main components: the control plane and the worker nodes.

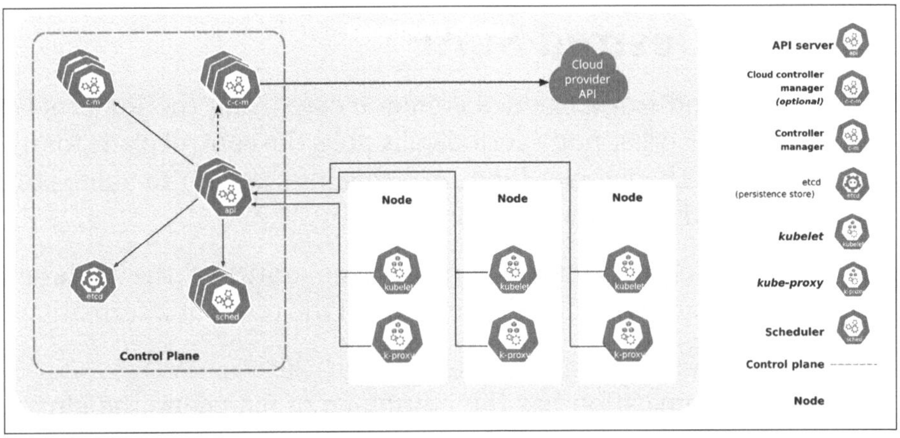

Figure 11.2: *Architecture of Kubernetes from the official documentation. source: https://kubernetes.io/docs/concepts/overview/components/*

Control Plane

The control plane manages the cluster and schedules workloads to the worker nodes. The control plane consists of the following components:

- **kube-apiserver**: This is the frontend component of the control plane and is responsible for exposing the Kubernetes API.
- **etcd**: This distributed key-value store stores Kubernetes configuration and operational data.
- **kube-scheduler**: This is responsible for scheduling workloads to the worker nodes.

- **kube-controller-manager**: This is responsible for running several controllers that manage various aspects of the cluster, such as the deployment controller, the replica set controller, and the node controller.

Worker nodes

The worker nodes are responsible for running the workloads. The worker nodes consist of the following components:

- **kubelet**: This agent runs on each worker node and is responsible for communicating with the control plane and running the workloads.
- **kube-proxy**: This is responsible for load-balancing traffic between the pods on the worker node.
- **Container runtime**: This runs the containers on the worker node.

Current vs Desired State

The control plane and worker nodes communicate using the Kubernetes API. The kubelet on each worker node periodically polls the control plane for updates to the cluster state. The kubelet then uses this information to start, stop, and manage the workloads on the worker node.

On the flip side, each kubelet also updates the status of the node and the container it is running by periodically sending all the relevant information to the Kubernetes API server.

This two-way communication has the advantage of managing the cluster as a whole, having all the information centralized and accessible from a single source of truth, and syncing the current state of the cluster to the desired state in an infinite loop using all the components mentioned earlier.

The main selling point of Kubernetes is that last part, that is, ensuring at all times that the current state is observed and managed to reach the desired state. For example, if you want two instances of your application running, the Kubernetes workload will ensure that it is the case unless you change it otherwise.

Figure 11.3: *The picture of a yellow bicycle.*
source: https://unsplash.com/photos/a-close-up-of-a-yellow-bicycle-with-a-basket-lRX-BRFJRFqY

Kubernetes Concepts

Kubernetes is a big topic and deserves its scope and dedication. There are excellent resources out there that dive deep into the concepts. But, for the sake of introduction and overview, we will introduce you to the most essential concepts in this ecosystem so that you understand the underlying terminologies.

Control Plane

The Kubernetes control plane is the set of components that manage the Kubernetes cluster. It is responsible for scheduling workloads to nodes, monitoring the cluster's health, and responding to events.

The control plane can be self-managed or cloud-managed.

Self-Managed Control Plane

A self-managed control plane is a control plane that you manage yourself. This means you are responsible for installing, configuring, and maintaining the control plane components.

Self-managed control planes can be complex to set up and manage, but they offer the most flexibility and control.

Cloud-Managed Control Plane

A cloud-managed control plane is a control plane managed by a cloud provider. This means the cloud provider is responsible for installing, configuring, and maintaining the control plane components.

Cloud-managed control planes are easier to set up and manage than self-managed ones, but offer less flexibility and control.

Which type of control plane should you use?

Consider a self-managed control plane if you have the expertise and resources to manage a self-managed control plane. However, if you are new to Kubernetes or need more resources to manage a self-managed control plane, consider using a cloud-managed control plane.

Here are some of the benefits of using a cloud-managed control plane:

- **Easy to set up and manage**: Cloud providers make setting up and managing a Kubernetes cluster easy. You can have a cluster up and running in minutes with a few clicks.
- **Reliable and scalable**: Cloud providers offer reliable and scalable Kubernetes clusters. You don't have to worry about managing the underlying infrastructure.
- **Secure**: Cloud providers offer secure Kubernetes clusters. You can be confident that your cluster is protected from unauthorized access.

Here are some of the benefits of using a self-managed control plane:

- **More flexibility and control**: A self-managed control plane gives you more flexibility and control over your cluster. You can customize the cluster to meet your specific needs.
- **Reduced costs**: Using a self-managed control plane may save money over time. This is because you are not paying a cloud provider to manage your cluster.

Ultimately, the best type of control plane for you will depend on your specific needs and requirements.

Nodes

A Kubernetes node is a worker machine that runs containerized applications. Nodes can be physical machines, virtual machines, or cloud instances.

Pods

A Kubernetes pod is the basic unit of deployment and management in Kubernetes. A pod is a group of one or more containers that are deployed and managed together. Pods share the same network namespace and resources, such as CPU and memory.

Deployments

A deployment is a declarative object that describes how to deploy a pod or set of pods. Deployments can be used to roll out new versions of your application or to scale your application up or down.

When you create a deployment, Kubernetes will create a replica set for the deployment. A replica set is a group of identical pods that are managed together. Kubernetes will ensure that the desired number of pods for the replica set is running. In short, Deployment creates ReplicaSet, ReplicaSet creates Pods, and there are one or more containers within each Pod.

Statefulsets

A StatefulSet is a Kubernetes controller that manages the deployment and scaling of a set of Pods. It is similar to a deployment, but provides additional features for managing stateful applications.

StatefulSets are designed to run stateful applications, which are applications that need to maintain a state or identity across restarts. Examples of stateful applications include databases, message queues, and key-value stores.

StatefulSets provides the following features for managing stateful applications:

- **Unique identity**: Each Pod in a StatefulSet is assigned a unique identity maintained across restarts. This allows the application to track which Pod is responsible for which data.
- **Ordered startup and shutdown**: StatefulSets start and shut down Pods in a specific order. This ensures that the application is started and stopped in a way that preserves its state.
- **Persistent storage**: StatefulSets can mount persistent storage to Pods. This allows the application to store data that needs to be preserved across restarts.

Services

A service is an abstraction that allows you to expose a pod or set of pods to other pods in the cluster or to the outside world. Services can be used to load balance traffic between pods and to provide a name and port for your application.

When you create a service, Kubernetes will create an endpoint for the service. An endpoint is a list of pods that the service exposes. Kubernetes will also create a load balancer for the service. The load balancer will distribute traffic between the pods at the endpoint.

Services can be used to expose your application to the outside world by creating a service for your application and then exposing the service to the outside world. For example, you could expose the service to the outside world through a cloud load balancer or a firewall.

Figure 11.4: *An athlete lifting weights.*
source: https://unsplash.com/photos/person-weightlifting-painting-vqDAUejnwKw

Creating Your First Kubernetes Cluster

Now that you have seen the definitions and introduction, it's time to look more closely into practical examples and get hands-on experience.

Firstly, we will need to create a Kubernetes cluster. There are countless tools out there that you can use to spin up a Kubernetes cluster, but here is a non-exhaustive list of possibilities:

- Using a managed Kubernetes cluster, such as AWS EKS, Azure AKS, Google GKS, and so on.
- Using one of the popular tools to quickly spin up a local cluster, for example, **`Docker Desktop Kubernetes,`** Kind, K3d, Minikube, Skaffold, and so on.
- Using Vagrant and manually provision and install the required dependencies.

For the sake of this book, we will follow the tradition and keep everything specifically Docker-related, as is the book's intention. Therefore, we will spin up a Kubernetes cluster using the Docker Desktop. You have seen instructions on installing Docker Desktop at the beginning of this book in *Chapter 2, Docker Architecture and Components*, but if you still don't have it installed, follow this link to get to the installation page:

https://www.docker.com/products/docker-desktop/

After ensuring you have Docker Desktop installed on your machine, you can open the application and create a Kubernetes cluster, as shown in the following screenshot.

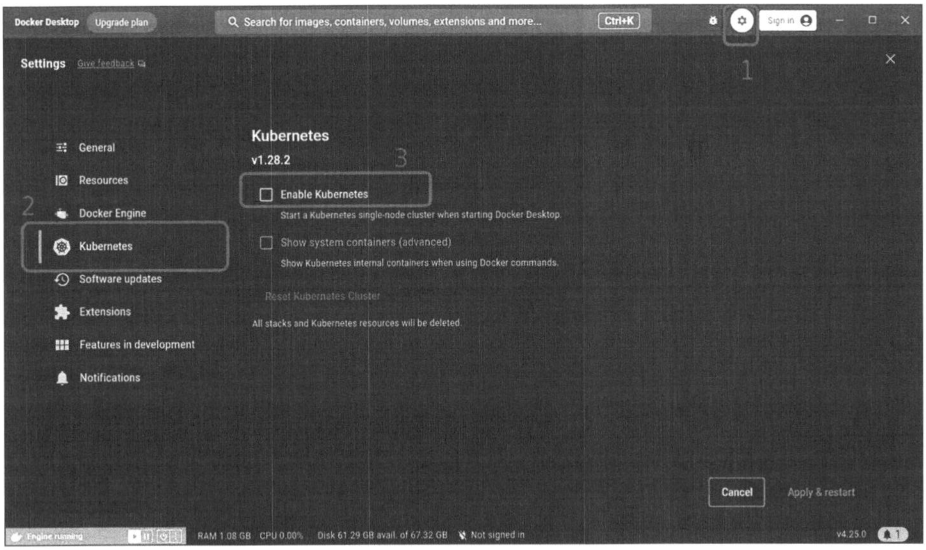

Figure 11.5: *Docker Desktop Kubernetes - part 1 (Screenshot by the author from Docker Desktop)*

After starting the Kubernetes cluster, you can see that it is running on the same page, just as seen in the following screenshot.

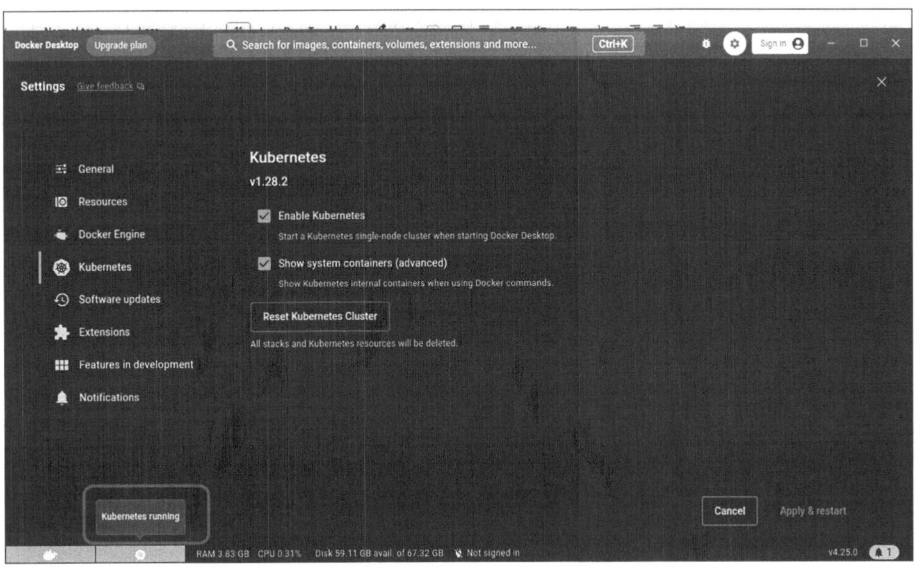

Figure 11.6: *Docker Desktop Kubernetes - part 2 (Screenshot by the author from Docker Desktop)*

Now that the server side is ready, it's time to get your Kubernetes client ready.

The most helpful client of Kubernetes is the `kubectl` CLI. It is developed internally by the Kubernetes itself, so you won't have to doubt its compatibility, as it is always up-to-date with the respective Kubernetes version.

To install **`kubectl`**, you can head over to the official documentation and download the binary for your platform from the following URL.

https://kubernetes.io/docs/tasks/tools/#kubectl

Here's the command to install the **`kubectl`** for an AMD64 machine as a demonstration.

```
version=$(curl -L -s https://dl.k8s.io/release/stable.txt)
curl -LO "https://dl.k8s.io/release/${version}/bin/linux/amd64/kubectl"
chmod +x kubectl
mv kubectl /usr/local/bin/
```

After this step, we have the server and the client set up, and we are ready to create our first Kubernetes-hosted application.

Creating Your First Kubernetes Application

Kubernetes API server exposes a REST API, which means if you can send an HTTP request to the server, you can instruct it to perform your tasks.

But that is just the implementation details since, from a client's perspective, we only need to write one or more manifest files in JSON or YAML format and pass them to the `kubectl` CLI. The rest is handled under the hood; we wouldn't need to worry about it. But I invite you to check out the official documentation to learn more.

https://kubernetes.io/docs

The best part, especially for beginners, is that we wouldn't need to write those YAML formatted files line by line. We can use most of the boilerplate coming right from the `kubectl` itself.

Let's show an example for better understanding.

Earlier in the course, you were introduced to Deployments, which, in a nutshell, ensure that a specific number of instances are running at all times. We will create a Deployment of an Nginx server inside our cluster.

To do so, we run the following command.

```
kubectl create deployment nginx \
  --image=nginx:1.25-alpine \
  --dry-run=client -o yaml > nginx.yml
```

This will give us the YAML definition in a file in the current working directory.

If we look at the file, we will see the following content.

```yaml
apiVersion: apps/v1
kind: Deployment
metadata:
  creationTimestamp: null
  labels:
    app: nginx
  name: nginx
spec:
  replicas: 1
  selector:
    matchLabels:
      app: nginx
  strategy: {}
  template:
    metadata:
      creationTimestamp: null
      labels:
        app: nginx
    spec:
      containers:
      - image: nginx:1.25-alpine
        name: nginx
        resources: {}
status: {}
```

You can see many attributes in this file that we may not be comfortable creating ourselves because we may miss some. Using the kubectl is almost always the go-to approach when creating resources from scratch since it gives you the boilerplate, and you can apply your modifications.

For example, we may want to change the image later on, or we may want to increase the number of replicas of this deployment. We can also add new attributes that are not present in this definition. You shall find a complete list of available keys in the official documentation.

Having this definition, we can modify the file as we desire and once finished, we can apply (that is, **create**) this Deployment using the following command.

```
kubectl apply -f nginx.yml
```

The output shall give you the successful execution result.

```
deployment.apps/nginx created
```

Now that we have created our deployment, we can check its creation status using the following command.

```
$ kubectl get deployment
NAME          READY   UP-TO-DATE   AVAILABLE   AGE
nginx         1/1     1            1           2m19s
```

As you can see, the deployment has stabilized and is now in the desired state.

We can even check to see if the child pod exists, as expected.

```
$ kubectl get pod
NAME                         READY   STATUS    RESTARTS   AGE
nginx-779cd7c47-hd9zb        1/1     Running   0          8m57s
```

Just as you expect, this pod is now running, and you can see under the Ready column that it has one out of its total one container running.

Now, let's try to access this Nginx service from our local machine.

The way for us to do that is to create another type of resource in the Kubernetes cluster called Service. The Service resource is responsible for routing the traffic within the cluster and traffic from outside to the respective Pods.

Creating a Service for our Nginx Deployment is done using the following command.

```
$ kubectl expose deploy/nginx --port=80 --target-port=80 --type=NodePort
service/nginx exposed
```

As you would expect, **kubectl** is your best friend in this and many other cases.

In this command, we are passing three options. In the first option, we specify the port number for this service. This port refers to the one exposed within the cluster, i.e., any other pod in the cluster can access this service through this port.

The target port specifies the port that the underlying Pod is listening on. In the case of Nginx, we know it is opening port 80 inside the container, but it might be different in other cases.

Lastly, we want this service to be of type NodePort, one of the four available options.

- **ClusterIP**: This type of service is only accessible from within the cluster by other pods. It cannot be accessible outside the Kubernetes cluster (unless alternative ways are taken).
- **NodePort**: This type of service is accessible from within the cluster and from all the worker machines running in the cluster. If you have three nodes in the cluster, this port number will be exposed to all three with the same number.
- **LoadBalancer**: This is a particular type that requires additional effort on top of Kubernetes to work correctly. It will expose the Service to the Pods within the cluster, the worker nodes within the cluster, and the outside world through the internet, for example, through one of the cloud provider load balancers. You may not be able to use this resource locally, but rather, operating a cluster hosted in the cloud is an option.
- **ExternalName**: This type of Service maps the Service to a DNS name, maybe a service hosted outside the cluster, for example, using a hosted database outside the cluster. You rarely use this resource, but when you need it, it's there for you when the day comes.

Unless you run a production Kubernetes cluster, you may only sometimes use the last two types of Service since they are more suited for non-localhost use cases.

For your reference, here is the YAML definition of the newly created service.

```
apiVersion: v1
kind: Service
metadata:
  creationTimestamp: null
  labels:
    app: nginx
    name: nginx
spec:
  ports:
    - port: 80
  protocol: TCP
  targetPort: 80
```

```
  selector:
    app: nginx
  type: NodePort
status:
  loadBalancer: {}
```

Now that we have created the Service, it's time to send traffic to the Nginx and see the result.

The way to do that depends on how you run your Kubernetes cluster. For our use-case, because we're using Docker Desktop Kubernetes, we can simply use `localhost`.

We first need to find the node-port of the Service.

```
$ kubectl get service nginx
NAME    TYPE       CLUSTER-IP      EXTERNAL-IP   PORT(S)        AGE
nginx   NodePort   10.106.183.30   <none>        80:32593/TCP   13m
```

You can see that the type of service is indeed **NodePort**. We seek the number below the `PORT(S)` column, right after the semicolon, which is 32593.

This port is randomly allocated; you can modify it to something memorable. The way to do that is either using `kubectl edit service nginx` and modifying the attribute **nodePort** or using the following one-liner in your CLI.

```
kubectl patch service nginx --type=json \
  -p '[{"op": "replace", "path": "/spec/ports/0/nodePort", "value":
32000}]'
```

This will change the node port to port 32000, which is easier to remember. Note that you can change this value to anything between 32000 and 32767.

The syntax of this command shouldn't scare you since you can get the exact location of the attribute you want to change just by looking at the YAML definition of the service when running the following command.

```
kubectl get service nginx -o yaml
```

After changing the node port, we can access the service from the localhost using the following command.

```
curl localhost:32000
```

This will give you the response coming from the Nginx server.

Congratulations, you have created your first application in Kubernetes.

For your reference, here is the YAML definition of the created deployment.

So far, this is similar to what you would have achieved with `docker run nginx:1.25-alpine`. But the thing that makes this approach different is not that Docker cannot do this. Kubernetes can do more; with Kubernetes, you can manage a fleet of machines and not just one, and you can coordinate the communication between different Pods, their storage, their rollout strategy, and much more. And just because you don't see all that is not happening in this book doesn't mean that it's not possible. It only means that we can only cover so far in one book chapter.

Creating Your First Statefulset

So far, you have seen how to run a stateless application. The application will not hold **state** or data between requests; you shall send an infinite number of requests in parallel or sequence, and each individual's result will not impact the one coming afterwards. This **state** can be stored in memory, database, or persistent volume.

Another characteristic of stateful applications is that they often require multiple pods to work together, and the order in which pods are started and stopped matters. This is an informal definition of stateful vs. stateless applications, but it shall suffice in the context of Kubernetes and what we aim to introduce.

Now that you have seen the definition, it's time to create a stateful application.

We will create a PostgreSQL database within the cluster with a volume attached for this demo. That way, upon restarts, the pod's data will be preserved, and we will keep the promise of durability to the clients of the database.

Creating **`StatefulSet`** is more involved than a simple **`kubectl create deployment.`** We can use the same CLI command to create the boilerplate and modify the content to match our desired state.

Pro tip: You can use **`kubectl`** for many other scenarios to create the boilerplate and modify the content to your needs. This way, you won't have to memorize countless keys and their indentation or exact syntax.

First, let's try to create a basic **`StatefulSet`** with CLI and only use terminal commands.

```
kubectl create deployment postgresql \
  --image=postgresql:16 --dry-run=client -o yaml | \
  sed ‘s/Deployment/StatefulSet/’ | \
```

```
  yq 'del(.spec.strategy)' | \
  tee postgres.yml
```

And with that, this is the content you will receive:

```
apiVersion: apps/v1
kind: StatefulSet
metadata:
  creationTimestamp: null
  labels:
    app: postgres
  name: postgres
spec:
  replicas: 1
  selector:
    matchLabels:
      app: postgres
  template:
    metadata:
      creationTimestamp: null
      labels:
        app: postgres
    spec:
      containers:
        - image: postgres:16
          name: postgres
          resources: {}
status: {}
```

This file is a valid Kubernetes object; you can easily create it inside the cluster. But one other requirement still needs to be met with this definition.

We want to persist the database data so that upon restarts or crashes, we don't lose the data, hence **stateful**.

The way to do that has a lot to do with how you set up your Kubernetes cluster. But if you have followed along and created your cluster using Docker Desktop, you should not worry too much about it if you're a novice or beginner with Kubernetes.

We will modify the earlier YAML definition as follows.

```
apiVersion: apps/v1
kind: StatefulSet
metadata:
  creationTimestamp: null
  labels:
    app: postgres
  name: postgres
spec:
  replicas: 1
  selector:
    matchLabels:
      app: postgres
  template:
    metadata:
      creationTimestamp: null
      labels:
        app: postgres
    spec:
      containers:
        - image: postgres:16
          env:
            - name: POSTGRES_HOST_AUTH_METHOD
              value: trust
          name: postgres
          resources: {}
          volumeMounts:
            - mountPath: /var/lib/postgresql
              name: data
  volumeClaimTemplates:
  - metadata:
      name: data
    spec:
      accessModes:
        - ReadWriteOnce
      resources:
        requests:
          storage: 10Gi
status: {}
```

The indentation matters a lot in these YAML definitions, and if you miss one space or mix and match tabs and spaces in the same file, you will get the relevant error on your screen.

The definition we have created so far will have the same effect as if I had run the following docker command:

```
docker run -d --name postgres -v data-postgres:/var/lib/postgresql
postgres:16
```

The Kubernetes scheduler will select a worker node for the pod of this **Statefulset**, which will be the same localhost machine in our case of Docker Desktop Kubernetes. Then, the **kubelet** on the worker node will abide by the scheduler's decision and create a pod on the machine. At every interval, the **kubelet** will update the status of its managed pods, the containers within them, and the underlying node by sending the updates to the Kubernetes API server.

These are implementation details, and you don't have to worry yourself too much if you don't know too much about the mechanisms inside Kubernetes since we're only giving you a glimpse of its many capabilities, introducing you to the main topics while showing a brief detail for each section that will help for the better understanding of the entire thing.

So far, we have created two applications, and we can check their status by running the following command.

```
$ kubectl get pods
NAME                     READY   STATUS      RESTARTS   AGE
nginx-6848fd9964-2dl6t   1/1     Running     0          100m
postgres-0               1/1     Running     0          10m
```

The second column shows one container in the pod (the number on the right of the slash) and one running (the number on the left). Essentially, the pod's only container is running.

The second application should have a volume attached to it, so let's check the existence of a **PersistentVolumeClaim**.

```
$ kubectl get persistentvolumeclaims
NAME              STATUS VOLUME                                   CAPACITY
data-postgres-0 Bound  pvc-778b69b8-b011-4505-9e5f-6655c4ece7c9 10Gi
```

Some columns were truncated for brevity, but you can see that the pods and the containers within them are running as expected, and the volume is present on the worker node.

Exposing the Service

You've already seen how to expose a service before when creating the Nginx Deployment and making it accessible from within the cluster and the worker nodes.

This time, we will use the same practice to expose the PostgreSQL database to applications within the cluster. This way, another pod can access the database to persist its information.

As before, we still cannot use **kubectl** expose to create a service for **Statefulset**, and you may need to define a YAML definition for advanced use cases. But there is a trick we can use to create a simple service without leaving the command line.

In Kubernetes, the Service heavily relies on the pods' labels as the upstream server. As such, if the label of a pod matches the one the Service is expecting, the traffic will be forwarded to the pod.

That said, we can find our PostgreSQL pod's label and create a service targeting it.

```
$ kubectl get pods --show-labels
NAME                        READY   STATUS    RESTARTS   AGE     LABELS
postgres-0                  1/1     Running   0          107m
app=postgres,controller-revision-hash=postgres-
686c6b8bf6,statefulset.kubernetes.io/pod-name=postgres-0
```

The last column shows a label with the key app and the value of **postgres**.

With that in mind, we can create a service with the following command, adding an option at the end to output the final manifest when the command is done.

```
kubectl create service clusterip postgres --tcp=5432:5432 -o yaml
```

The output will be similar to the following:

```
apiVersion: v1
kind: Service
metadata:
  creationTimestamp: "2023-11-11T06:13:21Z"
```

```
  labels:
    app: postgres
  name: postgres
  namespace: default
  resourceVersion: “4784”
  uid: 0efd6820-4d06-421f-86b3-41ce6f23342c
spec:
  clusterIP: 10.43.210.135
  clusterIPs:
  - 10.43.210.135
  internalTrafficPolicy: Cluster
  ipFamilies:
  - IPv4
  ipFamilyPolicy: SingleStack
  ports:
  - name: 5432-5432
    port: 5432
    protocol: TCP
    targetPort: 5432
  selector:
    app: postgres
  sessionAffinity: None
  type: ClusterIP
status:
  loadBalancer: {}
```

You can see in the `selector` field that it matches the first label of our `postgres` pod. This indicates that this service will work as expected, but we can also double-check to ensure the final state is what we wanted.

```
kubectl get endpoints
```

The output looks similar to the following:

```
NAME        ENDPOINTS         AGE
postgres    10.42.0.16:5432   2m54s
```

The IP you see under the endpoints column is the IP address of the pod.

```
$ kubectl get pods -o wide
NAME       READY STATUS  RESTARTS AGE  IP         NODE
postgres-0 1/1   Running 0        115m 10.42.0.16 docker-desktop
```

Some of the columns have been removed for brevity.

You can see that the pod's IP matches the endpoint of our newly created Service, proving that this Service is working as expected.

The next mission is to create a pod using this PostgreSQL instance as its database.

For this demo, we have picked the non-official WordPress application that supports PostgreSQL as its database; the official image only supports working with MySQL!

Creating Your First ConfigMap and Secret

To create the application, we must create some configurations and pass them along to the WordPress app to talk to the PostgreSQL in our cluster.

We have two files with the following content:

```
# wordpress.env
WORDPRESS_DB_HOST=postgres
WORDPRESS_DB_USER=
WORDPRESS_DB_NAME=postgres
WORDPRESS_TABLE_PREFIX=

# wordpress.secret
WORDPRESS_DB_PASSWORD=
```

You remember that we didn't specify any password for our PostgreSQL instance, and that's why the corresponding credentials in the WordPress config are also an empty string.

We will use these files to create two resources in our cluster.

One **ConfigMap** to hold the non-confidential values that we wouldn't mind having in plaintext.

Additionally, we'll create a secret resource that holds the credentials. The difference between **ConfigMap** and resource is subtle, but essential. **ConfigMaps** are not encrypted and their value are stored as plaintext in the underlying disk (the encryption of the disk is not taken into account).

However, secrets are usually encrypted in Kubernetes offering of Cloud Providers. You can also add your encryption solution for self-hosted Kubernetes clusters so that those values are always encrypted and inaccessible from the outside.

Another difference between **ConfigMap** and Secret is that the value is always Base64 encoded at the administrator layer and not shown as plaintext. That adds a thin layer of security, but you must remember that this is just an encoding and anyone can decode them without problem. Encryption, however, is a different story, and unless you have the key file that encrypted the value, you won't be able to find out about its decrypted value.

Remember that Docker Desktop Kubernetes does not encrypt Secret unless additional effort is added. But for the sake of our demo, since we're the only one operating on the localhost machine, we wouldn't mind about that! In production applications, it is strongly recommended to enable encryption through some means.

Back to our application, with the contents of the preceding two files for configuration, here's how to use the two resources to pass to the WordPress application.

```
kubectl create configmap wordpress --from-env-file=wordpress.env
kubectl create secret generic wordpress --from-env-file=wordpress.secret
```

To see the created values, we can run the following command.

```
kubectl get secret,configmap wordpress -o yaml
```

You can see that I can get more than one resource at a time with kubectl. In fact, `kubectl` is a very handy command, and we strongly recommend studying it thoroughly if you want to operate a Kubernetes cluster.

The output will look similar to the following.

```
apiVersion: v1
items:
- apiVersion: v1
  data:
    WORDPRESS_DB_PASSWORD: ""
  kind: Secret
  metadata:
    creationTimestamp: "2023-11-11T06:00:13Z"
    name: wordpress
    namespace: default
    resourceVersion: "4521"
    uid: 6d84a4cd-d010-4d9c-bc6b-ff0fa21fc507
  type: Opaque
```

```
- apiVersion: v1
  data:
    WORDPRESS_DB_HOST: postgres
    WORDPRESS_DB_NAME: postgres
    WORDPRESS_DB_PASSWORD: “”
    WORDPRESS_DB_USER: “”
    WORDPRESS_TABLE_PREFIX: “”
  kind: ConfigMap
  metadata:
    creationTimestamp: “2023-11-11T05:58:43Z”
    name: wordpress
    namespace: default
    resourceVersion: “4491”
    uid: de32eb40-b372-443c-bb77-8b7c9ed7fdec
kind: List
metadata:
  resourceVersion: “”
```

That's it for the configuration. We're ready to create the application and pass these values in.

As usual, we will use **kubectl** to create the boilerplate for us.

```
kubectl create deploy wordpress \
  --image=ntninja/wordpress-postgresql:5.0 \
  --dry-run=client -o yaml | \
  tee wordpress.yml
```

The result will look similar to what we saw earlier.

```
apiVersion: apps/v1
kind: Deployment
metadata:
  creationTimestamp: null
  labels:
    app: wordpress
  name: wordpress
spec:
  replicas: 1
  selector:
    matchLabels:
      app: wordpress
```

```
  strategy: {}
  template:
    metadata:
      creationTimestamp: null
      labels:
        app: wordpress
    spec:
      containers:
      - image: ntninja/wordpress-postgresql:5.0
        resources: {}
status: {}
```

Add the following lines to the container to fetch the newly created configurations using the editor of your choice.

```
apiVersion: apps/v1
kind: Deployment
metadata:
  creationTimestamp: null
  labels:
    app: wordpress
  name: wordpress
spec:
  replicas: 1
  selector:
    matchLabels:
      app: wordpress
  strategy: {}
  template:
    metadata:
      creationTimestamp: null
      labels:
        app: wordpress
    spec:
      containers:
      - image: ntninja/wordpress-postgresql:5.0
        envFrom:
          - secretRef:
              name: wordpress
          - configMapRef:
              name: wordpress
```

```
        name: wordpress-postgresql
        resources: {}
status: {}
```

Once all is ready, apply the deployment with the following command.

```
kubectl apply -f wordpress.yml
```

And shortly after the whole thing is stabilized, we can see the following status from the pods.

```
$ kubectl get pods
NAME                         READY   STATUS    RESTARTS   AGE
postgres-0                   1/1     Running   0          142m
wordpress-85f46c5b6c-52ddg   1/1     Running   0          44m
```

This shows that our pods have been successfully created. We can even see their logs as follows.

```
kubectl logs deploy/wordpress
```

We can also check the logs of the PostgreSQL application.

```
kubectl logs statefulsets.apps/postgres
```

Kubernetes Wrap up

That's it for our demo application. You have seen how to create stateless applications, as well as stateful. You have also seen how to create a service so that apps from within the cluster can communicate with one another.

You have also seen how to expose the applications to the worker node to be accessible from outside the cluster.

This will give you a good picture of the possibilities, features, and capabilities you will get operating a Kubernetes cluster.

This is by no means a complete guide. We won't be able to cover everything related to the Kubernetes cluster in a single chapter of a book. But that shouldn't stop you from exploring further in your adventure towards mastery.

Figure 11.7: *A mountain climber descending.*
source: https://unsplash.com/photos/a-man-running-up-a-mountain-with-a-sky-background-gj7WgSOIIu4

Conclusion

In this chapter, we have introduced you to Kubernetes and its basic concepts. We have seen how to create a Kubernetes cluster, deploy a stateless application, expose it to the outside world, and create a stateful application. This gives you a good foundation for understanding the power and flexibility of Kubernetes.

However, this is just the beginning. Kubernetes is a complex and powerful platform, with much more to learn. For example, we haven't covered topics such as:

- **Advanced networking**: Kubernetes provides various networking features, such as load balancing, service discovery, and network policies.
- Storage: Kubernetes supports a variety of storage providers, including persistent volumes, persistent volume claims, and storage classes.
- **Security**: Kubernetes provides several features to help you secure your cluster, such as role-based access control (RBAC) and network policies.
- **Monitoring and logging**: Kubernetes provides several tools to help you monitor and log your cluster, such as Prometheus and Grafana.

If you want to learn more about Kubernetes, many resources are available online and in print. We encourage you to continue your exploration of this powerful platform.

Kubernetes is a complex and powerful platform, but it is also gratifying. By mastering Kubernetes, you can unlock the full potential of cloud-native computing and build scalable, reliable, and secure applications.

Kubernetes is like a Swiss Army knife for cloud-native computing. It has a tool for every job and is constantly improving.

In the next chapter, we will cover some of the advanced Docker concepts we haven't discussed so far. We will return to storage, networking, and other topics that haven't been covered. So buckle up, and let's explore more.

References

Here are some references and useful links for readers who want to study further on the topic of Kubernetes:

Books

- Kubernetes in Action (Manning, 2022) by Marko Luksa
- Kubernetes Up and Running (O'Reilly, 2022) by Kelsey Hightower, Brendan Burns, and Joe Beda
- Kubernetes: The Complete Guide (Udemy, 2023) by Mumshad Mannambeth

Online courses

- Kubernetes Fundamentals (Coursera) by Google Cloud
- Kubernetes for Beginners (Udemy) by Mumshad Mannambeth
- Kubernetes Certified Kubernetes Application Developer (CKAD) with Practice Tests (Udemy) by Mumshad Mannambeth

Official documentation

- Kubernetes documentation: https://kubernetes.io/docs/home/
- Kubernetes tutorials: https://kubernetes.io/docs/tutorials/
- Kubernetes History: https://www.ibm.com/blog/kubernetes-history/

Community Resources

- Kubernetes blog: https://kubernetes.io/blog/
- Kubernetes Slack channel: https://communityinviter.com/apps/kubernetes/community
- Kubernetes Stack Overflow tag: https://stackoverflow.com/questions/tagged/kubernetes

Chapter 12

Exploring Advanced Docker Concepts

Figure 12.1: *A picture of a chain over a sea.*
source: https://unsplash.com/photos/brown-metal-chain-with-white-background-ipuiM-36tAg

Introduction

This chapter will discuss some advanced topics that haven't been covered before, and you might need one or multiple. The topics in this chapter are in no specific order and are here to aid you in better understanding the capabilities of Docker and the ecosystem around it. It will aid you in implementing specific use cases in your current and future projects. If you need to learn more, we encourage you to refer to the official documentation for a complete list of available features.

Structure

In this chapter, we will cover the following topics:

- Docker in Docker
- Rootless mode
- Dev Environments
- WASM
- Docker Extensions
- Docker Content Trust
- Runtimes
- Buildkit

Docker in Docker

The ability to run a container within a container may not be a day-to-day requirement of your job. However, there are some cases where this can prove hugely beneficial.

An example includes CI/CD pipelines where one or multiple worker machines have agents of the CI running inside the Docker, and you also want the CI jobs to run in Docker containers so that after the job is finished, the data and the state are disposed, and nothing is left to pollute the system.

Running CI in this way has other advantages, too. Suppose you want to test your application with different versions and dependencies and don't want them to conflict. If you run each job in a separate and disposable environment, such as Docker, and remove them after the job is done, you will get isolation as a first-class citizen. This can also help you save disk space where the artifacts and states of the job are no longer required once the job is finished.

Fortunately, Docker provides official support for this. You can simply run the Docker image named `docker:dind, short for Docker IN Docker (dind).`

Let's see an example of using Docker in Docker when using GitLab CI.

```
# source: https://docs.gitlab.com/ee/ci/docker/using_docker_build.html
default:
  image: docker:24.0.5
  services:
    - docker:24.0.5-dind
```

```
  before_script:
    - docker info

variables:
  DOCKER_HOST: tcp://docker:2375
  DOCKER_TLS_CERTDIR: “”

build:
  stage: build
  script:
    - docker build -t my-docker-image .
    - docker run my-docker-image /script/to/run/tests
```

As you can see in this example, the parent service used to run the scripts is not a regular Docker but a Docker in Docker. This means we'll be able to run containers from within the container, all of which will run on the same host machine, but with the advantage of having isolation among one another and not producing conflicting environments.

The same idea can also be used in a Docker Compose, as shown here:

```
services:
  dind:
    image: docker:dind
    privileged: true
    environment:
      DOCKER_TLS_CERTDIR: “”
    volumes:
      - /var/run/docker.sock:/var/run/docker.sock
    ports:
      - “2377:2375”
```

Running this compose file with docker compose up will give us a Docker in Docker service. To test if it is working, we can run the following command.

```
DOCKER_HOST=tcp://localhost:2377 docker ps
```

Running the container in privileged mode is dangerous, exposes us to security risks and attacks, and is highly discouraged. Yet, for our demo purpose, this shall be enough.

You can consider other options if you want a production-grade version of the same functionality. Examples include, but are not limited to, using the Docker acquired tool called nestybox. For further information, check their GitHub repository from the following URL.

https://github.com/nestybox/sysbox

Figure 12.2: A *gray bird flying.*
source: https://unsplash.com/photos/flying-gray-and-white-bird-mSZKEQd5ptA

Rootless versus Root Mode

Rootless and root modes are different ways to run the Docker engine on Linux systems. The root mode Docker engine runs with root privileges, while the rootless Docker engine runs with non-root privileges. This difference has several implications for security and usability.

Root mode Docker is the traditional way to run Docker on Linux systems. It is easier to set up and use than rootless Docker, but has many security risks. Because the Docker engine runs with root privileges, it has access to all of the resources on the system. If the Docker engine is compromised, an attacker could use it to take over the entire system.

Rootless mode Docker is a newer way to run Docker, designed to be more secure. It runs the Docker engine with non-root privileges, meaning it has limited access to the system's resources. This makes it more difficult for an attacker to take over the system if the Docker engine is compromised.

Rootless mode Docker is necessary because it provides a more secure way to run Docker on Linux systems. As Docker has become more popular, attackers have been increasingly targeting it. Rootless mode Docker makes it more difficult for attackers to take over systems running Docker.

In addition to the security benefits, rootless mode Docker also has some other advantages, including:

- It can reduce the risk of privilege escalation attacks.
- It can make it easier to audit the system.
- It can make it easier to isolate different applications from each other.

However, there are also some drawbacks to rootless mode Docker, including:

- It can be more complex to set up and use.
- It can have some limitations in terms of performance and flexibility.

The choice of whether or not to set up the easy and risky way or the more complicated and secure way depends on your environment and infrastructure. However, running the Docker engine in rootless mode is recommended if you have the resources and knowledge. Otherwise, you may restrict access to the Docker engine through other means, for example, firewall, private network, and so on.

Here are the steps to set up a rootless Docker Daemon in a Linux host machine.

```
sudo systemctl disable --now docker.service
dockerd-rootless-setuptool.sh install
```

We can check the runtime configuration using the following command to ensure the new Docker Daemon is rootless.

```
docker info | grep rootless
```

Dev Environments

When developing your applications locally, it is essential to have your application's dependencies installed. This requirement is crucial because you don't need to install those dependencies whenever you want to compile or run the app. If those dependencies have not changed, you want to install and use them once. You would want the identical versions installed on your peer's computer when they are working on the same code; otherwise, incompatibility between different versions can catch up to you when deploying the code into production.

That is precisely why Docker Desktop provides a neat solution to solve all that with Dev Environments. With that, you can make the process reproducible, repeatable, and effortless. You can even share it with your peers and colleagues, so they will get the same environment and dependency as you do.

In the modern day of software engineering, every programming language is trying to solve this in its own way; some might create an isolated environment using the filesystem, some others might create a lock file to ensure no mismatch happens between the dependencies across different environments, and what you see is what you get!

Docker Desktop takes a creative approach to tackle this. It uses tools built into code editors, allowing Docker to access code mounted into a container rather than on your local host. This isolates your machine's tools, files, and running services, allowing multiple versions to exist.

The examples provided here may not be the same if you're running a later version. Also, note that there is a risk that they will be discontinued, so proceed with the development integration at your own risk!

You can use Dev Environments through the intuitive GUI in the Docker Dashboard or straight from your terminal with the new `docker dev` CLI plugin.

Here are the screenshots that create a Dev Environment from a sample repository.

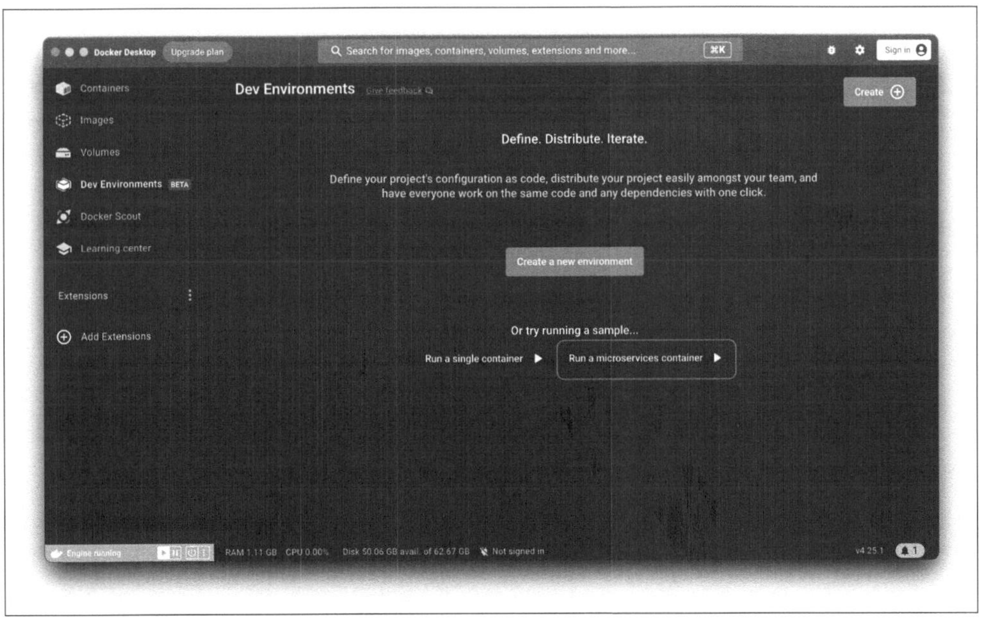

Figure 12.3: *Dev Environment initial page (Image by author from Docker Desktop)*

In the preceding page, you can select whether to create a new environment or import from an existing one.

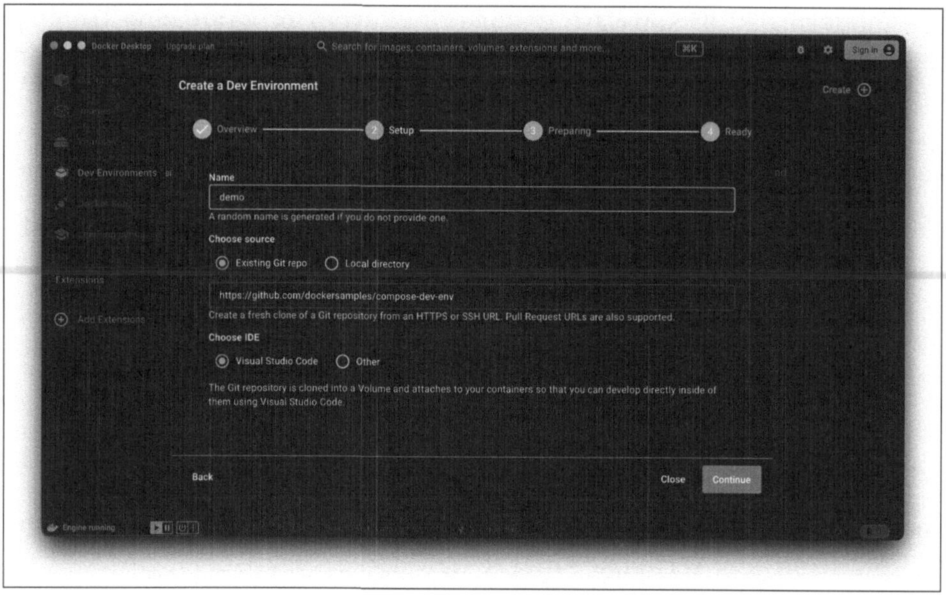

Figure 12.4: *Dev Environment setup page (Image by author from Docker Desktop)*

After specifying the information of the imported project, you will see the final summary page as follows.

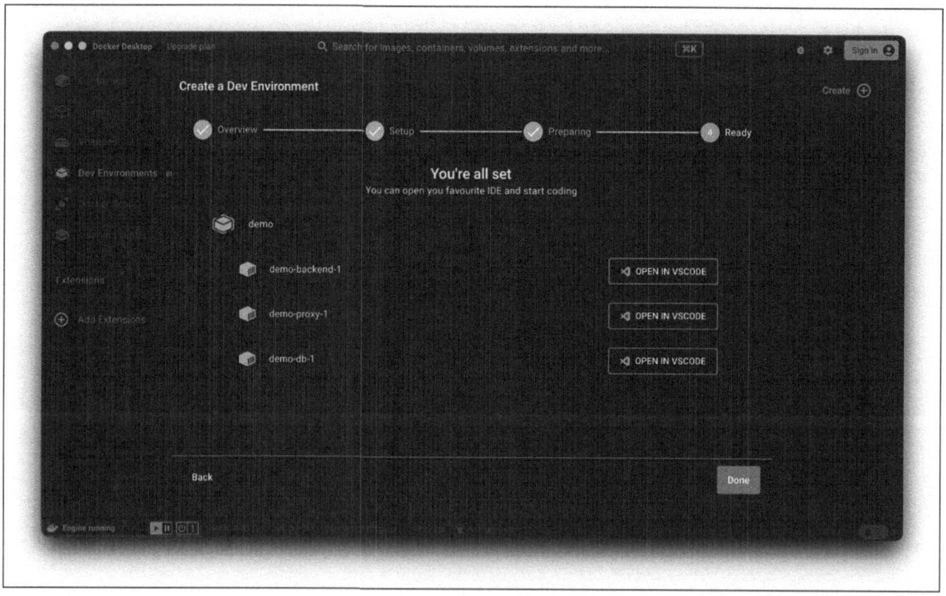

Figure 12.5: *Dev Environment summary page (Image by author from Docker Desktop)*

The only requirement for the repository URL, whether at the root or any of its subdirectories, is to have a file named `compose-dev.yml`. The contents of this file are identical to what we have covered in *Chapter 6: Docker Compose for Simplified Application Deployment*; they have the same syntax and definition.

You can even share this Dev Environment with your friend using either the repository URL or passing in the following format so that they will be redirected directly to the Dev Environment creation:

```
https://open.docker.com/dashboard/dev-envs?url=REPOSITORY_URL
```

For example, you can open up the following URL that will redirect you to the Dev Environment page to create a WordPress stack from the repository of this book.

https://open.docker.com/dashboard/dev-envs?url=https://github.com/ava-orange-education/Ultimate Docker for Cloud Native Applications/tree/main/chapter12/wordpress-mysql-dev@v0.1.1

As you can see, this is all powered by Docker itself, and all the capabilities around it that have emerged afterward is just leveraging the same technology. They wouldn't have to introduce another layer of complexity or config file with its learning curve.

There is nothing wrong with manually creating a compose file and spinning it up using the command line, and if that makes you productive, by all means, go for it. But if you want a streamlined approach that is easy to reproduce and collaborate, Dev Environment will be a good friend to you and your teammates.

WASM

WebAssembly (WASM) has gained much popularity among compiled programming languages such as Golang or Rust. It is a fast, light alternative to the containers we use on Linux or Windows machines.

What is WASM, and what problems does it solve?

WASM is a bytecode instruction set designed to be executed by web browsers and other virtual machines. It is a portable, lightweight, and secure format that can be used to run various applications, including games, multimedia, and web applications.

The idea behind WASM is to provide a way to run code on the web that is as efficient and performant as native code. In the past, web applications were typically written in JavaScript, which the browser interprets. This can be a slow and inefficient process, especially for complex applications.

On the other hand, WASM is compiled into a machine-code format that can be executed directly by the browser's CPU. This makes WASM applications much faster and more efficient than JavaScript applications.

In addition to being fast, WASM is also portable and secure. WASM applications can be run in any browser that supports WASM, and they are sandboxed to prevent them from accessing sensitive data or resources.

WASM solves some problems with web applications, including:

- **Performance**: WASM applications can be much faster than JavaScript applications.
- **Portability**: WASM applications can be run in any browser that supports WASM.
- **Security**: WASM applications are sandboxed to prevent them from accessing sensitive data or resources.
- It allows developers to write code that is as efficient as native code. This is important for applications that require a lot of processing power, such as games and multimedia applications.
- It makes it possible to write portable web applications across different browsers and platforms. This is important for developers who want to reach a broad audience.
- It makes it possible to write web applications that are more secure than those written in JavaScript. This is important for applications that handle sensitive data.

As a result of these advantages, WASM is becoming increasingly popular for writing web applications. It is a promising technology that has the potential to revolutionize the way we use the web. It is still under development, but several large companies, including Google, Microsoft, and Mozilla, are already using it. It is believed that WASM has the potential to become the standard way to write web applications in the future.

Fortunately, Docker also supports WASM, although it is in beta as of writing this book. The official documentation recommends not to use Docker WASM in production just yet, as it is subject to breaking changes until it becomes stable.

To enable WASM in Docker Desktop, we can modify the settings as shown here.

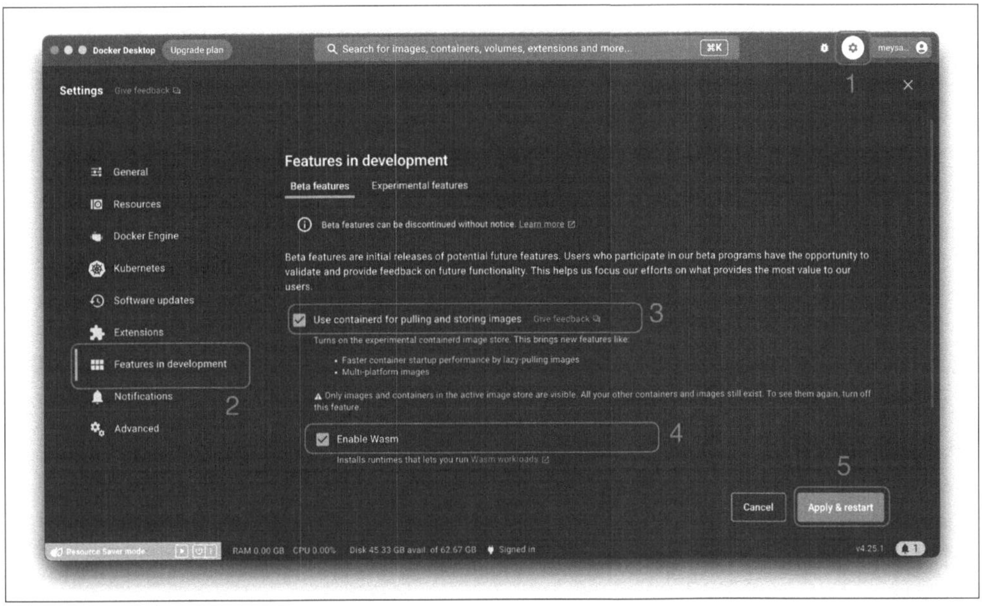

Figure 12.6: *Dev Environment initial page (Image by author from Docker Desktop)*

Applying the changes will take some time to install the dependencies, but after it is finished, this will enable WASM for your Docker Daemon. After that, creating and running a WASM workload **with docker is possible.**

Running WASM workloads in Docker can be as easy as running a container built for the WASM platform. An example is as follows:

```
services:
  app:
    image: secondstate/rust-example-hello
    platform: wasi/wasm
    runtime: io.containerd.wasmedge.v1
```

This example is taken from the official documentation, accessible at this URL: https://docs.docker.com/desktop/wasm/

Docker Extensions

Extensions are a way to enable the community and third-party tools to provide services and functionality on top of Docker. This encompasses many use cases, including but not limited to debugging, testing, security, and networking.

This way, if one or multiple organizations or individuals have a special requirement that is not met by built-in Docker tools or is not flexible enough for their environment, they can create their own custom tooling. They can even publish their extension to a wider audience of Docker users so that people can also benefit from it.

You can have zero, one, or multiple extensions installed without any hard limit on the number of extensions you can have.

You need to enable extensions from your Docker Desktop settings page, after which you can install any extension you require for your environment.

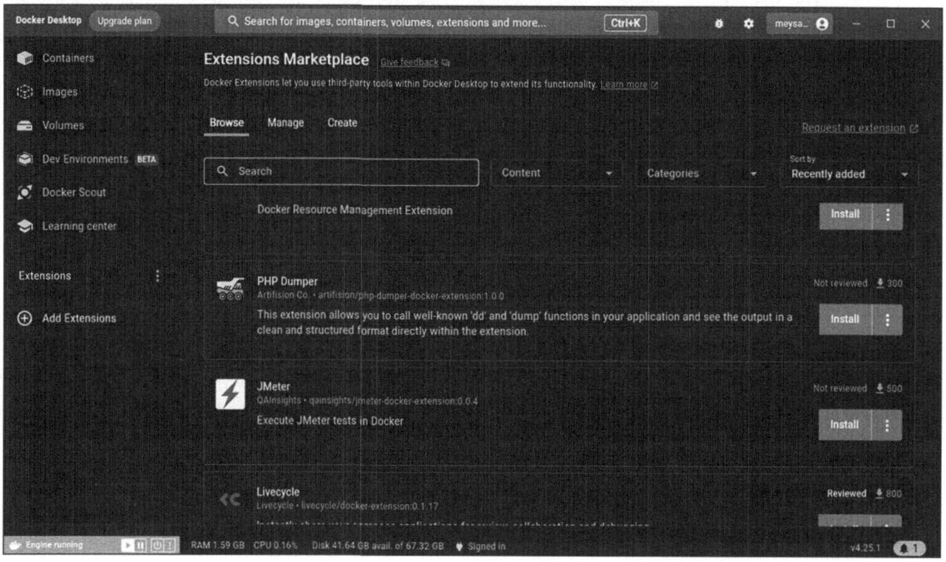

Figure 12.7: *Docker Extensions Marketplace (Image by author from Docker Desktop)*

As you can see in the preceding screenshot, there are many tools and extensions available at your disposal. You might have already heard of some of them, for example, the well-known JMeter performance testing tool, and some of them might not be that famous but still useful.

The whole point is enabling the community to extend the bare Docker further than what one company can individually. It will allow others to build open-source tools and enhance their brand awareness, as well as enable users of Docker to have a wide variety of tooling from a single platform.

If you ever find yourself in need of a certain aspect of your Docker image and container, make sure to look at extensions before reinventing the wheels. Someone else might have already built something you can integrate into your processes.

Docker Content Trust (DCT)

Docker Content Trust is a security feature that allows you to verify the authenticity and integrity of Docker images. This is important for ensuring that you are pulling images from trusted sources and that the images have not been tampered with.

Why is it necessary?

Docker Content Trust is necessary because Docker images are often pulled from public registries, which anyone can access. This means that it is possible for malicious actors to publish tampered images to these registries. If you pull an image from a tampered registry, you could be deploying malware or other harmful code to your systems.

Where is it useful?

Docker Content Trust is useful for any organization that uses Docker to deploy applications. This includes organizations of all sizes, from small startups to large enterprises. Content Trust is vital for organizations that deploy applications to production environments, where the stakes are high and the impact of a compromised image could be severe.

There are two main ways to use Docker Content Trust in a day-to-day job, including:

- **Sign your images**: If you are an image publisher, you can sign your images using Docker Notary. This will allow your users to verify that the images you publish are authentic and have not been tampered with.
- **Verify images**: If you are an image consumer, you can use Docker Content Trust to verify the authenticity and integrity of the images you pull. This will help ensure you are not deploying malware or other harmful code to your systems.

To use Docker Content Trust, you can install Docker Notary and set up a Docker registry that supports Content TrustHub. You will also need to configure your Docker clients to trust your Notary server. Once you have done this, you can start signing your images and verifying those you pull from registries.

Note that you can also use Docker Hub and Docker CLI without worrying about all this setup. Docker already hosts a Notary server online for public users.

Here are some specific examples of how Docker Content Trust can be used in a day-to-day job:

A software development team could use Content Trust to sign their images before they push them to a private registry. This would ensure that only team members could pull the images and that the images had not been tampered with.

A DevOps team could use Content Trust to verify the authenticity of images before they are deployed to a production environment. This would help ensure no malware or other harmful code was deployed to production.

A security team could use Content Trust to scan images for vulnerabilities before they are deployed. This would help to identify and fix vulnerabilities before they can be exploited.

Let's see a practical example to help you better understand the technicalities.

```
PASSWORD=$(head -c 12 /dev/urandom | shasum | cut -d ' ' -f1)
# persist the password in a file if you don't want to lose it
echo $PASSWORD > docker-trust-password.txt
export KEY_NAME=mastering-docker
export DOCKER_IMAGE=myuser/myimage
export DOCKER_CONTENT_TRUST_ROOT_PASSPHRASE=$PASSWORD
export DOCKER_CONTENT_TRUST_REPOSITORY_PASSPHRASE=$PASSWORD
docker trust key generate $KEY_NAME
docker trust signer add --key $KEY_NAME.pub $KEY_NAME $DOCKER_IMAGE
docker trust sign $DOCKER_IMAGE
export DOCKER_CONTENT_TRUST=1
docker push $DOCKER_IMAGE
```

After pushing your image with a signed key, the user of your Docker image will be able to verify the integrity of this image and verify it before launching it in their production environment.

```
docker trust inspect --pretty $DOCKER_IMAGE
```

Setting the **DOCKER_CONTENT_TRUST** is an important part that tells the Docker engine to enforce trust for all of the following commands:

- push
- build
- create
- pull
- run

Having such security measures in place will, as mentioned earlier, ensure that the user of a Docker image will not be at risk of image tampering. It's not hard to imagine that in the current age of internet and networking, having such access for adversaries can't be too difficult if they really have the will, and that's why you need to be prepared for that by verifying your source Docker images.

There are also community tools, such as cosign to sign your images before publishing them publicly. But we intentionally kept everything Docker-centric to keep the scope narrow. You are encouraged to visit the online documentation for other alternatives that suit your environment.

Figure 12.8: *Two youngsters doing acrobatics.*
source: https://unsplash.com/photos/a-man-holding-a-boy-on-his-back-on-a-beach-qVplzFXCTvw

Docker Stats

When deploying your application using Docker, you will need to monitor the resource utilization of your workload. Among many reasons, here are the top ones:

- **Early Detection of Issues**: Monitoring provides real-time visibility into the health and performance of applications and infrastructure components. This enables early detection of potential issues, such as performance bottlenecks, resource constraints, or error conditions, before they escalate into major outages or disruptions.
- **Proactive Troubleshooting and Resolution**: By identifying issues early, monitoring allows for proactive troubleshooting and resolution, minimizing downtime and maximizing application availability. Monitoring data can pinpoint the root cause of problems, guiding remediation efforts and preventing recurring incidents.
- **Capacity Planning and Optimization**: Monitoring data provides insights into resource utilization, helping identify potential capacity bottlenecks

and guide resource allocation decisions. This enables proactive capacity planning to ensure systems can handle the expected load and avoid performance degradation during peak demand.

- **Trend Analysis and Improvement**: Monitoring data can be analyzed over time to identify trends and patterns in application performance, resource consumption, and error rates. This information can drive continuous improvement initiatives, optimizing performance, resource efficiency, and overall application stability.
- **Compliance and Regulatory Requirements**: In many industries, monitoring is mandated by compliance and regulatory requirements to ensure the integrity, security, and reliability of critical systems. Monitoring data can provide evidence of compliance and support audits or investigations.

As such, Docker has a built-in capability to track the stats of your workload. Using the `docker stats` command, you can monitor how much CPU, memory, and IO your container(s) are using and proactively (de)allocate as required.

This will allow you to proactively respond to the demand for your application without losing availability.

For example, let's run a couple of resource-intensive containers and track their utilization.

```
docker run -d --rm --name stress1 colinianking/stress-ng \
  --cpu 2 --cpu-load 100 --vm 2 --vm-bytes 512M --fork 2 --timeout 120s
docker run -d --rm --name stress2 colinianking/stress-ng \
  --cpu 2 --cpu-load 100 --vm 2 --vm-bytes 512M --fork 2 --timeout 120s
```

Each of these containers will fork two processes, each of which using two CPU cores at its maximum capacity, with half a gigabyte of memory for two minutes.

If we take a look at the result from docker stats, we will see something similar to the following.

```
NAME     CPU %    MEM USAGE / LIMIT    MEM % NET I/O       BLOCK I/O     PIDS
stress1  582.54%  522.8MiB / 30.77GiB  1.66% 5.8kB / 0B    0B / 537MB    11
stress2  586.11%  522.3MiB / 30.77GiB  1.66% 5.46kB / 0B   0B / 1.34GB   11
```

As you can see, these are valuable information that can significantly help us track the resource utilization of our workloads. Next time you want to monitor your containers, docker stats can greatly help you.

Of course, using docker stats is not a scalable solution, so there are supplementary tools out there that can greatly help in monitoring the fleet of workloads across different machines.

One of the most popular tools is Prometheus. It has a lot of tremendous advantages in a production environment, which we don't have enough scope to cover. Still, for the sake of completeness, if we wanted to monitor a single Docker engine in a machine, the following would be a sample target rule.

```
- job_name: docker
  docker_sd_configs:
    - host: unix:///var/run/docker.sock
      port: 9323
      refresh_interval: 15s

  relabel_configs:
    - source_labels:
        - __meta_docker_container_name
      regex: ^/?(.*)$
      target_label: container_name
    - source_labels:
        - __meta_docker_network_ip
      target_label: container_ip
    - source_labels:
        - __meta_docker_container_network_mode
      target_label: container_network_mode
    - source_labels:
        - __meta_docker_container_id
      action: hashmod
      modulus: 1000000
      target_label: container_id
    - source_labels:
        - __meta_docker_port_private
      target_label: container_port
```

Daemon Configuration

Up until so far in this book, we have been using the Docker Daemon without any modification and only relying on the default configuration.

In certain environments, you may want to tweak and tune it to match your desired state. An example includes running the Daemon behind a TLS-enforced authentication so users won't anonymously send requests.

Another example includes running the Daemon behind a `(reverse-)proxy.`

To modify the behavior of the Docker Daemon, most configuration entries can be changed from `/etc/docker/daemon.json` file. Although some may require a change in the systemd service file. Note that changing the Daemon config requires a restart of the Daemon to reflect those changes.

Live Restore

One of the very useful configurations in Docker Daemon is the use of live restore.

The Docker daemon live restore configuration is a set of settings that allows Docker containers to remain running even if the Docker daemon becomes unavailable. This can be helpful for reducing downtime due to daemon crashes, planned outages, or upgrades.

Live restore offers several advantages, including:

- **Reduced Downtime**: If the Docker daemon crashes, live restore ensures that containers remain running, preventing service disruptions and minimizing downtime.
- **Planned Outages**: Live restore enables you to perform planned outages without affecting running containers, allowing for maintenance activities without impacting user experience.
- **Upgrade Continuity**: When upgrading the Docker daemon, live restore maintains container uptime during the upgrade process, ensuring a smooth transition to the new version.

To enable live restore, you need to modify the daemon.json file located in the `/etc/docker/daemon.json on Linux systems. Add the following line to the daemon.json` file:

```
{
  "live-restore": true
}
```

After adding this line, save the daemon.json file and restart the Docker daemon. The Docker daemon will now be configured to restore containers on startup.

While live restore provides significant benefits, it has some limitations, including:

- **Container Compatibility**: Live restore may not work for all containers, particularly those that rely on specific Docker daemon configurations that have changed between restarts.
- **Data Loss**: If the Docker daemon is unavailable for an extended period, containers may lose data or become corrupted.
- **Monitoring Requirements**: Live restore requires proper monitoring to detect and address daemon outages promptly to minimize downtime.

Consider the following factors when deciding whether to use live restore:

- **Application Sensitivity**: For mission-critical applications that cannot tolerate downtime, live restore can provide valuable protection.
- **Downtime Tolerance**: If downtime is not a major concern, live restoration may be unnecessary.
- **Monitoring Capabilities**: Ensure you have adequate monitoring capabilities to promptly detect and address daemon outages.

Remote Access

Another useful entry is remote access. Remote access in Docker daemon configurations allows you to connect to and manage Docker containers from a remote machine. This can be useful for managing Docker deployments on multiple machines or accessing Docker containers from a laptop or other device.

To configure remote access for the Docker daemon, you need to add the hosts array to the `daemon.json` file. The hosts array specifies the IP addresses and ports that the Docker daemon will listen on for remote connections. For example, the following configuration will allow the Docker daemon to listen on all IP addresses on port 2375:

```
{
  “hosts”: [“tcp://0.0.0.0:2375”]
}
```

After adding the hosts array to the daemon.json file, you need to restart the Docker daemon. Once the Docker daemon has restarted, you can connect to it from a remote machine using the Docker CLI. For example, the following command will connect to the Docker daemon on the machine with the IP address 192.168.1.100:

```
docker -H tcp://192.168.1.100:2375 info
```

TLS

Remote access to the Docker daemon must be secured using TLS (Transport Layer Security). This will encrypt all communication between the Docker daemon and the remote machine, preventing unauthorized access to your Docker containers.

To enable TLS for remote access, you need to generate a TLS certificate and key pair and add the following lines to the `daemon.json file:`

```
{
  "tlsverify": true,
  "tlscacert": "/path/to/ca.pem",
  "tlscert": "/path/to/cert.pem",
  "tlskey": "/path/to/key.pem"
}
```

After enabling TLS for remote access, you need to restart the Docker daemon. Once the Docker daemon has restarted, you will need to use the docker CLI with the `--tls` flag to connect to the Docker daemon remotely. For example, the following command will connect to the Docker daemon on the machine with the IP address 192.168.1.100 using TLS:

```
docker --tlsverify --tlscacert=/path/to/ca.pem \
  --tlscert=/path/to/cert.pem --tlskey=/path/to/key.pem \
  -H tcp://192.168.1.100:2375 info
```

Remote access to the Docker daemon can be a powerful tool for managing Docker deployments, but it is important to use it carefully. Make sure to secure your Docker daemon with TLS and to only allow authorized users to connect to it.

Figure 12.9: *A player holding two cards at the table.*
source: https://unsplash.com/photos/person-holding-white-and-black-playing-cards-bRqsXcEcKFw

Docker Alternative Runtimes

Docker uses a runtime to manage containers. The runtime is responsible for creating, starting, stopping, and deleting containers. It also manages the container's network and storage resources.

There are several different Docker runtimes available, each with its own strengths and weaknesses. Some of the most popular Docker runtimes include:

- **runc**: The default Docker runtime. It is a lightweight and efficient runtime that sets up process and namespaces that is comparable to Linux LXD containers but has evolved to be more.
- **containerd**: It is a popular container runtime that is cri-o and runs on runc to run the containers. It is a lightweight and efficient runtime that is based on the Open Container Initiative (OCI) specification.
- **cri-o**: An alternative to containerd that is designed to be more modular and extensible, relying on runc or Kata Containers. It is used by Kubernetes and other container orchestration platforms.
- **gVisor**: A sandboxed container runtime that uses a hypervisor to isolate containers from the host operating system. This can improve security and isolation but can also add overhead.
- **wasmtime**: A container runtime that uses WebAssembly (WASM) to run containers. WASM is a portable bytecode format that can be run in a sandboxed environment.
- **Kata Containers**: A container runtime that uses a highly optimized VM image and hypervisor to boot a VM is a few (hundreds) milliseconds.
- **youki**: An alternative container runtime to runc that leverages the Linux cgroup2 subsystem for efficient resource management and isolation of containers. It focuses primarily on container startup, while runc offers broader functionality.

The best Docker runtime for you will depend on your specific needs and requirements. If you are looking for a lightweight and efficient runtime, then runc is a good option.

If you have specific needs and use cases, you are recommended to read the documentation of each runtime and decide which one best suits you.

Buildkit

Docker BuildKit is a toolkit for building Docker images more efficiently and reliably. It is a more powerful and flexible alternative to the legacy Docker builder. BuildKit is necessary because the legacy builder is no longer able to meet the demands of modern containerized applications.

The legacy Docker builder was designed for a simpler time when Docker images were smaller and less complex. However, modern applications are often composed of multiple microservices, each with its own dependencies. This makes building Docker images more complex and time-consuming.

Docker Buildkit is the new default builder in recent Docker releases, starting with **Docker Engine version 23.0.**

BuildKit solves this problem by providing several features that make it more efficient and reliable, which are as follows:

- **Concurrent builds**: BuildKit can build multiple stages of a Docker image concurrently. This can significantly reduce build times, especially for complex images with many dependencies.
- **Cache-based builds**: BuildKit can cache the results of previous builds. This means that it only needs to rebuild the parts of an image that have changed since the last build. This can save a lot of time, especially for frequent builds.
- **Image export and import**: BuildKit can export and import images. This allows you to share images between different build environments.
- **Build plugins**: BuildKit supports plugins that can extend its functionality. This allows you to customize BuildKit to meet your specific needs.

In short, BuildKit is a necessary tool for building modern Docker images. It is more efficient and reliable than the legacy builder, and it provides several features that make it easier to build complex images.

Here are some additional benefits of using Docker BuildKit:

- **Reduced build times**: BuildKit can reduce build times by up to 50%.
- **Improved image consistency**: BuildKit can help to improve the consistency of images by ensuring that they are always built with the same dependencies.
- **Simplified build workflows**: BuildKit can simplify build workflows by making it easier to manage and share images.

You are recommended to use Docker BuildKit for building your Docker images. It is a powerful and flexible tool that can make your builds more efficient and reliable.

Custom Dockerfile Syntax

Using Buildkit to build the Docker images, you can specify an external frontend for the syntax of your Dockerfile.

That was a mouthful, so let's break it down.

If you build your Docker images using the normal and traditional way, you are always bound to the version of the Docker Daemon running on the machine. And if there's a new feature available in the Dockerfile syntax that you want to add to your application, you won't be able to unless you upgrade your Docker Daemon.

That has changed thanks to Buildkit. Using Buidlkit, you can specify which syntax you want to adopt in your Dockerfile, which in turn will pass that information from Buildkit down to the Docker Daemon about which syntax you want to have.

This way, you won't have to upgrade your Docker Daemon if you don't want to, but still be able to get the latest upgrades and features in the Dockerfile syntax.

This may sound abstract so far, so let's bring some examples.

Linked Copy

Starting with version 1.4, Buildkit is able to receive the `--link` in the COPY or ADD directives of the Dockerfile.

This allows an optimized caching layer in which the files that are being copied will get their own independent layer, and will not change due to the change in the earlier layers of the image.

Let's see an example.

```
# syntax=docker/dockerfile:1.4
FROM alpine
RUN apk add --update curl
FROM busybox
COPY --link myapp.js /app/
```

The first line of this Dockerfile is not a comment, contrary to what it looks like. It is rather metadata for the Buildkit to receive the latest update on the Dockerfile syntax version 1.4 and apply that when building your Dockerfile.

In this Dockerfile, the line that copies the source file will get its own layer, even when the earlier package installation has changed because of an update to the upstream.

This feature is extremely helpful for reducing your build time and using the caching technique of Docker layers. In the world of CI/CD, this means you will be billed less time for the time the CI job was running for your application.

Mount in Run

This is another example of a feature in the Dockerfile syntax that your Docker Daemon may not be fully upgraded to be aware of.

We are trying to use a secret inside the Dockerfile in this file. This is helpful if you don't want to expose the content of a confidential value to the builder or the user(s) of your Dockerfile.

```
# syntax = docker/dockerfile:1.3
FROM busybox
RUN --mount=type=secret,id=my-secret,target=/mysecret ls -lh /mysecret
```

To build a Docker image from this file, we can run the following command.

```
DOCKER_BUILDKIT=1 docker build -t external-dockerfile-syntax \
   --secret id=my-secret,src=/etc/hosts .
```

The `id` field must be the same, or you will not see the desired behavior.

As you have seen in the last two examples, specifying the syntax of your Dockerfile is extremely helpful in maintaining a consistent view of your Docker image across all machines and deployments.

It will help you to have the same behavior if you run it on your machine or on your colleagues'.

Docker Buildx

You have already seen Docker Buildx in *Chapter 9: Docker in Continuous Integration and Deployment*, where we talked about CI/CD integrations. But now that you better understand Buildkit, it's time to resurface the topic and explain it further.

Docker buildx is a Docker CLI plugin that allows you to build Docker images using BuildKit, the new Docker image builder. BuildKit is a more powerful and flexible alternative to the legacy Docker builder, and it can be used to build images more efficiently and reliably.

Docker buildx is a command-line tool that provides a high-level interface to BuildKit. It allows you to build Docker images on local machines, remote machines, or multiple machines in parallel. It also provides several features that make it easier to manage build workflows, such as caching and image pruning.

Note that Buildx allows for advanced options where `docker build` actually delegates to Buildx.

How does Docker buildx relate to BuildKit?

Docker buildx is a client that communicates with the BuildKit daemon. The BuildKit daemon is the server that executes the build workloads. When you run the docker buildx build command, Docker buildx sends a build request to the BuildKit daemon. The build request includes the Dockerfile and other build artifacts. The BuildKit daemon executes the build and returns the results to Docker buildx.

Why did Docker buildx come to be?

Docker buildx came to be to address the limitations of the legacy Docker builder. The legacy Docker builder can no longer meet the demands of modern containerized applications. Docker buildx is more powerful and flexible, and it can be used to build images more efficiently and reliably.

What problems does Docker buildx solve?

Docker buildx solves several problems with the legacy Docker builder, including:

- **Performance**: Docker buildx can build images more efficiently than the legacy Docker builder. This is because it can run builds in parallel and can cache build results.
- **Flexibility**: Docker buildx is more flexible than the legacy Docker builder. This is because it supports multi-stage builds and can be used to build images on multiple machines.
- **Reliability**: Docker buildx is more reliable than the legacy Docker builder. It is based on BuildKit, a more stable and mature technology.

You should use Docker buildx if you need to build Docker images that are:

- **Complex**: Docker buildx is well-suited for building complex images that require multiple stages or have many dependencies.

- **Portable**: Docker buildx can be used to build portable images for a broader range of environments.
- **Composed**: Docker Buildx can be used to compose images from different sources.

If you are building simple images that do not require any of these features, you can continue using the legacy Docker builder. However, if you need to build more complex or sophisticated images, switch to Docker buildx.

Here are some benefits of using Docker buildx:

- **Increased build efficiency**: Docker buildx can build images more efficiently than the legacy Docker builder. This is because it can run builds in parallel and cache build results.
- **Improved image reliability**: Docker buildx is more reliable than the legacy Docker builder. This is because it is based on BuildKit, which is a more stable and mature technology.
- **Simplified build workflows**: Docker buildx provides several features that make it easier to manage build workflows, such as caching and image pruning.
- **Support for multi-stage builds**: Docker buildx supports multi-stage builds, which allow you to build images in multiple stages. This can make your builds more efficient and help reduce the size of your images.
- **Support for remote builds**: Docker buildx can be used to build images on remote machines. This can be useful for building images requiring specific hardware or software access.
- **Support for parallel builds**: Docker buildx can be used to build images on multiple machines in parallel. This can significantly reduce build times, especially for complex images with many dependencies.

Figure 12.10: *A green door surrounded by potted plants.*
source: https://unsplash.com/photos/a-green-door-surrounded-by-potted-plants-4KaQH-fyl00

Conclusion

This chapter introduced you to some of the advanced concepts that haven't been covered in the earlier chapters. It gave you a glimpse of what Docker is capable of in real-world applications and production scenarios. You shall find yourself referring back to this chapter and the official documentation to freshen up on these topics and be able to integrate them into your platform.

In the next chapter, we will wrap up this book with some of the future trends and possibilities in the upcoming decade. We will look at what trends to keep an eye on, as well as what trends have lasted for a long time and can be expected to last for years to come. If you've stayed with us thus far, stay tuned for one last chapter to see what to expect from the world of containerization and software engineering.

Chapter 13
Future Trends in Containerization

Figure 13.1: *A person looking at the sky on a grass field.*
source: https://unsplash.com/photos/man-on-grass-field-looking-at-sky-JrZ1yE1PjQ0

Introduction

In the final chapter of this book, we will cover some predictions and future trends of containerization in the years to come. These predictions should not be taken literally but rather as an indication to help the readers level their knowledge and expertise in the fields more relevant to their niche.

These trends are neither facts, nor actuality, but rather a feeling of what comes next after all these years of development and software delivery using different approaches.

If you have followed us along thus far, buckle up for one last chapter to wrap this book up with some general leads on what to expect to see in the upcoming years, as well as some suggestions on what to keep an eye on if you want to sharpen your axe and stay ahead of the game.

Structure

In this chapter, we will cover the following topics:

- Multi-Cloud and Hybrid Cloud Environments
- Serverless Computing
- Edge Computing
- AI and ML in Containerization
- Observability and Monitoring
- GitOps and Continuous Delivery
- Microservices Architecture
- Cloud-native Development
- Service-mesh

The Rise of Multi-Cloud and Hybrid Cloud Environments

In the past, organizations typically relied on a single cloud provider to host their applications and data. However, this approach has several drawbacks, including limited flexibility, vendor lock-in, and increased costs. As a result, many organizations are now adopting multi-cloud and hybrid cloud strategies.

Multi-cloud refers to using multiple cloud providers, such as Amazon Web Services (AWS), Microsoft Azure, and Google Cloud Platform (GCP). This approach gives organizations greater flexibility and choice, as they can select the best cloud provider for each need. For example, an organization might use AWS for its computing needs, Azure for its storage needs, and GCP for its data analytics needs.

A hybrid cloud refers to a combination of on-premises infrastructure and cloud-based resources. This approach allows organizations to keep their sensitive data on-premises while taking advantage of the scalability and agility of the cloud. For example, an organization might keep its customer data on-premises but use cloud-based resources for its development and testing environments.

Benefits of Multi-Cloud and Hybrid Cloud Environments

There are many benefits to adopting multi-cloud and hybrid-cloud strategies, including:

- **Increased flexibility**: Organizations can select the best cloud provider for each need.
- **Reduced vendor lock-in**: Organizations are not reliant on a single cloud provider.
- **Improved scalability**: Organizations can quickly scale their resources up or down as needed.
- **Reduced costs**: Organizations can take advantage of the competitive pricing of cloud providers.
- **Greater control**: Organizations can keep their sensitive data on-premises.

Real-World Example

An excellent example of an organization using a multi-cloud strategy is Netflix. To host its streaming applications, Netflix uses multiple cloud providers, including AWS, Azure, and GCP. This approach allows Netflix to take advantage of the best features and pricing of each cloud provider, and it also helps to ensure that Netflix's applications are highly available and scalable.

Increased Rate of Kubernetes Adoption

Kubernetes has emerged as the de facto standard for container orchestration due to its comprehensive capabilities, widespread adoption, and strong community support. This will lead to even further adoption of Kubernetes for production deployment in the software delivery process. The reasons are countless, but let's look at some highlighted ones.

Kubernetes' Comprehensive Capabilities

Kubernetes provides a robust and feature-rich framework for managing containerized applications. It offers a wide range of capabilities, including:

- **Automated deployment and scaling**: Kubernetes can automatically deploy and scale containerized applications based on defined configurations. This simplifies the process of managing and scaling applications in production environments.
- **Self-healing**: Kubernetes can automatically restart failed containers and replace unhealthy nodes, ensuring the high availability and resilience of containerized applications.
- **Service discovery and load balancing**: Kubernetes facilitates service discovery and load balancing, enabling applications to communicate and distribute traffic effectively.

- **Resource management**: Kubernetes efficiently manages container resources, including CPU, memory, and storage, ensuring optimal resource utilization and application performance.

Widespread Adoption of Kubernetes

Kubernetes has gained immense popularity and adoption across the software development industry. Several factors drive its widespread adoption, including:

- **Open-source nature**: Kubernetes is an open-source project, making it freely available for anyone to use and contribute. This open-source nature has fostered a vibrant community and led to rapid development and innovation.
- **Vendor support**: Major cloud providers, including AWS, Azure, and GCP, offer managed Kubernetes services, making it easy to deploy and manage Kubernetes clusters in the cloud. This vendor support has further accelerated Kubernetes adoption.
- **Enterprise-grade features**: Kubernetes has evolved to meet the demands of enterprise deployments, offering features like role-based access control, auditing, and security enhancements. This has made Kubernetes a viable choice for enterprise applications.

Strong Community Support

Kubernetes benefits from a solid and active community of developers and contributors. This community provides valuable resources, documentation, and support, making it easier for new users to learn and adopt Kubernetes. The community also actively contributes to the development of Kubernetes, ensuring that it remains relevant and up-to-date with the latest technologies and trends.

Figure 13.2: *A photo of the Earth from outer space.*
source: https://unsplash.com/photos/photo-of-outer-space-Q1p7bh3SHj8

Serverless Computing: A Paradigm Shift in Application Development

Serverless computing has emerged as a revolutionary approach to software development, offering a paradigm shift away from traditional infrastructure management and towards a more agile and cost-effective model. In a serverless architecture, developers build and deploy their application code without worrying about the underlying infrastructure, such as servers, operating systems, and middleware.

Critical Characteristics of Serverless Computing

Several key features characterize serverless computing, which are as follows:

- **Event-driven execution**: Serverless functions are triggered by specific events, such as an HTTP request, a message queue update, or a timer event. This event-driven nature allows for efficient resource utilization and scalability.
- **Abstraction of infrastructure**: Developers don't need to provision, manage, or scale servers in a serverless environment. Instead, the cloud provider handles all infrastructure-related tasks, freeing developers to focus on their application logic.
- **Pay-per-use pricing**: Serverless computing follows a pay-per-use model, where developers are only charged for the resources consumed by their applications. This eliminates the need for upfront investments in infrastructure and makes serverless computing a cost-effective solution.

Advantages of Serverless Computing

Serverless computing offers numerous advantages over traditional server-based approaches, including:

- **Reduced operational overhead**: Serverless computing eliminates the need for developers to manage and maintain servers, significantly reducing operational overhead and costs.
- **Cost-effectiveness**: Serverless computing charges based on actual resource usage, leading to more cost-effective solutions than traditional server-based approaches.

- **Scalability**: Serverless computing automatically scales resources up or down based on demand, ensuring optimal performance and resource utilization.
- **Agility and innovation**: Serverless computing enables faster development and deployment of applications, fostering innovation and agility in software development.
- **Focus on core business logic**: Developers can focus on core business logic rather than infrastructure management, leading to increased productivity and efficiency.
- **Fault tolerance and high availability**: Serverless computing platforms are designed for fault tolerance and high availability, ensuring that applications remain operational even during failures.
- **Reduced vendor lock-in**: Serverless computing promotes vendor neutrality, reducing reliance on specific cloud providers and offering greater flexibility.
- **Continuous integration and delivery (CI/CD)**: Serverless computing aligns well with CI/CD practices, enabling rapid and automated deployment of code changes.
- **Microservices architecture**: Serverless computing is well-suited for microservices architectures, breaking down applications into more minor, independent services that can be easily deployed and managed.
- **Global reach**: Serverless computing platforms typically have a global network of data centers, ensuring low latency and high availability for applications worldwide.

Edge Computing: Bringing Computation Closer to the Edge

Edge computing is a distributed computing paradigm that brings computation and data storage closer to the location where it is needed. This approach contrasts with traditional cloud computing, where data is processed in a centralized cloud data center. By moving computation and storage to the edge, edge computing offers several advantages, including:

- **Reduced latency**: Edge computing reduces the latency between data generation and processing, enabling real-time applications and responses.
- **Improved bandwidth utilization**: By processing data closer to the source, edge computing reduces the amount of data that needs to be

transmitted over the network, conserving bandwidth and reducing network congestion.

- **Improved security and privacy**: Edge computing allows for data processing and storage within the local network, reducing the risk of data breaches and enhancing data privacy.
- **Enhanced scalability**: Edge computing scales horizontally, adding more edge nodes as needed to handle increasing workloads.
- **Reduced reliance on central cloud**: Edge computing reduces the dependency on centralized cloud data centers, improving resilience and availability in case of network disruptions.

Traction of Edge Computing in the Future

Edge computing is poised for significant growth in the coming years, driven by several factors, including:

- **The rise of the Internet of Things (IoT)**: The proliferation of IoT devices generates massive amounts of data that needs to be processed quickly and efficiently. Edge computing is well-suited for handling this distributed data processing.
- **Emerging technologies like 5G and AI**: The advancement of 5G networks, with their high bandwidth and low latency, will further enhance the capabilities of edge computing. Additionally, AI applications are increasingly being deployed at the edge to enable real-time data analysis and decision-making.
- **Growing demand for real-time applications**: The increasing demand for real-time applications, such as autonomous vehicles, augmented reality, and immersive experiences, necessitates edge computing to reduce latency and enable real-time responses.
- **Security and privacy concerns**: The growing emphasis on data security and privacy has led to a preference for processing and storing data closer to the source, which edge computing facilitates.
- **Edge-native applications**: Developing edge-native applications specifically designed to run at the edge will further accelerate the adoption of edge computing.

AI and ML in Containerization: A Convergence of Technologies

Integrating AI and ML into containerization revolutionizes how containerized applications are managed, optimized, and deployed. AI and ML bring automation, intelligence, and adaptability to containerized environments, enhancing performance, efficiency, and scalability.

Current Applications of AI and ML in Containerization

AI and ML are already being used in various aspects of containerization, including:

- **Automated container deployment and management**: AI algorithms can automatically analyze application requirements and infrastructure resources to deploy and manage containerized applications, reducing manual intervention and improving deployment efficiency.
- **Predictive resource allocation**: ML models can predict resource requirements for containerized applications, enabling proactive resource allocation and preventing resource bottlenecks.
- **Anomaly detection and failure prediction**: AI and ML algorithms can detect anomalies and predict potential failures in containerized applications, allowing for proactive remediation and preventing service disruptions.
- **Self-healing and self-optimization**: AI-powered container orchestration platforms can automatically detect and rectify issues in containerized applications, ensuring continuous availability and optimal performance.
- **Personalized user experiences**: ML models can analyze user behavior and preferences to personalize containerized applications and provide tailored user experiences.

Future Trends in AI and ML for Containerization

The future holds exciting advancements in AI and ML for containerization, including:

- **AI-driven auto-scaling**: AI algorithms will become more sophisticated in predicting and responding to load spikes, enabling containerized applications to scale up or down based on real-time demand automatically.
- **AI-powered security and compliance**: AI will play a crucial role in detecting and mitigating security threats in containerized environments, ensuring compliance with regulatory requirements, and protecting sensitive data.

- **ML-driven optimization of container images**: ML models will optimize container images by identifying and removing unnecessary components, reducing image size, and improving deployment efficiency.
- **AI-assisted container orchestration**: AI will assist container orchestration platforms in making intelligent decisions, such as workload placement, resource optimization, and failure recovery.
- **AI-powered container forensics and debugging**: AI will enable more efficient and accurate troubleshooting of containerized applications by analyzing real-time logs, metrics, and events.

Figure 13.3: *A lens pointing towards the city at night.*
source: https://unsplash.com/photos/shallow-focus-photography-of-person-holding-camera-lens-SYbDOjfSF3s

Observability and Monitoring

In the dynamic and complex world of containerized applications, observability and monitoring play a crucial role in ensuring these applications' health, performance, and reliability. Observability encompasses the ability to understand the internal state of a system and its behavior based on external signals. At the same time, monitoring focuses on collecting and analyzing data to track the system's performance and identify potential issues.

The Importance of Observability and Monitoring in Containerization

Containerized applications introduce a unique set of challenges for observability and monitoring. Due to their transient nature and container environments' distribution, traditional monitoring tools often fail to provide the insight needed to effectively manage and troubleshoot containerized applications.

Observability and monitoring tools designed explicitly for containerized environments provide several critical benefits:

- **Early detection of issues**: By continuously monitoring containerized applications, these tools can detect potential problems early on, allowing for quick remediation and preventing service disruptions.
- **Performance optimization**: Monitoring provides insights into application performance, enabling optimization efforts to improve resource utilization, reduce latency, and enhance overall application responsiveness.
- **Root cause analysis**: In case of issues, observability tools provide the ability to drill down into the root cause of problems, facilitating effective troubleshooting and corrective actions.
- **Security monitoring**: Observability and monitoring tools can detect and flag suspicious activity, helping to prevent security breaches and protect sensitive data.

Examples of Successful Observability and Monitoring Products

Several successful observability and monitoring products have explicitly emerged for containerized environments, including:

- **Prometheus**: An open-source monitoring system that collects and stores metrics from containerized applications, providing a comprehensive view of application performance and health.
- **Grafana**: An open-source data visualization platform that integrates with Prometheus and other monitoring systems to create dashboards and visualizations for analyzing containerized application metrics.
- **Jaeger**: An open-source distributed tracing system that tracks the flow of requests through containerized applications, providing insights into performance bottlenecks and potential issues.
- **Datadog**: A cloud-based monitoring and observability platform that provides comprehensive monitoring, alerting, and troubleshooting capabilities for containerized applications.

Widely Adopted Solutions for Observability and Monitoring

In addition to specific container-oriented tools, several widely adopted solutions are also being used for observability and monitoring in containerized environments:

- **ELK Stack**: A combination of Elasticsearch, Logstash, and Kibana, providing a powerful platform for collecting, analyzing, and visualizing logs from containerized applications.
- **Sysdig**: A comprehensive monitoring and security platform that provides visibility into containerized applications, including metrics, logs, and traces.
- **Splunk**: A data analytics platform that can be used to collect, analyze, and visualize logs, metrics, and other data from containerized applications.

Container Security: Shielding Applications in the Containerized World

Containerization has revolutionized how applications are developed, deployed, and managed, offering unprecedented portability, scalability, and agility. However, this transformative technology has also introduced new security challenges. As containerized applications become increasingly prevalent, container security has emerged as a critical area of focus for organizations seeking to protect their data, systems, and networks.

The Necessity of Container Security

The heightened focus on container security stems from several factors, including:

- **Increased attack surface**: Containerized applications present a broader attack surface than traditional monolithic applications. Each container represents a potential entry point for attackers, making it crucial to implement adequate security measures across the entire container lifecycle.
- **Ephemeral nature of containers**: The ephemeral nature of containers, where containers are created, run, and destroyed frequently, poses challenges in maintaining a consistent security posture. Security measures need to be dynamic and adaptable to this ephemeral environment.
- **Lack of visibility**: The distributed nature of containerized environments can make it challenging to gain visibility into the security posture of containerized applications. Organizations need comprehensive monitoring and observability tools to detect and address potential threats.

Evolution of Container Security

Container security has evolved significantly over the past few decades, driven by the increasing adoption of containerization and the growing sophistication of cyberattacks.

- **Early days**: Container security initially focused on securing the container image, the underlying operating system, and the container runtime environment.
- **Shift towards runtime security**: As container adoption matured, the focus shifted to runtime security, emphasizing the need to protect containers during execution.
- **Emergence of container security tools**: Specialized container security tools emerged, providing comprehensive monitoring, vulnerability scanning, and intrusion detection capabilities for containerized environments.
- **DevSecOps integration**: Container security has become integrated into the DevSecOps approach, emphasizing security throughout the software development lifecycle, including container design, deployment, and operation.

Future of Container Security

Container security is expected to continue evolving in several directions, including:

- **Automation and orchestration**: Automation and orchestration of container security tasks will become increasingly important to manage the complexities of securing containerized applications at scale.
- **AI and ML integration**: Artificial intelligence and machine learning (AI/ML) will play a crucial role in container security, enabling real-time threat detection, anomaly detection, and predictive analytics.
- **Shift left security**: The emphasis will shift further left in the software development lifecycle, focusing on building security into container images from the start.
- **Cloud-native security**: Container security will become seamlessly integrated with cloud-native security platforms, providing a unified approach to securing applications across on-premises, hybrid, and multi-cloud environments.

GitOps and Continuous Delivery: A Paradigm Shift in Container Management

Containerization has revolutionized application development and deployment, enabling rapid and scalable software delivery. However, managing containerized applications at scale poses significant challenges. GitOps and Continuous Delivery (CD) have emerged as a powerful combination to address these challenges and streamline container management.

Adoption of GitOps and CD

The industry is moving towards GitOps and CD for container management due to several compelling advantages, including:

- **Declarative Infrastructure**: GitOps provides a declarative approach to infrastructure management, where the desired state of the infrastructure is defined in a Git repository. This approach simplifies infrastructure management, reduces complexity, and promotes consistency.
- **Automated Deployment and Reconciliation**: GitOps automates the deployment and reconciliation of containerized applications, ensuring that the actual state of the infrastructure matches the desired state defined in Git. This automation reduces manual intervention and improves deployment reliability.
- **Continuous Delivery**: CD enables continuous delivery of containerized applications, allowing for frequent and incremental updates without disrupting production environments. This approach enhances agility and responsiveness to market demands.

Historical Solutions and their Limitations

Traditional approaches to container management, such as manual configuration and configuration management tools, have faced several limitations, including:

- **Complexity and Error-Prone Manual Configuration**: Manual configuration of containerized applications is error-prone and difficult to scale, leading to operational overhead and inconsistencies.
- **Configuration Drift**: Configuration drift occurs when the actual state of the infrastructure deviates from the desired state, leading to inconsistencies and potential outages.
- **Slow and Manual Deployment**: Traditional deployment processes are often slow and manual, hindering agility and responsiveness to changes.

Future Trends of GitOps and CD

GitOps and CD are poised to play an increasingly significant role in the future of container management. Here are some key trends to anticipate:

- **Integration with Container Orchestration Platforms**: GitOps and CD will integrate tightly with container orchestration platforms like Kubernetes, providing a unified infrastructure and application management approach.
- **Self-Healing Infrastructure**: GitOps will enable self-healing infrastructure, where the system automatically detects and rectifies inconsistencies between the desired and actual states, ensuring continuous availability and resilience.
- **AI and ML-Powered Automation**: AI and machine learning (AI/ML) will be integrated into GitOps and CD, enabling intelligent automation of tasks such as anomaly detection, predictive maintenance, and automated remediation.
- **GitOps as the Default Operating Model**: GitOps is expected to become the default operating model for container management, providing a consistent and declarative approach across different environments and platforms.

Microservices Architecture: A Journey from Monoliths to Loosely Coupled Microservices

Microservices architecture has emerged as a revolutionary approach to software development, breaking down monolithic applications into more minor, independent services that can be developed, deployed, and scaled independently. This modular approach offers several advantages, including increased agility, scalability, and resilience.

For a complete reference of community-approved guidelines on microservices, it is highly recommended to visit https://12factor.net website.

The Rise of Microservices

The rise of microservices can be attributed to several factors as follows:

- **The increasing complexity of software systems**: As applications have grown, traditional monolithic architectures have become challenging to manage and maintain. Microservices provide a more manageable approach to complex systems.

- **The need for agility and responsiveness**: In today's rapidly changing business landscape, organizations must adapt and respond to new market demands quickly. Microservices enable faster development cycles and easier deployment of new features.
- **The rise of cloud computing**: The proliferation of cloud computing has made it easier to deploy and manage microservices, as cloud platforms provide the infrastructure and services needed to run microservices effectively.

Critical Principles of Microservices Architecture

Microservices architecture adheres to several fundamental principles, including:

- **Small, independent services**: Each microservice represents a business capability developed and maintained independently.
- **Service-oriented communication**: Microservices communicate with each other through well-defined APIs, promoting loose coupling and enabling the independent evolution of services.
- **Decentralized data management**: Each microservice owns and manages its data, ensuring data autonomy and reducing the risk of data silos.

Benefits of Microservices Architecture

Microservices architecture offers several compelling benefits, including:

- **Increased agility**: Microservices allow for faster development and deployment of new features, enabling organizations to respond quickly to market demands.
- **Improved scalability**: Microservices can be scaled independently, allowing for efficient resource utilization and handling of fluctuating workloads.
- **Enhanced resilience**: Microservices are resilient to failures, as the failure of one service does not necessarily impact the entire application.
- **Simplified development and deployment**: Small teams can develop and deploy microservices independently, reducing development overhead and complexity.

Microservices and Containerization

Microservices and containerization are a natural fit. Containerization provides an ideal platform for deploying and managing microservices, offering isolation, portability, and resource management capabilities.

Future Trends of Microservices Architecture

Microservices architecture is expected to continue evolving in the coming years, driven by several trends, including:

- **Emergence of service meshes**: Service meshes provide an infrastructure layer for managing and orchestrating microservices traffic, enabling features like load balancing, circuit breaking, and observability.
- **Rise of cloud-native microservices**: Microservices are increasingly being developed and deployed on cloud platforms, taking advantage of cloud-native services and infrastructure.
- **Integration with AI and ML**: AI and ML are being integrated into microservices architecture to enable intelligent features such as predictive maintenance, self-healing, and anomaly detection.
- **Edge computing**: Microservices architecture is well-suited for edge computing, as it allows for distributed processing and decision-making at the edge.

Figure 13.4: *Two persons pointing spots on the map.*
source: https://unsplash.com/photos/person-in-red-long-sleeve-shirt-holding-white-and-blue-floral-textile-MU9CFBQKrOc

Cloud-native Development

Cloud-native development has emerged as a transformative approach to software development, specifically designed for building and deploying applications in cloud environments. It encompasses a set of principles and practices that optimize applications for cloud platforms' elasticity, scalability, and resilience.

Cloud-native Development Necessity

Several compelling reasons drive the adoption of cloud-native development, which are as follows:

- **Agility and Innovation**: Cloud-native development enables faster development cycles, easier deployment, and continuous integration and continuous delivery (CI/CD) practices, fostering innovation and agility in software development.
- **Scalability and Elasticity**: Cloud-native applications are designed to scale up or down seamlessly based on demand, efficiently utilizing cloud resources and handling fluctuating workloads.
- **Resilience and Fault Tolerance**: Cloud-native applications are built to be resilient, capable of recovering quickly from failures and maintaining availability despite disruptions.
- **Cost-effectiveness**: Cloud-native development promotes a pay-per-use model, where organizations only pay for the resources they consume, leading to cost savings and optimized resource utilization.

Cloud-native Development Minimum Requirement

Cloud-native development relies on a collection of technologies and practices, including:

- **Containerization**: Containers provide lightweight, isolated environments for running applications, enabling portability and simplifying deployment.
- **Microservices Architecture**: Microservices break down applications into more minor, independent services, promoting modularity, loose coupling, and independent development.
- **DevOps Practices**: DevOps emphasizes collaboration and automation between development and operations teams, facilitating faster feedback loops and continuous improvement.
- **Cloud-native Platforms**: Cloud platforms provide the infrastructure and services necessary to run cloud-native applications, such as container orchestration platforms and serverless computing services.

Cloud-native Development Aspects

Cloud-native development encompasses a wide range of aspects, including:

- **Application design**: Cloud-native applications are designed to be stateless, scalable, and distributed, leveraging cloud-native capabilities.
- **Deployment and management**: Cloud-native applications are deployed and managed using automation and orchestration tools, reducing manual intervention and improving efficiency.
- **Monitoring and observability**: Cloud-native applications are continuously monitored and observed to gain insights into performance, health, and resource utilization.
- **Security**: Cloud-native applications are built with security in mind, utilizing cloud-native security practices and tools.

Future Trends of Cloud-native Development

Cloud-native development is continuously evolving, with several emerging trends, which are as follows:

- **Service meshes**: Service meshes provide an infrastructure layer for managing and orchestrating microservices traffic, enabling features like load balancing, circuit breaking, and observability.
- **Edge computing**: Cloud-native development is expanding to the edge, enabling applications to be deployed and processed closer to the end-users, reducing latency and improving performance.
- **AI and ML**: AI and ML are being integrated into cloud-native development, enabling intelligent features such as predictive maintenance, self-healing, and anomaly detection.
- **Multi-cloud and hybrid deployments**: Cloud-native development adapts to multi-cloud and hybrid environments, enabling applications to be deployed across multiple cloud platforms or a combination of cloud and on-premises infrastructure.

Service Mesh and Container Networking

In today's containerized applications, service mesh and container networking are crucial in ensuring seamless communication, observability, and security. As containerization continues to revolutionize software development, integrating these technologies is expected to deepen, paving the way for more robust, scalable, and secure applications.

Service Mesh: The Enabler of Resilient and Secure Microservices Communications

A service mesh is a dedicated infrastructure layer that facilitates communication and management among microservices within a distributed application. It provides a centralized platform for implementing features, including:

- **Load balancing**: Distributes traffic across multiple instances of a microservice to ensure optimal performance and resource utilization.
- **Circuit breaking**: Isolates faulty microservices to prevent cascading failures and maintain overall application availability.
- **Observability**: Provides insights into microservice interactions, enabling real-time monitoring, tracing, and debugging.
- **Security**: Enforces authentication, authorization, and encryption to safeguard microservice communication and protect sensitive data.

Container Networking: The Foundation for Seamless Microservice Connectivity

Container networking forms the underlying infrastructure that enables microservices to communicate with each other and external services. It provides:

- **Network addressing and routing**: Assigns network addresses to containers and facilitates traffic routing.
- **Network policies**: Enforces security and traffic control rules to govern microservice interactions and protect the network from unauthorized access.
- **Network troubleshooting**: Enables debugging and troubleshooting of network-related issues in containerized applications.

Future Trends of Service Mesh and Container Networking

The convergence of service mesh and container networking is expected to drive several transformative trends in the future, such as:

- **Simplified Management and Automation**: Service mesh and container networking will become increasingly integrated, providing a unified management interface and automating tasks like network policy enforcement and traffic optimization.

- **Edge-aware Networking**: Service mesh and container networking will adapt to edge computing scenarios, enabling intelligent routing and traffic management for applications deployed at the edge.
- **AI-powered Networking**: AI and machine learning (AI/ML) will be integrated into service mesh and container networking, enabling predictive traffic analysis, anomaly detection, and self-healing capabilities.
- **Security-centric Networking**: Service mesh and container networking will prioritize security, providing advanced threat detection, intrusion prevention, and zero-trust networking features.

Be Prepared and Sharpen Your Axe

Now that you have seen some of the trends and future predictions, the next question is how to stay on top of your field to survive the fast pace of technological advancement.

Sharpening your axe is a necessary step for engineers to keep delivering their valuable products to the industry, and as such, here are some rough outlines for you to be prepared for what's coming up next:

- **Cultivate a Continuous Learning Mindset**: Embrace a mindset of lifelong learning and continuous improvement. Approach technology as a dynamic and ever-changing field, constantly seeking new knowledge and skills.
- **Engage in Active Learning**: Actively engage with new technologies and concepts. Experiment with new tools, frameworks, and programming languages to gain hands-on experience and practical understanding.
- **Follow Thought Leaders and Influencers**: Stay connected with industry experts, thought leaders, and influential figures in the software development community. Subscribe to their blogs, follow their social media channels, and attend webinars or conferences.
- **Participate in Online Communities and Forums**: Engage with fellow software engineers in online communities, forums, and discussion groups. Share knowledge, ask questions, and learn from the collective experience of others.
- **Contribute to Open-source Projects**: Get involved in open-source projects to gain practical experience, collaborate with experienced developers, and contribute to real-world software development efforts.
- **Attend Industry Events and Conferences:** Participate in industry events, conferences, and workshops to stay updated on the latest trends, learn from experts, and network with potential mentors and collaborators.

- **Enroll in Online Courses and Certifications**: Consider enrolling in online courses, certifications, and bootcamps to gain specialized knowledge and skills in emerging technologies or areas of interest.
- **Read Technical Blogs and Books**: Dedicate time to reading technical blogs, articles, and books to expand your knowledge base and learn from the experiences of others.
- **Practice Regularly and Build Personal Projects**: Practice coding and software development skills by building personal projects, participating in coding challenges, or contributing to open-source projects.
- **Mentor and Share Knowledge with Others**: Share your knowledge and expertise by mentoring junior developers, writing tutorials, or giving presentations at meetups or conferences.
- **Stay Informed about Business and Industry Trends**: Keep abreast of current business trends, emerging technologies, and industry-specific challenges to understand the context in which software development is applied.
- **Develop Strong Communication and Collaboration Skills**: Cultivate strong communication and collaboration skills to effectively work with other developers, stakeholders, and clients in a diverse and ever-changing environment.

Remember, staying ahead of the software development curve requires continuous learning, hands-on experience, and a willingness to embrace new challenges. By following these tips and guidelines, software engineers can effectively sharpen their axes and remain at the forefront of their field.

Figure 13.5: *Digital wallpaper of geometric shapes.*
source: https://unsplash.com/photos/geometric-shape-digital-wallpaper-oyXis2kALVg

Conclusion

As containerization continues to revolutionize the software landscape, it is evident that this technology is here to stay. Its ability to streamline application development, deployment, and management has made it an indispensable tool for organizations of all sizes and industries. For software engineers seeking to thrive in this ever-evolving field, gaining expertise in containerization is not just an option but a necessity.

The transformative power of containerization lies in its ability to break down monolithic applications into more minor, independent services; each encapsulated in a lightweight container. This modular approach fosters agility, scalability, and resilience, enabling organizations to respond quickly to changing market demands and build applications that can withstand the challenges of the cloud-native era.

The future of containerization is brimming with exciting possibilities. From integrating GitOps and continuous delivery to the emergence of service meshes and AI-powered networking, containerization is poised to play an even more prominent role in shaping the future of software development.

To stay ahead of the curve and outlast the relentless pace of technological advancement, software engineers must embrace continuous learning and equip themselves with the necessary containerization skills. This involves mastering the fundamentals of containerization technologies, such as Docker and Kubernetes, and exploring emerging trends like edge computing, cloud-native development, and service meshes.

The rewards for embracing containerization are plentiful. Software engineers who possess these skills will be well-positioned for career advancement, increased earning potential, and the opportunity to work on cutting-edge projects shaping software development's future.

In conclusion, containerization is not just a fad; it is a transformative force redefining how software is developed, deployed, and managed. For software engineers seeking to navigate the ever-changing landscape of technology, mastering containerization is not just an option but a crucial step toward ensuring their continued success and relevance in the years to come.

Final Word

If you have read the book so far, we want to thank you for the time you have invested in this material, and we hope you have gained the required knowledge we were aiming to convey at the beginning of this book.

To ensure you're prepared for real-world application deployment in today's modern containerization world, constantly practice your knowledge and apply it in different domains to gain a solid understanding of the capabilities and tooling you have at your disposal.

In this book, we have covered all the topics related to Docker containerization and many more. By now, you should have a good understanding of what problems containerization is here to solve, why it came to be, and how to apply it in your current and/or next project.

If you have found this book interesting, please write an honest review on online platforms and spread the word so that other people can also benefit from it.

You can contact the author through the available social platforms if you have further questions.

Thanks for reading this book.

APPENDIX A

All-in-One Cheatsheet

Here, you can see a list of commands you will need for your daily job. This can be a reference for you to get back to every once in a while to jog up your memory.

Each section is categorized in a sensible manner so that you can find your way around it effortlessly. It is not a complete list, as that is non-exhaustive, but rather the most common and most used commands you will encounter in your day-to-day job as a Docker specialist.

This list is taken, with granted permission, from the website **https://www.thinknyx.com** to be used as a guide for the readers of the Ultimate Docker for Cloud Native Applications book.

Docker Setup on CentOS

Install dependent packages and configure stable Docker repo on supported Centos OS version:

```
sudo yum install -y yum-utils
sudo yum-config-manager --add-repo \
  https://download.docker.com/linux/centos/docker-ce.repo
```

Reference: https://docs.docker.com/

Install the latest Docker Engine, Docker CLI, and **`containerd`:**

```
sudo yum install -y docker-ce docker-ce-cli containerd.io
sudo usermod -aG docker $USER
```

After running the **usermod** command, log out of your machine and log in again. If you're logged into a remote via SSH, close your connection and reconnect for the command to take effect. Remember that source **~/.bashrc** will not be enough for this.

Start and enable Docker service:

```
sudo systemctl start docker
sudo systemctl enable docker
```

Docker Host-Related Commands

Docker CLI and Docker Daemon version details:

```
sudo docker --version # Docker Command Line Version
sudo docker version # Docker Engine Version & Details
```

Docker host commands:

```
sudo docker system info # System-wide info, e.g., CPU, Memory, etc.
sudo docker system df # Docker storage usage info
sudo docker system prune # Release all unused docker objects
```

Docker - List Containers

Start a container in detached mode:

```
sudo docker container run -d httpd:latest
```

Start a container in the attached mode:

```
sudo docker container run -i -t centos:8
```

List containers:

```
sudo docker container ps # List all running containers
sudo docker container ps -a # List all containers, even if not running
sudo docker container ps -l # List the latest created container
sudo docker container ps -q # List short IDs of running containers
sudo docker container ps -aq #List short IDs of all containers


##### OR #####
```

```
sudo docker container ls
sudo docker container ls -a
sudo docker container ls -l
sudo docker container ls -q
sudo docker container ls -aq
```

Docker - Manipulate Containers

Stop a container:

```
docker container stop CONTAINER_ID_OR_NAME # signal SIGTERM (15)
docker container kill CONTAINER_ID_OR_NAME # signal SIGKILL (9)
```

Start a container:

```
docker container start CONTAINER_ID_OR_NAME
```

Delete containers:

```
docker container rm CONTAINER_ID_OR_NAME # Delete a container (requires
stop first)
docker container prune # Delete all stopped containers


docker container rm `docker container ps -aq` # Delete all containers
##### OR #####
docker container rm $(docker container ps -aq) # Delete all containers
```

Running a new process inside a container:

```
docker container exec -it CONTAINER_ID_OR_NAME /bin/bash
docker container exec -it CONTAINER_ID_OR_NAME uname
```

Container troubleshooting tips:

```
docker container logs CONTAINER_ID_OR_NAME
docker container stats # To display Memory, CPU, Network I/O, etc.
docker container top CONTAINER_ID_OR_NAME # To check the real process ID's
```

Docker - Images

List local images inside docker host:

```
docker image ls
```

To create a new image:

```
docker image build -t IMAGE_NAME:IMAGE_TAG CONTEXT_PATH
# Example
docker image build -t mastering-docker:v1 -f Dockerfile.dev $PWD
```

Save a running container as is to a Docker image:

```
docker container commit -a "John Doe <john@doe.com>" \
  -m "Update gcc" CONTAINER_ID_OR_NAME IMAGE_NAME:IMAGE_TAG
```

Tag a Docker image to a different name, similar to the Unix `ln` command:

```
docker image tag IMAGE_NAME:IMAGE_TAG NEW_IMAGE_NAME:NEW_IMAGE_TAG
docker image save IMAGE_NAME:IMAGE_TAG -o demo.tar
docker image load -i demo.tar
```

Push and pull images from and to Docker registry:

```
docker login -u USERNAME -p PASSWORD [REGISTRY_URL]
docker login -u john -p P@s5word myregistry.com
docker pull [REGISTRY_URL/]IMAGE_NAME:IMAGE_TAG
docker push [REGISTRY_URL/]IMAGE_NAME:IMAGE_TAG
docker pull myregistry.com/nginx:v1
docker push myregistry.com/nginx:v1
```

Delete images:

```
docker image prune # Delete all unused & Dangling Images
docker image rm IMAGE_NAME:IMAGE_TAG # Delete specific image(s)
```

Docker – Networks and Volumes

List Docker networks:

```
docker network ls # To List local Docker networks
```

Create a user-defined Docker network:

```
docker network create NETWORK_NAME [--driver DRIVER_NAME] \
  --subnet 192.168.0.0/16 --gateway 192.168.0.1
```

Add or remove network to containers:

```
docker network connect NETWORK_NAME CONTAINER_ID_OR_NAME
docker network disconnect NETWORK_NAME CONTAINER_ID_OR_NAME
```

Delete a network:

```
docker network prune # Delete All unused docker networks
docker network rm NETWORK_ID_OR_NAME # Delete specific network or networks
```

List Docker volumes:

```
docker volume ls
```

Create a user-defined volume:

```
docker volume create VOLUME_ID_OR_NAME
```

Delete a volume:

```
docker volume prune # Delete All unused volumes
docker volume rm VOLUME_ID_OR_NAME # Delete specific volume or volumes
```

Docker – Sample Dockerfile

Sample Dockerfile:

```
# Sample Dockerfile to Create a HTTPD Server Image based on centos:7
FROM centos:7
RUN yum install -y httpd
WORKDIR /var/www/html
COPY ./index.html .
EXPOSE 80/tcp
CMD ["httpd","-D","FOREGROUND"]
```

Docker command to build an Image using the preceding Dockerfile:

```
docker image build -t myusername/httpd:v1 .
```

Here, the . (dot) stands for the current working directory where Dockerfile is present.

Docker command to create and start a container using a newly created image:

```
docker container run -itd -p 80:80 --name=webcontainer myusername/httpd:v1
```

Index